"This text firmly establishes McShea as a leading contemporary scholar of French religious history. . . . In our time of resurgent national feeling throughout the West and much intra-Catholic disagreement about the nation's place in the world, the type of realism advocated by McShea in trying to understand what Catholics do, and how and why they do it, seems more necessary than ever."

—Samuel Gregg, *Catholic World Report*

"McShea's deeply original monograph is a must-read for scholars of early America. Authoritatively debunking the myth of French Jesuit missions as otherworldly, *Apostles of Empire* demonstrates that we cannot fully understand the history of North American imperial competition without French Jesuits."

—Gabrielle Guillerm, *American Catholic Studies*

"Thanks to McShea's meticulous research, these missionaries now appear less as ascetic martyrs devoted to saving Native American souls and more as worldly imperialists committed to spreading French civilization. In tracing the 'civilizing mission' back to the seventeenth century, this study upends current assumptions about the Enlightenment origins of modern French imperialism."

—Charles Walton, author of *Policing Public Opinion in the French Revolution*

"A meticulously researched, elegantly written, and precisely aimed salvo intended to demolish some of historiography's most cherished myths about the Jesuits in North America."

—Mary Dunn, *Journal of Jesuit Studies*

APOSTLES OF EMPIRE

FRANCE OVERSEAS:
STUDIES IN EMPIRE AND
DECOLONIZATION

*Series editors: A. J. B. Johnston,
James D. Le Sueur, and Tyler Stovall*

APOSTLES
of EMPIRE

The Jesuits and New France

BRONWEN MCSHEA

University of Nebraska Press
Lincoln

Substantial portions of chapter 2 were published as "Presenting the 'Poor Miserable Savage' to French Urban Elites: Commentary on North American Living Condition in Early Jesuit Relations" in *Sixteenth Century Journal* 44, no. 3 (Fall 2013).

The University of Nebraska Press is part of a land-grant institution with campuses and programs on the past, present, and future homelands of the Pawnee, Ponca, Otoe-Missouria, Omaha, Dakota, Lakota, Kaw, Cheyenne, and Arapaho Peoples, as well as those of the relocated Ho-Chunk, Sac and Fox, and Iowa Peoples.

Library of Congress Cataloging-in-Publication Data
Names: McShea, Bronwen, author.
Title: Apostles of empire: the Jesuits and
New France / Bronwen McShea.
Description: Lincoln: University of Nebraska Press, 2019. |
Series: France overseas: studies in empire and decolonization |
Includes bibliographical references and index.
Identifiers: LCCN 2018045055
ISBN 9781496208903 (cloth: alk. paper)
ISBN 9781496229083 (paperback)
ISBN 9781496214478 (epub)
ISBN 9781496214485 (mobi)
ISBN 9781496214492 (pdf)
Subjects: LCSH: Jesuits—Missions—New
France—History. | Indians of North
America—Missions—New France—History. |
Canada—History—To 1763 (New France) |
France—Colonies—America—Administration—History.
Classification: LCC F1030.8.M38 2019 | DDC 971.01—dc23
LC record available at https://lccn.loc.gov/2018045055

Set in Garamond Premier by Mikala R. Kolander.
Designed by N. Putens.

For my teachers, especially
Maureen and Kevin McShea

CONTENTS

ILLUSTRATIONS

ACKNOWLEDGMENTS

I wish to thank many individuals and institutions who helped bring this book into being, beginning with Alisa Plant, James Le Sueur, Ann Baker, Vicki Low, Courtney Ochsner, Rosemary Sekora, two anonymous readers, and all other editors, staff, and external advisers involved with the book's publication and marketing at the University of Nebraska Press.

I received generous support from Yale University for much of the initial research, writing, and travel that went into this book's development. Additional support was provided over the years by the American Catholic Historical Association, the Society for Reformation Research, the American Historical Association, the Institute for Advanced Catholic Studies, the Leibniz Institut für Europäische Geschichte (IEG) in Mainz, the Sixteenth Century Society, Harvard Divinity School's Center for the Study of World Religions (CSWR), and finally by Columbia University, the American Council of Learned Societies (ACLS), and the Andrew W. Mellon Foundation during my time as an ACLS New Faculty Fellow and Lecturer in Columbia's Department of History. Also helpful were staff at Yale's Beinecke Rare Book & Manuscript Library (especially Moira Fitzgerald), the Archives Jésuites at Vanves in France; the Archivum Romanum Societatis Iesu in Rome (especially Mauro Brunello), the Archives Nationales in Paris, the Bibliothèque Nationale de France at multiple Parisian sites, the Newberry Library in Chicago, Library Archives Canada in Ottawa, and the McCord Museum in Montreal.

Among the excellent historians from whom I was privileged to learn at Yale—and without whom this book would not exist—my adviser Carlos Eire has my warm gratitude, together with Charles Walton and Jay Gitlin. All three pored over early chapter drafts, offered constructive feedback on the project as it matured, and helped me engage effectively with scholarship on early modern Catholicism, ancien régime France, and colonial North America, respectively. Eire and Walton furthermore have been generous mentors since my time in New Haven. Conversations with other faculty, including Stuart B. Schwartz, John Merriman, and Steven Pincus, as well as Yale classmates including Taylor Spence, Sarah Cieglo, and Kathryn Gin, were likewise helpful.

Seeds for the book were planted earlier when I was an MTS student at Harvard Divinity School. Patrick Provost-Smith, formerly assistant professor there, introduced me to the Jesuit mission to New France as a research topic and encouraged my academic aspirations thereafter. Also inspirational at Harvard were conversations about the Jesuits and Catholicism's history with my friend James Edward Maschoff while he was a student at Harvard Law School. Later, not long before his tragic death on his thirty-third birthday from esophageal cancer, James helpfully assessed parts of an early draft of my manuscript. I miss him and hope he would be pleased with this final product.

Brad Gregory, a friend and mentor, generously read through the entire final draft of my manuscript. His care, even for small details, and his various suggestions for improvement helped me polish the text for publication. Earlier on, important feedback on parts of the developing manuscript was provided by Fredrika Teute and Nadine Zimmerli of the Omohundro Institute of Early American History and Culture as well as an anonymous reader for another press. Other scholars who were supportive in different ways at key moments while my project was maturing include Judith Becker at IEG, Jodi Bilinkoff, Charles Coleman, Alice Conklin, Markus Friedrich, John Grigg, Fr. James Heft, SM, Martha Howell, Robert Maryks, Eric Nelson, Adina Ruiu, Martina Saltamacchia, Daniel Wasserman-Soler, and Tara Windsor.

Many present-day Jesuits helped me bear this book to fruition. Fr. John

O'Malley read and commented on an early full draft, helped me rework a later draft of the introduction, and has been a mentor early in my career. Fr. Francis X. Clooney at Harvard's CSWR offered me a pleasant work space and renewed access to Harvard's magnificent libraries in 2013 and valuable global perspective on my particular group of early modern Jesuit missionaries. Frs. Robert Bonfils and José Antonio Yoldi welcomed me to the Jesuits' archives in Vanves and Rome, respectively, when I was a research novice. Fr. Mark Massa invited me to Boston College's School of Theology and Ministry in 2013 to teach on pre-Suppression Jesuit history; that chance to dig into the Society's development from multiple angles, in conversation with bright Jesuit scholastics, emboldened me to attempt a more ambitious book than I originally imagined. Fr. Matt Malone gifted me from *America Magazine*'s library a full set of Reuben Gold Thwaites's *Jesuit Relations and Allied Documents*; the ability to pore over passages from those volumes at a moment's notice, at home, helped my writing and revision process tremendously. Finally, Jesuit friends, including Frs. Sam Conedera, Ross Romero, Christopher Collins, Aaron Pidel, and Peter Nguyen, were more helpful than they knew by reminding me— by their presence and sometimes side-splitting humor—that the book I was writing was about real men of their same order, not icons or literary figments, and men who once labored, sorrowed, and rejoiced in real time. Sam, especially, helped bolster my spirits during some taxing final phases of the project and provided salutary feedback on a draft of the conclusion.

Other friends were important interlocutors and sources of cheer as my research grew into this book. I wish to acknowledge, in particular, Patricia Snow, whose friendship, encouragement of my writing, and devotion to the writer's craft per se helped me persevere through challenging stages of this project. Also I thank my college mentor and longtime friend Louis Miller, with whom I studied European intellectual history when he was an assistant professor at Harvard. At a time when I was unsure about the value of my own thoughts and capacity for advanced academic work, he helped me discover my calling to scholarship. Over many years since, he has helped confirm me in it. I thank, too, among others, Vivian Choi, Elbridge Colby, Ronald Distajo, Christopher Killheffer, Hanja Kochansky,

Florence Lotz, Victoria Gardner Misenti, Fr. Christopher Roberts, John and Eileen Safranek, Kristin Williams, and Sarah Yellin.

Finally, I am grateful to my family for the love and encouragement they have always given, solidifying the ground of all I do. A shout-out is deserved by each of my siblings, Colleen, Thomas More, and Brendan, the last of whom first got me curious about French North America long ago, in our woodsy childhood environs in Cornwall, New York, when for some mysterious reason he made us pretend to be characters at war with each other from *The Last of the Mohicans*. My sister-in-law, Elizabeth Purdy, was supportive during my postdoctoral year at IEG, when she and Brendan were also based in Europe, for U.S. Army duties. And I warmly thank my parents, Maureen (née McGowan) and Kevin McShea, originally of Woodside, Queens. More than a little of this book came into being during extended visits home to them as I took advantage of mom-cooked meals and blood-is-thicker-than-water forbearance with my artistic temperament. It is they who, standing on the shoulders of many humble, unsung educators—Catholic nuns, clergy, laypeople alike—first and most insistently over time taught me to write, read widely, think for myself, and care deeply for such things, whatever the earthly recompense. It is to my mom and dad, and to all my good teachers, that I dedicate this offspring of my spirit.

INTRODUCTION

As occasion arises, we must speak also of the earthly city.
—Augustine of Hippo

Between 1611 and 1764, 320 Jesuit priests and brothers departed France for mission posts in North America. While some labored in the Mississippi Valley, most ended up among the Native populations of New France—a vast territory that encompassed eastern Canada and the Great Lakes region.

A number of these Jesuits had grown up in Parisian privilege, others in provincial obscurity. Many had asked for overseas assignments when entering the Society of Jesus, but some were disappointed not to be sent to China or the Ottoman Empire. Still others had to accept the bitter pill that they would never hold more prestigious positions back home. Despite this diversity, each Jesuit's task in America was the same: to bring indigenous populations under the rule of Jesus Christ, share with them his teachings and the sacraments of the Catholic Church, and open to them the prospect of eternal blessedness with God and the saints in heaven.

Famously, a few of these men were killed while serving the mission. Isaac Jogues perished at the hands of Mohawk warriors in 1646. He and seven other Jesuits who died among the Iroquois and Hurons that same decade were quickly honored as martyrs by their confreres. Canonized centuries later in 1930, they are still venerated by Catholics the world over.[1]

Also increasingly famously, thanks to recent scholarship by Allan Greer,

Dominique Deslandres, and others, numerous Jesuits of New France devoted decades of their lives to adapting Catholicism to indigenous cultural forms. Some missionaries adopted nomadic lifestyles, following along with bands of hunter-gatherers such as the Montagnais of eastern Canada. Others labored in mission reserves such as Kahnawaké near Montreal, joined in mission work by Native American catechists and vowed celibates devoted to charity and penance. Among the latter was Kateri Tekakwitha, an Algonquin-Mohawk virgin ascetic who so impressed the Jesuits that, after she died in 1680, they immediately promoted her cause for sainthood—a cause that succeeded only in 2012, when Pope Benedict XVI canonized her.[2]

Unfamously, these same missionaries from the reign of King Louis XIII through the era of the Seven Years' War were enthusiastic, enterprising empire-builders for the Bourbon state. While spreading Catholic worship and teachings across the Eastern Woodlands, they recruited numerous Native Americans and fellow French people into New France's defense and expansion during wars with the Iroquois, English, and others. They and a transatlantic, lay support network also worked for the colony's cultural and infrastructural transformation according to elite, Parisian norms, and they strove further to import medicine and institutionalized poverty relief into wilderness spaces. In their view these worldly causes were sanctioned by divine providence, flowing from and further reinforcing their work of Christianization.

This book tells this forgotten imperial history of the Jesuit mission to New France, from its germination in Paris in the early seventeenth century to its quiet death under British colonial rule in the late eighteenth. Here the mission is observed not only at close range, with a focus on particular engagements with Native Americans, but also through a widened scope, revealing a transatlantic, Paris-based enterprise deeply imprinted by a Gallican and absolutist political culture during an early, optimistic phase of French national expansion.

Surprisingly, given the developed literature on the Jesuits and New France, this book is the first contemporary monograph on the mission to span the entire period of its history. Partly due to unevenness in the mission's paper trail, which is richer and more regular for the earlier phases, most accounts have covered events in the Saint Lawrence region in the first half of the seventeenth century. To respond to that literature with revisionist claims, this book also devotes significant space to the same era and region. At the same time, it covers developments well into the eighteenth century, across the Eastern Woodlands and Atlantic World, attempting chronological and geographical inclusiveness wherever feasible and useful to advancing central arguments. It is thus divided into two parts, the first on the mission's founding era and early decades of development, the second underscoring a longer-term story of continual warfare and metropolitan neglect as these shaped the Jesuit enterprise. The result is a history that spans two centuries, but one in which key political, social, and cultural themes are prioritized over narrative comprehensiveness, resulting in some chronological overlap between chapters.

Part 1 concentrates on the mission's founding era and better-documented early decades of development, from the 1610s to 1660s. It shows that missionaries under the leadership of Paul Le Jeune, François-Joseph Le Mercier, and others acted closely in concert with French political and mercantile elites, especially during the era of Cardinal Richelieu's royal administration. They utilized their special access to indigenous populations to help negotiate trade and military alliances for New France. They even sought to move events in favor of a French conquest of Iroquois Country. Additionally they collaborated with French lay elites to develop medical services and other charitable ministries for the poor in Canada, impart courtly French aesthetics and ideas of *civilité* to Native Americans, and transform woodlands and indigenous villages into secure, economically productive centers of trade and military preparedness. To advance these goals, the Jesuits vigorously promoted not only Native Americans' Christianization but also the cause of French empire in their best-selling *Relations de la Nouvelle France*, published annually in Paris from 1632 to 1673.

Part 2 covers a broader chronological sweep, accounting for both change and continuity in political, social, and cultural realities shaping the mission from the late seventeenth century through the eighteenth.

Drawing upon the later *Relations* and lesser-known archival and print sources, it demonstrates that the Jesuits' mission network expanded widely alongside only a weak French commercial and military presence during long periods of conflict, from the Iroquois Wars to the Seven Years' War that crushed French dreams of empire in America. Despite regular Jesuit protestations, French officials generally left New France, including fortified mission centers, in defensive positions in the face of Iroquois and English expansion. At the same time, French developers and officials left much of the day-to-day business of colonization and commerce with Native Americans to French émigrés, garrison commanders, and fur traders who were generally less devoted than the missionaries to the Bourbon state and French higher culture, let alone to finer points of Catholic morality where sex and alcohol were concerned. Moreover, this was the era of the French court's removal to Versailles and of rising skepticism among metropolitan elites about the value of New France per se and the need to convert anyone, anymore, to Catholicism. The Jesuits therefore struggled to communicate their wishes to royal officials and secure support for colonial projects from metropolitan elites. Thus, by the early eighteenth century, the missionaries had greatly moderated their ambitions for a French Catholic empire in America, due more to metropolitan neglect than to Native American resistance or English advances.

For all these frustrations the Jesuits consistently pressed the French imperial cause over the mission's *longue durée*, both in print in France and on the ground in North America. Also, right up to the Seven Years' War, they participated in colonial diplomacy and military conflicts, helping to muster French-allied mission Indians for campaigns against New France's enemies and serving as military chaplains for combined French and Indian forces. But above all they continually viewed their central work of pros-elytization in secular as well as spiritual terms. The Christianization of Native Americans was their specialized, and indispensable, contribution to a national-imperial effort in the Eastern Woodlands. Even as they grew discouraged about the will of most French colonials to advance empire in North America, the Jesuits increasingly looked to Native American leaders themselves as potentially a pan-tribal, aristocratic warrior elite for New France that would prove more loyal to the king of France and the values of *civilité* and *police* than many colonial Frenchmen seemed to be. In the process, although their this-worldly aspirations for New France ultimately came to naught, the missionaries laid the groundwork for more secularized, post-Enlightenment "civilizing missions" and efforts to recruit indigenous leaders into the service of imperial states.

Historiographically this book links Catholicism as French Jesuits first carried it to North America to a growing literature on the relationship of religion to empire in the early modern era.[3] In view of a longtime scholarly neglect of pre-Revolutionary French colonialism, this book is also part of a developing literature on Bourbon-era French empire specifically.[4] It is a response, as well, to ongoing discussions of the role of Catholic missionaries in French colonial contexts of the *modern* era, correcting misperceptions that enterprising missionary support for French imperial state formation was a nineteenth-century development. Jesuit activism for French empire is, rather, observable in the earliest decades of the seventeenth century, in advance of efforts by lay colonialists such as Jean-Baptiste Colbert, and centuries before the era of the Third Republic, when Catholic missionaries are believed to have been pushed by a decidedly modern, national-imperial zeitgeist to engage in aggressive boosterism for a secular *mission civilisatrice* across the globe.[5]

This study of the secular edges and metropolitan history of the mission also offers new appreciation for the integral role of laypersons in the enterprise—a phenomenon traditionally associated with the late eighteenth-century, evangelical Protestant missionary awakening and its lay, "voluntarist" associations.[6] For example the mission was closely tied to a lay confraternity in Paris, the Congrégation des Messieurs, classically studied by Louis Châtellier.[7] It also benefited from influential nobles such as François Sublet de Noyers, a secretary of state under Cardinal Richelieu, and the latter's niece, Marie-Madeleine de Vignerot, duchesse d'Aiguillon. Furthermore, publishers of Jesuit reports from New France, especially Sébastien Cramoisy, who produced the *Relations*, played a more active role in colonial developments than has been previously acknowledged. Attention to lay collaborators in turn helps illuminate the Jesuits' effort to shape colonial policy in favor of social goals that dovetailed with elite-driven charitable projects for Europe's poor in the same era.[8]

Lay participants in the mission also included Native American converts to Christianity who, in unpredictable ways, amplified and transformed what they had learned from the Jesuits.[9] In the Jesuits' view, lay participants furthermore included warriors from French-allied tribes, French soldiers, and colonial militiamen who killed in, and offered their own lives for, the defense and buildup of New France. Broadly understood, therefore, the mission was not strictly a clerical, religious project. The Jesuits rather conceived of their own labors as the spearpoint of a greater mission by the French and their new spiritual "brothers" and "sisters" in America to save souls, improve the earthly condition of an emerging transatlantic community, and defeat enemies of these causes.

Historiographical Interventions

The Jesuits portrayed in this book differ from those found in current narratives of New France and of Christianity in the Atlantic World. Despite much effort across several academic disciplines to historicize them, the Jesuits of New France remain trapped in iconic tableaux, especially of martyrdoms and wilderness reserves in which some but not all labored. With popular portrayals such as the film *Black Robe* reinforcing perceptions, the missionaries are seen as having been entirely focused on gathering up a harvest of Native American souls for heaven, rushing headlong into life-endangering situations to accomplish this, and setting up wilderness havens of Counter-Reformation piety and morality.[10] A dominant image is that of expatriated ascetics, fleeing with bands of Christian Indians from a rapacious, secularizing French civilization that threatened their thoroughly religious and moral project. The missionaries, further, are supposed to have been motivated toward utopian escapism by an extreme *contemptus mundi*, alleged to have been characteristic of their post-Tridentine Catholicism.[11]

At the same time a kind of Manichaean image of the Jesuits prevails, whereby they appear as both morally disapproving of their home culture in moments of precocious progressiveness and cynically dependent upon French power to access Native American souls. These contrary principles are generally held together in a narrative positing an evolved mission-ary opposition to the French colonial project—a divorce from it, so to speak, especially from its component of Indians' cultural assimilation or "Frenchification," following a brief marriage of convenience.[12] Having escaped to a surprising extent what Dana Robert has called "the icy grip of the 'colonialism paradigm'" that dominated academic discussions of Christian missions in the 1980s and 1990s, the Jesuit enterprise in New France has enjoyed up to this late hour a mythic status as somehow *attached* to French colonial history, but not really *of* it.[13]

Thus the mission's relationship over time with French imperialism has been thematized only in passing ways, despite the fact that a rich scholarly literature on the Jesuits of New France stretches back to the mid-nineteenth century.[14] Scholars have tended to focus on particular North American contexts of Jesuit activity, with limited reference to events and cultural shifts in Europe that influenced the enterprise and affected what the mis-sionaries reported in print and in private. Where scholars such as Greer and Deslandres have considered the mission's European connections and influences, they have tended to focus on what the mission drew from the supranational agendas of the Jesuit order and the Counter-Reformation Church. Such analyses are complemented and qualified here with new emphasis on the French imperial, Parisian base of the mission more than the Roman and ecclesiastical one. Especially at the leadership level, the Jesuits of New France were part of a larger, mostly lay network of French elites of a more Gallican and *politique* than ultramontane bent. With fresh readings of mission sources in light of this metropolitan milieu, the Jesuits' efforts to cultivate a royalist, Paris-centered, transatlantic French and Indian political community emerge from the historical record in sharp relief.

New emphasis on the metropolitan base of the mission and the mis-sionaries' this-worldly goals should not be mistaken for a suggestion that the Jesuits of New France were disloyal to the papacy or unmotivated by a corporate Jesuit identity that transcended other loyalties.[15] However, it is taken for granted here that despite aspirations to detached service to the universal Church and the Society of Jesus per se, many Jesuits maintained strong personal ties that preexisted or ran parallel with ties within their order.[16] Sometimes Jesuits' relationships with government officials and lay elites were more amicable than those they were required to maintain with their religious superiors.[17] Furthermore, the missionary experience intensified some Jesuits' identification with France, to which they not rarely longed to return—making all the more painful the spiritual detachment demanded of them in their ministry by the foundational counsels of the Jesuit order.

Although a book on the mission's French imperial history may strike some readers, initially, as retrogressively Eurocentric, this study has been conceived in response to a perduring *Americentrism* in conversations on the mission. Historiography on New France has come a long way since titles such as J. H. Kennedy's *Jesuit and Savage* (1950) were rolling off major university presses. Scholarship on the mission for nearly a half century has underscored Native American responses to Christianity, variously stressing resistance and conflict, receptivity and cooperation with missionaries, and the impact of Native American ways on the Jesuits themselves.[18] Discussions of French colonial experiences in North America also now tend to downplay metropolitan influences while playing up local dynamics in frontiers and borderlands. However, as Jay Gitlin has argued in *The Bourgeois Frontier* (2010), North America has much more of a "French" history than it is now customary to assume.[19] In exorcising chauvinistic, Eurocentric perspectives of the era of Francis Parkman from the history of colonial North America, scholars of the past few decades have, in a way, been *too* successful. This book is thus part of a larger effort among contemporary scholars of the French Atlantic World to achieve a truly transatlantic and transcultural historiography. At the same time, it is a proposal that we do not, while preoccupied today with all things "global" and "transnational," hastily write out national-imperial projects that are themselves critical data for deciphering why, and how, European missionaries were among the first actors systematically to bridge great cultural chasms of their time.

This book is offered, too, as a counterpoint to tendencies in scholarship on globalizing Christianity to advance idealist conceptions of European missionaries' Christianity as somehow cleanly separable from its historical culture of origin. The idea, where this particular mission is concerned, is that the purely spiritual core, or evangelical essence, of the Jesuits' project was gradually liberated after time in Indian Country from European imperial trappings, or rootedness in Western Christendom, through processes twentieth-century theologians identify as "inculturation" and even mutual conversion.[20] This book, differently, draws attention to the imperial, French purposes, not only evangelistic ones, discernible even in the missionaries' most culturally adaptive and experimental modes of Christianization. It highlights, too, a crystallizing Francocentric providentialism—an intensifying sense of the divine election of France and its allies—seen in mission sources over time. Indeed, this study comes to grips not only with the missionaries' theologically grounded perspectives on French expansion in the Atlantic World, but also with some Jesuits' willingness to sacrifice their own lives—and those of numerous others, Indian and European alike—on the altar of French empire, so identified did it become with the fulfillment, in an age dominated by the nation-state, of the Church's mission to all peoples.

Sources and Interpretive Approaches

This study of the mission from metropolitan and French imperial vantage points is not only overdue but logical, given that most sources available on the enterprise were long-distance communications between Jesuits on both sides of the Atlantic, and between the missionaries and a range of others including donors and colonial governors. Additionally, the most ample, detailed sources left by the missionaries were books published in Paris, intended not only to win support for overseas conversion efforts, but also to generate interest in New France per se among French elites.

Best known among these publications are the *Relations*, published annually in Paris from 1632 to 1673 by Sébastien Cramoisy and his grandson Sébastien Mabre-Cramoisy. Best sellers in the seventeenth century and reissued in later editions and translations, they have enjoyed a remarkable shelf life even to this day, and they remain a trove for scholars of early European ethnographic representations of Native Americans.[21] Their original dissemination by Cramoisy's press in the form of durable, octavo-sized volumes made later efforts at reprinting, translating, and studying them practicable for European and American scholars alike.[22] But the very readability and availability of the *Relations* have also led to overreliance on them as representative of the mission's history, even though their publication ceased more than a century before the mission's end.[23]

While drawing substantially from the *Relations*, too, this book freshly considers their metropolitan functions and reception while juxtaposing them with many other sources. These include the earliest histories of the mission and New France authored by Jesuits. An account in Latin by François Du Creux was published by the Cramoisy press in 1664.[24] A three-volume work later appeared in 1744 from the hand of Pierre-François-Xavier de Charlevoix, then serving as the mission's Parisian *procureur*.[25] We also have sections of the *Lettres Édifiantes et Curieuses* (1702–76)—a serial publication like Cramoisy's *Relations* but containing reports from all over the world—and articles from the Parisian Jesuits' academic monthly, the *Journal de Trévoux* (1701–82). Another source is *Moeurs des Sauvages Amériquains* (1724) by Joseph-François Lafitau, another of the mission's metropolitan procureurs.[26] This text has been assessed as a daringly sympathetic portrait of Native Americans. But it also served an imperial purpose: informing French officials about cultural dynamics in North America that needed to be taken into consideration for the French colonial effort to succeed.[27]

Given the public nature and European audiences of such sources, and given the *Relations'* fundraising purposes in particular, the value of these books as historical evidence has been debated by scholars, some of whom have read them with great suspicion.[28] Others have preferred to take what the Jesuits wrote more at face value, employing the texts as evidence of North American phenomena while still treating their propaganda function in France as a hurdle to be scaled.[29] Here the biases and practical functions of the sources—and the circumstances of their dissemination in France— are viewed as their most salient, useful features that help illuminate some of the understudied history of the pre-Revolutionary French empire and its religious culture. They are also interpreted as unique windows not only onto North American events, populations, and landscapes, but also onto dynamics in the metropole and the wider Atlantic World that the Jesuits knew and shaped.

Many other sources have been consulted for this book. These include originally unpublished missionary journals, correspondence between Jesuits and colonial officials and laypersons of interest, and mission superiors' private reports to Parisian provincials and the Jesuit General's office in Rome, termed *relations* and *litterae annuae*, respectively. In some cases the latter included details and word choices instructive in their difference from what appeared in Parisian publications.

Beyond the corpus of Jesuit-authored sources on the mission and New France, other early print and manuscript sources are relevant that either directly treat the Jesuits and New France or help contextualize mission sources. These include volumes of early French periodicals such as the *Mercure François*, Cramoisy imprints respecting other global missions of the same era, sources by non-Jesuit missionaries who worked in New France, travel writings on Canada and Louisiana by French soldiers and merchants, and communiqués by Canadian governors and other officials, including Colbert.

For each source employed for this book, care has been taken to be mindful of its original context of authorship and intended audience, and its sometimes simultaneous functions as reportage, dramatization, propaganda, and devotional literature. Generally, however, the sources are analyzed with several questions in mind: What do they tell us about the political and social functions Jesuits and their mission stations served in New France? How did the missionaries, Native Americans, and French laypersons perceive these functions? What do the sources reveal about Jesuit attitudes and agendas with respect to secular themes—government, warfare, trade, material culture, medicine, charity, aesthetics, the conditions of ordinary life—both in their own right and as they related to Christianization? How did the Jesuits view not only the progress of their mission and French expansion, but also the relationship of their endeavors to political developments, wars, commerce, and cultural trends across the Atlantic?

Men of This World

The Jesuits in this book may surprise readers already familiar with the martyrs and wilderness-bound pioneers of inculturation found in other accounts. Some of the missionaries, we will see, hobnobbed with duchesses and royal bureaucrats during visits home to France, working with them not only to fund religious ministries, but also to export to America urban French institutions such as charitable hospitals and schools. Sometimes profiting from their own seigneurial estates in New France, the missionaries also partnered with mercantile elites, urging investments in colonial trading, mining, and other development ventures so that the French might compete economically with other European powers. Other Jesuits served as guides and translators for French troops during wartime. A number were satisfied, while their confreres labored deep in Indian Country, to remain close by Quebec and Montreal, and even to return to France after a few years to teach or serve in administrative posts. Still others, especially younger Jesuits in the eighteenth century, saw their missionary careers cut short by events beyond their control. Julien-François Dervillé, for example, spent only three years in America before witnessing the suppression of the Jesuits by both his king and his pope. He was eventually martyred, not with a tomahawk in Iroquois Country, but with a guillotine, in the heart of revolutionary Paris before a jeering mob of his own countrymen.

Also appearing in this book are Jesuits who rarely counseled Native Americans to follow self-mortifying regimens like Kateri Tekakwitha's. Indeed, partly to ease the process of conversion and the formation of alliances with the French, the missionaries often advised young people asking for baptism to delay the sacrament until after a period during which they satisfied sexual urges by means of marriages *à la façon du pays*, or non-Catholic marriages in the local way. This was partly so that, if the marriages failed and more compatible Christian partners later appeared, strict Catholic prohibitions against divorce and remarriage would not apply, as ecclesiastical laws on marriage pertained only to the baptized. But it was also intended to encourage procreation among Native Americans tentatively well disposed toward the French and Catholic instruction, but who might have moved toward Iroquois or English alliances if badgered too much by missionaries on points of Catholic morality that seemed unreasonable to them or too difficult to honor.

In the chapters ahead, furthermore, are Jesuits who did not believe—despite higher aspirations toward Christ-like perseverance through agony—that non-violent acceptance of suffering and death was the only glorious path to heaven in North America. The missionaries often urged French colonials and Native Americans alike to risk their lives on the battlefield and win victories defending New France and expanding its borders, both for the glory of France and for Christ himself, understood as King of Kings and, in their hour of history, as particularly endorsing of French imperial expansion. And the same Jesuits who venerated martyred confreres and the ascetic Tekakwitha paid tribute, too, to individuals who skillfully wielded weapons, and lived to talk about it, against enemies of the French. For instance, in one *Relation*, mission leaders praised a young Nipissing Algonquin woman for her special favor with God, as evidenced by her "imploring Heaven's aid" before plunging a knife into the heart of an unsuspecting Iroquois man who—believing her when she offered to clean some beaver skins with it—had just lent her the implement.[30]

The Jesuits of New France, in short, were men planted knee-deep in an untidy world of politics, social pressures, and war—a world they helped create, and one that not rarely pulled them gravitationally away from the very Christian holiness to which they urged men and women to aspire. Despite their common cause as members of the Society of Jesus, they were a diverse group and much more preoccupied with the secular business of empire than we might expect to see among missionaries of the early modern era. And, whether posted in the Saint Lawrence River Valley, "flying missions" far from French settlements, or western spaces such as the Illinois territory, they were surprisingly abreast of happenings across the wider Atlantic World and labored for New France to embody urbane French values as well as reformed Catholic principles of order.

Early in the nineteenth century, the Oxford academic and Catholic convert John Henry Newman pleaded for more realism in discussions of Christianity among scholars and preachers of his day. He urged that

Christianity not be discussed as if it were a "dream of the study or cloister," exempt from the ordinary judgments of history. Christianity should be seen, rather, as "public property," having had long ago "passed beyond the letter of documents" and "thrown itself upon the great concourse of men." Accepting of, not obfuscating about, the more world-intruding than fastidious character of the faith he professed, Newman supported Christianity's critical assessment from secular, humanistic points of view: Christianity's "home is in the world," he insisted, "and to know what it is, we must seek it in the world, and hear the world's witness of it."[31]

In its dynamic relationship with a European imperial project, the Jesuit mission to New France illustrates something of Christianity's world-invading and world-affirming, not world-fleeing or utopian-idealist, character. The men of the mission, to be sure, were profoundly, self-sacrificially, and sometimes militantly motivated by the raisons d'être of the Catholic Church: to win souls to God, bring them the means of eternal salvation, and help them glorify God while sojourning on earth. But the Jesuits' transcendent horizons, and the religious beliefs and practices they cultivated in Native American communities, are from a certain vantage point just the *beginning* of their story—a story that in its twists and turns is as much about the city of this world as the city of God.

Let us look, then, for the missionaries and their Catholicism in the very this-worldly settings they inhabited and transformed. And let us look for them, indeed, not only in the fabled American wilderness into which they seem ever to be racing in other accounts, but also in one of the worldliest settings of early modern Europe: the teeming, factious, cosmopolitan city of Paris, where courtiers, merchant adventurers, and churchmen first joined together to bring to life an imperial vision called "New France."

NOTE ON PRIMARY SOURCES

Scholarship on the Jesuits and New France is indebted to two especially thorough, critically edited compilations of mission sources. The more recent is the nine-volume *Monumenta Novae Franciae,* edited by Fr. Lucien Campeau, SJ, and published in Rome by the Institutum Historicum Societatis Iesu between 1967 and 2003. This collection contains amply annotated French, Latin, and Italian sources from the mission up to the year 1661. The better-known, older collection is the seventy-three-volume *Jesuit Relations and Allied Documents*, edited by Reuben Gold Thwaites and published between 1896 and 1901 by the Burrows Brothers in Cleveland, Ohio. This collection contains annotated English translations of French, Latin, and Italian sources from the period 1610 through 1791 while including, in facing-page format, all sources in their original languages. Except where noted, I have chosen to cite Thwaites's older volumes instead of Campeau's when the same sources appear in both collections. I have done so from the considered judgment that Thwaites's volumes are sufficient in the great majority of cases. I have cited Thwaites, also, where Campeau's volumes are deficient—that is, for many sources postdating 1661. Also, readers wishing to consult cited material will have greater ease of access to Thwaites's volumes, which are available online and in more libraries. In instances where I have translated or revised others' translations of original texts, I have indicated so in the notes.

APOSTLES OF EMPIRE

PART I

Foundations and the Era of the Parisian *Relations*

CHAPTER I

A Mission for France

Writing home to Paris from "the middle of a forest" in Canada on June 6, 1632, Paul Le Jeune told his Jesuit superior that, after treading American soil for the first time—at Gaspé in eastern Quebec—he had asked some French laymen already there to build an altar so he could offer Mass. The priest added that, during his first act of divine worship in America, he was astonished that the texts from his missal that day included words from the Great Commission at the end of St. Matthew's Gospel. There, after rising from the dead, Christ says to his apostles: "All power is given to me in Heaven and earth. . . . Teach ye all nations; baptizing them in the name of the Father, and of the Son, and of the Holy Ghost."[1] Le Jeune took this as a "good omen" and declared that he and the small band of missionaries who had crossed the Atlantic with him were like "pioneers" in an army, digging "trenches" for "brave soldiers" who would later "besiege and take the place."[2]

Three decades later, working in Paris as metropolitan procureur or development officer for the mission to New France, Le Jeune urged King Louis XIV to send troops across the Atlantic to extend French colonial rule and Catholic worship into Iroquois, English, and Dutch lands. He would not live to see the commissioning of the Carignan-Salières Regiment for North American action in 1665, or receive news of its victories against "the little Turk of New France," as another Jesuit called the Iroquois at that time.[3]

Le Jeune was a leader not only of efforts to bring Native American populations into the Catholic fold, but also of a worldly enterprise of building up a French Atlantic empire. Throughout his career he would cast himself and other missionaries as a Christian army that wielded spiritual weapons against Satan and a host of indigenous "superstitions."[4] At the same time he would tirelessly promote North America's physical transformation through commerce, mining, agriculture, town-building, and actual military conquests by French troops and allied Indian warriors. He and other Jesuits were pioneers for France, as well as for Catholicism, in America.

Le Jeune was the first major author and redactor of the *Relations de la Nouvelle France,* published annually beginning in 1632. He served for many years as mission superior, and as an active missionary in and around Quebec, before serving the mission administratively in Paris from 1649 to 1662. His story opens a window onto the French metropolitan world in which the mission to New France was conceived, and upon which it would depend for decades for manpower, material resources, and moral support. The contours of that world, centered in Paris, also bring into focus the core concern of this book: a dynamic relationship between Catholicism and a sometimes militant French expansionism that is seen in numerous sources left behind by the missionaries.

A Young Jesuit in Bourbon Paris

Le Jeune was nearly forty when he received orders in March 1632 to cross the Atlantic and take up duties as mission superior at Quebec. At that time Quebec was a small French settlement and trading post overseen by its founder, Samuel de Champlain. In his first report on the colony, Le Jeune declared that, on the day he was given a Canadian assignment, "the joy and happiness" he felt was greater than any he had known in twenty years.[5] Those two decades before, he had been discerning a call to the priesthood and seeking admission into the Society of Jesus.

Le Jeune hailed from the French province of Champagne. He was born on July 15, 1592 into a respectable bourgeois, Protestant family of the Swiss Reformed persuasion. They lived in the small village of Vitry-le-François close to Châlons-sur-Marne (present-day Châlons-en-Champagne), a manufacturing town of about ten thousand inhabitants that had seen better days.[6]

The Huguenot community of Châlons lost a member in 1607 when Le Jeune, while still in his teens, was sacramentally received into the Roman Church. The young man's reasons for converting are unclear. But in becoming Catholic, he followed a path taken by many in Counter-Reformation France, including his king, Henry IV, who from Paris a hundred miles to the west ruled a large, divided realm still recovering from the Wars of Religion.

Le Jeune relocated to the royal capital in late September 1613, entering the Jesuit novitiate at Paris at age twenty-one.[7] Given the small social world of Châlons and its environs, it is likely Le Jeune was influenced in this path by the young Louis Lalemant, son of the bailiff of the local Comte de Vertus and later famous for his writings on spirituality. Lalemant, born in Châlons in 1578, had joined the Jesuits in 1605.[8] He later became Le Jeune's spiritual director.

Paris must have astounded Le Jeune. Teeming with nearly four hundred thousand inhabitants, it dwarfed Châlons and was many times over the largest city in France.[9] Quickly, too, Le Jeune would have met many young men like himself who had left behind a provincial existence for a cosmopolitan setting full of new possibilities. Going back to the days of Peter Abelard and Thomas Aquinas, Paris for centuries had been a magnet city for scholars and clerics on the make from all over Christendom.

The city was legendary in another way that would appeal especially to a young Jesuit. It was where Ignatius Loyola had formed the Society of Jesus with six of his friends, inside a small chapel atop the butte of Montmartre. This had occurred in 1534 on August 15, the Feast of the Assumption of the Blessed Virgin Mary.

Despite Loyola's Basque origins and his order's strong association with Spain, the Society was indelibly marked by its early French history. Four of its first ten members were from France or Francophone Savoy and, with Ignatius and others, had been educated in Paris.[10] Furthermore, by the late sixteenth century, the Jesuits were sought-after educators for elite children and confessors to high-ranking officials. By 1547, only a few years after Pope Paul III's formal approval of the Society, the Jesuits in France had secured the patronage of Guillaume du Prat, bishop of Clermont. By the end of his life the bishop had established three Jesuit colleges, two in the Auvergne at Billom and Mauriac, and another in Paris, where the school would be named Clermont in his honor. By 1575 there were fifteen Jesuit colleges in the kingdom, patronized by the duc de Nevers, the archbishop of Lyons, and other princely figures.[11] Jesuits even became court preachers and confessors of choice to the royal family.

Partly because they had catapulted so rapidly to such influence, the Jesuits faced fierce opposition in the French capital region throughout the same period. Plans for the Collège de Clermont were frustrated for years as members of the Parlement de Paris, the archbishop of the city, and officials at the University of Paris protested the venture. They were alarmed by the Society's Spanish connections and its innovative "fourth vow" of obedience to the pope, required of Jesuits when professing final vows to the traditional three of chastity, poverty, and obedience to religious superiors. More offensive still to many *parlementaires* was that during the Wars of Religion, many Jesuits collaborated with the militant, ultramontane Holy Union led by the Guise family, themselves major patrons of the order. And in 1594, after a student of the Jesuits failed to assassinate Henry IV, the Parlement banished the Society from its jurisdiction. Officials in Normandy and Burgundy followed suit.[12]

Paradoxically French Jesuits benefited from this period of exile, which lasted until 1603. Henry IV rehabilitated the Society to demonstrate the sincerity of his Catholic conversion and to assert royal power over the parlementaires. To secure Henry's favor, the Jesuits agreed to a stipulation in his Edict of Rouen that all members of the Society laboring in the kingdom be French-born or naturalized Frenchmen, and that all swear an oath of loyalty to the Crown.[13] This overlaid the troublesome fourth vow with (so to speak) a kind of fifth vow of allegiance to France. The requirement made the Jesuits of early Bourbon France an unusually nationally homogenous group of male religious, and one that in Paris, especially, took pains to demonstrate political loyalty. This patriotic corps of French Jesuits would fill positions in the mission to North America, distinguishing the enterprise from Iberian Jesuit missions in the same period, which included in their ranks not just Spanish and Portuguese men, but also Italians, Danes, men from the British Isles, and even men from the Middle East and mission lands themselves.[14]

When young Le Jeune arrived in Paris for his novitiate, the Society was enjoying rich fruits of this rapprochement with the monarchy. Henry had reopened Jesuit colleges, channeling money and favor their way. He also established eighteen new Jesuit colleges, taking a special interest in the Collège de La Flèche, housed in a magnificent château near Angers, where Le Jeune and many other Jesuits sent to Canada would undergo part of their formation.[15] Henry further approved the creation of a new level of Jesuit administrative bureaucracy in his realm, the Assistancy of France. This enabled the five Jesuit provinces of the kingdom to be overseen from a national perspective in Paris, rather than answer directly, one by one, to the Society's generalate in Rome as had previously been the case.[16] This new degree of autonomy from Rome was soon exhibited following the assassination of Henry IV by François Ravaillac. Once again under clouds of suspicion, the Jesuits in Paris issued a declaration of their allegiance to the French Crown and the special "liberty of the Gallican church."[17] They were quickly reprimanded by the Jesuit superior general, Claudio Acquaviva, and by Pope Gregory XV. Nevertheless the French Jesuits continued to promote a Gallican vision of the Church and a conception of the French monarchy as specially favored by God.[18] As a result even Parisian magistrates once hostile to the Society were by 1614 citing Jesuits' self-regulation under French law as exemplary.[19]

Amid such optimism about the Jesuits' relationship with the governing elites of France, Le Jeune in 1613 entered a brand new house of novitiate in the wealthy faubourg of Saint-Germain, close to Paris's bustling Latin Quarter. The building, the Hôtel de Mézières, close to the Église de Saint-Sulpice, had several years before been gifted to the Jesuits for their novices by Madeleine Luillier de Saint-Beuve and her nephew, the baron de la Bussière. Le Jeune and other aspiring Jesuits thus studied, prayed, and socialized in stately quarters furnished and supplied by wealthy patrons that included also the young King Louis XIII and his mother, the queen regent Marie de' Medici.[20]

In Saint-Germain Le Jeune was close to the administrative heart of the French kingdom in the period of the prince de Condé's machinations against the queen regent, the rare calling of the Estates General in 1614, and the young king's declaration of his majority. He was also just a few blocks from the River Seine—full in those days of commercial boat traffic and lined with fisheries and mills—at a point at which the newly reconstructed Palais de Louvre on the opposite bank stretched imposingly across one's line of vision. Paris as Le Jeune first encountered it was undergoing dramatic transformations as a result of Crown-sponsored projects. These included commercial-residential centers such as the Plâce-Dauphine, new bridges and quays, and land reclamation efforts in the Seine such as the creation of the Île de Saint-Louis out of two smaller islands.[21]

Just as Le Jeune entered the novitiate at Paris when its facilities were new, in 1622 he returned to the city for theology studies, after several years at La Flèche, Rennes, and Bourges, when the Collège de Clermont was in the first years of resurrected life. The college, established in 1563, was situated on the Rue Saint-Jacques in the Latin Quarter, close to the University of Paris. It had closed its doors during the period of Jesuit exile early in the reign of Henry IV and, due to parlementaire opposition, its reopening was delayed until 1618, when Louis XIII insisted the college was needed to ensure that talented youth would continue relocating to the royal capital.[22]

Le Jeune's second period in Paris, 1622 to 1626, was crucial for his professional formation. Also at Clermont at the time were the Parisian brothers Charles and Jérôme Lalemant, along with Barthèlemy Vimont from Lisieux. Vimont would eventually succeed Le Jeune as mission superior at Quebec. The Lalemants were the sons of Sieur Gabriel Lalemant, a *lieutenant criminel* of the early Paris police force who also judged cases brought to the city's criminal court.[23] Charles had met Le Jeune and Vimont at La Flèche during his own theology studies, and in Paris he served as principal of the boarding school at Clermont before being posted to New France in 1625. He was the first superior of the Jesuit mission there and would later precede Le Jeune, as well, in the office of metropolitan procureur of the mission. His brother Jérôme, who would also eventually serve in Quebec as mission superior, was by 1623 already a professor of theology at Clermont.[24]

Founding fathers of the mission thus knew each other first as peers, teachers, and students in Paris before their travels to New France. This Parisian network of Jesuits associated with the mission was tied to another at La Flèche. There a Jesuit named Enemond Massé, who in the early 1610s spent a very brief period in Acadie (present-day Nova Scotia and part of New Brunswick), was a member of the faculty from 1614 to 1625. He influenced many future missionaries to Canada: Le Jeune, Vimont, and Charles Lalemant; Alexandre de Vieuxpont, Claude Quentin, Charles Dumarché, and Nicolas Adam; and the femininely named Anne de Noüe, who was of noble lineage and who had earlier served Henry IV as an officer of the privy chamber.[25]

Perhaps due to his early contact with Massé and Charles Lalemant, Le Jeune in 1625 sent a letter to the Jesuit general in Rome, Mutius Vitelleschi, expressing a wish to be posted for missionary work, but not necessarily in America. In his reply Vitelleschi praised the young Jesuit's desire to labor apostolically "among barbarous peoples where, in human terms, there is no comfort." But he did not promise Le Jeune a missionary assignment, encouraging him rather to continue on the path of charity and obedience until the will of "good Jesus" for his future was brought more clearly to light.[26]

While in Paris as a theology student and new priest, Le Jeune had access to writings by Jesuits who worked as missionaries in different parts of the world, thanks partly to a publishing project of an enterprising young printer and merchant named Sébastien Cramoisy. In his print shop on the Rue Saint-Jacques, which catered to teachers and students at Clermont, Cramoisy produced and sold at affordable prices a number of French translations of missionary *relations*, the first appearing in 1624. This was Nicolas Trigault's translation of missionary letters from Japan, recounting martyrdoms endured by Christian converts there.[27] Around the same time Cramoisy printed more titles on Jesuit missions in East Asia.[28] Later in his own *Relations* from Canada Le Jeune would allude to details about China and Japan, likely gleaned from these books.[29]

Le Jeune at this time may also have drawn inspiration from the canonization of the first Jesuit missionary saint, Francis Xavier, in 1622. The first Jesuit to travel to India and Japan, Xavier was declared a saint along with Ignatius Loyola on March 12 by Pope Gregory XV. Several months later, as Le Jeune was about to commence theology studies, the Clermont faculty hosted a day of festivities to celebrate the canonizations. These were commemorated in a book published by Cramoisy, who also printed a French-language biography of Loyola at this time.[30]

Four years at Clermont furthermore brought Le Jeune near to persons of rank and wealth based in Paris. His spiritual director at Clermont, Jean de La Bretesche, was close to the family of Henri de Lévis, the young duc de Ventadour. Ventadour's uncle was Henry II de Montmorency, the viceroy of New France from 1620 to 1625. At La Bretesche's funeral late in 1624, Ventadour was persuaded by some Jesuits at Clermont to purchase his uncle's colonial office from the Crown. This action, accompanied by the duke's expressions of support for launching a Jesuit mission in New France, marked a turning point for Jesuits who hoped to be sent to North America. However supportive General Vitelleschi was in Rome, they needed patronage at the French court to launch any such mission.[31] Providing this, Ventadour turned his grand home close to the Jesuit novitiate in Saint-Germain into a center of activity devoted to New France. His salon was then frequented by Champlain, prominent merchants, nobles considering overseas investment, and Jesuits.[32] Ventadour would personally fund the expenses of the first group of Jesuits sent to Quebec in 1625: Charles Lalemant, Massé, and the future martyr Jean de Brébeuf.

After finishing at Clermont Le Jeune was not sent to Canada to join this group. Rather, in his mid-thirties, he embarked upon a professorial path of teaching rhetoric, first at the Collège de Nevers in Bourgogne. Then in 1629 he was given a prestigious teaching position at Caen in Lower Normandy. There he made important contacts while serving as chaplain to an elite laymen's confraternity. He offered spiritual direction to leading citizens of Caen, encouraging them to live prayerful lives dedicated to social and apostolic action. The following year he was sent to Dieppe, Normandy's premier port city, where he often preached publicly.[33] It was at Dieppe early in 1632 that he received orders from his Parisian provincial, Barthèlemy Jacquinot, to set sail for North America (see fig. 1).

French Expansion and Missions before 1632

The mission Le Jeune consecrated at Gaspé in 1632 was not the first French-sponsored Catholic enterprise in the Americas, but it was the first lasting one on the French imperial map. Compared to the Portuguese and Spanish, who had been active in the Atlantic World since the late fifteenth century, the French got off to a belated start with both missions and colonization.

The first French exploratory and colonial ventures overseas were the expeditions of Jacques Cartier and Jean-François Roberval in Canada in the 1630s and 1640s, Nicolas Durand de Villegaignon's ill-fated effort in Brazil from 1555 to 1559, and the short-lived enterprise of the Huguenots René de Laudonnière and Jean Ribault at Fort Caroline in Florida from 1562 to 1565. Later, in the wake of the Wars of Religion, French fisheries and trading posts began dotting North American and Caribbean coast-lines, on the Isle de Sable near Nova Scotia, the mainland of Acadie and Tadoussac at the confluence of the Saint Lawrence and Saguenay rivers, and the Isle Saint-Croix, today part of the U.S. Virgin Islands. All of these ventures proved to be short-lived.[34] Champlain's establishment at Quebec, beginning in 1608, would be the first successful French colony in the Americas.

As a Catholic kingdom, France in this period had to respect, if grudg-ingly, legal restrictions on its imperial aspirations imposed by the papacy since the 1490s. In the aftermath of Christopher Columbus's first voyage to the Caribbean, Pope Alexander VI reserved for Spain rights of trade and governance (known as the *patronato*) in the newly discovered Amer-icas and parts of Asia and Africa not already claimed by Portugal. Thus the French had to justify their presence in America in terms that would compel sufferance from the pope and other Catholic leaders in Europe. When King François I decided to pursue colonization, he sought Pope Clement VII's blessing in 1533, stressing his duty as a Christian prince to spread Christianity in places not yet penetrated by the Iberians. Clement compliantly interpreted his predecessors' bulls in practical terms: Iberian dominion did not apply in lands where no Spaniards or Portuguese were present.[35]

Shortly after, in 1534, Cartier first crossed the Atlantic, setting foot at Gaspé where his men planted in the ground a thirty-foot wooden cross that was emblazoned with the fleur-de-lis, the symbol of the French monarchy. This act came to symbolize French claims to most of North America, regardless of what the Spanish—and later the English—argued to the contrary. Echoing François I, Cartier promoted the cause of America's Christianization in an account of his voyages published in Paris in 1545. He offered a vision of Christianity's historical progression westward from the Holy Land to ancient Gaul. It was fitting, therefore, that the French should spearhead Christianity's further westward course across the Atlantic. He also evoked the role of France in the medieval crusades against Islam and stressed his kingdom's rivalry with the Iberian powers to bolster arguments for French activity in the New World.[36]

Despite such talk, Catholic missionary activity was not sponsored by France until Henry IV's time. And the first early modern French missionaries traveled eastward, to the Ottoman Empire.[37] However, Henry's Jesuit confessor, Pierre Coton, proposed a new Jesuit mission to Canada, an idea that appealed to the king. By this time missionaries had proven integral to rival colonial powers' progress in Latin America, and the remarkable growth of the Jesuits' institutional presence in the Iberian empires illustrated that order's special potential in serving European expansion abroad. Indeed, by 1603 the Jesuit province of New Spain already had seven colleges and a satellite vice-province in the Philippines and was recruiting men born in America, not just Europe.[38]

When Henry was killed in 1610 the future of French missions was suddenly in the hands of his widow. Fortunately for the Jesuits, Marie de' Medici retained Coton at court, despite false but persisting rumors of his involvement with the assassination. He was thus able, with the queen's *dame d'honneur*, Antoinette de Pons-Ribérac, the marquise de Guercheville, to arrange for the funding and transportation of two Jesuits to go to Acadie in 1611. Married to the governor of Paris, the marquise had just become the major backer of an Acadian colonial enterprise underway since 1605, led by the Huguenot nobleman Jean de Biencourt de Poutrincourt.

Poutrincourt had sought the Catholic noblewoman's aid after alienating Huguenot merchants at Dieppe with a decision to bring a diocesan priest, Jesse Fleuche from Langres, to his colony. But the marquise quickly leveraged her power over Poutrincourt in ways that distressed him. She required that two Jesuits join him across the Atlantic, her confessor Massé and Pierre Biard from Grenoble. She also bequeathed to the Jesuits stock previously owned by the former Huguenot investors in the enterprise, so that the missionaries could draw upon future profits from the fur trade to support ministries among Native Americans.[39] Poutrincourt was upset by the news that half of the expected profits of his enterprise would go to the Jesuits. This meant that he would not be able to fulfill his dream of creating a proprietary, agricultural colony in which he would recoup his family's honor, by setting himself up as a feudal lord, following losses suffered during the Wars of Religion.[40]

Tensions worsened between Poutrincourt and the Jesuits when the latter began scrutinizing Fleuche's mode of baptizing hunter-gatherer Mi'kmaqs and other Natives in Acadie. Following a centuries-old practice of expansionist Christendom, Fleuche would baptize first and teach Christianity second, even as the Mi'kmaqs presumed the ritual was simply a European way of sealing alliances.[41] Biard and Massé, by contrast, saw individual understanding as a prerequisite to sacramental incorporation into the Church. They also suspected that Poutrincourt favored mass baptisms simply so he could brag to potential investors about the conversion component of his project.

At any rate, the Jesuits' new mission had little time to develop, as Acadie was attacked late in 1613 by Samuell Argall, a Welsh pirate. Biard was taken to Jamestown in Virginia, where he was almost hanged. But he and Massé made it home to France, where they began publicizing the potential of colonial development and Catholic missions in New France.

Ensconced at the Jesuits' college in Lyons, Biard penned an account of his overseas experiences that went to print, in the same city, in 1616.

This first published Jesuit *relation* about Canada was as much an effort to attract royal officials and investors to New France as it was a report on what he and Massé had attempted in Acadie as missionaries. Dedicating the *Relation* to Louis XIII, Biard prayed in print that the young king might "one day plant the standard of the Cross with its *fleur de lys* upon the most distant infidel lands." Expressing desires for more than just a "Catholic" colony with sufficient "means to maintain it," Biard also made a case for French "rights" to vast territories in North America, over and above any "pretensions of the English."[42]

This language referred to a border dispute between France and England over lands between the thirty-ninth and forty-fifth parallels—that is, lands as far south as the Chesapeake Bay on America's eastern coast. Analyzing charters and other documents back to Cartier's time, the Jesuit asserted French rights to territories already claimed by England. From this point onward, French Jesuits in North America would continue to define "New France" in expansive terms that in theory would have justified French conquests all the way to Virginia. They would also sidestep the matter of the Spanish patronato. Biard himself dismissed Spanish claims to North America at a time when French claims across the globe were beginning to raise eyebrows in Rome, not just in Madrid and Lisbon.

Tellingly Biard criticized Poutrincourt's vision of a feudal, self-sufficient colony as impractical and old-fashioned. "It is great folly," he wrote, "for insignificant fellows to go [to New France], who picture themselves baronies, and I know not what fiefs and demesnes for three or four thousand *écus* . . . which they will have to sink into that country."[43] Instead Biard proposed sustained development by "several private houses in Paris," which nevertheless would not "greatly interfer[e]" with colonial affairs. Furthermore Biard was concerned that future colonial developers regulate more than Poutrincourt had the caliber of French colonists with whom Native Americans mixed socially and sexually. He wished for Native Americans to encounter well-mannered, pious, and public-spirited French farmers, tradesmen, and aristocrats, not men "flee[ing] the ruin of their families in France" or "covetous" of wealth and power.[44]

Biard's was the primary text on New France to which Le Jeune and other younger Jesuits were exposed before their own journeys to Canada. Furthermore its antifeudal, royalist, and French imperial tenor positioned the Jesuits well in the eyes of courtly officials, nobles, and merchants who would join together to transform Champlain and Ventadour's early efforts into a more ambitious enterprise.

Still, the Jesuits were not the first missionaries in Champlain's colony. Before Biard's *Relation* went to press, Champlain was persuaded by a court official from his hometown in Saintonge to recruit Franciscan Récollets for apostolic work in Quebec. Four Récollet friars thus arrived in Quebec in the spring of 1615, led by Denis Jamet of the order's Parisian province, and began preaching among the hunter-gatherer Montagnais and sedentary Hurons in the region.[45]

In the early 1620s the Récollets' future in New France seemed secure. They had a monastery and chapel in place, were planning a school, and welcomed more confreres from France. Among them was Gabriel Sagard, who lived for a time among the Hurons and compiled a dictionary of their language. Their labors were initially underwritten by Charles des Boves, a nobleman from Champagne with ties to the Guise clan.[46] But when Des Boves died unexpectedly in 1623, the young colonial viceroy Ventadour answered the Récollets' call for new support from France with Jesuits, not with a new patron. This was the context in which Charles Lalemant, Massé, and Brébeuf arrived from France in the spring of 1625, along with two consecrated lay brothers of the Society.

The Jesuits quickly met with resistance among Huguenot merchants in Quebec. Champlain, pragmatic as well as piously Catholic, had partnered with these men, Guillaume de Caën and other members of a joint-stock company backing the colonial enterprise at that time. Although Champlain favored the Jesuits, they were required to reside with the Récollets until the summer of 1627, even though the rhythm of a friary, with prayers in common several times a day, was in tension with the individuated approach to religious life prescribed in the Jesuit Constitutions. Relations between missionaries of both orders were amicable, however. Brébeuf and a friar named La Roche d'Aillon got along well and planned a joint mission to Huron Country.

Altogether, these first Jesuits in the Saint Lawrence River Valley, like the Récollets, felt their position in Canada to be insecure. In 1626 missionaries of both orders attempted to improve their situation by means of the printed word back in France. Friar Joseph Caron published a pamphlet that urged King Louis (whom he knew, having been tutor to the king's brother) to remove De Caën and his trading company from Quebec. Le Caron went so far as to question the competency of the Huguenot merchants to run a colonial enterprise. The Jesuits' approach was more politic. Lalemant sent several letters to France—to Champlain who was visiting Paris at the time, to the Jesuit and Récollet provincials, and to several others with financial interests in Quebec—alerting the recipients to poor conditions in the colony but without criticizing De Caën by name. He also sent a letter to his brother Jérôme, which ended up being published in Paris early in 1627. The letter was hawked as a pamphlet in the streets of the capital, at the instigation of the Jesuit Philibert Noyrot, who had recently been to New France to assess the situation with De Caën.[47]

The complaints against De Caën succeeded, but this was owed substantially to the fact that colonial policy was newly in the hands of Cardinal Richelieu, the prime minister, who wished to assert state control over Huguenot wealth and power following the short-lived Peace of La Rochelle. The cardinal took for himself the viceregal powers held by Ventadour and gathered a coterie of investors for a new colonial merchant monopoly. These included royal officers, merchants, and financiers from Rouen, Bordeaux, and especially Paris—but, conspicuously, no members of the Caën clan of Dieppe.[48]

Chartered in 1627, Richelieu's merchant company was called the Compagnie de la Nouvelle France and nicknamed the Cent-Associés (Hundred Associates). Granted a royal monopoly over all prospective French trade in North America, the Compagnie was to be exclusively Catholic in membership. In the meantime, Champlain—a company investor and increasingly ardent in his Catholicism—took up permanent residence in Quebec as acting governor.

This was part of a larger scheme by Richelieu to centralize control over French overseas engagements and to make France more competitive with other European powers. In this same period, Richelieu planned a major reorganization and expansion of the French navy. Furthermore, in accordance with the Code Michaud of 1626, he encouraged nobles to participate in overseas trade without risk of *dérogation*, or loss of Second Estate status.[49]

Although New France was now on stronger financial footing, its missions remained insecure. The late 1620s were turbulent years as France was, on the one hand, engulfed by flaring hostilities between Huguenots and the king's army, culminating in the Siege of La Rochelle. On the other hand, France was drawn into a war with England that spread to North America and resulted in the temporary loss of Quebec between July 1629 and March 1632. There was no missionary activity during this period.

However, barely a fortnight after the English and French signed a treaty at Saint-Germain-en-Laye that returned New France to Louis XIII, Richelieu signed an order, on April 14, 1632, that secured transatlantic passage for Paul Le Jeune and two other Jesuits. Sailing with Le Jeune only a few weeks later were the nobleman-turned-Jesuit De Nouë, who had already spent time in New France from 1626 to 1629, and Gilbert Burel, a consecrated lay brother of the Society who was an experienced cook and gardener. On board the same ship were three Capuchin friars. Richelieu's own confessor, his éminence grise Joseph du Tremblay, was the prefect of Capuchin missions based in France—missions then directed at Protestant England and the Ottoman Empire—and he had convinced the cardinal to allow his confreres to join the Jesuits in Canada.[50]

Conspicuously absent from the ship were any Récollet friars, who were shocked by the slight. In response Sagard authored an account of their work around Quebec prior to the English incursions. Published quickly in 1632 in Paris, the book was revealingly dedicated not to King Louis but to "the almighty monarch . . . Jesus Christ" and to a nobleman named Henry de Lorraine-Harcourt, whose family was distant from Richelieu and tied to the ultramontanist Catholic League.[51] In the book there was little enthusiasm on display for the French monarchy. The Récollets' attitude may have factored into Richelieu's decision to deny them renewed access to New France, together with the fact that the order was more compliant than the French Jesuits with new papal efforts to centrally regulate missions by means of the new Congregation de Propaganda Fide in Rome.[52]

The Jesuits of Paris were more comfortable with Richelieu's political and cultural aims and willing, too, to advocate for French ventures abroad in patriotic terms. Richelieu, in turn, was confident he could delegate to the Jesuits and Capuchins the task of advancing national interests across the Atlantic.

Lay Metropolitan Support and Sébastien Cramoisy's Press

In his *Relation* of 1616, Biard had pinned hopes for the Jesuit mission in America on "the ambition of the great" and "display of the rich." He had in mind the most resourceful French elites who could turn New France—"a horrible wilderness," lacking "ornaments and riches of the soul"—into a land as prosperous as France itself. He alluded in particular to great families in Paris with the wealth and management capabilities to conduct large-scale enterprises.[53]

The Jesuits of New France were well aware that their project could not succeed based on clerical zeal alone. Along with the Crown, a network of lay elites proved critical to the development of the mission relaunched at Quebec under Le Jeune's leadership. Two organizations were the main nodes of this network: the mercantile Compagnie de la Nouvelle France and a semi-secretive confraternity affiliated with the Jesuits, the Congrégation des Messieurs de Paris.

When Richelieu established the merchant company in 1627, each member invested three thousand livres in exchange for stock in a single seigneury devoted to the commercial development of all Canadian territory claimed by France.[54] The fur trade was to be the main source of profit. In turn the company was to build settlements in the Saint Lawrence River Valley and support Jesuit missions. Among the company's original members were sixty-two residents of Paris along with merchants, noble financiers, and royal administrators from further afield, especially Rouen. In time the Jesuits of Quebec would become stockholders.[55]

The Congrégation des Messieurs was a confraternity founded in Paris by the Jesuits and influential laymen—parlementaires, other nobles, prominent merchants, and royal and municipal officials. They convened regularly at the Jesuits' Maison Professe, a residence for leading priests who had professed final vows, on the Rue Saint-Antoine. The congregation was an exclusive fellowship in which personal and professional relationships were cultivated. Its aims were social and political as well as devotional. As historian Louis Châtellier has written, its goals were to unite members "in loyalty to the Virgin [Mary] and in a religion lived intensely" and "to create at all points a Catholic elite destined to surround and serve the Christian prince," helping him realize more fully "the Christian state."[56] Its lay character was critical. Its goal was not to build up a theocracy run by priests or arrange society wholly around Catholic worship but to infuse the spheres of political administration, military service, and social improvement with Christian virtue, elevating worldly society without effacing its secular character.

Prominent in both the Compagnie de la Nouvelle France and the Congrégation des Messieurs was the nobleman François Sublet de Noyers, a loyal member of Richelieu's administration. Sublet de Noyers represents well the metropolitan elites who by the 1620s were taking interest in the Jesuit mission and commercial ventures in New France. He was a major patron of the Jesuits in Paris, funding for example the construction of a new church for their novitiate in 1630.[57] His association with the Canadian mission became personal: in the *Relation* of 1637, Le Jeune mentioned that Sublet de Noyers adopted a Native American boy into his household.[58]

Sublet de Noyers was politically ambitious and from a recently ennobled family. He had a hand in many projects of state centralization under Richelieu. In Paris he resided in an elegant new *maison particulière* on the Rue Saint-Honoré close to the palace. When not in Paris he resided in other new homes at Fontainebleau, Rueil, and Dangu that well served his position in the royal bureaucracy, rather than setting himself up as a great feudal lord over his ancestral demesne in Normandy. A model "creature" of Richelieu, he served the Crown with diligence, first as a military commander in Champagne and Picardy engaged with constructing new fortresses and modernizing the French military, then as a secretary of state and superintendent of the king's buildings, overseeing royal construction and renovation projects.[59]

Another member of both the Compagnie and the Congrégation was Sébastien Cramoisy, the publisher of the *Relations*. Known in his day as "the King of the Rue Saint-Jacques," Cramoisy may have been the layman most crucial to the early success of the Jesuit mission to New France. He has been described as "a substantial citizen" of Paris who published more than twenty-five hundred books and numerous official publications for Louis XIII, Richelieu, and their successors.[60] Indeed Cramoisy produced a tenth of all books printed in Paris during his lifetime. This is impressive considering there were about seventy-five printing establishments in the capital at the height of his career and that Paris was one of the great centers of book production in the era (see fig. 2).[61]

Well before the Jesuit Le Jeune had arrived at the Collège de Clermont on the Rue Saint-Jacques in 1622, nearby on the same street the young and ambitious Cramoisy had turned the modest printing business he had inherited from his maternal grandfather, Sébastien Nivelle, into a thriving establishment. Chez Cramoisy, then both a residence and a print-shop, occupied the grand Maison de l'Écu de Bretagne close to Clermont and the University of Paris. Cramoisy lived there with his growing family, expanding his grandfather's business and turning the original print-shop into headquarters for an expanding network of other firms he bought out.[62]

Cramoisy had been born in Paris in 1585 to a bourgeois father, Pierre Cramoisy, whose family was connected to the duc d'Anjou and Alençon, the brother of King Henry III. Cramoisy's mother was Élisabeth Nivelle, the daughter of the Parisian *libraire* Nivelle, whom Cramoisy succeeded in 1606 at the age of twenty-one.[63] By virtue of these family connections, Cramoisy by 1612 was one of the top booksellers in Paris and by 1621 the official printer for Henry, the duc de Lorraine. Lorraine's first wife was a sister of Henry IV, and his second wife was Margherita Gonzaga, whose family was close to the Jesuits and included Medicis and Holy Roman emperors.[64]

Many of Cramoisy's early imprints were textbooks for the Jesuits at Clermont and other colleges in France, the Low Countries, and Germany. Cramoisy also produced scholarly works by Jesuits such as the humanist Jacques Sirmond and the theologian Denis Pétau, who taught Le Jeune.[65] And in 1625 he published Thomas Pelletier's *Apologie ou Défense pour les*

Pères Jésuites. This relationship with the Society helped Cramoisy establish himself internationally, in Antwerp, Brussels, and further afield.[66]

Young Le Jeune, who was interested in literary pursuits, frequented Cramoisy's *librairie* while studying theology at Clermont. By the mid-1620s he may have been on personal terms with the printer. The two young men had something important in common: just as Le Jeune by June 1625 had been in contact with the Jesuit general, Cramoisy, too, established a personal correspondence with Vitelleschi early in his career.[67] Indeed Cramoisy began to serve the general as virtually the Jesuits' official printer in France. In exchange the general would refer aspiring Jesuit authors to Cramoisy's firm.[68] Over time Cramoisy received an unusually high number of personal letters from Vitelleschi and his successors. Between 1628 and 1666 at least forty-seven letters were sent from the general's office to Cramoisy. The publisher even appears to have received more letters from the general than any other non-Jesuit individual in France—a list of personages that includes Cardinal Richelieu, Queen Anne of Austria, the prince de Condé, and various prominent churchmen.[69]

As important as Cramoisy's reputation was among the Jesuits, it would not have served the latter's hopes for the Canadian mission unless an association with him also guaranteed access to French elites interested in North American enterprise. Cramoisy was exceptionally well placed in this regard. He had been close to Richelieu since at least 1614, when the latter, as the young bishop of Luçon, arrived in Paris to represent the clergy at the Estates General. The Cramoisys and Nivelles for generations had been connected to the Richelieu family as vassals; Richelieu personally selected Cramoisy to print his first publication, a transcript of his speech to the Estates General.[70] Thereafter the ambitious bishop when outside Paris communicated with Cramoisy about events in the capital. Richelieu's meteoric rise to power in France began soon after, when he was chosen by Marie de' Medici as a close adviser. Cramoisy's star rose, too. In 1629 he was given a lucrative monopoly on documents printed for the Cour de Monnaies that regulated French currency. In 1633 he was named *imprimeur du roy*, an office granted to only a few printers. By 1640 he would be appointed as director of operations of the new Imprimerie Royale at the Louvre, working under the authority of Sublet de Noyers.[71]

In the meantime, on August 1, 1628, Cramoisy had signed his name as one of the Hundred Associates whom Richelieu had gathered for the colonial effort to New France.[72] In 1633 he was also named Parisian procureur for the Compagnie de la Nouvelle France. And several years later he was chosen to receive and transmit to Canada a large donation of funds from Marie-Madeleine de Vignerot, duchesse d'Aiguillon and Richelieu's niece, for a hospital she established in Quebec.

Although it is unclear who initiated Le Jeune and Cramoisy's project of publishing annual *Relations* from New France, the merchant company as well as the mission itself stood to benefit from it. Published reports by Jesuit missionaries would, as well, serve the Crown by confirming the pious purposes of French expansion into North America that were crucial, at the time, for justifying it against Spanish and English claims.

Thus in 1632 Le Jeune not only took the post of mission superior at Quebec. He also became a published author, when Cramoisy printed the first of what would be many mission reports he would send to Paris. His *Briève Relation* of that year was in the form of a letter to his provincial. Such *relations* had been a standardized form of communication between missionaries and their superiors since the earliest days of the Society of Jesus.[73] However, the rapid publication of a *relation* by a printer of Cramoisy's stature was unusual.

Considering the publication of Biard's *Relation* in 1616 as well as the fate of Lalemant's letter of 1626, it is unlikely Le Jeune had no thought that his first *relation* to Jacquinot might be circulated publicly. Furthermore a comparison between the autographed manuscript sent to Jacquinot and the first Cramoisy imprint suggests that publication was part of Le Jeune's original agenda in 1632. The original letter is entitled "Relation Briesve de Nostre Voiage" and is dated by Le Jeune "du milieu d'un bois, 16 août 1632."[74] The Cramoisy imprint, however, appears to have been based on a second, more polished redaction, now lost, dated August 28. The latter contained elaborations not found in the extant manuscript, including the personalizing detail that the mission superior had not experienced such happiness for twenty years as he experienced on the day he received orders to depart France for North America.[75] Other differences may be due to editing by Le Jeune, his provincial, or an assistant of Cramoisy's. These differences include more economical, energetic descriptions of scenes in Canada and more modish spelling and syntax consistent with the standardizing, elite Parisian French of the time. Also suggestive of a predetermined plan for publication is the quick turnaround between the receipt of Le Jeune's original report by Jacquinot, which could have arrived in France no earlier than late September, given the duration of even smooth Atlantic crossings at that time, and the publication of the edited version before the end of 1632.

The *Relations* became available for purchase as handsome, inexpensive octavo-sized volumes at Cramoisy's bookstore in the Latin Quarter.[76] They were a new kind of publication in France, attracting notice and becoming best sellers. Of course, they were not the first missionary writings published in the French vernacular.[77] A letter by Francis Xavier in Goa to Ignatius Loyola was translated and published in Paris as early as 1545.[78] Among other publications, there was a Parisian precedent for Cramoisy's own series of translations of Iberian and Italian Jesuit writings from around the world: between 1578 and 1586 Thomas Brumen produced a series of *Lettres* from Jesuit missions in Asia, South America, and Africa.[79] But Le Jeune's *Brière Relation* of 1632 stood out for its French authorship, French colonial context, and descriptions of very recent events. Readers of Le Jeune's first *Relation* understood, from the title of the text, that the events described had happened within the previous year. To be treated soon after to another, longer account by the same author, Le Jeune's *Relation de ce qui s'est Passé en la Nouvelle France en l'Année 1633*, and then to others in subsequent years, was a new kind of experience for French readers.

The *Relations* captured imaginations in part because of how strange the Native people, Canadian lands, and missionary experiences they described must have seemed. At the same time many early readers of the *Relations*—members of the Congrégation de Messieurs and the Compagnie de la Nouvelle France, court officials, other Jesuits, and their friends in Paris—would have already known something about Canada from Biard's

Relation, earlier writings by Cartier and others, and private conversations. These readers may have been struck by the *familiar* quality of Le Jeune's polished, sometimes ironic, rhetorician's voice addressing them from "the middle of a forest" across the Atlantic Ocean. His *Relations* had a "this-just-in!" quality associated more with private letters and French digests of European events, such as the *Mercure François* published by the Richer brothers in Paris since 1611. That they were journalistic and bore the stamp of the king's official printer distinguished them all the more.

The *Relations* also embodied and further cultivated the Jesuits' partnership with metropolitan officials and other elites. Nobles such as Sublet de Noyers and Richelieu's niece read them and afterward directed personal resources to the mission and other Canadian projects. At the same time, the early *Relations* were intended to inspire masses and other prayers in France for the mission. They succeeded in this, as at least one grand prayer service in Paris for the mission, held by the Ursulines, attests.[80]

Thematically the first Cramoisy *Relation* from New France was a mix of the familiar and the strange. The text opened with Le Jeune's praise of patrons who ensured his Atlantic passage. The Jesuit described how, at Le Havre, before departing France, he had paid respects to Richelieu's nephew, François de Vignerot du Pontcourlay, and thanked the curé de Havre and the Ursuline Mothers of the city for their hospitality while the Jesuits were passing through and making preparations. Le Jeune also described the new lands he and the others sailed past while entering the mouth of the Saint Lawrence River. He sighted land on June 1, 1632, which he was startled to see covered with snow so late in the year. But his initial impressions of the country, however harsh the weather, included positive comparisons with familiar things from home, such as the "large gray partridges" killed for food that were "as large as our chickens in France," and the glories of the Saguenay River, which the Jesuit believed was "as beautiful as the Seine." It was just after this remark that Le Jeune described how on Trinity Sunday he set foot on American land for the first time, to celebrate Mass at Gaspé. "Never did man, after a long voyage, return to his country with more joy than we entered ours; it is thus we call these wretched lands," he declared, signaling a sense of ownership over, and posture of pity toward, a continent he was encountering for the first time.[81]

Working for France's "Powerful Genius"

The contrast could not have been greater between the small band of Jesuits and other Frenchmen in Quebec in 1632 and the vastness of little-explored Canada before them. More fantastic still was the gap between their situation and the grand visions of empire animating them and their supporters in France. It is no wonder Le Jeune described himself as a mere pioneer, preparing the ground for a much larger army of Christian Frenchmen to come to America after him.

Yet once he set to work as superior of the reconstituted Jesuit mission to New France, Le Jeune proved hardly content to serve simply as a foot soldier for the colony and its Christianization. From 1632 to 1639 he directed experimental Jesuit evangelistic efforts among the Montagnais and other Algonquian-speaking peoples in the Saint Lawrence and Saint Maurice river valleys. He also oversaw the mission's successful expansion into Huron Country in the vicinity of Georgian Bay in Ontario. All the while, and into the 1640s when freed from some administrative duties, his artful composition of increasingly lengthy *Relations* for a major French press was enterprising. Working with Cramoisy, Le Jeune went beyond the call of his ordinary Jesuit obligations to communicate annually with his religious superiors in Paris and Rome (see fig. 3).

Additionally Le Jeune propagandized for the French Crown and especially for Richelieu's administration, among both Native Americans he encountered and, through print, his own countrymen. Illustrative was a ceremony held in Quebec to honor the birth of a dauphin—Louis "Le Dieudonnée," who would become Louis XIV, the unexpected issue of the long-estranged Louis XIII and Anne of Austria. Le Jeune and his confreres collaborated with company merchants and Champlain's successor, Governor Charles Huault de Montmagny, in organizing the ceremony and communicating its significance to local Indians who were gathered to witness it. Le Jeune described the ceremony in the *Relation* of 1640: "The *Te Deum laudamus* was chanted, and bonfires and fireworks were prepared with every device possible. . . . Fireworks were shot up towards Heaven, falling in golden showers . . . a fine night was illuminated by lighted torches; while the heavy thunder of the cannon resounded in . . . our great forests." According to Le Jeune, the display amazed some baptized Hurons who were watching and who wondered whether "the dominion of the French extended even over the realms of fire." But it is the Jesuits' response to the Hurons, publicized by Cramoisy, that reveals a conceptual, affective link between Christianity and French power that they sought to cultivate: "They were informed that Monseigneur the Cardinal contributed greatly to the maintenance of the Gospel laborers . . . sent to their country; this astonished them . . . and, had they not been Christians, they never would have believed that on earth men could be found willing to incur expense to assist them."[82]

Le Jeune and his confreres also attempted to elicit awe toward the Crown and French culture by urging indigenous leaders to send their children to France. Accounts of such travelers' responses to what they encountered were highlighted in the *Relations*. Also in 1640 Le Jeune boasted of a conversation he had had with some Montagnais following the return from France of one of their number, the son of a Chief Iwanchou:

> I said to them; "ask your countryman if what I told you of the greatness of our King and of the beauty of our country be not true? . . ." [Iwanchou's son] admitted that nothing had so interested him as the King, when he saw him . . . walking with his guards. He attentively observed all the soldiers, marching in good order; [they] produced a great impression on his eyes. . . . The King's piety was of powerful assistance to us in doing honor to our faith; for this good Canadian admitted that the first time he saw the King was in the house of prayer, where he prayed to Jesus. . . . As soon as this savage had seen the King, he said to the father who conducted him: "Let us go away. I have seen all, since I have seen the King."[83]

Regardless of what the young man meant, or whether he really said all this, Le Jeune wished to convey to French readers that the North American Natives were able—and ought—to return to their homeland with such impressions of France and its king.

Le Jeune's efforts to cultivate deference to the French Crown among Native Americans dovetailed with a propaganda effort within France itself during the era of the Thirty Years' War. Indeed the *Relations* of the 1630s and early 1640s served partly to enhance Richelieu's reputation during the lead-up to and early years of France's involvement in the war on the side of Protestant Sweden, the Dutch Republic, and England.

Cramoisy's *Relations* stood out from other missionary publications of the era because they were journalistic, akin to a new genre of French *annuels* and periodicals, such as the *Gazette de France,* which was launched in 1631 by a printer named Théophraste Renaudot, with Richelieu's backing.[84] Explicit links between the *Relations* and the new French political press under Richelieu include a report of 1632 about the mission that appeared in the *Nouvelles Ordinaires* edited by Renaudot. News that the Jesuits were to return to Canada was couched in criticism of Spain's reputation for cruelly exploiting resources and peoples in the Americas. The departure of Le Jeune and other Jesuits with members of Richelieu's new merchant company was hailed by Renaudot as something that had "rendered illustrious the beginnings of a colonial enterprise that [would] make passage [to America] very easy for Frenchmen zealous [both] for their religion" and "for the honor and peace of their nation." Furthermore the sending of the missionaries and members of the mercantile company would make it easier for other Frenchmen to "second the holy intentions" of Louis XIII, who desired to spread Christianity in the New World and who did not wish to create colonies simply to "plunder and enslave."[85]

Yet Richelieu's decision in 1632 to send Jesuits, in particular, to New France was in one respect surprising, given the political climate in the French capital at that time. At that point France had not yet entered into the Thirty Years' War as a combatant, but the cardinal was openly supportive of Protestant powers in the war, not the Catholic Habsburgs, who threatened France's position in Europe. Despite new Crown efforts to control the press, a veritable pamphlet war was raging between ultramontanists, who believed Richelieu's anti-Habsburg posture was a betrayal of the Catholic cause, and Gallican and politique enthusiasts of Richelieu's foreign policy. It was a period of factional strife at court over the same matter. The Society of Jesus was a major bugbear for the anti-Habsburg faction. This was partly because Jesuits were behind some of the most effective and reproduced tracts critical of French support of Protestant powers, such as the *Admonitio ad Regem* (1625).[86]

However, as had been the case in Henry IV's time, many French Jesuits bent over backward to prove their loyalty to the Crown in the lead-up to France's entrance into the continental war. For instance they recruited Pelletier, an associate of Richelieu's, to write a tract called *Apologie ou Défense pour les Pères Jésuites*, which distanced the French Jesuits from their pro-Habsburg confreres across Europe. Cramoisy published this book. Another Jesuit, Étienne Petiot, authored a volume commemorating Louis XIII's victory over the Huguenots at La Rochelle.[87] Others, most notably Pierre Le Moyne, went out of their way to praise the Crown's policies, and Richelieu as their mastermind, in the form of pompous poetry.

Unsurprisingly Le Moyne's publisher for one such work was Cramoisy. *Le Portrait du Roy passant les Alpes* (1629) lauded Richelieu as France's "grand Esprit," citing the cardinal's support of Christian proselytization in the Ottoman Empire as evidence he was helping France achieve its great destiny. France might also soon "make French the one and the other ocean," Le Moyne wrote, in order to "subject the whole infidel world," including nations that so far had "escaped the ships of Isabella."[88]

Several French Jesuits also contributed to collections of French and Latin odes that glorified Louis XIII and Richelieu and were compiled by François Le Métel de Boisrobert, a founding member of the Académie Française. Boisrobert's monumental works of propaganda were published by Cramoisy on the eve of France's entry into the war. In one of his dedications Boisrobert himself praised the "special glory of [the] age" in which France was enjoying the leadership of the "great genius [*Grand Genie*]" Richelieu, whom he called "the support of the state, the liberator of the fatherland, the author of its . . . most precious delights."[89]

Language in Le Jeune's early *Relations* resembled that of these works published by Cramoisy. The *Relation* of 1636 honored Richelieu as "the father of [New France], and the powerful genius [*le génie puissant*] who is to bring about, under the favor and authority of His Majesty, the designs of God for the conversion of this new world." The *Relation* of 1640—at the height of French involvement in the war, when many were questioning Richelieu's commitment to Catholicism—opened with a statement of gratitude for "the solicitude of Monseigneur the Cardinal for these [American] countries, and his donations for the Huron mission," a reference to a gift from his personal fortune that he had recently made to the Jesuits.[90]

By contrast, references to Rome and the papacy in the *Relations* were tepid where they appeared at all. One indirect reference to Pope Urban VIII appeared in the *Relation* of 1638, which was published, atypically, in Rouen and not by Cramoisy in Paris. In this same reference Rome was not named but indirectly alluded to as a place "beyond the Alps."[91] Furthermore Le Jeune and his confreres never in print described as "Roman" the religion they brought to America. Rather they emphasized the French character of their Catholicism and presented themselves as extending the boundaries of a church bound to the Bourbon monarchs.[92]

Urban VIII had been educated by Jesuits and was an enthusiastic advocate of Jesuit missions.[93] He was also pragmatic. In a move that dovetailed with Richelieu's efforts during the war for the Mantuan succession, Urban sought to protect the Papal States from Habsburg domination by supporting the Protestant duc de Nevers and opposing a Habsburg-backed rival, Charles Emmanuel I of Savoy. He never condemned France's alliance with Lutheran Sweden, and he maintained a posture of neutrality during the war.[94] All the same he was disliked in Paris, simply because he was the pope. He put the Jesuits of Paris in an awkward position, therefore, when he announced an indulgence for New France in 1637, expecting it to be publicized.

Le Jeune shared the news in understated terms in the *Relation* of 1638, the manuscript for which was sent to Jean le Boullenger, an obscure printer in Rouen, not to Cramoisy. The Jesuits may have deemed it prudent not to publish any allusion to the pope in Paris, where they were concerned to remain in good standing with the Crown and various elites. Regardless Cramoisy was miffed by the Jesuits' decision to go to Rouen and quickly secured an abbreviated second manuscript for 1638 from Le Jeune, publishing his own *Relation* of 1638. In it something new appeared, a "permission" by the Parisian provincial granting Cramoisy exclusive rights to all future *Relations* from New France. Granting such exclusive, long-term rights to a printer was unusual in the era. The timing underscores the importance of the missionary reports as wartime propaganda for the Crown.

The missionaries had few qualms about their project's appropriation for the French cause. Le Jeune, in particular, was well aware of political dynamics in France and sought advantage in them for the mission. In the summer of 1635 he sent a letter to Richelieu that began with the following praise of the prime minister:

> All Europe . . . regards you with admiration. . . . France owes her recovery to you, who dissipated the poison which was creeping into her heart. Alas, what misfortunes would have befallen her . . . if this poison had retained its strength in the midst of the state! The . . . allies of the most noble crown in the universe have not words enough to acknowledge your kind deeds, and its enemies no longer have courage in your presence. You know both when to make peace and war, as you possess equally goodness and justice. . . . The seas acknowledge your power, for it is you who have joined the new France to the old; and all these peoples, who do not yet know the true God, begin to . . . admire your authority.[95]

Here Le Jeune went beyond customary courtesies. He supported the cardinal's vision for French power in Europe and abroad. His allusion to the seas' acknowledgment of the cardinal's power, and to what united France with North America, referred to the fleet Richelieu had created for New France in 1629 under the command of the Compagnie de la Nouvelle France. This enterprise was part of a larger strategy of modernizing France's naval and trading capacities.[96] Le Jeune also showed himself to be solicitous for the merchant company, despite its early failures, while pressing Richelieu to assist it more than he had been doing. In doing so he cast himself as an admirer of the cardinal's power: "Monseigneur, you are all-powerful in this matter . . . a single glance of your eyes can protect, animate, and help [the merchants], and indeed all these countries, from which France can one day derive great benefits."[97] Such rhetoric evinced a sophisticated understanding of Richelieu's agendas for both France and the projection of his own, mythic image.

Furthermore when Le Jeune wrote that "all Europe" admired Richelieu, he knew this was not the case: nothing in European politics was more salient in the mid-1630s than the battle lines between supporters of the cardinal, France, and its mostly Protestant allies on one side and the supporters of the Spanish Habsburgs, Bavaria, and their mostly Catholic allies on the other. It has been posited elsewhere that when the Jesuit referred to the "poison . . . creeping into [the] heart" of France, he was alluding simply to the Huguenots, defeated at La Rochelle in 1628.[98] But for a well-informed clergyman like Le Jeune, La Rochelle was old news by 1635. Le Jeune's reference was to recently ousted members of the government who opposed Richelieu's growing authority over the affairs of France— grandees that included the king's own brother, Gaston d'Orléans, who was exiled in 1632 for conspiring against Richelieu's administration. The Jesuit was writing in the wake of the Day of the Dupes, the period of factional strife between Marie de' Meédici and her *dévots* (devouts) and Richelieu and his *bons François* (good Frenchmen), from which Richelieu arose triumphant, gaining the support of Louis XIII. The factions were locked in conflict over France's relationship with Spain.[99]

In his first letter to Richelieu, Le Jeune praised the cardinal for knowing "when to make peace and war." By the early 1630s it was no mystery to the well informed that France and Spain were headed toward war.[100] Before Le Jeune left France in 1632, Richelieu was already positioning France against Spain, aiding the Dutch, German Protestant states, the Danes, and eventually Sweden with large sums of money.[101] In 1634 readers of *Le Mercure François* encountered stories of Spanish preparations for war and of incidents such as the aggressive Spanish entrance into the ducal territories of Savoy the year before.[102] It is noteworthy, then, that Le Jeune made a frank allusion to Spain as among France's "enemies" in his letter to Richelieu. The Jesuit also urged the cardinal to encourage emigration to New France as a matter of policy that would aid in France's national security as well as relieve the economic burdens under which many in the kingdom suffered: "I have . . . heard it only with great regret, that a large part of the artisans in Spain are Frenchmen. . . . Must we give men to our enemies . . . when we have here so many lands . . . where colonies can be introduced which will be loyal to His Majesty and to Your Eminence?" When Le Jeune wrote this, he did not yet know that France had already declared war on Spain on May 19. In other words, he was one of Richelieu's *bons François*.[103]

In the *Relation* of 1636 Le Jeune argued similarly to the French public about the benefits of preparing a settler colony in North America that could support numerous French emigrants. But unlike the private letter to Richelieu, the *Relation* referred only obliquely to Spain. The mission superior presented his patriotic vision in more general terms, while using much the same language, in a discussion of French workers who left France for other countries.[104] Le Jeune dissembled because he wished to get his strategic point across while still obeying the Jesuit general in Rome, who in 1632 had forbidden all Jesuits from publishing anything that might offend any European princes during wartime without first running it by Roman censors.[105] Given the restrictions Le Jeune was under as an increasingly prominent Jesuit author in France in the 1630s, the limited remarks he penned in 1635 suggest he desired the triumph of France over its "neighbors" in and beyond Europe. His remarks in the *Relation* about shipbuilding, with their obvious relevance to the development of French naval power, support this interpretation as well.[106]

When reading the *Relations* in the context of Richelieu's political and military concerns, we must acknowledge that colonial matters were of secondary importance to Richelieu.[107] But we should not undervalue the unofficial work some did for the cardinal by informing the French public about North America, with a view to the future of France's colonial empire, even if it had to remain on the backburner during the war with Spain in Europe.

Le Jeune was well aware of New France's secondary importance in France, especially during wartime. In the opening of his *Relation* of 1637, he praised Richelieu simply for holding New France "in his heart."[108] The Jesuit also responded to questions put to him by various *personnes de condition*, or status, in France who were curious to know more about

Canada. The first and last related to the European war. One of Le Jeune's interlocutors asked if New France was "beyond the incursions of the Spaniard," to which the Jesuit answered that it was impossible for the Spanish to come by land. Moreover, a seaborne invasion would require tremendous effort. Ships from New Spain would have to bypass "the whole of Florida, and . . . all of Virginia, and all the other lands which belong to France, which are of vast extent."[109] This last remark was decidedly vague about which territories "belong[ed] to France" and could have been intended to suggest that the French could claim much of the land between Canada and Mexico.

Le Jeune also assured his readers that in New France the French did not fear any European invaders. He ascribed the colony's brief takeover by the English in 1629 to Champlain's lack of sufficient "food and powder and other munitions of war" from France. The ninth and last question in Le Jeune's list asked what sort of "merchandise" could be sent to France from America, including fish and furs, but also trees and other "materials with which to build [France's] ships." Le Jeune answered that the country was full of resources that would turn a great profit for enterprising French merchants as well as enhance French power, but that the "chief care" of all concerned with the colony was at the moment "to provide for lodgings, fortifications, and the clearing of the land" in order for "riches" later to be gathered in.[110] Clearly Le Jeune understood one of his roles to be that of opening ways to French empire on multiple fronts: Christianization, commerce, military and political expansion, and also the buildup of basic habitations and infrastructure in the Eastern Woodlands.

CHAPTER 2

Rescuing the "Poor Miserable Savage"

In the *Relation* from New France published by Sébastien Cramoisy in 1635, Paul Le Jeune offered what at first seems like unremarkable commentary on New World "savages" by a scholastically educated European of the era:

> It was the opinion of Aristotle that the world had made three steps . . . to arrive at the perfection which it possessed in his time. At first, men were contented with life, seeking . . . only those things which were necessary and useful for its preservation. In the second stage, they united the agreeable with the necessary, and politeness with necessity. First they found food, and then the seasoning. In the beginning, they covered themselves against the severity of the weather, and afterward grace and beauty were added to their garments. In the early ages, houses were made simply to be used, and afterward they were made to be seen. In the third stage, men of intellect . . . gave themselves up to the contemplation of natural objects and to scientific researches; whereby the great republic of men has little by little perfected itself. . . .
>
> Now I wish to say that our wandering Montagnais savages are yet only in the first of these three stages.[1]

Le Jeune was in his third year as superior of the mission based in Quebec. He was paraphrasing a passage from Aristotle's *Politics* in which neither seasoning in food nor discussions of clothing and architecture as artistic forms featured significantly. These were the Jesuit's preoccupations as a Frenchman of the early seventeenth century from a particular social milieu.

Explaining why some Native Americans were only in the first of Aristotle's three stages, Le Jeune might have been writing instead about numerous peasants in France who, too, lived beyond the world of abundance and refinement known to his urban-elite audience: "They cover themselves to keep off the cold, and not for the sake of appearance. . . . They cannot understand what we ask from God in our prayers. . . . They say . . . 'tell him that thou wishest to eat. . . .' In short, they have nothing but life; yet they are not always sure of that."[2]

Although patterns of labor, landowning, and economic hardship varied widely throughout early modern France, turning to prayer for basic necessities was a condition known to the majority of Le Jeune's countrymen, especially during subsistence crises in which some communities lost as much as 20 percent of their population to starvation and disease. Before he was a missionary Le Jeune was already familiar with populations that had little opportunity, while working the land and in preindustrial manufacture, to cultivate "gentleness" or "scientific researches."[3]

In Paris, Rennes, and other cities in which he resided as a young Jesuit, Le Jeune was surrounded by laborers, peasants, and beggars who lived at a subsistence level, often in crowded, unsanitary conditions. As a Jesuit, however, he socialized primarily with urbanized individuals from bourgeois and noble families. With respect to education, food and drink, and social rituals, these early seventeenth-century elites were increasingly concerned to establish distance between themselves and the common run of French society, and to identify with the neoclassical aesthetics, controlled but abundant displays of wealth, and centralizing political power of the French monarchy. Other Jesuits who authored portions of the *Relations* came from prominent or aspiring families of the same milieu. The Parisian brothers Jérôme and Charles Lalemant hailed from a family of *noblesse du robe*. François-Joseph Le Mercier, also Parisian, was the son of a goldsmith-turned-royal valet with privileged access to the king's chambers. Such was the social profile, too, of many of the *Relations*' readers.[4]

Remarks in the earlier *Relations* on indigenous American living conditions and religious culture included subtexts about France's own lower classes. They reveal an effort by the Jesuits to appeal specifically to metropolitan elites who identified with the newly evolving, courtly, and Paris-centered culture of consumption, aesthetic refinement, and self-conscious distance from France's peasants and urban poor.[5] The *Relations* alternately mirrored and redeployed elite attitudes toward socially marginal populations for the sake of both the mission and colonial development. Rhetoric in the *Relations* suggests, too, that the Jesuits sought to import this particular urban-elite culture—not yet fully ascendant in France itself—to New France together with Catholicism. The early *Relations* reveal, further, that Jesuits of the mission's founding era were convinced that severe poverty, and a lack of infrastructure compared to urban France, needed to be addressed by colonial developers before Native Americans' imaginative capacities for Christianity and for higher culture could truly flourish. The Jesuits thus sought to attract French elites' attention to the "misery" in which Native Americans were living by means of comparisons with the most wretched peasants and street beggars in France itself. In the process they gave voice and moral weight to new understandings of "Frenchness" itself as identified with exceptionally elite, urban experiences and attitudes.

In Le Jeune's commentary, in particular, are characterizations of elements lacking in the Eastern Woodlands as "French" at a time when many French elites would not have recognized such generalizations about a national culture. Such moments suggest that the act of writing about North American encounters contributed to the Jesuits' evolving understandings of a French Self in relation to a colonial Other.[6] However, beyond this, even in missionary writings penned thousands of miles from Paris, the French Self was being forged in relation to an Other much closer to home for the intended readers of the *Relations*: the lower classes that comprised the great majority of France's population. They, like colonized peoples, were increasingly the objects of social reform projects by government officials, churchmen, civic leaders, and new religious congregations and lay associations.[7] Missionaries such as Le Jeune did not stand apart from these developments while far from France. Rather, their experiences of Native

American cultures, and their drive to communicate with elite readers, heightened their self-consciousness regarding their French identity and what elements of their home culture they believed were best representative of it and worth importing to America.

"At the Best, Their Riches Are Only Poverty"

With readers such as the noble and upper-bourgeois investors in the Compagnie de la Nouvelle France in mind, Le Jeune in his first *Relation* of 1632 compared Native Americans to "French beggars who are half-roasted in the sun." His reference to beggars used the French term *gueux*, which connoted utter wretchedness more than the terms *mendiants* or *vagabonds* would have. Thus the Natives of North America were, in the Jesuits' view, exceptionally poor and miserable. They were worse off than French panhandlers and the most destitute peasants. They were so poor that even Native Americans who considered themselves wealthy simply did not comprehend their condition. So Le Jeune suggested when he wrote of two Montagnais families who stopped by the Jesuits' house in Quebec one day, asking to store several packages they described as "great riches" while away for several weeks on a hunt. In Le Jeune's estimation the belongings were worth little. "All their riches are only poverty," he wrote. Several years later he responded in a similar way to a Montagnais captain who wished to offer a gift to King Louis XIII: "I began to laugh, telling him that all their riches were nothing but poverty compared to the splendors of the King."[8]

Le Jeune was not the first Frenchman to link North American Natives' "savage" condition to a dearth of material goods. Jacques Cartier wrote a century earlier that "the whole lot of them had not anything above the value of five *sous*."[9] The phrase *pauvre sauvage* also appeared often in Samuel de Champlain's *Voyages*.[10] Gabriel Sagard, a Récollet friar who worked in Quebec in the 1620s, employed the phrase *pauvre sauvage* in his *Histoire du Canada*, but his emphasis was on their "poor souls" and he also referred to his Récollet confreres as "poor religious," referring to their voluntary poverty and solidarity with the poor, which were hallmarks of their Franciscan charism.[11]

Distinctively the Jesuits characterized poverty on both sides of the Atlantic as a problem to be fixed, not as a condition to be embraced for its spiritual rewards. They shared in a newer understanding of the Christian vocation, increasingly popular among pious elites of their time, whereby efforts to alleviate poverty supplemented, and increasingly supplanted, penitential asceticism. The missionaries therefore presented New France as a wide open field in which the wealthy might exercise Christian charity.[12]

Additionally the Jesuits highlighted colonization and trade as means of combating poverty on a large scale. This view of the social benefits of mercantile activity was then advocated in France only by a small, elite group, including the royal physician Théophraste Renaudot, who edited the weekly *Gazette de France*, the kingdom's first state-sponsored periodical. Renaudot advocated a systematic reform of France's charitable hospitals and workhouses that had existed since the early sixteenth century. Like the Jesuits of New France he rejected the notion, widespread at the time, that biblical passages such as "The poor you always have with you" were to be taken as injunctions against human efforts to eradicate poverty.[13] Le Jeune and his confreres did not echo the view shared by the Récollets and French Capuchins of the period, that God made numerous people poor to serve as Christ-like examples of humility to the rich.[14] Nor did they share a common view that mass poverty helped stabilize the body politic, which needed extremes of wealth and poverty to preserve order.

As early as 1616 Biard's *Relation* on the preliminary Jesuit effort in Acadie posed a dilemma to French elites, asking how it was possible that great material inequality, as well as spiritual inequality, could exist between those on either side of the Atlantic Ocean: "We breathe under the same sky. . . . Whence, then, comes such great diversity? Whence such an unequal division of happiness and of misfortune? Of garden and wilderness? Of Heaven and Hell?" Remarkably, given the era in which he wrote, Biard in response did not cite the American Natives' ignorance of Christianity or their moral failings. He suggested instead that great inequality, if it persisted between prosperous Europe and the New World, would be due to omissions of charity by those in France who had the means to change the situation.[15] For Biard a cycle of poverty—breakable by Catholic

France—was at the root of the spiritual misery he believed the Natives suffered: "Great poverty stifles the spirit," he wrote, "and overwhelms it with its . . . despotic sway, so that it can seldom . . . dream of something better. . . . Our poor savages . . . live only from hand to mouth. . . . They not only lack all literature and fine arts, but also . . . medicine."[16] Thus the Jesuit justified missions and empire on social and cultural grounds.

Several decades later Le Jeune linked colonial expansion to alleviating poverty within France itself, not just North America. In the *Relation* of 1637 he posited that many poor peasants in France who had "no bread in their mouths" might one day own land in North America and become "rich." He hoped New France would become a profitable colony that would provide new economic opportunities to ordinary French people and Native Americans alike. At the same time he articulated an elite prejudice about France's peasants, expressing pessimism that they could overcome their conservative, place-bound instincts and brave a transatlantic voyage. They would prefer to "languish in their misery and poverty," he opined, afraid of "losing sight of the village steeple." The Jesuit harnessed this prejudice to advocate colonial development, urging more forward-thinking "people of wealth and rank" to encourage and finance peasants' journeys to North America and even lead the way as emigrants.[17]

Le Jeune qualified these remarks by cautioning colonial developers not to send lots of ordinary farmers and laborers unless they were willing to sweat alongside the Montagnais and Hurons in clearing forests and preparing the soil for cultivation. New France with effort would become "a terrestrial paradise," he wrote, but only if "its first inhabitants [did] to it what Adam was commanded to do in that one which he lost by his own fault. God had placed him there to fertilize it by his own work . . . not to stay there and do nothing. I have more desire to see this country cleared, than peopled. Useless mouths would be a burden here."[18] The missionary's biblical allusion grounded this-worldly hopes for crews of industrious emigrants to arrive from France, to cut down trees and make the land fit for French-style farms and towns.

Early on Le Jeune hoped that because New France was "so immense," the project of clearing forests and tapping into potential mineral resources would provide employment for struggling French day laborers and artisans, including miners and shipbuilders. Workers remaining in France might also then find better employment, due to the increased demand for labor following the emigration of some competitors for jobs. New France's buildup, he added patriotically, would not only "banish famine from the houses of poor workmen," but would "strengthen France" and "weaken the strength of the foreigner," by which the Jesuit meant, at that time, the English and the Spanish.[19] His vision was one of economic development and the production of wealth on both sides of the Atlantic, for workers and their families and, nationally, for France. France's fortunes, Le Jeune urged Cramoisy's readers, would be tied to colonial successes and a refusal to let lands, labor, and new opportunities for socially oriented Christian charity go to waste.

Interpreters of the early *Relations* have sometimes attributed to the Jesuits a utopian desire to set up a "new Jerusalem" of agricultural reserves in which they would be able to teach a primitivized Christianity to Natives while shielding them from a corrupt European civilization.[20] However, passages in the *Relations* sometimes taken as evidence for this suggest something rather different when considered in broader context. Le Jeune and his confreres were concerned to teach Native Americans to live according to new, urban-elite understandings of what "Frenchness" entailed. They wished to segregate Natives specifically from emigrants who did not live in a disciplined, law-abiding way, deferential to religious and political authorities. In this vein Le Jeune warned readers of the *Relations* that "vice" would migrate from France to New France if French officials allowed persons from "certain places in old France"—and morally and spiritually from "Cedar and Babylon," so to speak—to "slip" into the country. Instead Le Jeune hoped upstanding French families would migrate that were "prepared to observe the laws that will be established there."[21] The Jesuit made coded references to French regions and social groups that were not yet submissive to the "reins of government" under the centralizing administration of Richelieu, or to the spirit of religious reform in France attempting to discipline the people and root out old "superstitions." The Jesuits were discriminating as to the quality of potential settlers from

France because of the social imprint they would make on New France and its indigenous missions. They hoped for a metropolitan emigration policy consistent with their aims.

Mission sources furthermore resound with indications that economic development and Christianization were closely linked in the Jesuits' understanding. In this vein the language with which Le Jeune sometimes wrote of mundane matters such as the fur trade is worth pausing over:

> In contemplating the affairs of New France, I seem to see an aurora emerging from the profound darkness of the night, which, lighting up the surface of the earth with its golden rays, finally changes into that great ocean of light brought in by the sun. The great losses incurred by these gentlemen in the early infancy of their company are indeed like a most heavy night. . . . The lilies died here; the few French who dwelt here were strangers in their own land. In short, these immense provinces could aspire to no higher fortune than to be made a storehouse for the skins of dead animals, than to fill savage mouths, to support elk, beaver, and great quantities of trees. Behold to what height the glory of New France could attain under the bondage of the foreigner, or under the administration of those who love it only for its spoils! But, God having poured out his blessings upon this new company, that night has been scattered; and now the dawn of a mild and peaceful prosperity is spreading along our great river. This makes us hope that the sun of plenty will follow these happy beginnings, every day advancing until it reaches the highest point of its apogee, never to descend therefrom.[22]

Trained in rhetoric, Le Jeune was an expressive writer who moved easily between measured, sometimes ironic language and purple prose. Even so this passage from the *Relation* of 1637 is startling. It is one of the most mystical moments in the mission sources. Yet its subject matter is the renewal of French trade in Canada by the Compagnie de la Nouvelle France and the Jesuits' hopes for a well-regulated economic program for New France.

In Le Jeune's vision the colony's spiritual health depended on the success of Richelieu's trading company. Its associates and directors were active participants in "extending the Kingdom of Christ" throughout New

France.[23] Furthermore the French monarchical state would oversee in a unique way the progress of a "mild and peaceful prosperity"—likened to a never-setting sun!—rather than an economic regime based on stripping colonial lands of mineral wealth and other "spoils." Le Jeune subtly swiped at the English, who controlled Quebec from 1629 to 1632, and the Spanish, whose record in extracting New World wealth was infamous. At the same time he was not at all critical of French people interested in profiting from American ventures. Rather he believed such activities would be blessed by God, yielding profits over the long term, if pursued in a spirit of moderation, loyalty to France, and Christian piety.

Le Jeune's links between transatlantic trade, French power, and the material and spiritual uplift of Native Americans resemble but also predate Anglo-Protestant missionary programs that emphasized commercial, settlement-based solutions for converting indigenous populations. The latter have been thought to contrast with a supposedly more traditional, less mercantile and nationalistic, outlook among Catholic missionaries of the early modern era.[24] Yet it is clear that the Jesuits early on presumed that French economic expansion would ground the cultivation of Catholicism in the Eastern Woodlands. They were more optimistic about the dynamic relationship between wealth and the spiritual health of society than were members of other orders, such as the Récollets, who stressed purely spiritual motives for colonization. They diverged, too, from prominent French thinkers of the era such as the Jansenist abbé de Saint-Cyran, who insisted that material abundance was a stumbling block to spiritual progress.[25]

As Le Jeune put it, the poor, including peasants in France who might emigrate to Canada, would more "easily find [the goods] of Heaven and of the soul" if surrounded by more of the "goods of the earth."[26] He even characterized the missionary effort as planting "seeds" that would yield "the fruits of Heaven and of earth" and "blessings, both corporal and spiritual."[27] A "terrestrial paradise" would emerge not simply on the ground of Christian conversions but also, more prosaically, on Canadian spaces cultivated by human enterprise. And, in time, the colony would become less dependent on France and capable of profiting a larger French Atlantic empire—not just through the fur trade, but also with fisheries, cash crops, mines, metalworks, lumber, and shipyards.[28]

"Voilà, Their Fine Eating"

New France as Le Jeune first experienced it was far from the paradise he envisioned, partly because it was sorely lacking in the food and wines that urbanized French elites like himself took for granted. The early *Relations* contain vivid passages on Native American foodways in which the priest presented himself as a bon vivant suffering in a gustatory desert. But while it may seem unremarkable at first that a Paris-trained Jesuit would comment in this way, Le Jeune's identification with a "French" diet of particular elements missing in North America is intriguing for its appearance as early as the 1630s.

French cooking had a high reputation in Europe by the sixteenth century, and the French capital's reputation as a culinary capital was well established by Le Jeune's day. In his younger years in Paris Le Jeune became accustomed not only to venerable guilds of butchers, bakers, and grocers, but also to *rôtisseurs*, *charcutiers*, sauce-makers, and proprietors of family-style *tables d'hôte*. While he dined relatively modestly as a member of a religious community, he knew what it meant to eat well. In the *Relation* of 1640 he identified the "grande nombre de rôtisseurs" as among the French capital's chief attractions.[29]

Le Jeune's references to Parisian food punctuated stark portrayals of Montagnais cuisine. The Montagnais were "only fed like dogs," he wrote in the *Relation* of 1635, and "their most splendid feastings are . . . only the bones and leavings of the tables of Europe." He warned Jesuits who might follow him to America that they would have to do without meat most of the year and content themselves with water as a beverage. "Voilà, the delights of the country," he said. "Bread, wine, the many kinds of meats, fruit, and a thousand refreshments that are in France have not yet come to these countries." Other Jesuits of the mission penned similar remarks.[30]

In descriptions of meals offered by his Native American hosts, Le Jeune used irony directed toward cultivated French readers. In 1634 he noted that the Montagnais used oil the way the French used sugar: "They use it with their strawberries and raspberries . . . and their greatest feasts are of fat or oil. . . . Voilà, their fine eating."[31] In the original French, Le Jeune specifically said, "Voilà leur bonne chère"—an expression then just beginning to be used in the modern, figurative sense of "a fine meal," rather than the old Latinate sense signifying a pleasant face or manner.[32] The full impact of Le Jeune's irony would have been sensible to urbane readers for whom the phrase had the new connotation, making them conscious of an especially wide gap between American Natives' ideas of a feast and their own.

Le Jeune's discussions of Montagnais cuisine included subtexts about French peasants. For example the Jesuit wrote, "A certain peasant said in France that, if he were King, he would drink nothing but grease; the savages do drink it very often, and even eat and bite into it, as we [French] would bite into an apple. When they have cooked a very fat bear, or . . . beavers in a kettle, you will see them skim off the grease . . . with a large wooden spoon."[33] Here Le Jeune made one dietary practice then common in France (relishing animal fat) seem exotic and another that was uncommon (eating apples) seem typically French. France's common people, who could not afford meat most days of the year, and to whom butter and cheese were often unavailable, prized the flavor and nutrition that fats and oils added to diets of bread, meal, and soup. In the seventeenth century even bourgeois of some means who drizzled fats on bread and sometimes served it with berries would not have found Montagnais customs so very strange. In contrast the regular enjoyment of fresh fruit was less common throughout France. In Le Jeune's day, apple orchards were rare outside of Normandy. Ripe fruit was expensive, especially in Paris, and sometimes was used as a status symbol on elite tables.[34] Thus the priest's reference to apples as something ordinary to himself and his audience was socially coded.

Montagnais cuisine centered on roasted or raw moose, beaver, and other game meat; pike, sturgeon, and other fish, often smoked; cornmeal, sometimes available from trade; and a variety of root vegetables, berries, and nuts. Meals were seasoned with little except animal fat prized during times of plenty. However, although staples differed based on local ecosystems, the contrast with rural French cuisines was not so great as Le Jeune rhetorically cast it. Based on his urban, elite experience of "French" cuisine, he mentioned how put off he was by the Montagnais habit of dipping strawberries in animal fat, by the absence of salt in their meals, and by the lack of herbal seasonings and sauces. He further highlighted as evidence of poverty in North America what were considered to be festive, hearty meals provided to the Jesuits by the French émigré residents of Quebec, for which a number of different items were stewed in a single pot without salt. Governor Champlain himself on at least one occasion served the missionaries a stew of peas, bread-crumbs, prunes, and water. Le Jeune referred to this meal as a "banquet" with definite irony, employing the French word *mets,* which then had the connotation of great platters served separately in a several-course meal.[35] In doing so the priest revealed that his own palate had been conditioned—as only some French elite palates had been by then—by what food historian Susan Pinkard has called an early seventeenth-century "revolution in taste." Specifically, a new "analytic" aesthetic of cooking was just at that time spreading outward from elite homes in Paris, characterized by keeping apart sweet, salty, sour, tart, or spicy flavors and enhancing the natural flavor or each item with salt, another condiment, butter, flour, or some combination of these.[36]

Le Jeune's construction of "French" dietary norms as a foil to Native Americans' is also seen in his references to wine. He noted that the Montagnais would drink warm water or broth out of a common pan with the same "satisfaction" that a person "in France [would] drink wine from a crystal glass." Wine, of course, had been enjoyed in European taverns, monasteries, barracks, and great halls for centuries, but in Le Jeune's day it was not yet the national drink of France. It was common on tables in wealthier houses but, except on important feast days, the great majority of the population typically consumed water from ponds and streams, beer and cider, and a very diluted *demi-vin.* Most of Le Jeune's countrymen enjoyed decent wine only a few days of the year, and they certainly did not drink it in crystal glasses.[37] Le Jeune's urban-elite outlook on proper "French" beverages was further in evidence in his remark, in 1634, that the Montagnais drank "rainwater . . . with as much enjoyment as they drink the wine of Aï in France." The wine of Aï, or Aÿ, had only recently achieved renown in Europe's royal courts. It was the most prized wine from Le Jeune's native Champagne and the ancestor of Dom Pierre Pérignon's champagne, which would appear late in the seventeenth century. In Le Jeune's day the wine of Aï was inaccessible, if not unknown, to most French people.[38]

Commentary on food and drink in the early *Relations* has on occasion been taken as proof of a generalized Jesuit "wonder" at how different Native American ways were from "civilized" Europe's.[39] On closer inspection, we see that Le Jeune rhetorically exaggerated such wonder to appeal to French literate society, with its increasing aloofness from impoverished, uncultured people closer to home. His contrasts between indigenous and "French" diets reified a new culture of gustatory refinement while drawing attention to basic ways in which French colonization could transform North America.

Native American eating behaviors receive similar treatment in the early *Relations*. In 1634 Le Jeune noted how one Montagnais man received a bowlful of peas from the Jesuits: "He threw aside the pewter spoon that had been given to him, and took the big pot-ladle to eat with, observing no other law of civility than what his great appetite suggested. . . . Voilà, all the social graces [*honnesteté*] they know about." The priest added, with relief, "Those who know us [better] do not . . . indulge in such gross incivilities in our presence."[40] He used the words *civilité* and *honnesteté*, which had specific connotations among elite French readers of the day. Referring to public-spiritedness, urbanity, and consideration of others before self, *civilité* was gaining new traction in France, whereas *courtoisie*, emphasizing the ceremonial, was still the ordinary word for elite rituals at table and the like.[41] Le Jeune's frequent use of *civilité*, reserving *courtoisie* for refined modes of address, would have seemed modish to Parisian readers of the 1630s.[42] His construction with *honnesteté* emphasized a Montagnais lack of knowledge of social graces or rational behavior. Paired with "Voilà leur bonne chère," his phrase "Voilà toute l'honnesteté qu'ils sçavent" pointed not toward a well-established French understanding of good manners but to a new preference among some French urban elites for graceful, rational refinements upon feudal customs and the martial virtues traditionally prized by the upper nobility. It would not have occurred to Le Jeune to note behaviors such as double-dipping in a common pot, or eating on the floor, and then to exploit them rhetorically to win support for his mission, had he not been sensitive to a growing urban-elite intolerance of these very same behaviors still common across France.[43]

"The Cabins of This Country Are Neither Louvres nor Palaces"

Descriptions of Native Americans' ordinary life in the early mission sources included expressions of horror toward sanitary conditions, dwellings, and domestic arrangements. In the early years of the mission, sometimes having to shelter and dine with Montagnais and Huron families while away from Quebec, Le Jeune and his confreres experienced discomforts that they readily dramatized in the *Relations*.

On October 12, 1633, Le Jeune accepted the invitation of an elderly Montagnais woman to join her family for a meal. "They roasted an eel for me upon a little wooden spit," he later reported of the visit, adding, "They presented it to me upon a small piece of bark. . . . [A] little boy, having handled the roasted eel, which was very greasy, used his hair as a napkin, and the others rubbed their hands on the dogs. The good old woman, seeing that I was looking for something upon which to wipe my hands, gave me some powder made of dry and rotten wood. . . . They have no other towels."[44] On another occasion Le Jeune underscored the absence of table linens during meals with indigenous families. The lack of infrastructure in New France exacerbated the discomforts this caused: "To carry linen with you would require a mule, or a daily washing; for, in less than no time, everything is turned into dish-cloths in their cabins." He noted with distaste that the Montagnais wiped hands on their own hair, or the fur of domesticated animals, during mealtimes. Also serving as "hand-towels" were shoes and pine branches.[45]

Le Jeune referred to hand-towels and even napkins made of "Holland linen" as if they were commonplace in France, reinforcing his depiction of North America as a place of severe want. Yet the practice of offering napkins to dinner guests was a recent development in his homeland.[46]

Most ordinary French people in Le Jeune's day were still unaccustomed to wiping their hands on individual cloth napkins. Notably Le Jeune said nothing about the absence of eating utensils in North America, probably because the use of forks was not yet universal even in courtly French circles at the time. The use of hands to eat greasy meat was not yet considered impolite in the social contexts the Jesuit knew best, which made table linens all the more crucial for maintaining decorum.[47]

On the whole Le Jeune presented himself to French readers as horrified by the sanitary conditions in North American domestic spaces. He devoted an entire section of the *Relation* of 1635 to the "filthiness" of the Montagnais lifestyle.[48] Greasy plates of bark would be double-dipped into common pots, sometimes with animal hairs stuck to them. Noting the high incidence of scrofula among the Montagnais, Le Jeune blamed unsanitary ways of preparing foods and healthy persons' indiscriminate sharing of meals with the sick.[49]

Such conditions were related to the limited domestic spaces, furnishings, and household implements then available in North America, especially among hunter-gatherers such as the Montagnais. Dogs, with whom the Jesuit sometimes had to live in close quarters and share meals, competed for space with human beings because in the cold weather, while sheltering in makeshift Montagnais cabins, they had nowhere else to go. Keeping dogs inside cabins, and also crowding in many men, women, and children— something that distressed the celibate missionaries—helped preserve warmth. This was a practical necessity that Le Jeune described as strange and "intolerable."[50] Yet such living arrangements were hardly unthinkable in Le Jeune's home country at the time. The homes of poorer peasants were quite small, sometimes shared with animals and lacking raised beds and other furniture, and unconducive to privacy. Even larger homes in the countryside often contained one large room that served as kitchen, bedroom, and living space all at once. In urban spaces it was common for whole families to crowd into one-room apartments. "Filthiness" was common in French homes, especially in the urban spaces familiar to Le Jeune, where dysentery was surpassing starvation as a leading cause of death. As a Jesuit he had been decently housed in Paris, but other students of his generation in Paris were familiar with dirty, rented rooms infested with insects and swept up in a world of prostitutes, criminals, and penniless laborers looking for work.[51]

Le Jeune's confrere Jean de Brébeuf was familiar with the larger cabins of the Hurons but also asserted that the typical living conditions of the North Americans were worse than those known to France's poorest populations.[52] At the same time, in descriptions of Montagnais and Huron homes, the Jesuits seemed less concerned to draw precise comparisons to living spaces in France than to dramatically foil North American domiciles with France's newest architectural wonders. Before recounting at length some excruciating experiences he had while living with Montagnais hunters in the winter of 1633–34, Le Jeune again employed irony, calling a small, circular cabin made of branches, bark, and packed-in snow a "beautiful Louvre."[53] Similarly Brébeuf wrote a year later, "The cabins of this country are neither Louvres nor palaces, nor anything like the rich buildings of our France."[54] In such references the Jesuits not only affirmed the physical superiority of French architecture over everything they found in North America. They also appealed to readers most familiar with the newer French palaces that dominated some urban cityscapes, especially in Paris. These included Marie de' Medici's Palais de Luxembourg, which was under construction while Le Jeune was living in the French capital, and of course the Louvre itself, which had undergone remodeling from Henry IV's time, trading a medieval, fortress-like heaviness for the Italian palazzo style and magnificent size that dominate Parisian vistas to this day.[55]

Such buildings projected the new aesthetics and *gloire* of their masters and were also a boon for the artisans and laborers hired for their construction. At the same time they masked realities of poverty and poor sanitation to which Le Jeune and Brébeuf could not have been strangers when they described the "filth" and squalor they found in North America. In the early seventeenth century, as Karen Newman has explained, everybody in Paris, "no matter what their position in society, grew quickly used to the smells of bodies, food, excrement, coffee, animals, and the . . . mud of the streets."[56]

Writing of the dirt, smells, and domestic arrangements they observed in North America, the Jesuits connected their mission to a newly ascendant, elite culture of refined tastes, sociability, and identification with the gloire of the French Crown. The Jesuits hardly shunned discomfort or poverty, but they described these things in terms of degradation, as needing alleviation by those who had the means and taste to change them. They were to be endured only until a time when New France would begin to resemble modernizing spaces in Paris and other French cities.

Le Jeune may also have been concerned, when writing from North America—a place with which most urbane French readers would want nothing to do—to establish his mission's bona fides as connected to the world of wealth and privilege on which it so depended for success. There was shrewdness of this sort at work in every description of unappetizing foods and the look and feel of Montagnais dwellings. Such shrewdness is also apparent in descriptions of conditions travelers faced in North America. Le Jeune wrote ironically of the "inns" of Canada, by which he meant "the woods themselves." In the *Relation* of 1635 he compared such "inns" to those supposedly found all over France: "In the discomforts of a journey in France, villages are found where one can refresh and fortify one's self; but [here] the inns that we encountered and where we drank, were only brooks."[57]

It simply was not the case that inns were readily available to travelers throughout France. In more populated areas there were certainly comfortable inns for travelers, but only travelers of means could afford to stay in them. Poorer travelers got what they paid for—filthy lodgings shared with strangers or even animals—if they could afford the journey to begin with and were not among the many who, during times of famine, were forced from their homes to look for work and beg for shelter.[58] Le Jeune was alluding to nicer inns such as La Couronne in his native Châlons-sur-Marne, a place at which Montaigne himself had once lodged, calling it "a beautiful hostelry" where "the food is served on silver plates."[59] Le Jeune was struck by the absence of any such accommodations in North America, and he wanted readers of the *Relations* to know what the Jesuits had to endure while traveling to meet new groups of potential Christian converts. The message to Parisian elites was that the missionaries were willing to suffer not only to bring souls into the Catholic Church, but also in the hope that, through a successful colonial enterprise, North America might come to know some of the comforts, wealth, and cultural achievement his readers took for granted.

"I Mocked Their Superstitions"

The Jesuits' descriptions of "poverty" and "misery" in the daily life of Eastern Woodlands peoples extended from the material to the spiritual planes. Telling in this regard is an anecdote in Le Jeune's *Relation* of 1638. In the spring of the previous year, a young Montagnais woman, recently baptized with the name Anne, had died after suffering a long illness. She was one of numerous victims of epidemic disease that ravaged populations in eastern Canada between 1634 and 1640. The Jesuits buried Anne "in the Christian way," which for the Montagnais meant not interring her body with personal belongings, such as the clothing she had worn, as was their custom based on a view that such objects would be needed in the afterlife. Her parents, who were not Christian, had nevertheless followed another Montagnais custom of wrapping some of her hair in a small package made of tree bark, which they were to retain as a keepsake or bequeath to another close relative. However, the package had by mistake been buried with Anne's body and, the day after her funeral, her parents wanted to retrieve the memento. They expressed their wishes to Le Jeune through a messenger, but the Jesuit promptly forbade the action, adding in his account in the *Relation* for that year that he then "mocked their superstitions" to the go-between, telling him—"laughingly"—to "take a little moose hair" to give to the girl's father. The moose hair "would be just as useful as that for which he had asked," Le Jeune explained. The messenger, we are told, himself "began to laugh, and went away."[60]

Of all the Montagnais customs Le Jeune might have singled out for ridicule, the salvaging of a lock of hair from a corpse was a strange choice for a Catholic priest of his era, especially considering the Jesuit's own assertion that Anne's soul had probably gone straight to heaven because of the holy life she had led since her conversion.[61] The desire to preserve some token of a loved one's physical remains—especially if the person was believed to have gone quickly to heaven—was hardly opposed to

Catholic dogma or cultural practice. In Catholic Europe personal effects and even corpses of reputedly holy persons were regularly chopped up by relic-seekers. The Jesuits themselves famously exploited the relics of their saintly confreres: for example, Francis Xavier's right arm was on display at the Gesù in Rome by 1614, well before the saint's beatification and canonization. Rather than mocking Anne's parents for their "superstitions," Le Jeune might have employed the occasion as a teaching moment, expressing sympathy and explaining how Christians honored dead persons who had lived well. Instead he invited onlookers to laugh with him. In doing so he amplified his critique of Native American material existence, positing a relationship between what Anne's parents valued materially with what they valued spiritually. The problem was not so much that they infused meaning into a physical object, but that they did so with a *trivial* object—a mere lock of hair "wrapped in some bark."

Other Jesuits of the mission engaged in similar mockery of what they saw as Native Americans' impoverished conceptions of what was worthy of reverence. Writing for the *Relation* of 1638 from the Saint Joseph mission in Huron Country, Le Mercier encouraged readers to laugh at the expense of another young woman—also a Christian convert—and her father. The man claimed that his daughter had had a dream before she died, in which she had met her recently deceased sister in "the Heaven where the French went . . . where she had seen a vast number of Frenchmen, wonderfully beautiful, and some savages." The sister in the dream was wearing a beaded bracelet given to her by the Jesuits, so the dying woman, upon waking from her dream, wished for beads of her own to take to heaven. Her father relayed the request to Le Mercier, who said sarcastically of him, "Truly, a man with exalted ideas of Heaven."[62]

In the early *Relations* the Jesuits' criticism of Native American "superstitions" underscored their agenda of rescuing the Natives from poverty. Their critique of indigenous approaches to the afterlife and the supernatural expressed more than simply a religious agenda of replacing them with Catholic ones.[63] Also, while catechesis was centrally important to the Jesuits, Le Jeune and his confreres did not believe that erroneous beliefs were generally the source of the Natives' degraded condition. Commentary in the *Relations* suggests the reverse, that the missionaries saw poverty as a root cause of religious error and enslavement to sin and the devil, not a symptom of or punishment for these things.

The Jesuits began their critical study of Native American religious culture as soon as they arrived in Canada. From the first they had little respect for what they encountered. Le Jeune did not want to dignify the spirituality of the Montagnais with the word *religion*, writing in the *Relation* of 1635 that the word *superstition* was more appropriate to describe, for example, their uttering of short incantations to the spirits of animals before going on a hunt. Likewise, in a remark reminiscent of Bernard Groethuysen's increasingly "enlightened" Catholic bourgeois, who complained of French peasants who offered prayers to fend off storms harmful to their crops, the mission superior complained that the Montagnais devoted many prayers for the coming of spring, "or for the deliverance from evils and other similar things . . . crying out as loudly as they can, 'I would be very glad if this day would continue, if the wind would change' etc."[64]

The Récollets who had arrived in Canada before the Jesuits had also characterized Native American religious culture as a collection of "superstitions." Yet where Sagard, for example, had stressed the strangeness of those "superstitions," casting them as tools of the devil, who "play[ed] with [the Hurons] and [held] them fast in his snares," the Jesuits in their early encounters were more thoroughly dismissive. Sagard had a horror of Huron religious culture because he viewed the world as swarming with warring devils, angels, interceding saints, and the inscrutable spirit of the God whom he worshipped. In his view the Hurons were mistakenly worshipping demons, and they needed to be awed away from "superstitions" by the rival power of Christian prayers.[65] Le Jeune, by contrast, revealed aloofness toward those who believed prayers should be used for the needs of daily life, dismissing also the Montagnais' enchanted conceptions of stars, animal bones, women's menstrual cycles, and other phenomena in the natural world.[66]

At the same time, Le Jeune was concerned with the Montagnais' limited understanding of the extent and grandeur of the world as it was known to well-traveled, educated Frenchmen like himself. In the *Relation* of

1635 he posed a series of questions to Montagnais interlocutors both to challenge their conception of the afterlife and to prove how little they knew of the world:

"First, where do these souls go, after the death of man and other creatures?" "They go," they say, "very far away, to a large village situated where the sun sets." "All your country," I say to them (meaning America), "is an immense island, as you seem to know; how is it that . . . the souls of all things that die or that are used, can cross the water to go to this great village that you place where the sun sets? Do they find ships all ready to embark them and take them over the water?" . . . "And how . . . can they ford the great ocean . . . which surrounds your country?" . . .

At last, I told them that the Europeans navigated the whole world. I explained to them and made them see by a round figure what country it was where the sun sets according to their idea, assuring them that no one had ever found this great village.[67]

Elsewhere Le Jeune lamented how limited the Montagnais' horizons seemed to be in forming their prayers: "O, my God, what prayers they make! In the morning . . . they shout . . . 'Come, porcupines; come, beavers; come, elk'; and this is all of their prayers." Praying for the arrival of animals to hunt was, of course, a central ritual of nomadic, Montagnais existence. The Natives believed that animals were endowed with souls and that real communication took place in moments of prayer between human and animal souls, involving the assertion of control over the animals' destinies by hunters.[68]

Le Jeune was dismissive of such conceptions of the soul, writing: "[They] persuade themselves that not only men and . . . animals, but also all other things, are endowed with souls . . . they imagine the souls as shadows. . . . They say the souls drink and eat, and . . . give them food when any one dies, throwing the best meat . . . into the fire."[69] The first part of this passage has been interpreted elsewhere as proof that, compared to Eastern Woodlands peoples, the Jesuits—as European Christians per se—were operating with a stingy conception of who, and what, possessed a soul.[70] Yet European Christians in the tradition of Aristotle and Thomas Aquinas believed that flora and fauna, if not rocks and heavenly bodies such as stars, possessed souls of a kind, if not the rational, immortal souls possessed by human beings, and that even inanimate objects had a metaphysical essence or quality that made them what they were.[71] The problem Le Jeune presented to metropolitan readers regarding Montagnais belief was not its ascription of souls to animals, plants, and other things. More precisely, it was that the Montagnais conception of the human soul was not distinguished enough from the physical body of its possessor and that a view of the afterlife followed upon this that conflicted with a core Catholic belief: that death involves a painful (but only temporary, until the general resurrection) rending of the soul from the flesh.[72]

However, important as such principles were in Le Jeune's opposition to Montagnais burial rites, the Jesuit had other objections less rooted in traditional metaphysics and Christian theology. He objected to wastefulness, and he objected, again, to what he regarded as the limited *material* horizons of the Montagnais. Throwing meat into the fire for a deceased relative was a problem for Le Jeune in the same way that the eat-all feasts the Montagnais ritually held before hunts were a problem: it prevented communities from developing more economical attitudes toward food that would save them from always living on the brink of starvation.[73] Montagnais conceptions of departed souls' enjoyment of food were also a problem because the food the Montagnais imagined their deceased relatives to be eating was simply unappetizing. Le Jeune posed several more questions to some Natives about departed souls: "I ask them, 'What do these poor souls eat . . . ?' 'They eat bark,' they said. . . . 'I am not astonished,' I replied, 'that you are so afraid of death . . . there is hardly any pleasure in . . . eating old wood'. . . . 'What are these poor souls hunting during the night?' 'They hunt for the souls of beavers, porcupines, moose, and other animals.'"[74] Le Jeune simply could not accept that hope for such an afterlife could satisfy his interlocutors.

Reporting from Huron Country, Brébeuf also wrote about "superstitions" regarding the afterlife, emphasizing that the Hurons obscured moral distinctions between right and wrong and the justice of being punished in the afterlife for vicious behavior. Brébeuf, however, was convinced to a degree Le Jeune was not that supernatural forces were at work among the Natives. Convinced that most preternatural activity among non-Christian peoples was of the devil, he claimed, "It is the devil [who] deceives them in their dreams . . . he speaks by the mouth of some, who having been left as dead, recover health, and talk at random of the other life." At the same time, the Jesuit was confident that it was "really God whom they honor[ed], though blindly."[75]

But even Brébeuf's relatively optimistic, if less rationalistic, view of Huron religion had limits: "God of truth, what ignorance and stupidity," he exclaimed in 1637 after describing their view of the afterlife, a "village" where "souls" went "hunting, fishing" and valued "axes, robes, and collars" just as they had before death. He hoped that someday "these poor people" would be "enlightened by Heaven" and would "laugh at their own stupidities."[76] Importantly, Brébeuf's contempt for Huron conceptions of the afterlife did not stem from theological objections to a physical dimension. The problem, rather, was that the "axes, robes, and collars" they wanted with them after death were so basic—the treasures of "poor people."

Elsewhere Brébeuf saw as proof that the devil was at work among the Hurons that their material horizons, not only their spiritual horizons, seemed so limited. He argued that "the devil keeps them so strongly attached" to their feasts as "a means of rendering them more brutal, and less capable of supernatural truths." They were thus "slaves of the belly." But it was not because the "belly" was unrelated to religion that the Hurons were rendered "brutal" by their feasting. It was because they invested very basic foods and ways of eating with profound meaning—foods and ways the Jesuits found disgusting. There were so many more wonders *in* the world, not just beyond it, from which they might benefit and for which they might eventually thank God. In this vein Brébeuf quoted a line from Virgil's *Aeneid*: "Perhaps one day you will even delight in remembering this," that is, that the Hurons would one day smile, looking back on the state of brutality in which they had formerly lived.[77] The stanzas he referred to concerned Aeneas's hope that his companions would someday enjoy comforts of life— beyond venison from hunts and old wine carried from Sicily—that, under embattled conditions during their epic journeying, they had had to forgo.[78]

Le Jeune was more explicit than Brébeuf about connections he saw between faulty conceptions of the divine and low standards of living. The irony, for Le Jeune, was that in focusing prayer on basic things such as food, rather than on higher blessings, the Montagnais remained in a state of poverty where the basics of life were concerned: "These people, who place their ultimate happiness in eating, are always hungry."[79] Without a "science," "philosophy," or vision of "paradise" that looked beyond the means of physical survival, the Montagnais, in Le Jeune's view, could not comprehend that there were better modes of physical existence, let alone spiritual existence, that could be desired and cultivated.

In the missionaries' understanding, erroneous theological and philosophical conceptions were only to a limited extent to blame for the Natives' poverty and low living standards. At the same time, poverty was itself to blame for frustrated progress toward higher cultural and religious achievements. Indeed Le Jeune and his confreres believed that for Christian views of the soul to take root in North America, and for the ultimate joys and peace of heaven to be desired, the Natives needed to be educated to desire greater *earthly* pleasures and comforts than the bare necessities of life. Le Jeune's critiques of Native "superstitions" made it clear that he believed Christianity was as much about gracing "the present life" as it was about leading souls to heaven after death. The Jesuit drove home this point by describing the kind of life in which the Montagnais shamans seemed satisfied to see their countrymen remain: the shamans would often take the "dainty pieces" of the meat roasted on any given day while their fellows would listen attentively to their prophetic stories amid the "cold" or the "heat," the "annoyance of the dogs," and ubiquitous "sickness." Fewer statements in the *Relations* are more damning of the religious horizons of the Montagnais than Le Jeune's characterization of one shaman's "paradise" as the mere "pleasure of his jaws."[80]

Natives as Carnival "Maskers," "Sorcerers," and "Charlatans"

The solutions initially proposed by the Jesuits for countering indigenous "superstition" did not strictly emphasize instruction in Catholic doctrines and rituals. Such instruction was of course important to the missionaries, but more urgent at times was improving the conditions of daily life in North America. The Jesuits believed that the Natives needed to be weaned from the influence of "sorcerers" by becoming accustomed to material comforts known to the French. The religious problem would be addressed in part by economic and social changes, by which Native Americans would enjoy, regularly, a bountiful diversity of finer foods and reside in clean, solidly constructed homes with nice furniture, drapes on the windows, and raised beds with clean linens.

The Jesuits also believed that the Montagnais, Hurons, and other populations would be compelled away from "superstitions" by the cleanliness and orderliness of schools that they initially had thought of establishing, not just by the ideas taught in them. Children would learn, along with their catechism lessons, to behave and dress in a more refined way. A small school begun in Huron Country was described as a place that "pampered" young people with finer clothing and with "furnishings, linen, and other necessary things."[81] Students were also taught to "set the table" before meals, as well to control their bodies and behavior "after the French manner."[82] Accustoming the young to desire and *need* material conditions that their families of origin had never known was so crucial to Le Jeune that he likened his feelings of disappointment over one young Huron who had abandoned the school to the agonies suffered by the crucified Christ.[83]

The missionaries' social critiques of indigenous ways are reminiscent of contemporaneous reformers' views of popular customs and beliefs within Europe itself. Notably, in his first encounter with Native Americans, Le Jeune compared the Montagnais not only to "beggars" but also to "maskers who run about in France at Carnival time," because of the paint on their faces. Subsequent comparisons in the *Relations* between Native Americans and Carnival revelers in France were more critical and call to mind the rhetorical war between Lent and Carnival in elite-driven reform agendas targeting popular culture in early modern Europe.[84]

Le Jeune made his opinion of Carnival clear when he praised a Frenchman who was living in Canada for eschewing "the licentiousness which is carried on in other places" during the pre-Lenten festivities.[85] He also likened the religious incantations of the Montagnais to calls of puppeteers in France and the "vivacious" sound of "the Provençal." One Montagnais "juggler commenced to whistle, in a hollow tone ... then to talk as if in a bottle ... then to howl and sing, constantly varying the tones ... disguising his voice so that it seemed to me I heard those puppets which showmen exhibit in France." The impressions that Le Jeune gave both of disdain for, and amusement by, Montagnais religious culture were of a kind with the self-conscious distance from the popular classes and provincial populations that Jesuits in urban France were cultivating in their colleges.[86]

Brébeuf, as well, had harsh words for Carnival in a passage from 1637 about a festival he observed while living among the Hurons: "I would have liked several Christians to be present at this sight ... they would have been ashamed of themselves, seeing how like these people they act in their carnival follies. ... You would have seen some with a sack on the head, pierced only for the eyes; others were stuffed with straw around the middle, to imitate a pregnant woman. Several were naked as the hand, with bodies whitened, and faces as black as devils, and feathers or horns on their heads; others were smeared with red, black, and white."[87] For Brébeuf, what linked the feasting Hurons to European Carnival revelers was their foolishness and disorderliness. In such remarks about Carnival and Native American customs, there was a note of disdain not simply for the way they seemed inharmonious with Lent, but also for the cultural degradation they implied. It was not just disorderly for men to dress up as pregnant women. It was tasteless, and amusing only to those not yet uplifted into a state of sociability.

References to Carnival in the *Relations* form a concrete, transatlantic link between the Jesuits' agendas for New France and those of their confreres in France itself, who were attempting to bring populations into greater conformity with courtly, urban-elite social norms, not just the reformed Catholicism of the Tridentine era.[88] Perhaps also eminently expressive of a Catholic, sacramental understanding of things, infused with values imbibed among the urbane in France, the alleviation of poverty and the cultivation of *civilité* mattered in and of themselves to the missionaries as fruits of spiritual progress.

Complementing French Jesuit criticisms of peasant religiosity in their own country, the missionaries linked France's popular classes to the "poor miserable savage" of the Canadian wilderness. They thus took advantage, to stress the urgency of their work in New France, of increasing social distance between urban elites and the popular classes of France, who were most often the targets of top-down reform efforts. This is seen in a quotation of 1638 from Le Mercier on acts of torture and cannibalism exacted upon an Iroquois prisoner by a group of Huron villagers. Le Mercier connected the story and the "superstitions" he blamed for the horrors to the "disorder" seen in some French cities due to gangs of youths: "It often happens in the best cities of France that when a troop of children get to fighting with their slings, a whole town with its magistrates has considerable difficulty in quelling this disorder.... Yet we are full of hope, and these new [missions] ... will be ... so many forts whence ... we shall completely overthrow the Kingdom of Satan."[89] There was a connection in Le Mercier's mind between cruel acts of torture in North America and unruly behaviors of some French crowds, like the youth abbeys famously discussed by Natalie Zemon Davis.[90] The common problem was deeply rooted local "customs," and the solution was a reform effort linking the public profession of Christianity to the tightening of social controls by governing authorities.

Moreover, in their commentary about Native American religiosity, the Jesuits employed the same terms for indigenous shamans that French elites used to marginalize popular healers in France. These included the terms "jugglers" (*jongleurs*), "sorcerers" (*sorciers*), and "charlatans." Using such terms, the Jesuits positioned themselves on one side of an unsettled debate regarding the legitimacy of various behaviors in France as well as in Canada. They did so, again, by taking familiar French phenomena and recasting them as strange, associating them with North American savagery and opposing them to what was "French," as in the following passages by Le Jeune from 1638:

> Last winter, a little child being very sick, one of their jugglers entered his tent and summoned the soul of this poor little one; he had some trouble in catching it, but at last he took it in his hand, placed it upon the child's

head, and by dint of blowing made it reenter the body, and thus the child began to revive. . . . Such ideas appear so ridiculous to us in France that it seems as if the first word ought to dispel them.[91]

We call them sorcerers. . . . We have no other name to give them, since they even do some of the acts of genuine sorcerers—as, to kill one another by charms, or wishes, and imprecations . . . by poisons. . . . They have no other physicians. . . .

These charlatans sing and beat their drums to cure the sick, to kill their enemies in war, and to capture animals.[92]

Le Jeune's use of the terms *jongleurs* and *charlatans* to belittle native healers and dismiss their rituals as "ridiculous" was also not a neutral rhetorical strategy for a French writer of the early seventeenth century. At the time, a lively debate was taking place in Paris about the benefits, if any, provided by popular, unofficial healers—often termed *charlatans* and *jongleurs* but not yet universally with negative connotations—in contradistinction to university-trained physicians who were officially incorporated into the medical profession.[93]

The negative connotation of *charlatan* was not established definitively in high French society until late in the seventeenth century, although formal, literary attacks on unofficial healers had begun to appear late in the previous century in France. The debate reached such a pitch that many Paris-trained physicians, especially, were dismissing as charlatans, quacks, and empirics those doctors who had been trained in the medical faculties of provincial universities, as well as most doctors trained outside of France.[94] By calling Native shamans "charlatans," Le Jeune and his colleagues both reified the negative connotations of such terms and sought to turn elite attention toward the lack of even basic European-style medical knowledge and treatments in North America.

The missionaries were connected with elites who would have been especially receptive to rhetoric that bolstered the cause of learned, "rational" medicine. Most notably their publisher Cramoisy sat on the boards of his parish hospital of Saint-Jacques, a reformed hospital in Dieppe, a hospital founded in Quebec itself by Cardinal Richelieu's niece, and eventually the revolutionary Hôpital Général de Paris.[95] But even before Cramoisy's time, the missionary Biard had employed such rhetoric in his 1616 *Relation* on Acadie. Biard dismissed local Mi'kmaq healers as "jugglers, liars, and cheats," whose "science" consisted solely in "knowledge of a few simple laxatives, or astringents, hot or cold applications, lenitives or irritants for the liver or kidneys, leaving the rest to luck." At that time only a few years had passed since the physician Thomas Sonnet de Courval had issued his satirical attack on "charlatans," provoking defensive parries from, among others, Anthoine Girard or "Tabarin," a famous Parisian healer who set up shop in the Place Dauphine, eventually to retire as a rich gentleman in Orléans.[96]

In their discussions of Native as well as French "sorcerers," "charlatans," and "jugglers," the Jesuits offered social as well as religious critiques: such healers were medically ineffective and, holding their countrymen in thrall, kept entire populations trapped in cycles of poor health and poverty. It was the duty of the pious, more advanced "French" to rescue the "poor miserable savage" in North America from such conditions. The French would do so, Le Jeune proposed, partly by importing into New France the blessings of a new, prosperous French economy, as well as charitable institutions intended to alleviate both poverty and disease. They would show the Montagnais and Hurons that there were more inviting and effective paths toward earthly happiness, not only happiness in heaven, than those to which they had been accustomed before the French came.

The Jesuits were confident that all of this would come about through a joint effort of dedicated missionaries like themselves, the French Crown, the merchant company, and wealthy metropolitan laypersons of "merit" and "condition."[97] The missionaries dramatized particular aspects of North American life that would shock such readers as utterly beyond the pale even of the lowest standards of decency, civility, and human comfort in their own country. The early *Relations* thus inverted an older literary device of making the non-European Other more familiar in order to more easily incorporate them into traditional systems of thought and justify missionary and colonial activity. The Jesuits focused on aspects of North American living conditions that were not so unfamiliar to Europeans and rhetorically cast them as more alien to "French" modes of life than they really were. This suggests something more intentional and creative than simply giving voice, following the shock of American difference, to a new consciousness about what made the French "European."[98] The early *Relations* also featured something quite distinct from the earlier literary devices seen in the writings of Montaigne and Jean de Léry, who employed contrasts between Native and French ways of life to rebuke Europeans for sins such as avarice and sectarian violence. The Jesuits employed contrasts, more positively, to attract elites to projects of conversion and social uplift in the New World.

Just as they would adapt to circumstances in North America to advance their Catholic mission, the Jesuits marshaled the printed word and aspects of elite culture in France to influence urbane readers whose Paris-centered vision of French *civilité* had social as well as religious implications for populations on both sides of the Atlantic. They urged French elites to help North America rise above Aristotle's first stage of "necessity" and to see New France as a land of both spiritual and secular opportunity to which they might direct some of their wealth and influence. The missionaries hoped to enlarge French horizons to encompass transatlantic opportunities for charitable and commercial endeavor. In their view the French had the capacity to help entire nations reach Aristotle's second and third stages of development, which French elites were already enjoying near to perfection in the more exclusive *quartiers* of Paris.

CHAPTER 3

Surviving the Beaver Wars
and the Fronde

Late in 1655, a courier was robbed by bandits somewhere on the long road from La Rochelle to Paris. Lost in the attack were mail items from America intended for the former missionary Paul Le Jeune, then residing in the aristocratic Marais district of the French capital. One of these was mission superior François-Joseph Le Mercier's manuscript for the *Relation* planned for publication in the new year.

This would be the first time in over two decades the Jesuits would have no *Relation de la Nouvelle France* for the French public. At this time, France was recovering from the Fronde civil wars (1648–53), so the elites for whom the *Relations* were intended were preoccupied with crises at home. There were also new political dramas playing out, as when that April an increasingly assertive, teenaged Louis XIV embarrassed his cooler-headed prime minister, Cardinal Jules Mazarin, by bursting into the chambers of the Parlement de Paris, riding crop in hand, to rebuke the members for affronts to royal authority.[1]

Aware of all this, Le Jeune as Parisian procureur, or chief development officer, for the mission was determined to give *something* to Sébastien Cramoisy, so that New France would not disappear completely from view among people of means and influence on whom the Jesuits counted for support. So he made do with two brief letters he had received from Quebec that year, binding them together with introductory comments and news about English and Spanish attacks on French ships carrying aid and merchandise to Canada. He included, too, news of Mohawk violations of a recent peace reached between French colonists and the Iroquois nations. The Mohawks had even killed a Jesuit—a consecrated layman of the Society named Jean Ligeois who had been shot, beheaded, and scalped while doing reconnaissance on Mohawk movements.[2]

Ligeois was just the latest of a number of missionaries killed in the era of the Beaver Wars in the Eastern Woodlands. Between 1642 and 1649 eight other Jesuits had perished at the hands of American Natives. Not long after, they were honored by their confreres as saintly martyrs. These were Isaac Jogues and Jean de Brébeuf, killed in Iroquois Country and Huron Country respectively in 1646 and 1649; René Goupil, who had only recently entered the Society of Jesus and had traveled with Jogues into Mohawk territory in 1642; Jean de Lalande, a *donné*, or lay assistant, of the Jesuits; and Antoine Daniel, Noël Chabanel, Charles Garnier, and Gabriel Lalemant, the last of whom was the nephew of Jérôme and Charles. Dramatizing their stories in the mid-century *Relations*, mission leaders shifted rhetorically into hagiography, hoping to confirm the mission and French colonization in North America as divinely ordained.[3]

At the same time, portraits of the martyrs were part of a new Jesuit press strategy in the era of Anne of Austria's regency. By the close of the 1640s, following the devastation of Huron territory by the Iroquois and the closure of missions there, Le Jeune and other mission leaders faced a public relations nightmare in Paris. How could they convince prospective supporters that their projects were still viable, given flaring intertribal conflicts in which Jesuits themselves were dying? Furthermore, the French Crown was strapped for cash and manpower toward the end of the Thirty Years' War and faced insurrections at home, deploying troops against Frondeur rebels in Paris and across the kingdom. Parisians caught up with the Fronde included the publisher Cramoisy. With such reliable supporters distracted from America, would the Jesuits continue to receive even basic aid for their mission, let alone for more ambitious goals that now included a French offensive in Iroquois Country?

Accounting for the mission's fortunes during the troubled period of both the Beaver Wars and the Fronde, this chapter details the Jesuits' early, little-known efforts to get the Crown to better secure New France against attacks and to launch a war of conquest in Iroquois Country. It also connects the story of the most famous mission martyr, Jogues, to these machinations for war. Furthermore the chapter shows how the Jesuits, in order to keep New France's needs in the French public eye at this time of crisis, downplayed developments in the colony that might have alienated potential supporters. Instead they dramatized French and Native American casualties of the early Iroquois conflicts.

A Political Mission in France

Early on New France had a royally appointed governor and was managed by the state-sponsored Compagnie de la Nouvelle France. Richelieu had essentially farmed out the development of the colony to traders, settlers, missionaries, and Native Americans who could be recruited to the French Catholic side. In short there was hardly yet any political regime in the colony, which by 1640 consisted of small settlements at Trois-Rivières, Sillery, Quebec, Beauport, and on the Côte de Beaupré.[4]

During the Thirty Years' War the missionaries buttressed France's Catholic reputation within Europe with their popular *Relations*. But in return the Crown provided little for New France's development and security. The war was significantly to blame. It was expensive and absorbed the attention of government officials.[5] So by 1640 the colonial enterprise was stalling. The merchant company had failed to turn a profit since 1632. The settler population around Quebec numbered about two hundred, falling extremely short of the three thousand projected in the company's charter. Around the same time, a new settlement, Ville Marie, was planned at the site of present-day Montreal, which only stretched thinner already scarce colonial resources.[6]

Ville Marie was from the start imperiled by Mohawk hostilities against Algonquian-speaking tribes in the vicinity. The Jesuits blamed this on Dutch traders who had been selling firearms to the Mohawks and other Iroquois nations, although in reality the Mohawks were suffering a drop-off both in Dutch gun sales and the beaver supply at a time when the fur trade was becoming more necessary for their survival. Having failed to maintain peace with their traditional rivals, the Hurons, the Iroquois attempted to negotiate with the French. This was a challenge, as the new colonial governor, Charles Huault de Montmagny, was committed to an alliance with the Montagnais, other Algonquian-speaking tribes, and above all the Hurons themselves.[7]

On June 5, 1641, 350 Mohawk warriors arrived at Trois-Rivières with an offer of peace in exchange for French firearms and tolerance of their war with the Hurons. Montmagny employed the fur trader Jean Nicollet and the Jesuit Paul Ragueneau as emissaries, attempting to convince the Iroquois to accept peace on French terms: no guns and no more attacks on the Hurons. Put off by this, the group left Trois-Rivières and a Mohawk band attacked Ottawa allies of the French that winter.[8]

Knowing the Mohawks would be a formidable enemy, Montmagny commissioned Le Jeune to return to France to alert Richelieu of the weak position of New France and to propose that new fortresses were needed throughout the Saint Lawrence region, along with men and arms to fill them. He was also tasked with urging Richelieu to oppose the Iroquois in North America, but in a way that would not jeopardize the Franco-Dutch alliance in Europe at a crucial juncture in the war against the Habsburgs.

Le Jeune was preceded in this return to Paris by a letter to Richelieu sent by the superior of the Huron mission, Jérôme Lalemant. Lalemant emphasized the perilous proximity of the English and Dutch to New France, claiming the Dutch, especially, "fortif[ied] the courage" of the Iroquois, whom he characterized as "enemies of God and of the state." He urged Richelieu to prevent the English and Dutch from securing a "foothold" in North America, by breaking up their friendship with the Iroquois. Otherwise the French could not develop a profitable colony and the Catholic mission would be cut off from necessary supports.[9]

Le Jeune was energetic and approaching fifty when he returned to Paris after almost a decade overseas. By late 1641 the capital city included a new charm for Jesuits: the order's magnificent new Église de Saint-Louis on the Rue Saint-Antoine in the Marais district. Its first stone had been laid by Louis XIII prior to Le Jeune's departure for America. On the Feast of the Ascension, 1641, Richelieu offered the church's first Mass, with the royal family, prominent nobles, and leading citizens of Paris such as Cramoisy in attendance. With the Bourbon coat of arms and a statue of the medieval crusader-king Louis IX high on its towering façade, the church symbolized the warm relationship that the Jesuits then enjoyed with the Crown and Parisian elites.[10]

Le Jeune's reception at court was no exception. As his confrere François-Joseph Bressani reported to General Vitelleschi, the primary author of the best-selling *Relations de la Nouvelle France* was fussed over by Queen Anne, the duchesse d'Aiguillon, and others "as if he were an angel from Heaven." The queen also tried to convince him to stay in France as her spiritual adviser.[11]

Afterwards Le Jeune met with D'Aiguillon, who took his case to her uncle, Richelieu. The cardinal quickly pledged aid for fortifying key locations of French-Huron trade, promising 10,000 livres to support men and arms and 3,000 livres for a fortress at the mouth of what the French had named the Richelieu River. Linking Lake Champlain and the Saint Lawrence, the smaller river was regularly used by the Hurons and Iroquois as a channel for canoes loaded with furs and other trade goods. The fortress, also named for Richelieu, went up quickly at the site of what is today Sorel-Tracy.[12]

Le Jeune had hoped for more than this. He lobbied unsuccessfully for a French offensive against the Iroquois and the Dutch, insisting to Crown officials that there was no hope of conciliation with the Iroquois and that France should forcibly take lands in present-day upstate New York that overlapped with the Dutch West India Company's claims. This plan met with fears of reprisals against France by the Dutch Republic, then a key ally in Europe. But Le Jeune believed the Iroquois would surrender quickly in the face of real French force, and that any such colonial conflict with the Dutch would not escalate.[13]

The Jesuit's request did not fall entirely on deaf ears. In a meeting with Secretary of State Sublet de Noyers, Le Jeune was told the cardinal would soon be convinced to combat the Iroquois and push Dutch traders out of Acadie, if not move in on New Netherland. Encouraged, Le Jeune wrote to Richelieu from Dieppe while awaiting passage back to America. He thanked the cardinal for Fort Richelieu while urging him to do more to handicap the Iroquois and the Dutch in the long term, so that "peoples south of New France" could be brought "to Jesus Christ" and "the commerce of the French" could be extended.[14]

In the *Relation* published in 1642 the Jesuits continued to press for military aid.[15] In their public comments they exaggerated the Iroquois threat to New France while downplaying their additional designs on New Netherland. They depicted the Iroquois as cannibals who might obstruct French commerce, colonization, and Christianization entirely in North America if the French were unwilling to "*exterminate* them."[16]

Obfuscating about Le Jeune's fuller purposes while in Paris, mission superior Barthèlemy Vimont claimed in the next year's *Relation* that the "state of affairs" in Canada had compelled *him*, not Montmagny, to send Le Jeune to France, so that he might explain how Iroquois "incursions" were harming a "newborn church." Privately Vimont told General Vitelleschi a different story. It was the governor's idea to send Le Jeune to France, and the priest was released from ordinary religious duties to lobby for fortresses, money, men, and arms.[17]

As the missionaries pushed for a French show of force in the Eastern Woodlands, their effort was blunted by Jesuit leaders in Paris. Rather than amplifying Le Jeune's message to metropolitan officials, mission procureur Charles Lalemant expressed uncertainty about Le Jeune's political activities to Étienne Charlet, then the top French Jesuit in Rome.[18] Not long after, also in the spring of 1642, Provincial Jacques Dinet in Paris complained to Vitelleschi of "errors" he believed his confreres in Canada were committing. Among other things Dinet objected to Le Jeune's dealings with Richelieu, D'Aiguillon, and Sublet de Noyers. Apprised of Dinet's concerns, Le Jeune defended the mission to Vitelleschi, emphasizing the high esteem in which it was held at the French court. Le Jeune boasted, too, of the funds he had been promised for New France.[19]

The fact remained, however, that Crown support for the colony was still minimal by the close of 1642. Le Jeune and his confreres blamed Dinet, Lalemant, and other Jesuits in Paris. Brébeuf complained to Vitelleschi that, although Richelieu and the king were well disposed toward New

France, the colony and its missions had no reliable Jesuit intercessor in France.[20] Without a man in Paris to regularly press their cause at court, the missionaries feared their strategy against the Iroquois and Dutch would go unrealized. As it happened, although Dinet was at this time replaced by a more sympathetic provincial, Jean Filleau, Cardinal Richelieu himself was dead before the year was out.

Louis XIII's death followed soon after, in May 1643. Sorrows in France thus framed Jesuit narratives about tragedies in North America. In the *Relation* of 1644, the missionaries grieved the loss of both "Louys the Just" and the great cardinal-statesman. Vimont also explained that the Jesuits still awaited "with joy and hope" the assistance Richelieu had promised, for they trusted that "the persons to whom divine providence has committed the government of New France ha[d] no less zeal and power" than the cardinal "to succor these poor countries." Vimont expressed trust in "the good will" of the new regent, Anne of Austria, regarding "the salvation of [the] savages" and the defense of New France.[21] But such public expressions of confidence in the Crown masked new missionary doubts.

A Martyr for Christ and for New France

In the early years of Anne's regency, while France was still preoccupied with war in Europe, the Jesuits continued to stress New France's need for military and financial assistance. However, following Richelieu's death, they fell under new scrutiny in Paris for their association with the Compagnie de la Nouvelle France. They were accused of partaking directly in trade and profiteering in Canada.

The missionaries defended themselves in the *Relation* of 1644, printing a declaration signed by influential stockholders in the Compagnie. These included Jacques de La Ferté, a canon at the prestigious royal chapel of Saint-Chapelle. In response to accusations that the priests were partaking in "shipments, returns, and commercial transactions" in New France, the directors insisted the Jesuits "had no part in the traffic of merchandise." The text was accompanied by words of insistence, probably Le Jeune's, that Jesuits hardly "expose[d] themselves to horrible dangers" across the Atlantic simply to "traffic [in] dead skins." Rather, "only God and the salvation of souls [made] them leave their native land . . . to go in quest of fires and torments in the midst of barbarism."[22]

But this was the first real opportunity the Jesuits had to refer credibly to "horrible dangers" and "torments" they suffered in New France, apart from the ordinary discomforts of living amid peoples whose lifestyles they deemed primitive. In 1644, in time to fend off critics and put an exclamation point on Le Jeune's lobbying for a French offensive in Iroquois Country, they had a dramatic story to tell about a new sort of hero who embodied their mission's true spirit.

This Jesuit hero, as depicted in Paris, was "clothed like a savage . . . like Saint John the Baptist," and resided without complaint as a prisoner among Mohawks very hostile to the French. He was very different from Le Jeune and his confreres as they had first represented themselves in the *Relations*. This missionary never mocked indigenous "superstitions" or the deprivations and "incivilities" he endured. Nor did he appear, at first glance, to be interested in the grand designs of France's political ministers and merchants. Instead he was "a living martyr," a "suffering confessor," a man "joyful and contented in the land of pains and sadness."[23]

His name was Isaac Jogues. He had recently been captured by a band of Mohawks that subjected him to beatings and mutilated his left hand. Eventually, in October 1646, while in Mohawk territory a second time near present-day Auriesville, New York, he would be killed.

Jogues was born on January 10, 1607, in Orléans. From a family of merchants, lawyers, and government officials, he joined the Jesuits in Rouen at seventeen. In 1636, while teaching grammar at the local college, he was ordered to join the young mission across the Atlantic. During his first six years in North America he worked among the Hurons at Ihonatiria and Sainte-Marie. In the spring of 1642 he was chosen to represent the interests of the Huron missions at Quebec.[24] His capture by the Mohawks on his return to Huron Country, subsequent torture and rescue by Dutch traders, and voluntary return to Mohawk lands where he would die are among the most iconic episodes of Jesuit history (see fig. 4).

Like other Jesuits of the mission, Jogues was a patriotic Frenchman devoted to the security and success of New France. The first public accounts of his experiences were originally intended not only to praise his heroism and win support for the mission, but also to strengthen the case for French empire and the hoped-for war against the Iroquois and New Netherland.

The day Jogues was taken prisoner, August 2, 1642, he was returning to Huron territory from Quebec in the company of twenty-five Huron warriors and fur traders and two lay Jesuits: René Goupil, who was trained in medical work, and the multilingual Guillaume Couture, who served as an interpreter. Their captors were about three hundred Mohawks who had recently attacked the Huron village of Onontchataronon, slaying and kidnapping many, and who were monitoring points along the Saint Lawrence, targeting canoes manned by Hurons trading with the French.[25] The Hurons with Jogues were carrying French firearms to their countrymen to help fend off Iroquois attacks—firearms Governor Montmagny had exchanged for Huron baptisms into the Church.[26] The presence of three Frenchmen among them did not help their cause. Once captured, Jogues and the rest of the party were beaten, humiliated, and tortured. Jogues's second and third fingers on his left hand were chopped off. This mutilation would interfere with his ability to offer Mass, due to Catholic rubrics for priests' proper handling of the Eucharistic host.

The authors of the *Relations* unapologetically mingled praise of Jogues's commitment to Christianity with accounts of his diplomatic activities for Montmagny and with calls for French attacks on the Iroquois and Dutch. In 1644 Vimont informed the French public of Jogues's regular communications with Montmagny while in captivity. Jogues for instance had warned the French of impending Iroquois attacks—using Dutch guns—against the Hurons. Additionally he had urged Montmagny not to let "regard" for himself or Couture (Goupil had already been killed) prevent the French from serving "the glory of God" by militarily thwarting Iroquois plans for an Iroquois-Huron state friendly to the Dutch.[27]

Vimont framed news of Jogues's captivity with criticism of the Dutch and calls for French military buildup in the Eastern Woodlands. He suggested that, despite the Dutch alliance with France in Europe, the Dutch in America were bent on an anti-French strategy, encouraging the Iroquois to harass the French and their indigenous allies to the point of destroying

New France. The Jesuit hoped his *Relation* would result in more French aid to New France, to fight the Iroquois and end the Dutch double-dealing.[28] With this goal partly in mind, Cramoisy published Vimont's accusations and the story of Jogues's ordeal in the midst of the continental war in Europe. This amplified the missionaries' calls for more French troops in North America and for a real show of force against the Iroquois.

Although Vimont's account of Jogues's sufferings was penned while Jogues was in captivity, the *Relation* in which it appeared was actually published after Jogues had been rescued by Dutch traders and returned to France late in 1643. By the time it went to press early in 1644, Jogues was ensconced at Rennes, writing about his ordeals and rescue. In the meantime Le Jeune had accompanied Vimont's draft to Paris in order once again to lobby the Crown on Montmagny's behalf. He frankly informed General Vitelleschi—who simply wished him success—that he was back in France to continue pressing for military aid against the Iroquois.[29] While in Paris Le Jeune also appended a chapter to Vimont's text, quoting some of Jogues's letters from Rennes.[30] In them Jogues underscored that he had ended up in the proximity of the Dutch because armed Mohawks with whom he was traveling were welcomed into Dutch settlements to trade. The Jesuit further relayed intelligence he had received in one Dutch settlement that the Mohawk village into which he had been adopted (the Iroquois commonly adopted war captives) had become "excited against the French" and that he would be killed upon his return.[31]

The reason for this was that the villagers had learned of Jogues's communications with the French. A Huron taken by the same Mohawks, but who had become hostile to the French while in captivity, had grown suspicious toward the priest. He had asked disingenuously if Jogues had any letters to mail to the French at Fort Richelieu, which he and some Mohawks could deliver. Realizing this was a ruse, Jogues had included a letter for the delivery that alerted the French to the "designs" he suspected the band had on the French and of the quantity of firearms he had observed among France's "enemies."[32] As soon as the French at Fort Richelieu had perused the packet of letters, they turned their guns on the party that had delivered them. The Huron and his Mohawk companions had fled the scene, and the villagers with whom Jogues had been residing with apparent contentment began debating an appropriate punishment for his treachery.[33]

Jogues had known that his warning to the French, if discovered by the villagers, would exacerbate already tense relations between the Mohawks and the French and French-allied nations. He had also known his perceived act of treachery could result in torture and death. He risked such things, however, "for the public good [*le bien public*]," as he put it, "and for the consolation of our French and of the poor savages who listened to the word of our Lord."[34] He expressed his willingness to die among the Mohawks in both political and religious terms. This willingness was wrapped up in readiness to expose the Huron warrior and his companions to French fire at Fort Richelieu, whatever the consequences. He acted to protect his fellow Frenchmen and their allies from what he suspected— but did not know for certain—were hostile intentions from a small band of armed men. "The public good" for which he was willing to die was the stability and future of a French Catholic colony. Contrary to what later hagiographic accounts would suggest, his devotion was not strictly directed to spreading the Gospel and giving sacraments to Native American neophytes. He was ready to die for both Christ and New France.

According to Jogues's recollections at Rennes, some Dutchmen from Rensselaerswyck secured his freedom from the Mohawks with a monetary gift worth 300 livres. By mid-September 1643 he was safe in New Amsterdam on the southern tip of Manhattan, where Governor William Kieft ensured his well-being until he could travel to France that winter. He was in a disheveled state—"in want of all things," as he put it—when he reached Rennes. But he was not wanting in useful information about the Iroquois and the rival European colony in which he had resided for several months. Following his time of recuperation in France, he produced a report for colonial officials, entitled *Novum Belgium*. It was finalized at Trois-Rivières in August 1646.[35]

Novum Belgium contained details about the harbor at the mouth of what later was called the Hudson River, with its capacity for traffic and by "the largest ships," as well as the developing fortifications, artillery, and manpower protecting New Amsterdam. Jogues offered observations, too, about the cargo and points of origin and destination of West India Company ships stopped at Manhattan during his time there. He included similar information about Rensselaerswyck upriver and about the capacity of the adjoining river for large, loaded vessels. At the same time, he mentioned points of weakness in New Netherland, such as the "wretched little fort," Fort Orange, with its several Breteuil cannons and swivels.[36]

In his report Jogues also noted the generosity of the West India Company toward settlers who came into the Dutch territory. Despite a formal law barring any but Dutch Reformed Christians, the Company welcomed and outfitted settlers from various European countries, regardless of whether they were Reformed, Lutheran, Anabaptist, or even Catholic. The Dutch patroons, furthermore, did not charge tenants rents like some of the landlords of New England. Envy on New France's behalf may have animated the Jesuits' observation that New Netherland's climate was mild, its soil excellent, and its harvests abundant, including those of "European fruits" such as apples, cherries, and even peaches appearing as late as October. And Jogues observed with interest—perhaps as a point of instruction for French officials reading his report—that trade was "free for everyone" in the Dutch colony, which meant that the Iroquois and other Natives met with "a good market price" when dealing there.[37]

Jogues reported, as well, on conflicts that arose after his sojourn in New Amsterdam between the Dutch and the Delaware-Algonquian-speaking Lenapes, traditional rivals of the Iroquoian-speaking Susquahannocks. Kieft had destroyed Lenape villages, spurring a new alliance against New Netherland by several Algonquian-speaking tribes in the region. The Jesuit painted a picture of escalating conflict, with the Dutch emerging as brutal perpetrators and victors. He provided casualty numbers and estimates of property damage suffered by the Dutch and noted the swiftness with which the Dutch had raised a militia with English assistance, resulting in massacres of indigenous men, women, and children.[38] Information about this conflict, Kieft's War of 1643–45, had more than historical value for Jogues and his audience: knowledge of Native groups with grievances against the Dutch was useful for those

French, including the Jesuits, who were contemplating an invasion of Iroquois and Dutch-controlled lands.

A myth about Jogues's single-minded devotion to evangelism has been perpetuated over the centuries by more than pious hagiographers inspired by his unimpeachable willingness to die in service to Christ. No lover of Catholicism, Francis Parkman long ago described the Jesuit's visit to France in the winter of 1643–44 in these terms: "The Queen, Anne of Austria, wished to see him; and when [he] was conducted into her presence, she kissed his mutilated hands, while the ladies of the Court thronged around him. . . . These honors were unwelcome to the modest and single-hearted missionary, who thought only of his work of converting the Indians."[39] But the original account of this meeting, appearing in the *Relation* of 1647, is more reflective of the three-dimensional author of *Novum Belgium*—a committed missionary much concerned with French expansion and mindful of worldly matters useful to French officials. The queen, according to Jérôme Lalemant, was not only moved by Jogues's sufferings, but also by the idea that a man stood before her whose "great adventures" surpassed tales of derring-do in the old romances. And she was moved to "compassion" specifically by the proof, seen in Jogues's mutilated hand, of "the cruelty of the Iroquois."[40] The original account of this courtly meeting was intended, in part, to stir up anti-Iroquois feeling.

Lalemant went on to describe how Jogues returned to New France not simply to establish a new mission among the Iroquois but ready to serve again as Montmagny's agent in Iroquois Country.[41] Indeed, throughout the spring and summer of 1646, Jogues—dressed as a layman!—served as the governor's representative among the Mohawks. A tentative peace had been reached between the French and the Mohawks, and the Jesuit, with New France's chief engineer Jean Bourdon, hoped to convince the Mohawks to set up defenses against other Iroquois less friendly to the French. However, Jogues caused offense by affirming that the French planned to establish independent, direct trade with the Onondagas, no longer depending upon the Mohawks as intermediaries.[42]

After describing Jogues's diplomatic visit, Lalemant wrote for the *Relation* of 1647, before he knew of Jogues's death, "Father Isaac Jogues, entirely attentive and devoted to this mission ... thought of nothing but undertaking a second voyage" into Iroquois Country, since "he could not endure to be so long absent from his spouse of blood."[43] But Jogues's devotion was displayed by both his desire to preach Christianity among the Mohawks and his willingness to serve Montmagny. In some modern accounts Jogues has been described as botching a French effort at the time to maintain peace with the Mohawks.[44] However, in view of the Jesuits' ongoing machinations for a French conquest in the region, it appears Jogues assisted a larger strategy by dividing Mohawk opinion about the French and buying the French time with those Iroquois who were wavering on whether war or peace with the French was better in the long run.

Jogues, for his part, was hopeful for New France in the face of the hostility he met in Iroquois Country. In September 1646, the month before he was killed, he was optimistic for the future of commerce, material improvements, and political stability in New France. In a letter written from Montreal to a Jesuit friend in France, he underscored "the trade which the country now has," which was giving New France "a notable change in its appearance" and "greater comfort in all respects." He went on say that the colony was "no longer ... as rough as before," that it was yielding "good wheat and other conveniences of life," and that the fur trade with the Hurons was especially thriving. With a note of sarcasm, he added, "I do not know whether this will catch the eyes of the gentlemen of the [merchant] company, who barely could furnish shipping when they had the trade."[45] Like his lay travel companion Bourdon, who was an energetic proponent of French commerce, Jogues celebrated the recent end of the monopoly held by the Compagnie de la Nouvelle France because it had not effectively advanced French commerce in the country.

Jogues would take his worldlier hopes for New France to the grave. During a fateful, final stay in Mohawk territory, he and another Jesuit, Lalande, were killed by an anti-French faction at the village of Ossernenon—Jogues by tomahawk on October 18, and Lalande the next day while trying to recover his confrere's corpse from the Mohawk River. With news of these events, and of subsequent Iroquois assaults on Huron villages occurring coterminously with a civil war breaking out in France, the many surviving Jesuits of the mission began fearing that New France's worst days were still ahead.

Maneuvers during the Fronde

The Jesuits lost invaluable men during the Beaver Wars of the 1640s. Adding to their tribulations, they also lost Huron territory as a mission field after devoting many resources to it for over a decade. Following a series of Iroquois attacks, the Huron mission collapsed when fleeing Hurons torched and abandoned many of their own villages between 1647 and 1649. The diaspora was hastened in the spring of 1649 by waves of Iroquois terror after several battles between a thousand-man army of mostly Mohawks and Senecas on one side and the Hurons north of Lake Superior on the other, including those residing near present-day Midland, Ontario, at mission centers named Saint-Louis, Saint-Ignace, and Sainte-Marie-au-Pays-des-Hurons.[46]

As the crisis unfolded, the Jesuits and colonial leaders looked desperately to France for support. But even metropolitan elites most concerned with the mission were newly preoccupied at the time with the domestic French crisis known as the Fronde. A two-phase civil war, the Fronde was a reaction to the increasingly unchecked exercise of monarchical power by Cardinal Mazarin and the queen regent. An uprising in Paris in mid-1648, led by parlementaires and politically charged urban crowds, gave way by 1650 to a revolt by princes and nobles across the kingdom.

The Jesuits in Quebec had received news of the Fronde in July 1649. Shortly after, Superior Jérôme Lalemant learned of terrible scenes in Huron territory, including the deaths of his nephew and Brébeuf.[47] The coincidence of such catastrophic events prompted Le Jeune's third and final journey home to France, which resulted in his appointment as Parisian procureur for the mission. Despite the drain on mission manpower at this time, Le Jeune's talent for courting French elites was deemed critical for helping the mission survive the transatlantic storm.

Upon his return to Paris, Le Jeune learned that the mission's loyal friend, Cramoisy, had joined the Parisian resistance against Mazarin and Louis II de Bourbon, the prince de Condé, whose army's blockades of the capital region resulted in food shortages and some starvation. Cramoisy was moved to take a prominent role in the rebellion partly because he had grievances against Mazarin, who was holding up funds owed to the Imprimérie Royale after casting out of the government Cramoisy's patron, Sublet de Noyers, another friend of the mission. As the new director of the Imprimérie Royale, Cramoisy employed the position to undermine Mazarin.[48]

Cramoisy was close to parlementaires and other Parisian elites opposed to Mazarin's administration, given his prominent position, since 1636, as a *juge consul* of the capital city. He had also served as an elected *échevin*, or magistrate, of Paris, a post from which he had just retired when, in late summer 1648, inhabitants of the city began erecting barricades in fear of Condé's troops.[49] His activities during the Fronde multiplied, distracting from his ordinary business. He commanded a militia in the Latin Quarter after panic swept over Paris on January 6, 1649, when it was learned that the royal family had departed the city in advance of Condé's siege. He and other leading publishers also aided the Parlement de Paris with their printing presses, distributing *mazarinades* and copies of *arrêts* that ordered the creation of a citizen army and the reestablishment of law and order once the parlementaires settled with Mazarin at Rueil in March. And once the Fronde of the Princes was underway, Cramoisy continued to aid political opposition to Mazarin while fulfilling services to the Crown, after the now-rebellious Condé had allied with Spanish troops to try to topple Mazarin's government.[50]

It is testament to the youth and haphazard state of the Bourbons' overseas empire at the time that no significant uprisings occurred in tandem with the Fronde in any French colony. Royal authority was, after all, not palpably present in New France or Caribbean possessions such as Martinique. Indeed colonial leaders were left more definitively on their own due to metropolitan preoccupation with the domestic crises. Some pursued partnerships with other Europeans, outside the inchoate French mercantile system.[51]

The missionaries, Governor Montmagny, and the latter's successor in Québec, Louis d'Ailleboust de Coulogne, were forced by the Fronde to rethink their anti-Iroquois strategy along such lines. Without informing their metropolitan support network, they attempted to negotiate a military alliance with New England, in the hopes of strengthening New France's position vis-à-vis the Iroquois and the Dutch.

This little-known episode of the mission's history involved Gabriel Druillettes, a Jesuit originally from Limoges. He had been working among the Abenakis when Governor D'Ailleboust sent him on several diplomatic missions to New England. During the fall and winter of 1650–51 the priest was the guest of the governors of Massachusetts Bay and Plymouth. Spending most of his time in Boston, Druillettes served as New France's official envoy to New England, as he described himself in 1651 in a letter to John Winthrop the Younger in Connecticut.[52] The letter revealed awareness of events in Cromwellian England at the time and included ecumenical appeals to Winthrop and other Connecticut leaders to join New France in saving Native American fellow "Christians" from Iroquois aggression. Claiming to speak for the Abenakis, too, Druillettes offered the Connecticut and Massachusetts governors "ample commercial advantages, and considerable compensation for the expense of the war" in exchange for "auxiliary troops." He proposed subduing the Mohawks in the same way that Connecticut had recently "subdued the ferocity of the Naragansets." In an account of his visits in New England, Druillettes described what both D'Ailleboust and the Jesuits were urging as "an offensive war," capable of "exterminating" the Iroquois.[53]

The governors of New England had made the first overtures regarding a trading partnership. By 1650 D'Ailleboust and the Jesuits had reason to hope they would agree to a military alliance, too. Druillettes received encouraging signs from officials in New England, but rumors of a coming war between France and England finally dissuaded them from joining forces with New France and its indigenous allies.[54] France had in fact supported the royalists during the English Civil War, and by 1652 the Commonwealth government was naming the French as targets in letters of marque to privateers. War did not openly erupt, however. Regardless, in a second diplomatic tour of New England, accompanied this time by a Montagnais Christian, Noël Negabamat, Druillettes learned that the Plymouth leaders had most of all opposed going to war with the Iroquois, out of concern it would result in war with New Netherland—probably what Druillettes and those who had sent him had had in mind all along.[55]

The Jesuits said nothing in the *Relations* about Druillettes's failed political mission to New England. Public reporting on Jesuit attempts to negotiate trade and military deals with English colonists—unbeknownst to Queen Anne and Cardinal Mazarin—would not have gone over well with metropolitan officials or critics of the Jesuits at any time, let alone at a time when France and England were at loggerheads with mutual trade embargoes.

The responsibility for keeping Druillettes's story out of the *Relations* rested with Le Jeune, now ensconced in Paris as mission procureur and final redactor of the drafts sent to Cramoisy's typesetters. Better informed than his predecessor about events and challenges on the ground in New France, Le Jeune was now also in close proximity to Cramoisy and others in the French capital who cared for the colony and its missions but who were preoccupied with the Fronde. Concerned to maintain lifelines between New France and its support network during a period of crisis on both sides of the Atlantic, Le Jeune and the mission superiors communicating with him began tailoring their overtures to French elites in ways that resonated powerfully in the regency era's climate of alarm and confusion.

For one thing they scripted the content of the *Relations* more than in the past. They began using a new title for the annual imprints: no longer *Relations de ce qui s'est passé en la Nouvelle-France*, but now *Relations de ce qui s'est passé de plus remarquable és missions des Pères de la Compagnie de Jésus, en la Nouvelle-France.*[56] The *Relations* now highlighted "remarkable" events such as the terrible deaths of Jogues and Brébeuf and the sufferings of the Hurons in the Beaver Wars with the Iroquois. They also underscored the fear and anxiety in which French settlers in the Saint Lawrence region were living and occasions, too, when lay Frenchmen perished at the hands of the Iroquois.

In the *Relation* of 1650, the draft of which Le Jeune carried to Paris in his final transatlantic journey, the Jesuits framed news of a massive Huron refugee crisis in terms that would inspire sympathy among those preoccupied with the Fronde. In place of the usual two-part *Relation* authored partly by the Quebec superior, Le Jeune gave to Cramoisy a brief, power-ful *Relation* authored solely by Ragueneau, who had been working with Brébeuf and the younger Lalemant in Huron territory. Ragueneau by 1650 was caring for Huron refugees at the new mission station of Saint-Marie on the Isle Saint-Joseph, known today as Christian Island in Georgian Bay. This *Relation*, postmarked from a lonely and perilous new mission outpost, opened with the assertion that Christianity was progressing among the Hurons in ways "more notable than ever," appearing to some Natives with new "luster" precisely because they were now experiencing tremendous suffering. Some Huron families, "constrained to abandon their goods, their houses, their country," preferred "to die from privations" rather than suffer "a more cruel death" at the hands of the Iroquois. "What consoles us," Ragueneau added, "is that Heaven becomes enriched by our losses, and is filled with the spoils of this Church militant." The Hurons, he proposed, truly now formed a new, young church that bore upon it "the true mark of Christianity," which was "the cross of Jesus Christ."[57]

Amid his accounts of Huron suffering, Ragueneau shared with France the news of Brébeuf and Gabriel Lalemant's gruesome deaths in the Iro-quois attacks on the Saint-Ignace mission in March 1649. He depicted the ultimate outrage of cannibalism enacted upon the still living bodies of his confreres: "Before their death, both their hearts were torn out, by means of an opening above the breast; and those barbarians inhumanely feasted thereon, drinking their blood quite warm, which they drew from its source with sacrilegious hands. While still quite full of life, pieces of flesh were removed from their thighs, from the calves of their legs, and from their arms—which those executioners placed on coals to roast, and ate it in their sight."[58]

Such images of unholy feasting by the Iroquois were juxtaposed with equally horrific images of starving, baptized Hurons. Forced to abandon their settled, agricultural lifestyle and forage in unfamiliar woodlands, they quite differently were forced by awful need to cannibalize deceased family members in order to survive.[59]

The *Relation* of 1650 drew special attention to Huron refugees, facing death, who bravely tried to defend themselves against the Iroquois. Le

Jeune even had Cramoisy, extraordinarily, print up a second edition of the *Relation* that dramatized this more than the first. It depicted Hurons enduring "a state of famine more terrible than war" and struggling to "fortify themselves" in new, unfamiliar environs to fend off further Iroquois assaults.[60]

The *Relation* of 1650 not only saw unusual, hasty re-edition by Cramoisy but was also republished in French and in translation by other printers in and outside of France.[61] This suggests that new effort was made to seek aid outside of France, from which little was forthcoming during the Fronde. It also suggests that the *Relation*'s dramatic stories gained the mission new notice within France, despite the ongoing civil war. The harrowing tales of Brébeuf and young Lalemant's martyrdoms had something to do with this. At the same time, scenes of starving men, women, and children forced to barricade themselves against a fierce enemy would have resonated with Parisian citizens who had prepared for attacks by Condé's forces. By January 1649 Cramoisy himself, while leading militiamen in his quartier, had become involved in monitoring food supplies and aiding Parlement's rationing efforts during Condé's blockade, directing grocers and other shopkeepers to stay open for business despite fears of pillage by hungry mobs.[62] Although their situation was different from the Hurons', Cramoisy and his readers in early 1650 were not altogether strangers to the experiences of fear, hunger, and rushing to build makeshift fortifications that were dramatized in the *Relations*.

By late 1652, as Le Jeune and Cramoisy prepared the *Relation* of 1653 for press, this was even more the case. Once the Fronde of the Princes set in, there was a major subsistence crisis. In Paris and other cities across France it was not an uncommon sight to see large numbers of men, women, and children dying of starvation, and suffering, too, from the aftershocks of massacres and pillaging by both royal and Frondeur armies.[63]

Penning most of the *Relation* for 1653 in Paris, Le Jeune drew an unambiguous connection between the besieged Hurons and the French Frondeurs who, as he put it provocatively, were combating "Iroquois as barbarous as those of America." In the opening chapter on "the war with the Iroquois," he also likened the suffering Hurons to young David in the

Hebrew scriptures: when still a shepherd, the Psalmist was trained by God "in the use of a sling [*fronde*], to give him victory over a giant." The French word *fronde*, and the image of a young, future king bravely standing up to Goliath, were intended by the politically savvy Le Jeune to appeal both to readers sympathetic to the original *frondeurs* and those horrified by powerful princes, who with Spanish allies were in open conflict with the teenaged, Louis XIV's monarchy.[64]

Le Jeune used such parallels to press forward with his long-standing campaign to secure more French assistance for a war against the Iroquois. He insisted that, despite the destruction of the Huron missions and the ongoing refugee crisis, the Iroquois problem was one that French leaders could "easily remedy, nothwithstanding the disorders of France," if only they would assert a will for it. Interestingly, however, when referring to French leaders, the politic mission procureur—perhaps hedging his bets— did not speak of Queen Anne, Cardinal Mazarin, or any other French official by name. He instead employed a generic phrase he had not used before: "les hautes puissances."[65]

Notably, in contrast to the glowing language toward the monarchy and Richelieu in the earlier *Relations*, during the regency period there was a definite moderation in enthusiasm toward the Crown in the missionaries' published writings. Brief, polite thanks to the queen appeared in the *Relations* of the mid-1640s through early 1650s whenever royal support was secured for New France, but that is all. For example, Anne sent a small force of twenty-two French soldiers to the colony, which Lalemant tersely called an act of "kindness" by a queen who then had grandiosely declared herself to be "the mother and protectress of her French and savage subjects" in America.[66] And the name of Richelieu's successor, Mazarin, is nowhere to be found in the *Relations*. Rather, newly appearing in the *Relations* of the period, and in private missionary communications, were frank complaints about the failure of the Crown to help New France. Among these complaints was that funds the queen had sent with the twenty-two soldiers had not covered even basic expenses. The Jesuits had to lodge and feed the men on their own dime and even repair their broken firearms and tend to their sick and wounded.[67]

Metropolitan neglect of New France remained a concern of the missionaries throughout the 1650s. Late in 1652 Ragueneau and Jean de Quen each complained to General Goswin Nickel in Rome that, although the missions continued to be threatened by the Iroquois, no military assistance was forthcoming from France. Toward the end of the decade, Ragueneau—who had witnessed an Iroquois massacre of some Hurons—was still complaining of New France's dire situation, expressing wishes to Nickel that French troops would soon be commissioned to subdue the Five Nations.[68]

In the meantime a Jesuit mission reserve near Quebec, Saint-Joseph de Sillery, which already had palisades, was surrounded with stronger defensive walls and mounted with cannons.[69] And in August 1653 the new colonial governor, Jean de Lauson, ordered the Jesuits' primary residence in Quebec to be turned into a fortress—complete with gun ports and bastions—in advance of expected Iroquois attacks.[70] This was despite the fact that, at the Iroquois' instigation, a general peace was being discussed.

Efforts by Jesuits such as Simon Le Moyne to secure that short-lived peace of 1654, so that a mission to the Iroquois might truly commence, have been underscored in other historical narratives.[71] Yet there is evidence, too, that the missionaries in the years following understood their new access to Iroquois Country as a prelude to a French conquest. In 1656 the first Jesuit mission in Iroquois Country, Sainte-Marie de Gannentaha on the northeast shore of Lake Onondaga, was established as both a mission and a redoubt for French soldiers. Two years prior Le Jeune in a letter to Nickel had matter-of-factly described the planned mission as a fortress—in a literal, not spiritual or metaphorical, sense.[72] And the *Relation* of 1658 frankly reported that French workmen at the site had constructed good lodgings for the missionaries as well as "a good redoubt for the soldiers . . . on an eminence commanding the lake and all surrounding places." In the meantime, the Jesuits posted to this mission, along with fifteen French soldiers, visited the village of Onondaga seventeen miles away. They were welcomed as representatives of the French, with whom the Onondagas wished to trade.[73]

Furthermore the Jesuits downplayed the peace of 1654 in the *Relations*. This corresponds with a general pattern of underreporting news of positive cultural and political developments in New France throughout the era of the Fronde and its aftermath. An example of the kind of news left out of the *Relations* in the period is the staging of high French theatrical tragedies in Quebec between 1646 and 1652. Private journal records kept by the superiors of Quebec in this period reveal that, on at least three different occasions between the winter of 1646 and the spring of 1652, the playwright Pierre Corneille's tragedies *Le Cid* (1636) and *Héraclius* (1647) were staged at the *comptoir*, or warehouse and counting-house, Quebec. The plays, performed before an apparently pleased audience of Native Americans, colonial officials, leading French families of the colony, and of course Jesuits, were still then au courant among Parisian theatergoers.[74] In the earlier years of the mission the Jesuits would have boasted of such events to urbane readers back home. To have reported such news at mid-century, however, might have given the impression that the situation in New France was not so dire as the Jesuits were insisting.

Mission superiors' journals of the period offer additional snapshots of the Jesuits' life and various events in New France that were left out of the *Relations* of the period. For example, in January 1649 the missionaries in Quebec were enjoying bottles and even kegs of "Spanish wine" as well as roasted turkey and other foods that had been unavailable in the early years of the mission. The missionaries also noted with satisfaction that the first executions under French law had taken place: specifically, public hangings of a rapist and a teenage girl convicted of theft.[75] The journals of the period record, as well, various pleasant social calls between the missionaries, colonial officials, and other persons of rank in and around Quebec.

In short, although New France was certainly in crisis in the late 1640s and early 1650s, the situation was not as desperate as the *Relations'* stark emphases on Iroquois cruelty and treachery made it appear in France.

A New Holy War for the "Heirs of Saint Louis"

The Jesuits' lowered expectations for royal aid to New France were only temporary. By the late 1650s, as stability returned to France, the missionaries renewed their requests for soldiers, armaments, and provisions—not only to protect settlements along the Saint Lawrence, but also to launch a war of conquest in Iroquois and Dutch lands. Further, once it was clear young Louis XIV would be a strong ruler, Le Jeune and his confreres reasserted their imperial vision for New France in bolder terms than ever.

Peace and unrivaled dominance in Europe came to France in 1659, in the form of Mazarin's diplomatic achievement, the Treaty of the Pyrenees. The next year, with the Fronde fully in the past, twenty-one-year-old Louis triumphally entered Paris and prepared to take the reins of government from Mazarin, who was dead by early 1661. In this optimistic moment France was finally poised to take serious advantage of commercial and colonial opportunities overseas.[76]

The Jesuits shared in this optimism after securing approval from the Parlement de Paris in 1658 to launch new missions, anywhere they wished, in the Americas. That same year Louis had purchased Martinique from the Parquet family, which had previously purchased it from Richelieu's Compagnie des Isles d'Amérique. By 1660 French Jesuits in communication with Le Jeune were established in Martinique, where their sugar plantations, worked by slaves, were among the largest on the island.[77] Thus earlier Jesuit aspirations regarding Martinique's economic potential, published by Cramoisy in Richelieu's day, began to come to fruition.[78]

In the early 1660s Le Jeune and the Jesuits of New France understood that prospects for plantation colonies were making the Caribbean the new center of gravity for French activity in the Atlantic World. But their own hopes remained pinned on North America, where much had been invested—including Jesuit blood—for decades, and where they believed that, but for the Iroquois, the French had an opportunity to build an empire that would yield profits of many kinds. Lands south of the Saint Lawrence were especially fertile for agriculture, so in addition to the fur trade, the Jesuits were convinced that an expanded New France would produce vast amounts of timber, fish, and mineral wealth. Given unexplored regions to the west, New France also held out the promise of a northwest passage to the East Indies, which the French were also eyeing for trade and colonization in the face of weakening Portuguese power.[79]

With such concerns in mind along with North America's Christianization, Le Jeune and two other priests—one in Quebec and another deep in Canada's interior, at a place called Nekouba along the Ashua-pmushuan River—publicly entreated their young monarch to fight a "holy war" in Iroquois Country. With the *Relations* of 1661 and 1662 the Jesuits informed the French public, with not a little hyperbole, that "every-where" the Iroquois were slaughtering, burning, and even *eating* newly baptized Native American Christians. They were frightening away from the French other potential converts and cutting off trade lines, imperiling New France's future. They were also killing ordinary Frenchmen, not only missionaries, who were working to build up the colony.[80] The missionary writing from the uncharted region around Nekouba called the Iroquois "the little Turk of New France," expressing disbelief that the Five Nations were such a menace to French expansion in North America when their numbers were small compared to forces France was used to fighting in Europe.[81] Mission superior Jérôme Lalemant in Quebec further hoped that the Jesuits' reports of Iroquois cruelty would "rekindle in the French that zeal and ardor which, of old . . . rendered France so glorious through the Crusades."[82]

Lalemant's *Relation* of 1661 petitioned the king for at least two regiments of French regulars, partly because, in the Jesuit's assessment, the French settlers in Canada were incapable of defeating the Iroquois on their own through militia activity, given the depleted strength of the Hurons and their other indigenous allies.[83] Furthermore, fortifications and natural defenses in the Saint Lawrence region were weak, despite efforts in Richelieu's time to secure Quebec. Settlers in isolated farms were therefore subject to surprise raids by Iroquois war parties that knew the terrain, especially nearby forests, much better.[84] The solution to all this, according to Lalemant, was a new French crusade into Iroquois Country that would preserve New France, open the gates of heaven to numerous Natives, and give the French a new "glory" that was worthy of the "heirs of the great Saint Louis." According to the Jesuit, Louis IX had centuries earlier "planted the *fleur de lis* in the heart of the Crescent," but Louis XIV now had a new opportunity to "make a Holy Land of one that is infidel." The venture only required will: "Let France but wish to destroy the Iroquois, and he will be destroyed."[85]

Le Jeune elaborated that Louis XIV might even win the crown of sainthood himself should his armies advance through Iroquois Country. In the opening of the *Relation* of 1662, the mission veteran addressed the king directly:

> Sire: Behold your New France.... "Save me," she cries. "I am about to lose the Catholic religion. The fleurs-de-lis are about to be snatched from me. I will no longer be French.... I will fall into the hands of foreigners, when the Iroquois have drained the rest of my blood....
>
> If you consult heaven, they will tell you that perhaps your own salvation is dependent on the salvation of many peoples who will be lost if they are not aided by ... Your Majesty. If you consider the French name, you will know, Sire, that you are a great king who, in making Europe tremble, should not be scorned in America....
>
> By saving... your French colony and souls from a great number of nations, they will all be obliged to pray to God that he should bestow upon you the name of "Saint," as he has your illustrious ancestor, whose zeal you would imitate in undertaking a holy war.[86]

Rhetoric about holy war in the *Relations* has largely been whitewashed from tellings of the mission's history. Where noted at all, it has been interpreted in exclusively spiritualized terms or as evidence of a fanatical idealism, characteristic of a militant fringe out of touch with political realities of the seventeenth century.[87] But crusade rhetoric was not archaic among French elites at the time. In the early 1660s young Louis was planning to assert royal control over a long-neglected New France and to consolidate a growing network of overseas colonies and trading stations. He was also hungry for personal and national gloire and looking for opportunities to deploy idle regiments of his great army—a force of unprecedented size in Europe—following a period of stalemate in the Cretan War with the Ottoman Empire.[88] Le Jeune and other Jesuits believed, probably correctly, that France could easily afford new action in an American theater. The lull in tensions with the Turks, combined with indications at court that direct rule over New France was imminent, occasioned a new missionary sales pitch for a westward, transatlantic crusade that would appeal to political elites who had been focused, while thanklessly assisting the Venetians, on a more traditional conflict with an Islamic power in the eastern Mediterranean. Although the missionaries had been pressing for years for a war of conquest in Iroquois lands, they did not deploy the rhetoric of holy war until this era of the Cretan War and increasing noise across Europe about a possible united Christian-European front against the Turks in Hungary.[89] Thus militant words constituted a pragmatic rhetorical strategy, well within the bounds of respectable European speech two decades before the Siege of Vienna.

Le Jeune's appeals to Louis were his last published words on New France, as he retired from the position of procureur in 1662 and was replaced by Ragueneau. Ragueneau had also proven himself enterprising on behalf of a militaristic, anti-Iroquois strategy. Late in 1661 he wrote a letter to the prince de Condé, whom he knew from earlier days in Bourges. The prince had just been welcomed back to court after years of disgrace for his behavior during the Fronde. One of the first things he did in this period of royal clemency was to promise the Jesuits of Quebec that he would use whatever renewed influence he had to raise a force of French soldiers for Canada. Ragueneau expressed to Condé his concern that some aid the king had recently promised the new colonial governor, Pierre Dubois D'Avaugour, would be insufficient. He urged the receptive prince to inform Louis that a single regiment—commissioned to subdue the Iroquois, by advancing through New Netherland, and then maintained as a standing force—would put an end to the Jesuits' concerns about the Iroquois.[90]

Ragueneau worked in concert with Governor D'Avaugour, who further urged the prince to inform the young king not only of the promise of the Saint Lawrence region, but also that it would be easy for him to control "two states as large as France" in America if he simply exerted the will. The only stumbling block was the Iroquois, whom the governor was sure could be destroyed by three French regiments, or at least handicapped by one. D'Avaugour further informed Condé that Jesuits including Ragueneau, then heading the colony's general council, had served the king and the good of New France better than anyone else up to that point.[91]

The Jesuits' campaign for military intervention in New France was furthered by the publication of the first official history of the mission in 1664, François Du Creux's monumental *Historiae Canadensis*.[92] Cramoisy published the work after it was vetted by Le Jeune.[93] Du Creux himself was a professor of rhetoric at the Jesuits' Collège de Bordeaux. He had never set foot in North America, but beginning in 1643 he interviewed missionaries who had returned from Canada and pored over the *Relations* and unpublished mission records available to him.[94] Although in the form of a history of the Jesuits' work in New France up to that time, Du Creux's Latin narrative was dedicated to Louis XIV and lamented, in its first pages, that New France was "torn and crushed by the cruel Iroquois."[95] In his dedication Du Creux went on:

> Most Christian King, will you not avenge this insult to God and to yourself? Will you who have . . . imposed the terror of your arms upon the whole of Europe, permit these assassins to go unpunished? Will you allow an armed band of robbers to wander with impunity, affronting the name of France? . . .
>
> Your subjects, Louis, expect that you will send adequate forces to take vengeance upon the perfidy of the Iroquois and to guard Church and State in Canada. . . .
>
> When the Iroquois have been subdued, the infant Church in Canada will arise . . . your kingdom and the kingdom of Christ will be propagated at one and the same time far and wide.[96]

The *History* contained tales of sudden Iroquois attacks on unsuspecting Huron villagers and French farmers.[97] Numerous passages alleged Iroquois treachery against the French following the peace of 1654. The book concluded with a dark passage about a "base plot" by the Iroquois "to destroy utterly the French, both priests and laymen."[98]

The deaths of Jogues, Brébeuf, and the other Jesuits of course featured prominently in Du Creux's narrative, which has traditionally been presumed to have been intended primarily to lay groundwork for the martyrs' canonizations.[99] Yet the cry of *vengeance* for the martyrdoms rings out from the first pages of the *History*. Jesuit suffering and deaths were to justify Louis XIV's vigorous intervention into conflicts that had been plaguing the mission and hampering French trade and colonial development.

The martyrs in the *History* also served as mouthpieces for a vision of French power and cultural superiority. Du Creux attributed a speech to Jogues—probably invented, but plausibly declaimed to Mohawk villagers a few months before he was killed—in which he spoke of cultural developments that would follow if the Mohawks joined with the French. Du Creux called Jogues "the envoy of the French," dutifully "discharg[ing] the task assigned to him by Montmagny," which was to encourage Mohawks who were hostile to New France to abandon their Dutch alliance and partner with the French instead.[100] The speech, resembling nothing in the *Relations* from Jogues's time, linked the priest's martyrdom to the cause of spreading French civilization as the Jesuits were newly defining it:

> You have often heard . . . of the glory of the name of France, of the majesty of the Most Christian King, of the extent of his kingdom and of its strength and riches; there is no happier kingdom in all Europe than France, and Europe is the only place in the world where happiness exists. . . . In France they know everything in Heaven and earth, they have all the arts, their cities are populous, they wear beautiful clothes, they have large and beautiful houses and public buildings, they are polite, elegant, and refined; and most of all they know, they worship, and they serve the high God who made the stars and the sun. . . . Would it not be better to live in peace with such a nation?[101]

Du Creux went on to say that, during his last days among the Mohawks, Jogues made no "public mention of . . . the Faith" but engaged individuals about Christianity only "in private."[102]

The *History* was another call to French arms against the Iroquois. At the same time it commemorated Louis XIV's assertion of direct rule over New France in 1663 and attendant efforts to newly control and expand his world empire. Du Creux referred to the "French Empire" (*Gallici Imperii*) in a way few had done, given perduring opposition in Catholic Europe to any powers but the papacy and the Holy Roman Empire laying claim to the ancient mantel of imperium.[103] The book was also dedicated, secondarily, to the merchants of a new trading monopoly, the Compagnie Française des Indes Occidentales, which had been established in 1664 by the king's first minister, Jean-Baptiste Colbert.

The Jesuits were clear during the optimistic early years of Louis XIV's personal rule that the "temporal interests" of France were at stake and were an important goal of their work in New France, even while insisting that the "eternal" interests of Christendom, led by the "most Christian kingdom" of France, were the most important reasons to pursue imperial hegemony in North America.[104] Together with Du Creux's *Historia* and many private communications with French officials, the *Relations* of the early 1660s were the culmination of a two-decade campaign by the Jesuits to shape French imperial policy in favor of more aggressive shows of force and cultural self-confidence. Indeed the *Relations* of this period were the most baldly nationalistic of the series, evincing refreshed hope that the missionaries' long-harbored imperial vision for France and North America would soon be realized. A French crusade against the Iroquois would result, the Jesuits were sure, both in a "beautiful French kingdom" in North America and "a great Christian empire," fittingly ruled by a descendant of Saint Louis (see fig. 5).[105]

CHAPTER 4

Exporting and Importing Catholic Charity

In November 1669 a middle-aged Jesuit named Charles Albanel was tending to Montagnais Natives at the Mission de la Sainte Croix near Tadoussac, a fur-trading center some one hundred and thirty miles northeast of Quebec. He wrote of this small mission that it "might have passed for a hospital" after some Frenchmen dropped off there twenty sick persons who "resembled monsters rather than human beings," so ravaged were they by the latest of many smallpox epidemics to hit the region since European contact the century before.[1]

More Frenchmen stopped by and urged Albanel to come tend to a "cabin full of dying persons" discovered at Isle Verte on the opposite shore of the Saint Lawrence. With some French sailors' help, the priest carried food, medicine, and the sacraments to the "living skeletons" he encountered there. He administered theriac, a traditional European plague remedy just then becoming widely available in French markets due to the publication of a formula long monopolized by the Venetians.[2] The Jesuits employed theriac with success at various mission stations in New France. But in this instance the medicine failed. The *Relation* of 1671 informs us that Albanel and the French laymen were soon lugging corpses to a graveyard.[3]

Native American populations' decimation by smallpox and other European-borne diseases is a familiar, terrible story. In the Eastern Woodlands many populations were thinning out by Champlain's time, because disease had traveled northward through trade routes and ecosystems affected earlier by Spanish colonization.[4]

The Jesuits' response to epidemics among indigenous populations has been regarded as medically backward and almost purely spiritual in focus. In other accounts of the mission, Jesuits are portrayed as rushing to sick Natives' bedsides at the hour of death—to catch souls just in time, so to speak, with baptism and last rites.[5] However, greater attention to the social dimension of the mission and Jesuit collaborations with laypersons and women religious in charitable ministries reveals efforts, advanced for the time, to provide this-worldly remedies to the sick, as well as food, shelter, and other material assistance to the destitute and infirm. Many of these efforts in and beyond the Jesuits' mission stations were successful, unlike Albanel's in 1669. Over time they were the fruit not only of Jesuit collaboration with other French persons but also with Native American Christian converts. Furthermore these efforts were not a marginal appendage of a mission that was almost entirely spiritual in orientation. They were central to the Jesuits' enterprise in New France, conceived less as a means of luring vulnerable Natives to Christianity than as a vital embodiment of the Jesuits' Catholic faith and that of the French and their new Native American coreligionists.

The Jesuits' social-charitable ministries in New France are best represented by several large-scale projects, beginning with an experimental mission village called Saint-Joseph de Sillery. Sillery has heretofore been seen as a center of religious and moral instruction in which the missionaries initially, but unsuccessfully, strove to "reduce" (permanently settle) and "Frenchify" Native Christians. It has not been appreciated as the center of social charity it was envisioned to be and eventually became. At Sillery Algonquin and Montagnais nomads were provided with medical services by both the Jesuits and Augustinian nuns who joined them there. They were also provided with food, homes, tools for farming and artisanal production, and end-of-life care. Assistance was financed and dispensed through a joint effort of male and female missionaries, merchants of the Compagnie de la Nouvelle France, and wealthy donors on both sides of the Atlantic.

Additionally, in the late 1640s and 1650s, the Jesuits collaborated with laypersons, such as the colonial landowner Éléanore de Grandmaison, in a large-scale effort to feed, shelter, tend medically, and resettle thousands of Huron refugees who were forced from their villages by the Iroquois attacks of 1648 and 1649. Many of these Huron refugees were already baptized Catholics and migrated toward French settlements in numbers that caught missionaries and colonists alike off guard.

Beyond all this the Jesuits over many decades partnered with metropolitan elites, French officials, colonists, and mission Indians themselves in a range of social-charitable projects throughout their expanding mission network. These included dispensing medicines to Indians distant from colonial hospitals and financially assisting Christian Indian widows and orphans whose husbands or fathers had died fighting as allies of the French in wars against the Iroquois.

However, despite promising beginnings, the charitable components of the mission were not very successful over the long term, if success is to be judged against the Jesuits' ambitions for widespread poverty relief, access to the best medicines then available in France, and general material uplift according to urban-elite standards of the time. This is partly because French laypersons did not help to expand the mission's charitable components to the extent the Jesuits had envisioned. But this was not due simply to a lack of interest. Rather, conditions in both New France and France itself, as well as on the high seas—where ship journeys were infrequent and sometimes imperiled by piracy and war—frustrated timely communication about specific charitable needs and the transport of alms and personnel for services such as hospital work. The Jesuits' social ministries were especially difficult to develop in a colonial setting in which the French population remained quite small: there were only about three thousand French inhabitants by 1660, few of whom had the means to serve as bountiful patrons of large-scale charitable works such as those increasingly common in French cities. The ministries thus remained overly dependent upon metropolitan assistance that simply was not to be had without a struggle in the era of the Thirty Years' War, the Fronde, and later conflicts back home. And even when donations crossed the Atlantic, they were not readily transported into mission locales that, even when not beset by the ongoing Iroquois Wars, were often several days away by foot or small canoe from Saint Lawrence port towns.

Despite their frustrated development over the long term, the Jesuits' social-charitable ministries in New France deserve attention that has been lacking in prior studies of the mission. This inattention is due, in part, to a general neglect of the Jesuits' frequent collaboration with laypersons—many of them women—as well as with female missionaries of other religious orders. Tensions, rather than productive relationships, between the all-male, priestly Jesuits and these other groups have here-tofore attracted more scholarly interest.[6] It is also sometimes assumed that active lay involvement in the Christian missionary movement is an eighteenth-century missiological development, attributed especially to Pietist and evangelical Protestant breakthroughs in this respect, and not something to be found in post-Tridentine Roman Catholic enterprises.[7] But when we shift focus to references in the mission sources to Jesuit col-laboration with religious women as well as with laypersons, an intriguing, developing world of early transatlantic charitable activity comes into view. Indeed the mission to New France begins to resemble, and cast new light on, the more developed and well-studied world of Reform-era European charity—a world in which we know that Jesuits, other religious, lay elites, and government officials all played prominent roles.[8] Furthermore we come to see that the Jesuits of New France understood their mission as something more than the sum of their own particular, religious ministra-tions. Rather, laypersons were *expected* to participate in it and to enlarge it, especially by advancing—as was fitting for their worldly state of life—the corporeal, this-worldly life of the Church and the exportation to America of the infrastructure of a generous, charitable, and well-ordered French Catholic society.

And assist the mission in such ways many laypersons did, although over time not in the sustained way the Jesuits originally envisioned. Unfortu-nately many of the names of the Jesuits' lay collaborators went unpublished: the *Relations* are full of references to individuals who aided charitable projects but asked to remain anonymous.[9] But the mission sources do reveal the identities of some prominent figures who aided the mission. These include the duchesse d'Aiguillon, Richelieu's niece; François Sublet de Noyers, one of Richelieu's secretaries of state; Bernardin Gigault de Bellefonds, marshal of France under Louis XIV; and Marguerite d'Alégre, the marquise de Baugé, who for a number of years sent money and supplies to a medical mission among the Abenakis.[10] Also among the high-profile laypersons who assisted charitable causes in Canada was Sébastien Cramoisy, the publisher of the *Relations*, who took a particular interest in the improvement of medical ministries in New France. While individuals such as D'Aiguillon and Cramoisy do of course appear in some accounts of Reform-era French charity, they generally come across as passive underwriters or interfering lay elites who constrained the spiritual energy and creativity of French religious, such as Louise de Marillac's Daughters of Charity.[11] Yet the colonial story pushes us to consider how critical lay action was when it came first to exporting Reform-era charity across oceanic distances and then to importing it into early North American terrains with little urban development and infrastructure.

Social Charity at the Sillery Reserve

In 1641 readers of the *Relations* learned of a young Algonquin who had been abandoned by his tribe about sixty kilometers from the Sillery mission. He was ill, and his people were nomads who could not afford to linger long in one place during hunting season. They made the sad but not unusual decision to leave him to die. But an Algonquin resident of Saint-Joseph learned of this and passed on word to Jean de Quen, a priest of the mission whose work included assisting Augustinian hospital nuns with their ministries. De Quen and a French layman then searched for the sick man and brought him to the religious women, who nursed him back to health. Once recovered, the patient asked the Jesuits to teach him Christianity and baptize him, so impressed was he with the "great love" that had been shown him by the French. Or so it was reported by Paul Le Jeune, who had ghostwritten parts of mission superior Barthèlemy Vimont's *Relation* that year. "Charity works miracles," Le Jeune editorialized in Paris. "It changes savages into children of God."[12]

With this and similar reports in the *Relations*, Le Jeune wished to encourage wealthy readers in France to continue offering social-charitable assistance to distressed Natives. In this regard he had recently succeeded in a dramatic way with the duchesse d'Aiguillon. In the *Relation* of 1635 he had expressed the Jesuits' desire to develop a central area where many sick, starving, and elderly persons could be brought and cared for, with a hospital on site like the *hôtels-dieu* devoted to charitable services in Paris, Caen, and other cities he knew well. The Jesuits of Quebec initially had taken such persons into their residences, but only men, not women, and fewer than they hoped to assist. Le Jeune proposed to his readers that a colonial hôtel-dieu, run by nuns trained as nurses, could receive "all the sick people of the country, and all the old people."[13]

D'Aiguillon, inspired by these words, had arranged in 1636 to purchase land in Quebec from the Compagnie de la Nouvelle France and to build the Hôtel-Dieu de Québec, a charitable hospital to be staffed by the newly reformed Augustinian Canonesses Regular of the Mercy of Jesus. These nuns, known commonly as Hospitalières, already ran a hospital for the poor in Dieppe in Normandy—known also to Le Jeune from his pre-missionary stint in that city, and one of several hospitals whose board of directors included the publisher Cramoisy.[14] To establish the Canadian hospital on a sound footing, D'Aiguillon by 1639 had provided a great sum for that time of 40,540 *livres tournois*—almost half the amount she later gave, more famously, to help establish the Hôpital Général de Paris in the 1650s. The noblewoman's main conditions for this endowment were that the hospital be dedicated "to the blood of the Son of God, shed in order that mercy might be granted to all men," that all nuns who labored there be devoted to "service of the poor," and that any priest who offered Mass in the hospital chapel share in the same spirit.[15]

While D'Aiguillon was planning the hospital, another large charitable gift to the mission was finalized by the Chevalier Noël Brûlart de Sillery, a Knight of Malta and erstwhile ambassador to Spain. Entrusting 32,000 livres tournois plus annuities to Le Jeune, Sillery wanted to sustain a new mission complex in which nomadic Natives could settle. His gift was supplemented by funds from François Derré de Gand, *commissaire général* of the colonial merchant company, which was earmarked for the first two families to settle in the mission—Montagnais families headed by Christian converts named Nanaskoumat (baptized François Xavier), and Negabamat (baptized Noël, after the chevalier himself). The site chosen for this new mission, Saint-Joseph de Sillery, was a fishing cove frequented by Algonquins, about a two-hour walk southwest of Quebec. Within a few years various Montagnais and Algonquin families joined the original two, typically residing seasonally, not full-time, so they could hunt for part of the year, both for sustenance and for the new French fur trade. There was some initial thought among the French that the Sillery families would settle full-time into farming, but the Jesuits, merchants, and colonial governor quickly realized the impracticability of the scheme.[16]

Le Jeune and other Jesuits believed that Native American families were attracted to Sillery in part because of rumors they heard about "assistance" the French intended to give them. In the early *Relations*, the experimental Sillery mission was often described in terms of help, almsgiving, and charity. Sillery was also publicized in France as a place where housing, food, tools for farming and building, as well as medicines and care for the sick would be freely offered to Natives for their bodily, this-worldly well-being. The *Relation* of 1641, for example, attributed to Negabamat these words: "The French love us. . . . They succor not only those who are baptized, they aid us . . . to cultivate the land . . . and . . . with lodgings; they relieve us in our sicknesses, they provide for us in our want, without . . . expecting any recompense."[17]

Negabamat had experienced the mission's charitable services firsthand, but in a way that illustrates the challenges faced by the Jesuits and Hospitalières in dispensing both their major noble patrons' transatlantic charity at one and the same time. In 1639 Negabamat and Nanaskoumat both took ill from smallpox, caught from Algonquin traders. Nanaskoumat was immediately carried from Sillery to Quebec—a journey of several hours on foot, even without a heavy load—where the first group of Hospitalières, led by Mother Marie Guenet de Saint-Ignace, were tending to other smallpox victims. But Negabamat's journey to Quebec was delayed because he feared leaving his pregnant wife alone at Sillery. He and the Jesuits were sure his end was near by the time he was lodged in the new Hôtel-Dieu de Québec. He recovered, however, and was eventually able to return to Sillery, but not before the Hospitalières became overwhelmed by a further influx of smallpox patients and an exhausted De Quen, traveling back and forth from Sillery to assist the nuns, contracted the disease himself. Given how many of the sick in Quebec came from the direction of Sillery upriver, the Jesuits, Hospitalières, and colonial authorities decided on the spot, before informing D'Aiguillon in Paris, that the hospital should be relocated to Sillery itself. The duchess approved the plan once she learned of it, in part because she expected it would lead to Christian conversions "at the beginning of sicknesses" more often than among patients "near death."[18]

Conversions were, of course, a major goal of the Jesuits and the Augustinians at Sillery, but the missionaries and their patrons strongly preferred conversions accompanied by renewed bodily health. In the *Relation* of 1643 the missionaries advertised in Paris the high recovery rates they were seeing at the hospital: only six of three hundred patients treated by the nuns had died over the preceding twelve months. The Jesuits also underscored the sanitary, orderly, as well as prayerful and godly conditions in which the Hospitalières were able to treat patients—conditions then identified among French urban elites with new, socially oriented projects of Catholic renewal.[19]

Sillery and its hospital also innovated upon the French models in their deliberate distance from Quebec, the developing, if very small, "urban" capital of New France. As D'Aiguillon noted when approving the relocation of her Canadian Hôtel-Dieu, Sillery served better than Quebec as "a refuge for the sick" and place of food distribution for "the poorest" of New France, by which she meant nomadic hunter-gatherers. While the residential hôtels-dieu and parish hospitals of Reform-era France tended to be located in the heart of cities, where street beggars and migrant laborers were primary targets for social charity, the colonial context required that French alms and medical care be accessible to nomadic woodland populations beyond settlement peripheries. Infrastructure being minimal at that time outside of French settlements and trading ports along the Saint Lawrence, keeping Sillery well supplied with medicines, bed linens, foodstuffs, and other items sent from Quebec and France was not only physically challenging but also considerably expensive, given the high cost of labor in the colony. As Barthèlemy Vimont noted in the *Relation* of 1644, "the day's time of a man, which amounts here to no less than thirty or forty *sols*, has often been employed for going to Québec [from Sillery] in quest of a few herbs or a half dozen eggs for the sick." But the Jesuits and Augustinians were certain that the benefits to the local population of Sillery's location far outweighed the inconveniences. As Vimont put it, it was easy enough for the French in Quebec, when they got sick, to travel to Sillery, "but the sick savages [were] unable to go to Québec, and thus it would have been a hospital for savages, without savages."[20]

Although Montagnais families were the first to reside in Sillery, members of other tribal groups were welcomed in Sillery's early years, including Sokoki-Abenakis and Hurons. The Montagnais' traditional, pre-Christian custom of marrying and adopting especially able-bodied "outsiders" for the purposes of trade and security was behind this, in part. At the same time, traditional ceremonies of welcoming strangers were augmented at Sillery by new practices, encouraged by the missionaries, of taking in ill and wounded strangers and ensuring they were cared for at the hospital or nourished back to health in ways that had generally been impracticable for the hunter-gatherers in the past. For example a Sokoki warrior was received at the mission late in 1642 while "covered with wounds and sores," as Vimont put it in a *Relation*, following time as an Algonquin hostage. Leading Montagnais men of the village brought him to the hospital nuns and a surgeon attended to him while many mission residents looked on. He was pleased to find there another Abenaki-speaking man who, while ill and received by the Sillery residents himself, had been baptized with the name Claude by the Jesuits. The warrior, according to Vimont, was "astonished" by the "charity" shown to him equally by the Frenchwomen and Natives of different tribes. Once healed he left Sillery with an intention of telling others about the strange sort of "affection" he had encountered there. Vimont mentioned, additionally, that four Huron travelers were welcomed to Sillery around the same time, seeking treatment for one among them after hearing of the hospital from Jesuits working in their region. Another of the four knew some Christian prayers and said them at the hospital bedside of his sick companion, who also recovered and returned with his friends to their people.[21]

We cannot know from the *Relations* how commonplace such scenes were at Sillery. But we know that by 1643 De Quen and other Jesuits were regularly assisting the Hospitalières in medical work at the mission, going beyond normal duties of offering sacraments, preaching, and teaching catechism. The nuns tended to the sick in their hospital ward while teaching them about Christianity. They also provided Montagnais families, primarily, with food and supplies, afforded by D'Aiguillon and others' support. The Jesuits, for their part, offered medicines, food, and other goods to Atikamekw Natives, especially, who were also beginning to settle into the village, traveling in from the Saint Maurice River region southeast of Quebec.[22]

The mission provided some Sillery families with French-style wooden homes, constructed by French émigré day laborers whose wages were provided by anonymous donors. The Jesuits referred to these benefactors as "persons distinguished in virtue and in merit" when publicly thanking them in their *Relations*. In advertisements to additional prospective donors, the missionaries described the homes in detail, explaining that more were planned pending further metropolitan assistance. Courting sympathy among upper bourgeois and aristocratic readers, the Jesuits pointed out that the homes were for the "principal savages" of Sillery, while the ordinary residents remained in "cabins of bark . . . waiting until we can procure for them also some small buildings." They underscored that the homes contained lofts where the semi-nomadic Natives could securely store their belongings, in ways they could not in the past, while away from the village for lengthy periods.[23]

In Sillery's early years the Jesuits sought metropolitan support for wages to sustain more French workmen to build these homes for Montagnais and Atikamekw residents, who clustered on opposite ends of the mission. Skilled carpenters, especially, were able to charge more for their labor in New France than they could back home. This labor cost was a source of frustration both for the Hospitalières, who expended much of

D'Aiguillon's funds on it, and the Jesuits, who envisioned many more French-style cabins than they were able to see constructed at Sillery. "The few workmen who are to be found," Le Jeune complained in the *Relation* of 1642, "do not hire themselves out for a piece of silver, but for loads of gold."[24] As a result most residents remained in small, mobile structures of indigenous design and make.

Money itself was not easily transported to New France, further adding to the challenge of building up Sillery's charitable ministries. In an age long before wire transfers and even paper currency, the latter of which was not widely used by the French until the Revolution of 1789, monetary donations that were literally in the form of heavy chests of coins were sometimes held up in France. Indeed a substantial portion of D'Aiguillon's initial outlays for the hospital—along with some Hospitalières themselves—almost did not make it across the Atlantic. In 1640 the merchant ship *L'Espérance* was menaced at its French port of departure, Le Havre, by some enemy ships—probably Spanish, as this was the time of the Thirty Years' War. Because of who she was, D'Aiguillon in dramatic fashion was able to use her clout at court to ensure the ship's safe passage: she got her uncle, Richelieu, to order forty amply-armed naval ships to convoy *L'Espérance* into safer Atlantic waters. The vessel arrived in good time at Quebec, where the nuns, with money in tow, disembarked to travel on to Sillery.[25]

That same year the Chevalier de Sillery died in Paris, a few months shy of his sixty-third birthday. In theory this was actually good news for the Sillery mission, as it meant the major part of his gift for the village—20,000 livres tournois contracted the year before and contingent on his death—was to be released and sent to Canada. However, the monies were held up in France for a number of years—a problem not easily counterbalanced by others' gifts, given the distance of the colony and the infrequent transatlantic passages of the merchant company's ships.[26]

Despite this setback other French laypersons stepped in to serve as benefactors for Sillery, as we saw in the case of donors who funded the construction of French-style homes for the residents. Still others, including members of the colonial merchant company, covered some of the cost of medical services, food, clothing, bed linens, and tools with which the

Sillery residents could more easily live off lands that were themselves cleared at the expense of private donors. Le Jeune also thanked in the *Relations* an unnamed "lady of merit and rank" who stepped in with additional funds for D'Aiguillon's hospital after learning the endowment was falling short, partly because D'Aiguillon's almsgiving was spread out across multiple charitable endeavors by the early 1640s. It was just at this time, indeed, that D'Aiguillon began providing for various ministries of Saints Vincent de Paul and Louise de Marillac, with whom she is more famously associated than with the Jesuits and Hospitalières in Canada.[27]

Another metropolitan layperson, connected to both the merchant company and D'Aiguillon, proved to be more reliable than most in assisting charitable causes in New France: the Jesuits' publisher Cramoisy. From the beginning Cramoisy was involved with the transmission of D'Aiguillon's initial gifts for the hospital, in his capacity as procureur for the Compagnie de la Nouvelle France. In later years Cramoisy would prove to be a loyal, reliable agent of charity for New France, especially for the Hospitalières at Sillery. From 1658 to the time of his death in 1669, he exercised notarized powers of procuration for the colonial hospital. By then the hospital was based permanently in Quebec, not Sillery, at the original site chosen by D'Aiguillon, following orders by Governor Charles Huault de Montmagny to secure the nuns' and patients' safety during a time of escalating conflict between the French and the Iroquois. Also, Quebec was struggling to provide for a growing number of smallpox victims in its immediate vicinity.[28]

Over the years Cramoisy regularly purchased medicines and supplies for the Hospitalières using his own money and funds from D'Aiguillon and others.[29] He was also in regular contact with the Jesuits about medical needs in their missions, and he used the *Relations* to solicit donations to meet them. Some years he would append to the imprints lists of needed "drugs and other articles" requested by the Augustinian superior in Quebec, instructing readers of the *Relations* to deliver any donations to his home in Paris, which served as a depot for transatlantic almsgiving.[30] At least one relative of Cramoisy's, his cousin Madame Boudreau, sent gifts to Canada for the hospital by this channel.[31]

Where social ministries were concerned, the missionaries' relationship with Cramoisy was a double-edged sword. Around the time the Jesuits first began to attract major donors, they decided to have the *Relation* of 1638 published in Rouen, not Paris. This decision offended Cramoisy, who secured exclusive rights to the *Relations* thereafter. The Jesuits chose Rouen that year partly to thank, and further cultivate, a new donor based nearby at Caen, Madame de la Peltrie, who had agreed to sponsor an Ursuline seminary for girls in Quebec. They also hoped to reach other potential benefactors based in Normandy's prosperous Atlantic port cities. Peltrie and several others were thanked profusely, but anonymously, in the first chapter of this Rouen *Relation*.[32] However, required thenceforward to publish the *Relations* in Paris, the missionaries later found it more difficult to quickly reach wealthy elites who resided most of the time in Rouen and other French cities rather than in the royal capital. The effects that a less centralized press campaign might have had on the development of the mission's charitable ministries of course cannot be known, but less dependence on Paris and courtly circles might have enabled steadier growth over the long term.

In any event, charitable ministries continued at Sillery for many decades, up to 1687, when its residents abandoned it, many of them relocating to the Jesuits' new Mission de François-de-Sales, treated later in this chapter. However, insufficient medicines and other supplies at Sillery sometimes resulted in great losses of life for the community during periods of epidemic, as in 1670. Over time, too, the Jesuits hoped to replicate the Sillery mission, with its charitable emphases, in other locations such as Trois-Rivières and Rivière-des-Prairies. They commenced talks about this with wealthy patrons, including D'Aiguillon. But these plans did not materialize, partly because the main French settlements that were to have served as intermediate support centers were increasingly at risk from the escalating Iroquois Wars.[33]

The Huron Refugee Crisis

Between 1634 and 1648, Jesuits including Jean de Brébeuf and Jérôme Lalemant oversaw a modest but successful missionary effort among sedentary

Huron villagers in what is today southeastern Ontario. French colonial leaders since Champlain's time had cultivated trading ties with the Hurons that had facilitated Jesuit access and strengthened with Jesuit influence. Some of the missionaries' early success in spreading Christianity among the Hurons stemmed from effective medical treatments they administered, as François-Joseph Le Mercier reported of his work with a Jesuit donné in the village of Ihonatiria.[34] But along with the benefits they brought to Huron communities, ties with the French also exacerbated the confederacy's long-standing rivalry with the Iroquois. Conflict escalated in the early 1640s. Iroquois raids on Huron villages peaked at the end of the decade, the era of Brébeuf and other Jesuits' martyrdoms. Numerous Hurons were slaughtered while those who survived the raids fled in a diaspora of many thousands.

Huron refugees migrated not only westward, toward what became known as a result as Lake Huron, but also eastward, toward other missions including Sillery, and toward Quebec and Montreal. The Jesuits, Hospitalières, and lay population of New France thus were confronted with a humanitarian crisis of a magnitude they had never experienced.

Before the worst of the refugee crisis, collaborative efforts to feed famine victims were already underway at Montreal and Trois-Rivières among the missionaries, habitants, and merchants of New France. Then, as Huron refugees began to arrive in the French settlements by the summer of 1648, the nuns and Compagnie merchants pooled limited resources to construct a cabin for some refugees in the courtyard of the Sillery hospital. The Jesuits, for their part, hosted a number of Huron refugee families on lands they corporately owned at Beauport (today a northeastern borough of Quebec City).[35] Additionally their relocated Mission de Sainte Marie on Christian Island, or what the Hurons called Gahoendoe, received as many as ten thousand refugees. With lay assistance, the Jesuits fed, clothed, and sheltered them as best they could, although the *Relations* hint of great struggle. "We [have] tried to assist them out of our poverty," wrote Paul Ragueneau in 1649, "to clothe the naked, and to feed those poor people. . . . [But] every day the number increases, as well as their miseries."[36]

Missionaries and laypersons found their resources stretched to the limit in the effort to aid the Hurons, many of whom had become Christian and who, unlike the Montagnais, were a settled, agricultural people unaccustomed to negotiating survival on the move. Foraging for food in unfamiliar spaces while seeking haven from the Iroquois, many starved before reaching the French. Those received at Sillery, Sainte Marie, and the colonial centers were often emaciated upon arrival, some having resorted to eating loved ones' corpses to survive.[37]

For relief on the scale that was needed, the Jesuits turned once again to Paris with Cramoisy's help. As we saw in the previous chapter, in 1650 the publisher produced two editions of the *Relation* for that year. The first included a description by Ragueneau of starving Natives who looked like "corpses unearthed"—men, women, and children who had "neither corn, nor acorns, nor garlic, nor fish" and yet had to labor beyond their strength "to clear new forests to make new cabins, and erect palisades, in order to secure themselves."[38] The second edition included an appended section at the end, drawn from letters received at Paris after the typesetting of the first edition, which drew special attention to the plight of the Hurons who were both starving and trying to defend themselves against the Iroquois. The *Relation* of the following year included more shocking images painted by Ragueneau's pen:

> We were compelled to behold dying skeletons eking out a miserable life, feeding even on the excrements and refuse of nature. . . . Even carrion dug up, the remains of foxes and dogs, excited no horror; and they even devoured one another, but this in secret; for . . . the Hurons . . . regard with no less horror the eating of their fellow countrymen than would be felt in France at eating human flesh. But necessity had no longer law. . . . Mothers fed upon children; brothers on their brothers; while children recognized no longer, in a corpse, him whom, while he lived, they had called their father.[39]

This passage was a cry for much more charitable assistance from France, specifically for the Huron allies of the French colony—allies who in many cases were Christian and whom the Jesuits also described as pitifully trying to extend charity to one another amid their own miseries. In the *Relation* of 1651 Ragueneau expressed hope that God would "grant genuine feelings of a truly Christian charity [toward the Hurons] to all those who have so rich an opportunity to put it into practice," especially as the Jesuits were near to "exhaust[ing their] own resources," becoming "powerless to continue [their] charities" without lay assistance. The hospital nuns, too, according to Ragueneau, were also running out of resources at a time of extreme need.[40]

Despite the widespread dissemination of such reports, little assistance arrived from France during the worst of the crisis. Ragueneau, while tending to the Hurons, complained in March 1650 to the Jesuit general in Rome that he had received no letters from Europe in the previous twelve months, despite all the Jesuits had reported on the crisis. The *Relations* indicate that limited assistance for the Hurons did arrive from France in the winter of 1651–52, transported by the delayed fleet that had disembarked in October 1651. The *Relation* of 1652 included a bit of positive news about the Jesuits' and Hospitalières' work at Sillery, which was once again able to "serve . . . as a refuge for the Christian savages in their necessities."[41] However, metropolitan aid fell far short of the Jesuits' hopes. This was due, in part, to the fact that key lay elites in the mission's metropolitan network were preoccupied with the social and political hemorrhages of the Fronde civil wars.

It was at this time that Cramoisy, along with D'Aiguillon and other personages in the French capital, began to strategize for the establishment of the revolutionary Hôpital Général de Paris in order to rein in the city's population of street beggars. As a result of the political disorders of the Fronde, that population was multiplying and straining older charitable institutions such as the Hôtel-Dieu de Paris and the parish hospital of Saint-Jacques, with which Cramoisy was involved as a member of its board of directors.[42] It was not by coincidence that Cramoisy, who was also preoccupied with various aspects of the Fronde, was remiss for the first time in 1650 in providing his usual and expected annual assistance for the Hospitalières, who communicated disappointment and alarm to him in a letter he remorsefully appended to the *Relation* of 1651. They stressed that the hospital courtyard was full of Huron refugees who exhibited "such poverty and such devotion," unlike anything they had seen before, and that the hospital was lacking in linens and medicines even for its ordinary services.[43]

As the Jesuits continued pressing for aid from France for the Hurons, they received major assistance for the refugees from Éléanore de Grandmaison, a propertied laywoman in Quebec. Notably, Grandmaison and her husband, François de Chavigny, resided as newlyweds at Sillery, not in Quebec, and eventually further out with their five children on the Chavigny seigneury on the Isle d'Orléans just east of Quebec. In March 1651 she signed a contract with the Jesuits to give to some Hurons use of her extensive lands at the Isle d'Orléans.[44]

Madame de Grandmaison in subsequent years collaborated with the Jesuits for her new tenants' subsistence, medical needs, and further instruction in Christianity. She formed close bonds with some Huron tenants, especially widowed women and orphaned children—no doubt from special sympathy, as her own husband, Chavigny, had died while she was still relatively young and raising five children. By 1653 the Jesuits were able to report that, with Grandmaison's help at the Isle d'Orléans, the Hurons with the assistance of French laborers were harvesting "a tolerably good quantity of Indian corn" on newly cleared land, but also that the Jesuits were hoping to aid those still without "enough for their maintenance . . . with the charitable contributions that will be sent to us from France."[45]

In other words the mission was still short of sufficient aid several years after the Iroquois devastation of Huron Country. This was still the case in 1658, when Le Jeune—at this point mission procureur in Paris—reported that many Huron Christians had to travel "a distance of thirty or forty leagues" to Quebec "to be regenerated and to resume their former spirit of fervor." The lack of more French settlements, infrastructure, and economic development farther afield from the towns and estates along the Saint Lawrence made such journeying necessary. As a result, some Hurons stayed as long as they could in Quebec, "to share," as Le Jeune put it, "in our spiritual and material alms." The Jesuit went on to say that the Hurons in Quebec were desperately hoping "that the liberality and charity of the French will be strong enough to burst the bonds of their slavery," adding his own wish that the French might soon settle among the Senecas in

Iroquois Country. This was because the Jesuit believed that the Senecas, if they partnered with the French, had the wherewithal to "display the same liberality" toward the refugees, given their relative prosperity as a settled, agricultural people.[46]

Diversifying Charitable Ministries and New Transatlantic Challenges

Although significant resources obtained by the Jesuits for social ministries were directed toward Sillery and Huron refugees in the mission's early decades, the Jesuits over time collaborated with laypersons in a diverse array of charitable efforts throughout their expanding mission network. These included lay sponsorship of Native American women, in the form of dowry funds and land plots with French-style homes. Such gifts were intended to help secure marriages with Frenchmen and baptized Native men alike. The *Relations* of the 1640s refer to anonymous donors in France who provided gifts on an individual or family-by-family basis. Some metropolitan elites, however, established "perpetual foundations" to fund dowries and other supports for multiple Native American couples and families over a long period. These donors included wealthy nobles and upper bourgeois who were childless and who, according to Jérôme Lalemant, "believed that they [would] gain children for God and for themselves, by this manner of holy adoption, and thus perpetuate their names" in New France, even as their names might be lost to memory in France itself. Lalemant expressed special commitment to facilitating such lay-driven designs of perpetuating French family legacies in America, which reflected the patriarchal, honor-oriented culture of the ancien régime. Some Huron families among whom Lalemant was working even agreed to take their unseen French patrons' surnames.[47]

Beyond laboring for metropolitan Catholic charity to be imported into North American settlements and wilderness spaces, the Jesuits over time also promoted charitable initiatives by materially advantaged and socially prominent Native Americans. We find in the *Relation* of 1653 the following report on Noël Negabamat, one of the leading men of Sillery: "That excellent neophyte knows how to dispense the goods that God and men have given him to the poor Christians, who he considers as his children.

He succors the old women, the poor widows, and the orphans—giving them bread, peas, Indian corn, eels, and even robes." Furthermore, in a drafted *Relation* that was to be published in 1674 but never went to press, the missionary Dablon highlighted the conversion of "a good Huron woman" who had acquired the habit of "bestowing alms" on her poorer neighbors. "It is a pity," the Jesuit opined, "that this charitable soul has not so much wealth as our great ladies in France. Ah, how many monasteries and hospitals would she not found! How many thousands of poor would she not assist!" Later in 1682 Claude Chauchetière reported that the wife of a leading Iroquois Christian of the mission of Saint François-Xavier near Montreal frequently assembled other "devout women . . . who call[ed] themselves sisters" and "deliberat[ed] together upon what [was to] be done for the relief of the poor in the village." He added: "There are women who have shared their fields, thus taking bread from their very mouths, as it were, to give it to new arrivals in the village—people who are not yet in a position to do anything for them in return—in order to win them for God." Elsewhere, in a letter to the Parisian provincial in October 1683, the mission superior and future metropolitan procureur Thierry Beschefer noted that the Iroquois who became Christians also became very charitable toward others, for example bringing large amounts of corn, meat, and other foodstuffs "to the poorer savages," especially on Christian feast days and during the season of Advent.[48]

What the Jesuits ascribed in such cases to Christianity's taking root among mission residents was in fact a complex process—more complex than they articulated—that did not so much involve the imitation of French benefactors and charitable persons as it did the integration of Christian ideas and practices of spiritually inspired social charity with traditions of gift-giving and hospitality among Eastern Woodlands peoples. It is well known from the work of Daniel Richter and others that leading members of Iroquois and other Eastern Woodlands societies would traditionally display their high, respected position not through displays of personal wealth, but through gift-giving to others, sometimes to the point of appearing poorer than their fellow villagers from the standpoint of European observers. The point here, however, is that the apparent increase of charitable activity among mission Indians along recognizably Christian, apostolic lines—tending to the sick, caring for widows and orphans, feeding the destitute and infirm—was an encouraging sign to the missionaries and their support network that metropolitan charity was at least being transported in *spirit* across the Atlantic on a large scale, if not very substantially in material terms.

The challenges faced by the Jesuits in importing Catholic charity from France become clearer when we examine the missionaries' understudied engagement in medical work among indigenous communities far afield of Sillery and the colonial hospitals staffed by others. By 1659 those hospitals included one in Montreal, established the decade before by the lay Société de Notre Dame. Distant from such institutions and the colonial infrastructure developing around them, the Jesuits generally could offer only primitive medical services, usually in the form of a single missionary who tended to smallpox victims or to those suffering from war wounds. Missionaries in such situations, such as Jean Pierron, who worked among Mohawk and Onondaga Iroquois villagers in the early 1670s, only sometimes had supplies of European medicines, which they dispensed usually in Natives' homes or in the open air.[49]

Sometimes, however, the Society's medical missions were conducted on a larger scale, specifically when Jesuits were able to procure major support from metropolitan lay elites and the French Crown. Important benefactors in this regard were Bernardin Gigault de Bellefonds, a leading general and marshal of France, and the wealthy Huguenot-turned-Catholic Paul Pelisson, court historian to Louis XIV and eventually abbé de Cluny. These men in the early 1680s petitioned the king for, and then arranged on his orders, a significant shipment of diverse medicines to the Jesuits working among the Onondaga Iroquois. The missionary Jean de Lamberville, while working in the central Onondaga village, reported to a contact in France on the good the gift had done, while also clarifying that such medical missions remained hampered by their distance from the mother country: "The medicines ... have procured for many people health of body and of soul. ... [But] it is not easy ... to have these precious medicines brought into this region. ... The charitable hand of His Majesty, and of those who have given us these medicines by his orders, has stretched out to the very depths of our forests."[50]

Another metropolitan layperson of note who assisted the Jesuits' medical ministries in New France was Marguerite d'Alégre, marquise de Baugé and wife of the marquis d'Urfé and Baugé, scion of an ancient house in Anjou. Her eldest son, Louis, was bishop of Limoges from 1677 to 1697, and her second son, François-Saturnin, was a missionary with the Sulpicians of Montreal. Marguerite herself regularly communicated with the Jesuits in Canada and devoted significant resources to charitable efforts for the Abenakis. Initially her donations were directed toward Sillery, but by the late 1670s the Jesuit medical mission she sponsored was given its own location, at the Chûtes-de-la-Chaudière (Chaudière Falls) near present-day Lévis in Quebec. The Abenakis began arriving in large numbers in the region, seeking refuge from the English during and after King Philip's War. Sillery's resources for feeding, sheltering, and medically tending them were stretched to the limit, so Jesuits including Jacques Bigot, a native of Bourges in his late twenties at the time, secured steady financial support for the Abenakis from the marquise. Until her death in 1683 she annually sent money and supplies, including textiles for new, clean clothing and bedding. Her assistance enabled Bigot to establish the Chûtes as a permanent place of refuge for additional arrivals from Abenaki territory in Maine, on lands granted to the Jesuits by the governor of New France in 1683. This mission was named after Saint François de Sales, a bishop of Geneva who was also by 1665 the first canonized alumnus of the Jesuits' Collège de Clermont in Paris.

The Mission de François-de-Sales from the start included a small hospital, run by Bigot, who claimed it was "no less crowded than that of the nuns" in Quebec. This hospital depended greatly upon the marquise's largesse, however. Upon her death, the medical services offered at the Chûtes diminished considerably. In October 1684 Bigot communicated about this dilemma to François de La Chaise, confessor to Louis XIV and Jesuit provincial at Paris at the time: "I must [now] suffer in beholding the suffering of the poor people whom I shall not be able to relieve. . . . I believe that some will not escape, and that several may even languish through the winter. Nearly all have pledged everything that they had—porcelain, collars, glass beads, embroideries of porcupine-quills, guns, cutlasses—in order to have some clothes to cover them in the ague-chill of their fever."[51] Bigot also complained to La Chaise that little assistance was forthcoming from France to the Chûtes, even after other Jesuits had spread the word about its needs before and after the marquise's death. As a result the Hospitalières and Ursulines had been sharing some of their own scarce resources to help Bigot's mission.[52]

Bigot would go on to serve in the Abenaki mission for many more years, eventually to die of scarlet fever, which he caught from patients he was tending. He was soon after lauded as a "skilled apothecary" in a report to Paris by Joseph Germain, together with a lay brother of the Society of Jesus named Jacques Boussat, who had also died in the same way: "We may say that both died in the field of honor—that is, in the exercise of the most perfect charity; for they caught the disease while visiting, consoling, and attending the sick. . . . This they did day and night . . . the brother taking medicines for the sick, which cured many."[53]

Obtaining charitable gifts for medical and other social ministries in New France became more difficult after 1673, the last year the *Relations* were published in Paris. Although not always as effective as the Jesuits wished, the *Relations* had been critical from the 1630s through the early 1670s in widely soliciting assistance in the timeliest way possible across the oceanic distance. They had even helped in the recruitment of personnel for particular charitable efforts. Furthermore the Jesuits had regularly broadcast through the *Relations* the Hospitalières' needs, not only their own, to a wider public. Messages of concern penned by the mother superior about the future of the hospital at Sillery, and of metropolitan assistance generally in New France, were included in chapters devoted to the hospital's work in a number of early *Relations*. In 1643, for instance, the Jesuits reported that the hospital had fewer European-style raised beds, mattresses, and blankets than were needed by the number of patients in residence. Moreover, the hospital's drug supply for that year—prescribed to more than a hundred and fifty patients in 1642 alone—was depleted.[54] In the *Relation*, Mother de Saint-Ignace's quoted words expressed anxiety about Sillery's distance from French elites and political supports upon which charitable institutions in France itself were highly dependent: "The hospitals of France have been founded by kings, princes, and princesses, very richly; and with all that, they would not subsist if . . . persons of merit did not bestow generous alms on them, and if the parliaments and tribunals did not apply the fines to them: *the ocean excludes us from all these aids*. There are in France persons who holily maintain here . . . the support and relief of a savage family; but few persons think of the support of a patient, and of furnishing him with linen or bedding."[55] This passage underscores how necessary printed communications by a publisher of Cramoisy's profile were for medical missions of even modest scale to flourish in French North America.

Significantly, Jesuit assistance to the Hospitalières in Paris did not end with the space given to them in the *Relations*. For a time the Jesuits' metropolitan procureurs assumed extra duties as procureurs for the missionary women in Canada. This is because the Hospitalières in Quebec were mainly in communication with their motherhouse in Dieppe, not with the Augustinian canonesses in Paris, and thus had more difficulty accessing wealthy elites and court officials in the French capital than did their Jesuit counterparts. When Le Jeune was appointed to his new metropolitan position in 1649, he began to mediate between the nuns overseas and benefactors in France, including D'Aiguillon and the merchant Antoine Grignon of the French province of Aunis, to ensure continued sustenance for the women's medical mission.[56] Forty years later the Jesuit procureur for French American missions, Jacques Vaultier, was still serving not double but triple duty as unofficial procureur for the Hospitalières and the Ursulines in Canada.[57]

The *Relations* had also at times included stories of particular Native Americans' responses to specific charitable gifts. In the *Relation* of 1653, for example, Ragueneau expressed a wish that metropolitan benefactors of the Sillery charities "might witness the sentiments of gratitude" that the residents had for them, "and hear the fine speeches they [made] in regard to them." He added further that mission residents appreciated "that persons . . . of worth and condition, like captains or captains' wives, [chose to] do them a kindness from a thousand leagues' distance," and that such facts helped to give them "a high idea of the [Christian] faith."[58] Ragueneau went on to inform French readers of the love some women at Sillery expressed toward a group of unseen patrons—a group of charitable, aristocratic women in particular—attributing to one of the Sillery women these thoughts and sentiments: "They have nothing before their eyes prompting them to love us, while we see . . . their alms. They love us for the love of God, who has bidden them to do good to the wretched; and we love them also for the love of God, whose will it is that we should love those who . . . do good to all the world. . . . God, who gives them this compassion for us . . . is our father, as they are our mothers."[59]

Such remarks hint not only at the terms in which the Jesuits sought to convey Gospel messages to the Natives through examples of metropolitan almsgiving, but also at how they attempted to forge, through print, personal attachments among metropolitan benefactors to distant individuals and communities that received their charity. Such attachments are reminiscent of the affective bonds that ideally arose in patron-client relationships in ancien régime society. Bridging the great oceanic divide, stories of grateful Native Americans that the Jesuits presented in print to benefactors stood in for the face-to-face interactions that were crucial to the patronage system and to Reform-era charitable ministries in French cities and towns. The latter, we know, tended to be parish-based or municipal institutions and were supported by wealthy elites and government officials who lived close enough to see the enterprises in action and to assess their fruits and long-term viability.

When the *Relations* ceased publication, however, the Jesuits had to cultivate patron-client relationships for their social ministries in new ways. They came to depend more than in earlier days on private transatlantic communications and on meetings in prospective patrons' homes and at the French court. But the court itself was less accessible to the missionaries than in the past, as this was also the era when Louis XIV transferred the court from Paris to Versailles. Thus in the last decades of the seventeenth century the missionaries modified their mode of securing French patronage for social ministries. Mission sources indicate an increasing dependency on royal assistance more than help from private families, but it was assistance that was typically now requested through chains of nobles who had to compete for access to the king in the new epoch of royal absolutism. We saw earlier in this regard the example of Pelisson and Bellefonds's help in securing royal assistance for the Jesuits' medical mission among the Iroquois. We have another example in the Jesuits' petitioning of King Louis, in February 1692, through his controller-general and secretary of the navy, the comte de Pontchartrain, for a royal fund to support the "many poor widows and orphan children" of Iroquois Christian warriors who were fighting loyally alongside the French in the Nine Years' War. Such charity from the king would, the Jesuits shrewdly reminded Pontchartrain, give the Iroquois Christians "a new and very attractive reason for continuing their [military] services, seeing that after their death their wives, their children, and their poor relatives would not be forsaken."[60]

In earlier decades the Crown had not been uninvolved with charitable efforts overseas: the assistance given by the Compagnie de la Nouvelle France to Sillery and to the Huron refugees was partly funded by the French monarchy, which sponsored the merchant company and covered a significant portion of its overhead costs. Furthermore, Louis XIII and Anne of Austria had given personal gifts of funds to the Jesuits and the other missionary orders, some of which were earmarked for charitable assistance to "the poor" in New France. But under Louis XIV the Jesuits more regularly sought royal assistance for their charitable as well as evangelistic efforts, partly because they no longer regularly accessed a wealthy reading public through the *Relations*.

"Give to Many Poor People, and to Many Kinds"

Pursued and established with much fanfare in the early decades of the mission, the Jesuits' charitable ministries in New France were frequently frustrated by insufficient infrastructure and supplies, the high cost and scarcity of skilled labor in the colony, and metropolitan elites' irregular attention to such problems. On top of this, charitable gifts that were forthcoming from France were sometimes stolen at sea. In 1655, for example, a donation of 12,000 livres from Queen Anne, some of it designated for mission Indians' sustenance, never arrived in Canada because the ship transporting it, *L'Escu de Nimègue,* commanded by the Dutchman Richard Foder, was caught in the crosshairs of the First Anglo-Dutch War and intercepted by the English off the coast of Le Havre.[61]

Despite such setbacks there is a notable, continual refrain in the mission sources of Jesuit hopes to alleviate destitution and wretchedness, not only ignorance of the Christian God and his ordinances, among various Native Americans they encountered. The missionaries and their lay collaborators furthermore sought to counteract challenges they faced in exporting Catholic charity from France to America while the colonial infrastructure remained primitive. Notable in this regard was the steady commitment to charitable ends of the colonial merchant company. Though struggling to turn profits in the fur trade, the Compagnie de la Nouvelle France was generous many times toward poor and sick Natives.

The Jesuits frequently used the *Relations* to reach and subtly pressure already committed donors while advertising to potential new ones. It is noteworthy that they did so from the 1630s forward, and specifically for overseas social-charitable ends, inasmuch as pioneering activity in this regard has previously been credited to English Protestant missionaries in New England from the late seventeenth century onward—missionaries who, furthermore, tended to discuss Native American poverty in meta-phorical and spiritual terms, not material ones.[62]

It is not so surprising, perhaps, that Jesuits departing cities such as Paris and Dieppe in the 1630s and 1640s would attempt to reproduce overseas something of the new social-charitable activism of the Catholic Reformation in France, itself spearheaded by figures such as De Paul and Marillac and lay elites such as D'Aiguillon. But the mission's social ministries in a colonial setting cast new light even on that well-studied, expanding European world of charitable action.

For one thing the transatlantic scale of the Jesuits' charitable ambitions, if not achievement, is striking for the seventeenth century. In the mission's early years the Jesuits envisioned a future in which metropolitan elites would help alleviate poverty and disease among *all* the Natives of the Eastern Woodlands. They would do this, furthermore, by means of diversified charitable initiatives: hospitals, housing projects, food distribution, dowry funds for young Native women, institutionalized stipends for war widows and orphans, and so on. This effort to marshal metropolitan, lay wealth and energy for multiple charitable services at once, and for varied Native American communities far across an ocean, differs from the more intimate, localized, often parish-based and municipal charity that was the norm in Reform-era France.[63]

The colonial ministries' scope and contours reflect principles current at the time among Parisian Jesuits, in particular, seen for example in the writings of Étienne Binet, provincial at Paris from 1634 to 1638. Earlier in 1627 Binet published a book with Cramoisy entitled *Le Riche Sauvé par la Porte Dorée du Ciel*. Dedicated to the wealthy "lords and ladies of Paris," it encouraged prudent investment of wealth in multiple charities at once, using maritime trade as a model: "Do like those who trade overseas: they divide up their money among many ships, so that if one of them does not arrive, voilà, their money is still secure. Give to many poor people, and to many kinds, so you can be sure some among them will arrive in Heaven."[64]

For Binet almsgiving was a path for the rich not only to attain salvation, as was commonly thought in Christian Europe up to then, but also to win special glory in heaven. Binet sought to relieve wealthy French readers of nagging worries (elicited often by preachers of the mendicant orders) that in order to "gain heaven," they needed to pursue a life of "rude austerity," "harsh fasting and rigors," or the "shedding of blood or tears." Instead men and women of means could partake in secular society, moderately enjoying its pleasures while also uniquely embodying God's own "liberality," by giving some of their time and wealth to the poor. Furthermore, in Binet's vision, the "best alms" were "the biggest [and] most ready-made, according to the value of things"—a remark clearly intended for persons of significant means. Among the projects Binet encouraged, therefore, were building hospitals, providing legal assistance to poor orphans and the "disgraced poor" when they were summoned before civil authorities, and sponsoring young women who needed dowries to make decent marriages. He also urged as especially fitting pursuits for those of worldly means and influence the creation of scholarship funds for poor children and the paying off of prisoners' debts.[65]

Le Jeune in his early *Relations* promoted a similar view of the special ability of the most wealthy and influential to assist large numbers of people—indeed to transform society on a large and even global scale—and by such means to attain exceptional glory in heaven. He urged his readers to assist the "poor" and "miserable" Natives of New France, who were needy in both physical and spiritual ways. His view is best expressed in a passage from the *Relation* of 1637: "Blessed are those who contribute from their means to this generous enterprise. There are many rich persons in the world, but few of them are chosen for these great works. To have the riches of the earth, is a blessing of the earth; to use them for Heaven, is a blessing of Heaven. To so use them as to gather up and apply the blood of Jesus Christ, this is to *participate in the merits of the apostles, to range one's self in the number of the most intimate friends of Christ.*"[66]

Le Jeune authored a veritable new beatitude—"Blessed are the very rich who give to the world's poor"—to accompany, from the Gospels, "Blessed are ye poor, for yours is the kingdom of God" and "Blessed are ye that hunger now: for you shall be filled."[67] To suggest that sending money, manpower, and other resources to an overseas colony was "to participate in the merits of the apostles," and enjoy especially intimate friendship with Christ, was a different sort of Gospel indeed. This Gospel for New France was not embarrassed by riches but depended radically upon the resources of the most prominent French elites.

Another distinctive feature of the Jesuits' social ministries in North America was their emergence from an intentional, if not smooth-going, pooling of resources by the several missionary orders in the colony, merchants and private benefactors on both sides of the Atlantic, and sometimes also the French state. A similarly collective, jointly private and public effort has been noted in studies of early French colonial for-profit ventures.[68] In this respect the Jesuit mission to France was closer than previously imagined—in aspiration and worldview, if not realization—to *modern* French Catholic missions of the era of the *mission civilisatrice*, given the latter's simultaneously privately funded and state-supported hospitals and vocational schools.[69]

Decades after the Jesuits are believed to have turned against Native

Americans' assimilation into French society as a prerequisite for their Christianization, remarks such as this one continued to be published in Paris: "Oh, if [only] these poor people had the aids and the means that Europeans had in abundance for accomplishing their salvation. . . . Oh, if they saw something of the magnificence of our churches . . . [and] extensive charities that are maintained for the benefit of the poor . . . I am sure that they would be greatly affected thereby."[70] These are the words of Claude-Jean Allouez, writing in 1670 from the mission of Saint François Xavier among the Winnebagos in the Green Bay area of the present-day U.S. state of Wisconsin. Such words were a call for more French development in America, inclusive of Catholic social ministries. Allouez, like so many of his confreres, hoped to reach personages in and beyond Paris who had the means to support not only large-scale social-charitable ministries in Quebec and Montreal but also infrastructural development, so alms might readily be supplied deep in the American interior.

However, the success of any such transatlantic enterprise by the French hinged not only on the involvement and goodwill of metropolitan lay elites, but also on the fortunes of French trade and political power in the Eastern Woodlands. And over time, the Jesuits faced the increasingly harsh reality of ongoing colonial warfare and metropolitan neglect of New France's commercial and military position. The extensive, almost boundless ambition for social-charitable initiatives seen among the first and second generation of missionaries would eventually give way to frustration and grim realism. By the eighteenth century, Jesuits accustomed to the rising living standards of the elite quartiers in French cities lamented that Native Americans generally lived at a level of poverty that most Europeans would find intolerable. Joseph-François Lafitau, for one, observed that nearly all Native Americans still inhabited "only miserable hovels or thatched huts," like those of "men born in the world's infancy" and those "known to antiquity under the names of *mapalia* or *turgaria*, designations which are all suitable to give a perfect picture of misery."[71] Such remarks evince a much-evolved consciousness, compared to early in the seventeenth century, of a vast and even widening gap in material and infrastructural conditions in Europe versus North America—a gap that would require much more effort and time to overcome than the French up to that time had devoted to it.

In the end the Jesuits' social-charitable ambitions in North America outstripped what they were able to bring to fruition, due over time to insufficient funds, personnel, and metropolitan interest. Nevertheless, even their frustrated efforts reveal that the post-Tridentine Catholicism they brought to America was more bound up than previously imagined with a cultural shift traditionally associated with the Enlightenment rather than Reform-era missions: an increasing identification of European, and especially French, colonialism with a this-worldly mission of uplifting "poor" and "miserable" nations through social welfare projects.

LE R P PAVL le IEVNE enflamé d'vn s⟨.⟩ zele pour la conuersion des Infideles Sauuages de la Nouuelle France fut le premier qui
les suiuit dans les bois les frequenta receut leur humeur, et en apri⟨t⟩ leur langue la reduisit en preceptes; il n'est pas croyable combien il souffrit de
froid, de chaud, de faim en ses courses dans les rigueurs de plusieurs Riuieres et Estés parmy ces barbares qui le plus souuent estoient sur le poinct de l'assom-
mer, et dont il a esté miraculeusement tiré, ce sont les preuues de son ardeur pour l'augmentation de nostre Religion pour la gloire de Dieu, il
passa Dix-sept ans dans le Canada, d'ou apres auoir fait l'Ombre de commerciens de ces Infideles, il fut rapelé en L'ancienne France son pays
natal pour les affaires de cette Mission, et en estre le Procureur, pour l'Interest de laquelle il a agi auec soing continuel, jusquà ce qu'il rendit
sa bien-heureuse Ame entre les mains de Son Sauueur chargé de Merittes et consommé dans les trauaux spirituels le 7.ᵉ d'Aoust 1664. agé de 72 ans

P⟨ ⟩ louÿes sculpsit et excudebit.   Cum priuilegio Reg⟨.⟩ 1665.

FIG. I. Posthumous portrait of mission superior and procureur Fr. Paul Le Jeune,
SJ (1665). Courtesy of Library and Archives Canada, Ottawa.

Sebastianus Cramoisy Regis Architypographus, Regiæ Typographiæ Lupareæ Director, Vrbis Parisiensis Exconsul, Pauperum Administrator. Vixit annos 83. Obyt anno 1669, die 29. Ianuary.

Ægid. Rousselet sculp. 1642.

FIG. 2. Portrait of Sébastien Cramoisy (1642), publisher of the *Relations de la Nouvelle France* and lay collaborator with the mission's social charitable ministries. Courtesy of Library and Archives Canada, Ottawa.

RELATION

DE CE QVI S'EST PASSE'
EN LA
NOVVELLE FRANCE
EN L'ANNE'E 1638.

Enuoyée au

R. PERE PROVINCIAL
de la Compagnie de IESVS en
la Prouince de France.

Par le P. PAVLE LE IEVNE de la mefme Compagnie,
Superieur de la Refidence de Kébec.

A PARIS,
Chez SÉBASTIEN CRAMOISY, Imprimeur
ordinaire du Roy, ruë fainct Iacques,
aux Cicognes.

M. DC. XXXVIII.
AVEC PRIVILEGE DV ROY.

FIG. 3. Cover page of the *Relation* of 1638 published in Paris by Cramoisy after securing rights of first edition to all subsequent *Relations* by the Jesuits of New France. Courtesy of the Beinecke Rare Book and Manuscript Library of Yale University.

P. ISAACVS IOGVES vande Societeyt IESV wort in CANADA met een byl het hooft
ingheslagen opden 18 October 1647. Twee Fransche Iongmans steruen de selue doot

FIG. 4. *Martyrdom of Father Isaac Jogues S.J. in Canada* (ca. 1660), by Adriaen Millaert
after Abraham van Diepenbeeck. Courtesy of the McCord Museum, Montreal-M2209.

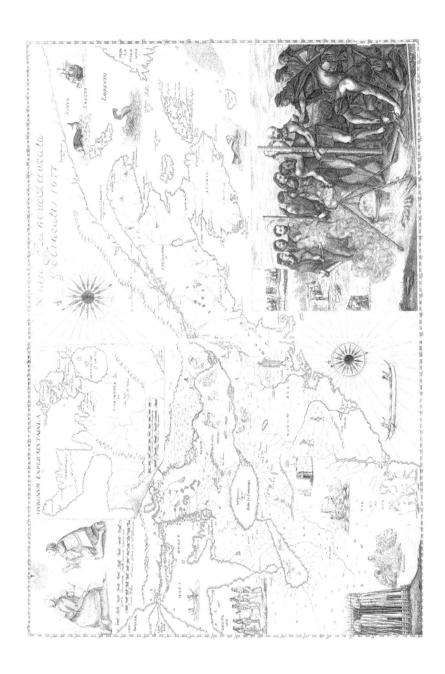

FIG. 5. *Novae Franciae accurata delineatio* (1657) by Fr. François-Joseph Bressani, SJ.
Courtesy of Library and Archives Canada, Ottawa.

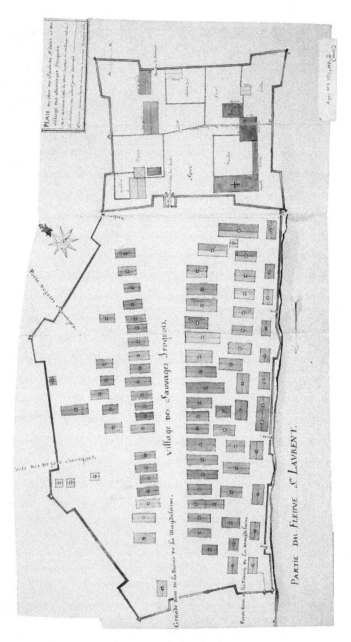

FIG. 6. Map of the Sault Saint Louis fortress and mission village (1752) near Montreal, home to many Iroquois Christian warriors and allies of the French. Courtesy of Special Collections, the Newberry Library, Chicago.

PART 2

A Longue Durée of War and Metropolitan Neglect

CHAPTER 5

Crusading for Iroquois Country

In 1667 a Nipissing Algonquin woman and her teenage daughter were captured by an Iroquois war party. The Jesuit Claude-Jean Allouez was preaching among their people at the time, near Lake Nipissing in Ontario, in the northeastern part of what the French called the Pays d'en Haut, or Upper Country. The priest reported on the women's escape in a *Relation* published the following year: "One day, when [the two women] found themselves alone with a single Iroquois . . . the girl told her mother that the time had come to rid themselves of this guard, and flee. To this end she asked the Iroquois for a knife to use on a beaver-skin that she was ordered to dress; and at the same time, imploring Heaven's aid, she plunged it into his bosom. The mother . . . struck him on the head with a billet of wood, and they left him for dead. Taking some food, they started forth in haste, and . . . reached their own country in safety."[1] Allouez was sure to include that the women were faithful Christians. They therefore received "extraordinary succor" from God in their hour of need.

The women were two of many Native Americans commemorated by the Jesuits for acts of bravery, and at times aggression, against Iroquois enemies during periods of both war and tenuous peace in the Eastern Woodlands. At the time of the women's defeat of their Iroquois guard, the French were at war with the Mohawks while the rest of the Five Nations had agreed to a peace with New France, resulting in new trade and Jesuit activity in Iroquois Country. By the time Allouez's story circulated in France, the

Mohawks, too, had agreed to a peace, opening up new possibilities not only for Christianization in the region, but also for the French to shift resources to westward expansion.

Allouez himself played an important role in a ceremony of possession on June 4, 1671, in which a French military officer claimed the entire Great Lakes region for Louis XIV. A great cross was planted, the heraldic symbols of the Bourbon monarchy were posted to a tree, and the "Te Deum" was sung as representatives of indigenous nations looked on. At this gathering, hosted at the Jesuit mission of Sault-Sainte-Marie established three years earlier, Allouez served as a go-between, communicating the imperial intentions of Simon-François Daumont de Saint-Lusson who had been deputized by the colonial intendant Jean Talon. In a speech in an Algonquian language that was paraphrased in French in the *Relation* of 1672, Allouez underscored the unparalleled military prowess of the king across the Atlantic whom the indigenous leaders were invited to accept as their overlord: "When he attacks, [Louis XIV] is more terrible than the thunder. . . . He has been seen amid his squadrons, all covered with the blood of his foes, of whom he has slain so many with his sword that he does not count their scalps, but the rivers of blood he sets flowing." The Jesuit added especially disingenuously, "No one now makes war upon him, all nations beyond the sea having most submissively sued for peace."[2]

The Jesuit knew his indigenous audience had insufficient information to contradict this portrait. Louis did not sully his manicured hands and magnificent lace cuffs in such ways when reviewing troops. Nor was the Sun King so dominant in Europe at the time. The War of Devolution had recently concluded, and Louis had to surrender territories recently taken in the Spanish Netherlands to England, the Dutch Republic, and Sweden. Also, the king was about to face William of Orange and other formidable enemies in a war in the Rhineland that would last until 1679.

Nevertheless the 1660s and 1670s were an optimistic time for Frenchmen with empire in mind. The authors of the *Relations* were no exception. In this period the Jesuits not only reported on wartime events that affected their mission but articulated afresh their dreams of a Bourbon-ruled world empire. Much of their optimism hinged on their young monarch. Mission superior François-Joseph Le Mercier, for one, expressed confidence in 1671 that Louis at last would "put Jesus Christ . . . in possession of what was promised Him by God, His . . . heritage, an absolute empire over all peoples."[3]

Le Mercier was especially pleased with Louis's decision of 1665 to send an army regiment to New France in order to pacify the Iroquois. The modest campaigns subsequently pursued by this Carignan-Salières Regiment enabled the Jesuits to recommence missionary activity in Iroquois Country, but the Jesuits hoped this was a prelude to the conquest and incorporation of the region into New France. They were soon disappointed. On the one hand, the Crown never directed significant power or resources to the region, even after the English—who had absorbed New Netherland into their empire in 1664—cultivated new trade with the Iroquois, positioning themselves for an eventual absorption of the country. On the other hand, different Frenchmen who dreamed of empire, such as Saint-Lusson and the explorer René-Robert Cavelier, sieur de La Salle, saw the temporary peace achieved in 1667 as an opportunity for western adventures, not new assertiveness in Iroquois Country.

An ironic result was that Jesuits such as Allouez accompanied French traders and soldiers westward and were able to launch new missions—among the Ottawas and Illinois, for example, who became crucial allies of the French while becoming more vulnerable to the Iroquois, who now also more freely expanded westward. We thus find Jesuits, in the late seventeenth century, scattered throughout the Eastern Woodlands and preoccupied with new political challenges. In the west, the missionaries sought a delicate balance between cultivating French alliances, partly by means of Christianization, and seeking redress from French officials who blithely expected trade with new western allies while offering in return little protection from the Iroquois. And, in Iroquois Country itself, missionaries soon found themselves driven out of the region together with many Iroquois Catholic converts of their mission. They were left in a defensive position with French colonists in the Saint Lawrence River

Valley, as colonial leaders regrouped for new military engagements with both the Iroquois and the English.

Throughout this period mission leaders tried to shape French-Indian relationships in favor of a final defeat of the Iroquois and an absorption of their lands into New France. Remarkably the Jesuits even continued to agitate for a conquest of Iroquois Country *after* the Great Peace of Montreal of 1701, which was seen by Governor Louis-Hector de Callières as the end of Iroquois threats to New France.

In the meantime, in the American theaters of the Nine Years' War and the War of the Spanish Succession, in both of which some Iroquois fought as allies of the English against the French, Jesuits ministering among the Illinois, Hurons, French-allied Iroquois, and refugee Abenakis served French imperial war efforts. Some served as military chaplains and occasionally wielded weapons themselves. Others served at the colonial governors' pleasure as interpreters and go-betweens, helping negotiate alliances and truces. Above all the missionaries labored to cultivate pro-French feeling among Christian converts and their wider kin networks. In tandem they encouraged military readiness among mission Indians, whom they expected to take up arms alongside the French against the Iroquois and the English, and whom they regularly heroized for their skill and bravery in battle.

This chapter showcases the missionaries' primarily positive—sometimes theologically validated—posture toward offensive, not only defensive, war against those seen as enemies of French expansion and Catholicism in America. The Jesuits understood Christian conversion and heroism as unfolding *through*, not *despite*, the colonial-era violence that surrounded them. Their rhetoric about warfare, especially about combatting the Iroquois, has largely been whitewashed from the mission's history. Where noted at all it has generally been overspiritualized or too readily interpreted as metaphor. Correcting the record we will see that even the Jesuits' more well-known emphasis on Christ-like suffering—as seen in the missionary martyrdoms and the asceticism of converts such as Saint Kateri Tekakwitha—requires rerooting in a context of mundane militancy on behalf of French Catholic expansion, however frustrated the latter was over the long term.

The Carignan-Salières Campaigns and the Iroquois Mission

In June 1665 Jesuit hopes for a stronger French military presence in North America materialized when eight companies of the Carignan-Salières Regiment arrived under the command of Alexandre de Prouville de Tracy, the new lieutenant general of New France. More companies arrived in the ensuing months, forming a force of 1,200 men. Some of the soldiers had combat experience fighting the Ottomans in Hungary and the eastern Mediterranean. Tracy himself had conducted other operations in the Atlantic World before his Canadian assignment, repossessing Cayenne from the Dutch and installing new governors at Martinique and Guadeloupe.[4] These tasks were part of Louis XIV and Jean-Baptiste Colbert's efforts to put all French Atlantic trade in the hands of the Compagnie Française des Indes Orientales, just established in 1664.

The regiment's formal mission was to subdue Iroquois threats to French trade. This fell short of the Jesuits' requests. Le Jeune and Jérôme Lalemant had earlier petitioned for at least two regiments of the king's massive army so that the Iroquois might be entirely overthrown and their fertile lands incorporated into the French empire.[5] Nevertheless the missionaries enthusiastically welcomed the Carignan-Salières troops, assuming their planned campaigns were a prelude to a greater show of "the terror of French arms" that would subject the Iroquois to Louis XIV's rule.[6] A sympathetic observer, Mother Marie de l'Incarnation of the Ursuline school in Quebec, recorded that the Jesuits encouraged the soldiers and colonial populace to regard the coming fight as "a holy war . . . for the glory of God."[7]

Several Jesuits supported the Carignan-Salières campaigns in immediate ways. Paul Ragueneau advised Commander Tracy on where to build redoubts for defending against Mohawk raids. Based on the Jesuit's recommendations, several small fortresses were constructed in strategic locations, including Saint Thérèse along the Richelieu River, en route to Lake Champlain—a lake that the Jesuit superior, Le Mercier, hoped would become the site of a greater fortress that would allow the French to "command" Mohawk territory.[8] Other Jesuits served as military chaplains for the regiment and additional forces of colonial militiamen and Native American allies. These were Charles Albanel, a donné named Charles Bocquet, and the young priest Pierre Raffeix, later attached to the Sault-Saint-Louis mission for converted Iroquois. According to Le Mercier the chaplains spurred on the men to acts of martial self-sacrifice. Additionally, several Jesuit brothers and donnés served as guides and interpreters.[9]

The Carignan-Salières campaigns were incommensurate with the Jesuits' rhetoric of prospective conquest. Early in 1666 a combined French and Indian force moved into Mohawk territory in what proved to be a disastrous effort. The men lacked adequate supplies for the harsh winter. Many suffered frostbite. Tracy lost about four hundred men. From September through November, six hundred of Tracy's troops, another six hundred colonial militiamen, and a hundred Native American allies—many from Jesuit missions—tried again, setting fire to Mohawk villages while sustaining significant casualties from surprise attacks. The Mohawks, for their part, suffered mostly material, not human, losses.[10]

As these dispiriting campaigns played out, Le Mercier and a Burgundian Jesuit named Pierre-Joseph-Marie Chaumonot helped negotiate a peace between the western Iroquois nations, who had chosen to parlay while the Mohawks kept fighting, and the French and their Algonquin and Huron allies. Complex negotiations unfolded over several sessions throughout 1666, in both French and Iroquois council settings. The Mohawks, while not devastated by the French, decided in the spring of 1667 to accept a peace eventually concluded at Quebec on July 10. It required that all Iroquois nations, as well as nations allied with the French, had to respect one another's right to hunt and trade in territories traditionally deemed their own. Also, at the Mohawks' request, French traders and Jesuits would reside among the Iroquois to facilitate trade with New France and counterbalance losses from decreased trade with Dutch settlers in what had recently become the English Province of New York.

Modest as all this was, and signifying no forfeiture of independence by the Iroquois, Le Mercier wrote of a great French victory in the *Relation* of 1668. He expressed the Jesuits' renewed hopes, too, not only for the Catholic conversion of all the Iroquois, but for the further expansion and development of New France, now that "fear of His Majesty's arms" had filled the Iroquois "with alarm, and compelled them to seek [French] friendship." North America, he was sure, would now see "a veritable New France" come into being—a place in which his countrymen could bring to fruition "the possibilities of [the country's] wealth, and ... resources."[11]

The Jesuits sent into Iroquois Country had different plans than their newly welcoming hosts. In addition to incorporating as many Iroquois as possible into the Catholic Church and a French empire, they envisioned transforming the country into something like France's profitable wine-producing regions. A young priest from Lyons named Jacques Bruyas, for example, was assigned to live among the Oneidas. He deemed their terrain especially "beautiful" and suited to vineyards that would "yield as well as they do in France," if only sufficient manpower were directed toward clearing and working the land. Eventually, he hoped, Oneida territory would be dominated by large country estates that yielded abundant produce and therefore be more beautiful still.[12]

Le Mercier himself envisioned increased commerce between Iroquois Country and the French settlements along the Saint Lawrence, with many Iroquois resettling among the French while the French began settling in Iroquois Country. He hoped also that safe roadways in all directions would be developed in regions cleared of dense forest. But all of this would only be possible, he stipulated, if the French kept the Iroquois "in a state of fear," policing Iroquois cantons with the soldiers Louis XIV had decided to keep in New France. The mission superior therefore applauded Governor Daniel Rémy de Courcelles for sending out patrols from the new fortresses of Sainte Anne and Saint Jean to keep the Iroquois "in a state of alarm."[13]

Jesuits threatened Iroquois villagers with harsh French reprisals for any future harm done to their countrymen. Jacques Frémin of Reims stood up before the chiefs of six Mohawk villages late in 1667 to apprise them of a coming era of French law and order. The Mohawks would be treated as "subjects" of Louis XIV, he explained, and there would be public executions for any who acted violently against a French person. To make his point clear, Frémin asked several men to plant a tall pole in the ground and drape a porcelain necklace from the top. "In like manner," Frémin warned, "should be hanged the first of the Iroquois who should come to kill a Frenchman or any one of our allies." The message was effective enough that, on the spot, a Mohawk leader released several captives to the French and offered ground for a chapel in his village and Iroquois laborers for the project.[14]

The missionaries who moved into Iroquois Country during this moment of tentative peace wished to convey an unsubtle connection between Catholic teachings and rituals and the coercive mechanisms of French law and policing. This was Bruyas's meaning when, as the *Relation* of 1669 recorded, he asked "souls zealous for the conversion of the savages" on both sides of the Atlantic to pray to God that "our Iroquois continue in a state of humiliation and fear," so that "in a short time we shall be able to ... reduce ... spirits of blood and cruelty to the gentleness [*douceur*] of Christianity."[15]

Telling, too, are words in the same *Relation* attributed to an Onondaga ambassador named Garakontié, who had recently helped the Jesuits build a chapel in his own village and, at the invitation of the French, traveled to Quebec to present himself to the governor and intendant. "I wish ... that I could thank our great King Louis," he reportedly said to the colonial officials, "for having desired [not] our total ruin, but merely our humiliation."[16] Not long after, Garakontié asked for baptism and was given the name Daniel, while sacramentally entering the Church. The name honored the governor, now his godfather, who fêted Garakontié after the baptismal Mass to demonstrate to other Iroquois in the vicinity how much the French valued the conversion of prominent members of their nations. In subsequent years Garakontié would lead a pro-French faction among his people, helping the French establish a new fortress in 1673 near Lake Ontario while alienating some of his countrymen who were beginning to favor an alliance with the English.[17]

The Jesuits intentionally contributed to this polarization, stoking conflict within family groups while cultivating conversions. Unsurprisingly, many Iroquois by the 1670s came to see the Jesuits as a threat to the unity and independence of the Five Nations. Cayugas and Senecas, especially, who favored trade with the English, began to see the Jesuits and the French generally as enemies who should no longer be permitted to reside among them as diplomatic hostages. By 1682 the Cayugas expelled the missionary Étienne de Carheil. Other Jesuits were forced to leave Iroquois Country, too. Two exceptions were the brother priests Jacques and Jean de Lamberville, who remained in Onondaga territory because their medical services were valued. By the mid-1680s it was dangerous not only to be a missionary in Iroquois Country, but also to be an Iroquois convert to Christianity.[18] Thus a number of Iroquois began practicing Catholicism in secret while others relocated nearer to the French. They were drawn especially to the mission at Sault-Saint-Louis near Montreal, the central village of which the primarily Mohawk residents referred to as Kahnawaké. This well-fortified mission, with its growing population of Christian and French-allied Iroquois warriors, would prove critical to the defense of New France in a new period of war.

Western Expansion and Renewed War

Despite their modest outcome with respect to Iroquois Country, the Carignan-Salières campaigns marked a turning point for French ambitions in the Pays d'en Haut. Encompassing lands around the Great Lakes and the Ohio River Valley, it was home to diverse peoples: Hurons, Otta-was, Miamis, Potawatomis, Illinois, and others. Most had suffered from Iroquois raids in prior decades or were soon targets of new, expansionist Iroquois activity.[19]

Several Jesuits, including Jacques Marquette and Claude Dablon, accompanied French fur traders and soldier-explorers into the region to found new missions. They established Sault-Sainte-Marie in Michigan's Upper Peninsula in 1668 and, in 1671, Saint-Ignace de Michilimackinac on the northern side of the Straits of Mackinac. Close to an existing Ottawa village, the latter became a magnet for French and Native Ameri-can traders. From it Jesuits including Allouez would assist in negotiating new trade and military partnerships. Missionaries also used Saint-Ignace as a launching point for more western missions, including in Kaskaskia, the central village of the Illinois Confederation.

The Jesuits in the Pays d'en Haut readily served as go-betweens for the French and potential trading and military partners while quickly discovering challenges this role entailed. Peace with the Iroquois ironically meant that the Iroquois were now freer to compete for hunting grounds traditionally claimed by western nations. They sought captives from those nations to replenish populations back in Iroquois Country. This new Iroquois aggression caused groups such as the Ottawas and Miamis to welcome the French, whose missionaries promised them military protection. At the same time the western nations were not in this period firmly allied with one another, so rivalries—for example between the Miamis and Illinois—resulted at times in openness to Iroquois overtures regarding trade and protection, thereby catalyzing Iroquois expansion in the region. The Jesuits at Michilimackinac quickly deemed this a problem for New France at a time when English traders who partnered with the Iroquois were pursuing westward opportunities, too. The missionaries soon came to favor, as the lesser of two evils, renewed war between the French and the Iroquois given the alliances that would strengthen in the face of a common enemy—alliances among the western nations themselves, and between at least some of those nations and the French.[20]

A second phase of the Iroquois Wars opened by 1680, after a joint Iroquois and Miami attack on the Illinois at Kaskaskia. Then the Iroquois turned on the Miamis, who had been trading with the French. Fearing similar treatment from the Iroquois, especially after a Seneca leader named Annanhae was killed by an Illinois trader at Michilimackinac, the Ottawas, Hurons, and others in the vicinity of this new mission attempted to negotiate with the Iroquois instead of expelling them.[21]

At this time the Iroquois attacks in Illinois Country occasioned a serious accusation by La Salle against several Jesuits of the Seneca mission. He spread a rumor, which he communicated to Governor Louis Buade de Frontenac in Quebec, that the young and inexperienced Julien Garnier and the veteran missionary Raffeix had incited the attacks with Allouez's knowledge. There is no evidence to support or refute the claim, but La Salle may not have been a trustworthy source. He disliked Jesuits as a rule, likely from an early life experience as a Jesuit novice before changing careers to soldiery. He also had ambitions for French expansion southward through the Mississippi Valley, rather than into the Pays d'en Haut.[22]

The leading missionary in Iroquois Country at this time, Jean de Lamberville, vigorously rebuffed La Salle's attacks on the Jesuits, reminding Frontenac how his confreres had advanced New France's cause for decades. He then boldly warned the governor, to the point of blaming him for the fact, that although the Illinois would likely fight with spirit against the Iroquois, the Miamis would not be dependable allies for the French. The Miamis would side with the Iroquois because Frontenac had, without consulting them, gone forward with an attempt to negotiate a peace with the Iroquois. He had also equivocated when promising them French "protection" in the event of Iroquois attacks.[23]

Lamberville was horrified by a recent Onondaga attack on the Miamis and Illinois in which hundreds had been slaughtered, cannibalized, or taken prisoner.[24] He feared, too, that French officials were not taking seriously the new threat to New France posed by westward Iroquois expansion. He conveyed to Superior Thierry Beschefer and Governor Frontenac his concern that French forces in Canada remained insufficient to stand successfully against the Iroquois in a great war that was on the horizon.[25]

Just at this time when the Jesuits urged Frontenac toward better diplomacy in the Pays d'en Haut and forceful opposition to Iroquois expansion, he was recalled to France. His replacement, Joseph-Antoine Le Fèbvre de La Barre, was a newcomer to Canada but a naval officer of wide experience. He had served as an intendant in Paris during the Fronde and enforced royal law in the Auvergne and the French West Indies.

The Jesuits urged a sympathetic La Barre toward a new French offensive against the Iroquois. They were concerned especially that gains they had made in the Pays d'en Haut would be lost if the French did not act against the Onondagas, in particular. On October 10, La Barre met with the priests Beschefer, Dablon, and Frémin at the central Jesuit residence. Also present were the intendant, the bishop of Quebec, and other leaders of New France. The Jesuits pressed for an offensive against the Onondagas, whom they believed were incited by the English and would cripple New France's trade. They also stressed that the Iroquois were now poised to control Michilimackinac, Lakes Erie and Huron, and the Baie des Puants as well as to shut down missions and French trade in the region.[26]

However, there was general concern at the meeting that New France's defenses remained primitive and that a fight with the Iroquois required more troops from France than the "thousand good men bearing arms" the missionaries and lay authorities then could muster. Those men, French and Indian, needed furthermore better "storehouses of provisions . . . in places distant from settlements," so that "they might subsist in the enemies' country long enough to destroy [the Onondagas] altogether."[27] The newest French fortress at the juncture of Lake Ontario and the Saint Lawrence, named for Frontenac, also needed to be better supplied. In short, the Jesuits—based on their firsthand knowledge of the terrain, infrastructural weaknesses, and dispositions of various Indian groups— cautioned La Barre regarding exigencies he should expect.

The assembled agreed that a successful anti-Iroquois campaign required more royal assistance, especially in the form of at least three hundred more soldiers to be garrisoned at Fort Frontenac and at La Galette, another new fortress closer to Onondaga territory. The missionaries also sought from France additional supplies, funds for new colonial naval ships, and indentured laborers who could be distributed among the French settlements to ensure timely production of crops while able-bodied militiamen were away on campaign.[28]

As had been the case in the past, however, metropolitan aid against the Iroquois was not forthcoming. In the years ahead the number of French regulars posted in Canada rarely surpassed eight hundred men at a time. The Crown also proved stingy with respect to gifts for Native American leaders, which were crucial in French-Indian diplomacy, especially when forming new military alliances.[29] Thus from the time of La Barre's administration, Jesuits regularly expressed frustration over the defensive posture in which New France remained in the face of Iroquois and English colonial advances.

In 1683, with the goal of securing French trade with the western nations, La Barre set up camp on the southeastern shore of Lake Ontario, planning to meet the Iroquois in battle. His manpower and supplies were limited.

The Jesuits assisted La Barre by raising an army of "200 good Iroquois soldiers" from the missions of La Prairie de la Magdelaine and Sault-Saint-Louis. Writing to the new secretary of the navy, the marquis de Seignelay, La Barre expressed appreciation for the Jesuits' role in the muster and the "good will" toward the French observed among the mission Iroquois.[30]

However, instead of frightening the Iroquois away from hunting grounds claimed by the French and their allies, La Barre instead saw his army weakened by hunger and disease. In 1684, when he arrived in Iroquois Country, he hoped to trick the Onondagas into submitting to French demands, without having to suffer further losses in a drawn-out fight. But a chieftain named Garangula ridiculed La Barre for what was obviously a bluff, adding defiantly, "We [Onondagas] are born free. . . . We may go where we please."[31]

The Nine Years' War and the Peace of Montreal

In the fall of 1688 Louis XVI went to war over territories in Europe against England, the Habsburg powers, the Dutch, and other members of the Grand Alliance. The North American theater of this war opened amid conflicts that had already broken out between New France and the Iroquois. La Barre's successor, Governor-General Jacques René de Brisay de Denonville, planned an assault on the Senecas in the summer of 1687. In the meantime, he used the Jesuit Jean de Lamberville's trusted position among some Oneidas and Onondagas to invite their leaders to Fort Frontenac to discuss peace and trade. Lamberville learned too late that Denonville planned to arrest the delegation. The governor's soldiers also captured Iroquois inhabitants of the nearby villages of Kenté and Ganneious. Altogether at least thirty Iroquois were captured and sent to the galleys in France.[32] Afterward Denonville and two thousand men, including many mission Indians, marched to the Seneca heartland. They were frustrated to find the village of Ganondagan abandoned and burning. They returned to Canada after only minor skirmishing, but not before building another fortress, this time at the juncture of Lake Ontario and the Niagara River.

Lamberville was outraged that Denonville had abused his trust. All the same he continued in loyal service to the governor while among the

Iroquois, especially following debilitating Iroquois reprisals against French settlers and their farms. Accompanied by a French army officer he regarded as a good friend, Lamberville helped negotiate a new peace over the winter of 1687–88—a peace the Jesuit knew fully this time was just another ruse. As he confided to a Jesuit correspondent in China, the goal was to "gain time" for the French "until the King should send aid that might resist these [Iroquois] and at the same time sustain [a new] war against the English." This time the staged negotiations succeeded, but the peace was short-lived after Huron allies of the French, frustrated with what looked like appeasement of their old enemy, independently renewed hostilities sooner than the French desired.[33]

Lamberville next served a French squadron. On at least one occasion he took up a weapon to assist the men during Iroquois skirmishes. He boasted to his confrere in China of an attack they sustained while crossing a lake. Greatly outnumbered, he recounted, "we defended ourselves very well for three quarters of an hour," but just when the Iroquois force proved overwhelming, "Heaven . . . sent us a wind, which swept us away from their fury." Lamberville survived other sorties while serving a larger group of 140 troops in February 1688. While unscathed himself, he rushed to give absolution to numerous Frenchmen gravely wounded in combat. Later, while in a fortified position with the survivors' garrison, the priest and many of the men contracted scurvy. They had no access to water, fresh food, or firewood while surrounded by Iroquois and heavy snows. Scores of men died but Lamberville was rescued by a French officer he earlier had befriended, who arrived with a group of French soldiers and mission Indians specifically to extricate the priest. Dragged in a sled by dogs and soldiers over difficult, snow-covered terrain, the Jesuit barely survived a harrowing journey during which Iroquois warriors were tracking behind. At one point he fell through ice, but the dogs hitched to the sled tenaciously pulled him to safety. The Jesuit was sure to record that, during his two-year recovery in Montreal, the French Crown covered his expenses, because he had "contracted [the] illness while serving the soldiers."[34]

Reflecting on this aborted war in Iroquois Country, Lamberville expressed severe disappointment with the defensive posture in which the French remained in Canada decades into the colonial effort. Denonville and his forces had executed the war poorly, leaving the Iroquois and the English too secure. However, the Jesuit excused the colonial officials and blamed instead metropolitan leaders' preoccupation with the main theater of the Nine Years' War in Europe.[35]

Other Jesuits tried to aid Denonville's failed invasion. Mission superior Beschefer, for his part, was in communication in the fall of 1687 with a royal councillor named Esprit Cabart de Villermont, who had asked for updates on the campaign. The Jesuit communicated the colony's dire need for stronger defenses and more manpower. He also underscored that, in the meantime, a group of three hundred pro-French Iroquois, Algonquins, Abenakis, and Hurons of the Jesuits' missions made up half of the army that had mustered at Montreal that summer. These Indian warriors, Beschefer noted, were "of very great assistance to the French," especially as they could navigate densely wooded terrain with facility.[36]

Jesuits of a later generation would look back on the era of the Nine Years' War as a discouraging turning point for long-harbored visions of a French conquest of Iroquois Country. Pierre-François-Xavier de Charlevoix from Picardy, in a history of New France he published in 1744 while serving as mission procureur in Paris, lamented that at the time the war broke out, the French were unable to press forward with a plan to take both Iroquois Country and English New York. He mourned especially the lack of French resolve to take Manhattan, with its excellent harbor. Although there were plans under consideration in this regard, colonial leaders had delayed acting, only to be put on the defensive by the English and their Iroquois allies.[37]

This unfolded at the start of Frontenac's second term as governor-general. Denonville was needed in France as Louis XIV mounted an offensive in the Rhineland, so Frontenac was recommissioned to govern New France, which was at that point deemed strategically unimportant by metropolitan officials. Upon his return to Quebec, Frontenac found a colony once again in terror of the Iroquois, following the Lachine Massacre of August 5, 1689, in which twenty-four men, women, and children perished in Montreal and ninety others were taken captive. The next year, Anglo-American militiamen attempted an invasion of Quebec that Frontenac's army—which included mission Indians—fended off.[38]

Additional Iroquois raids on the French and their allies followed. At the time, veteran Jesuits who had been involved with the Iroquois missions and the cultivation of western alliances registered frustration with how the French were surprised by the attacks. Étienne de Carheil, a fifty-seven-year-old priest from Brittany who had been posted at Michilimackinac in 1686 after years among the Cayugas, criticized Frontenac and his staff for not being better prepared at the time of the Lachine Massacre. At the same time, he let it be known that the Hurons and Ottawas were displeased with what seemed to them the blind eye the French were turning toward the Onondagas, who had recently violated the terms of a peace treaty with the French by launching new attacks in their heartland.

Carheil communicated his views to Frontenac in 1690, stressing several points. On the one hand, Huron and Ottawa leaders were considering whether to enter into their own new alliance with the Iroquois and the English and to abandon friendly relations with the French. This was because the French had failed to provide any of the protection they had promised against the Iroquois. Claiming to be amplifying the opinion of many western indigenous leaders, Carheil accused the French colonial authorities of cowardice in the face of the Iroquois—a damning charge to be leveled in that era, especially against sword-bearing nobles of Denonville and Frontenac's rank.[39] The Jesuit further charged that the French generally returned Iroquois prisoners without demanding the release of their own. And he concluded with the accusation that the French had abandoned their allies dishonorably, out of self-interest and fear of a real fight, while still expecting the Hurons, Ottawas, and other missionized communities to take up arms in New France's defense whenever needed.[40]

Frontenac took Carheil's accusations to heart and agreed that New France endangered itself by appearing fearful of war before the Hurons and the Ottawas. However, the governor also blamed his predecessor for the situation in which he found himself and insisted his own hands were tied. Although he favored a more aggressive campaign into Iroquois

Country and the English territories, the Crown was not sending sufficient men and resources for such an enterprise.[41]

By 1693 Frontenac's army, without reinforcements from France, was able to harass the Iroquois and English in the Massachusetts and New York borderlands but not to mount anything like the conquest of Iroquois Country and New York for which the Jesuits had been hoping. Several years before, prior to Denonville's departure for Europe, colonial authorities had proposed at court a plan to take New York from the English and absorb the Iroquois into the French empire. Jesuits approved the plan, believing an invasion was justified because the English were arming the Iroquois while hoping to make them subjects of the English Crown and mount their own invasion of New France.[42]

But French officials failed at the time to authorize the conquest or provide forces and supplies for it. Looking back some decades later, Charlevoix identified a lack of good understanding at court that continuing to leave New France in a defensive position with respect to the expansionist Iroquois and English would prove more costly over time than "once for all" removing the English threat to New France altogether and subjecting the Iroquois to French rule. Instead court officials informed Frontenac that they could send no reinforcements and that "a vigorous *defensive* seemed . . . at the juncture most consonant to [the king's] service and the security of the colony."[43]

Throughout the Nine Years' War Frontenac insisted he had the will but not the means or permission to launch a serious offensive against the Iroquois. Furthermore, just at this time, the king upon the advice of his council urged the colonial governor to withdraw men from Michilimackinac and other parts of the Pays d'en Haut.[44] It became clear at this point to colonial leaders and the Jesuits that the Crown for the time being was not going to assist them, except in token ways, with New France's security and further development. Instead, as war dragged on in both Europe and North America, fighting in the latter was done less by the French and English themselves and more by Native American forces allied to either side.[45]

The Jesuits attempted on their own to press for reinforcements and more weapons from France for Indian fighters from the missions. They stressed to the secretary of the navy, Louis II Phélypeaux de Pontchartrain, how much the mission Indians—especially from Sault-Saint-Louis—were doing in the king's service. As one Jesuit put it in a memorial of February 1692, "almost half of these savages [of the Sault] have perished while fighting as brave men against the English, and against the Iroquois, their relatives, and other savages, our enemies." The mission Indians also warned the French of Iroquois movements in the woods and they frequently "attacked the enemy on land and upon the water." They preoccupied themselves so much with war—honoring promises made in deals with the French—that there were not enough able-bodied men at the Sault with time enough to provide for their own families. The Jesuit hoped that Pontchartrain would be moved not only to send aid for widows and orphans of the mission whose male family members had perished in the war, but also—if he could not deliver more men—large cannons, other armaments, and gunpowder to shore up the mission's defenses.[46]

By the late 1690s French-allied Indians at Sault-Saint-Louis and other missions were weary from fighting. They resented that the French sent so few of their own men into battle against the Iroquois. They also were more ambivalent about fighting for the French against the Iroquois, who were kin to many of them. Thus toward the end of the war, without Jesuit objections, mission-based warriors avoided fighting wherever possible.[47]

Nevertheless the Iroquois themselves were considerably weakened by the fighting of the preceding years. Thus when an opportunity arose to negotiate a new peace with the French, following the appointment of a new governor-general, Louis-Hector de Callières, Iroquois leaders moved quickly to join the discussion. Keeping their own interests and independence in mind in the face of the increasingly rivalrous French and Anglo-American powers, they collectively moved toward neutrality, resisting pressure from the Europeans—especially the Jesuit Bruyas, on the French side—to accept terms that would have required subjection to either Louis XIV or England's William and Mary.

At sixty-five, Bruyas was an obvious candidate to represent French interests to the Five Nations. He had spent difficult years among the

Oneidas and the Mohawks before taking charge in 1679 of Sault-Saint-Louis, where he labored until his appointment in 1693 as superior in Quebec. He had experience with Iroquois council meetings and knew the Mohawk language well, having authored in it a catechism, a prayer book, and a grammar.[48]

When the French embassy arrived in Onondaga territory on August 10, 1700, Bruyas exhorted representatives of the Five Nations to regard the governor of New France not as a "brother," but as a "father" to whom they should be obedient and loyal. He encouraged them to disregard promises they had made to the governor of New York—who was merely their "brother"—suggesting that the English secretly wanted to enslave them rather than to treat them generously, as Callières planned to do if they submitted to the French king.[49] Significantly, Bruyas cited earlier Jesuit missionary efforts in Iroquois Country as a reason the French could now demand political incorporation.[50]

Bruyas's proposals were earnestly considered by pro-French factions among the Senecas, Oneidas, Cayugas, and to a limited extent the Onondagas, all of whom sent delegates to Quebec to speak further with Governor Callières and his men. In June 1701 Bruyas was commissioned again to persuade the more resistant, pro-English Onondagas and Mohawks to accept a French alliance. However, another faction emerged during the discussions, moving the initially pro-French parties across the Iroquois nations to choose neutrality, while the Mohawks, unsurprisingly, chose an alliance with the English.[51] In short, not a single Iroquois nation accepted Louis XIV as an overlord. However, the neutral nations agreed to trade with the French and permit missionaries again to reside among them.

Callières was satisfied with this outcome, regarding it as an achievement that freed the French in North America to focus militarily on the English.[52] The Jesuits, differently, were disappointed. In fact, their hopes for a French conquest of Iroquois Country did not subside even with the Great Peace of Montreal.

For Carheil, a veteran of difficult missions in Iroquois Country and the Pays d'en Haut, the Peace merited in response only a more strident articulation of the decades-old Jesuit cause célèbre:

The Iroquois must be completely tamed and reduced to subjection; and we [the French] must take possession of his country, which is much better than those of all the nations [of the Pays d'en Haut]. He is the only enemy who we have to dread, or who disputes with us the trade of the savages, which he tries to attract to the English. *What reason was there for not consenting to destroy him in the war* that we had undertaken to wage against him? *Why was he spared?* What would we lose by destroying him, now that his nation is so small in numbers? *His destruction and the possession of his country would secure for us the trade of all the savage nations up here.* Nothing would remain to be done but to settle the boundaries of our commerce and of that of the Misissipy [*sic*], so that one might not clash with the other.[53]

Carheil penned these words in a letter to Callières in 1702 while serving at the Mission de Saint-Ignace among the Ottawas and the Hurons. As had been the case earlier when he represented the western Indians' interests to Frontenac, Carheil found himself communicating a grievance. The French had accepted the peace with the Iroquois despite the latter's insistence on neutrality, partly to shore up trade with the Iroquois in and around Fort Frontenac, or Catarakouy, as the locale was originally known to the Indians. The problem was, the beaver the Iroquois traded at Fort Frontenac primarily came from the Pays d'en Haut. Thus rivalries over beaver and hunting grounds between the peoples around Michilimackinac and the Iroquois would flame up again, but now without any guarantee of protection of the western nations by the French, who were now friendly with the Iroquois. Carheil posed the question to Callières: "Should we lose the Iroquois's beavers by his destruction? Would they not revert to our savages, and from them to the colony?" Events would preclude the French from answering these questions.

Queen Anne's War

In 1701 a war seen by many as the first true "world war" broke out in and far beyond the Atlantic World. The War of the Spanish Succession, called Queen Anne's War by the Anglo-Americans, was primarily about trade, especially the slave trade.[54] While the heaviest fighting was in Europe, and while from a strategic perspective in France the defense of Canada was a secondary concern, the conflict spilled across the Atlantic and exacerbated long-standing intertribal conflicts that greatly affected the Jesuits' missions.

Fighting first broke out in North America in 1702 between the English and the Spanish, and between their respective Indian allies, in the frontier regions of Florida and the Carolinas. In Canada, because of the peace with the Iroquois, the Saint Lawrence settlements initially seemed more secure from English and allied Indian attacks than the French settlements and fisheries in Acadie and other parts of the Atlantic seaboard.[55] Thus Callières's successor as governor-general, Pierre de Rigaud, the marquis de Vaudreuil, preoccupied himself in 1703 with plans to invade New England with assistance from the Abenakis, many of whom were baptized Catholics due to Jesuit activity at the Mission de Saint-François-de-Sales.

Just prior to the Peace of Montreal, the Jesuits relocated this Abenaki mission in a way that proved strategically significant during the new war. Originally located at the falls of the Chaudière River close to Quebec, the Jesuits decided at the end of the seventeenth century to move it to Odanak, about seventy miles northeast of Montreal. Odanak was a village inhabited by several hundred Western Abenakis who had not yet embraced Christianity. The mission residents themselves had wished to migrate in this direction toward their traditional homeland north of the present-day U.S. state of Vermont. The Jesuits followed them. Many of the mission residents were Eastern Abenakis who had been attracted to the original Mission de Saint-François-de-Sales as a haven from the Iroquois and the English.

The relocated mission was conceived from the start as both a mission and a French fortress. According to the deed that gifted lands near Odanak to the Jesuits in 1700, the governor and intendant of New France deemed it "fit for the service of the King and the benefit of the colony to establish the Abenaki and Socoki Indians with Jesuit missionaries" on those lands, and "to anchor religion among the said Indians."[56] The Abenakis, in turn, agreed to a trading monopoly with the French family that had given the lands to the missionaries, that of Marguerite Hertel and her son Joseph Crevier.

The mission's history was closely bound up with that of this elite French colonial military family. Hertel's husband, Jean Crevier, had in 1693 been taken captive during an Iroquois raid on the original, unfortified site of Saint-François-de-Sales, and he had died from wounds after being tortured and nearly burned alive before his rescue by Peter Schuyler, an English major stationed at Albany. Marguerite had also lost a son, Louis, in a French-Abenaki raid against the English at Salmon Falls in New Brunswick led by her brother, Joseph-François Hertel de La Fresnière, and her nephew, Jean-Baptiste Hertel de Rouville, who would eventually serve as commandant of Fort Dauphin on Cape Breton. During the War of the Spanish Succession, Rouville would command a force of French soldiers joined voluntarily—and not by coincidence—by scores of Abenaki warriors who, with their own families, had moved to the relocated mission at Odanak. They were drawn to it possibly more for its fortified structure (four-sided with bastions at the corners, in a traditional European style) than for the religion to which the Jesuits were winning converts there.[57]

Rouville's small army of French regulars—accompanied by about fifty Canadian militiamen, some two hundred Abenakis, and a number of Hurons from Lorette and Iroquois from Sault-Saint-Louis—engaged in the famous raid on Deerfield in Massachusetts in March 1704. They killed more than fifty settlers and took another 120 as prisoners of war. Abenakis from Odanak, under French commanding officers, would go on to participate in more raids throughout New England during the war.[58]

Some New Englanders captured in these raids, including small children, were brought to the mission of Sault-Saint-Louis and adopted into Catholic Indian families. The Jesuits tolerated such kidnappings despite protests from anguished relatives in New England, seeing them as opportunities to catechize the captives and persuade them to renounce Protestant heresies. The hope was that many in time would freely choose to remain among the French and Indian Catholics. Some eventually did.[59]

Among their retaliatory campaigns in the wake of Deerfield, the English with their American militia and Indian allies planned for a massive assault on Quebec, by both land and sea, in the summer of 1711. Admiral Hovenden Walker departed from Boston Harbor with a fleet of nine warships and numerous other smaller vessels, carrying nearly 14,000 men in total. At the same time an army of 1,500 Anglo-American soldiers, militiamen, and allied Indians, including at least 600 Iroquois, gathered north of Albany under the command of Francis Nicholson, former governor of Virginia. They intended to march toward Quebec and reinforce Walker's men. Rumors that Iroquois fighters were joining in confirmed the Jesuits' fears at the time.[60]

After learning of the planned assault on Quebec, Jesuits throughout New France daily led public prayer services and petitioned the Blessed Virgin, especially, to intercede with God for a French victory.[61] In a letter to the French Jesuit assistant in Rome, missionary Joseph Germain painted a picture of a colony in terror of a zealous Protestant horde while yet expressing confidence that, despite the strength of the English and their Iroquois allies, the French and their own allies would prevail:

> All the inhabitants of Canada . . . were convinced that not only the pres-
> ervation of their temporal goods, of their wives, of their children, and of
> their lives were at stake, but also that of the Catholic, Apostolic, and Roman
> religion. . . . They were sure that in all the churches they would witness . . .
> altars overturned; images broken; priests and laymen ill-treated, murdered,
> or sent as slaves to . . . heretical countries. . . . All the inhabitants of Canada
> were convinced that it was God's cause, and that they would be fighting
> for God, and also that God would combat for them. Accordingly, they . . .
> determined . . . that they would have shed the last drop of their blood
> rather than yield.[62]

What unfolded in lieu of such devastation was accounted a miracle by the Jesuits. The ground force broke up as a result of Iroquois dissension, and Walker's great fleet was blown off course by powerful winds. Eight of his vessels crashed into rocks near Isle-aux-Oeufs near the Gulf of Saint Lawrence. Hundreds of men, nearly half of Walker's force, were lost at sea. Mangled, bloodied bodies washed up onshore, where they were discovered by locals who had been fearing the rumored invasion. The site of the disaster, one of the worst in British naval history, was thereafter known as Pointe-aux-Anglais. Three days after the ships had crashed, Walker and his officers canceled the invasion and returned to New England. As it happened, that was on August 25, the feast day of Saint Louis of France.

Celebrating this unexpected turn of events Germain wrote, "Is it possible to find a more visible and miraculous protection on the part of divine providence, of the Blessed Virgin, and of the holy angels, on behalf of this poor colony? ... All are ... thoroughly convinced that ... the defeat of our enemies is an extraordinary and miraculous manifestation of divine providence in our behalf."[63] Decades later Charlevoix echoed Germain's interpretation of the events of 1711: "In the manner in which the two great armaments were scattered ... the French colony could not but recognize a Providence which watched singularly over its preservation."[64]

But discernible in the Jesuits' gratitude for God's assistance of the French against the English was frustration with French officials who had left New France in a defensive position for so long that it had to depend on supernatural aid merely to survive. As late as 1744 Charlevoix still fixed on the perdurance of Iroquois autonomy as evidence of chronic error and neglect by French officials. At best New France by his time could survive only if the British colonies and the Iroquois fell into a state of "mutual antipathy" and the Iroquois coexisted peacefully with the French primarily out of a "fear of being crushed" if they took up arms again.[65] This was a fear the Jesuits themselves, for over a century, had more than anyone tried to stoke, but rarely with the success for which they had hoped and asked others to pray.

Warfare and Conversion

Even as they agitated over decades for a French conquest of Iroquois Country, the Jesuits hoped steadily for Iroquois conversions to Catholicism. They saw no contradiction in this. Indeed they believed that the Iroquois, as a bellicose people among whom the excellent warrior was the most honored social type, would only come to respect the French and their religion by means of a great, martial humiliation. We saw this in the words of Bruyas in his early missionary days, and in the words treasured by the missionaries from the Onondaga convert, Garakontié, when he thanked the French for humbling but not destroying his people. Garakontié personified Jesuit hopes for an imperial future in which defeated but impressed Iroquois warriors would begin to embrace Catholicism and French rule and encourage others to do the same.

The Jesuits wrote in multiple registers about Iroquois cruelty and barbarism, which they contrasted in exaggerated terms to what they observed among other indigenous peoples and the French. On the one hand, echoing biblical and patristic providentialism regarding wars that God allowed to test his chosen people's fidelity, they fixated on the Iroquois as enemies that *needed to be there*—to help prove that the mission and French colonial effort generally were divinely sanctioned. For example, in his original calls for a French "holy war" in Iroquois Country, mission superior Jérôme Lalemant cited Saint John Chrysostom and wrote, "God leaves us the Iroquois in our midst with the same intent wherewith he left the Canaanites in the midst of the land . . . he gave to his people." Then, citing Judges 3:2—"that the generations of the sons of Israel might learn to fight with their enemies and be trained in war"—he added, "Our Frenchmen would have learned no other warfare than that upon moose and beavers . . . had not God given them the Iroquois to be their Canaanites."[66] Indeed the Jesuits seem to have believed that God particularly permitted the Iroquois Wars to unfold, in order to elevate and sanctify the French colonial effort. The conflicts, requiring willing sacrifices of life and limb, widened New France's horizon beyond a narrow focus on material gains from the fur trade and gave its French and Indian participants opportunities to exercise higher virtues, such as courage and love of king, country, and Christ.

On the other hand, the Jesuits wrote about the Iroquois' war-oriented culture in ways that suggest they wished to understand it better, so that they could develop a mission strategy that would make both Catholicism and French alliances and rule more attractive to them. Lalemant, for one, noted with admiration that the Iroquois, especially the Mohawks, excelled at warfare like the ancient Parthians, "who gave the Romans much trouble," and often displayed a "courage" like that of "the bravest warriors of Europe."[67] Less complimentary, the missionary Bruyas said later that the younger Onondaga Iroquois he encountered were "reared and nourished in war, and would never choose peace [with the French or anyone] if the old men . . . did not compel them to it." Their "passion for killing," he concluded, was "so great that they willingly [would] go 300 leagues . . . to remove one scalp."[68]

Given the Jesuits' challenging experience with the Iroquois since Jogues and Brébeuf's time, and given, too, the time-sensitive competition with the Dutch and then the English over indigenous alliances, a military offensive to protect existing alliances and to awe the Iroquois into submission seemed a legitimate way to advance Catholicism and French rule in North America. But beyond this, the missionaries were convinced that war was a kind of *language*—perhaps the most effective language—through which the power of the Christian God and the merits of the French who had long honored him could begin to be impressed upon Iroquois imaginations. Mission superior Claude Dablon expressed this view in 1674 when he confessed that the Iroquois were generally unimpressed with the Jesuits' talk about God. Rather, he claimed, "they believe only what they see." To open their skeptical minds to Christianity, given how focused they were on war and taking captives, it would be necessary to "subdue them to the Faith by . . . the fear of arms."[69]

Linking Christianization to violence in this way, the missionaries diverged from an emergent French Catholic strain of pacifism in the wake of the Thirty Years' War. One representative, Blaise Pascal, cited as a proof of Christianity's truthfulness that Jesus urged his followers to *be slain* by their enemies, not to *slay* their enemies as other religious founders, such as Muhammad, did.[70] By the 1690s, precluding the legitimacy of holy wars, the Abbé de Fénelon was teaching the heir to Louis XIV that "war is an evil which dishonors the human race," and that only defensive wars to preserve one's kingdom were legitimate.[71]

Furthermore, the Jesuits of New France echoed nothing of the pacifism of some missionaries of prior eras, such as Bartolomé de Las Casas, and little even of the moderate positions of neo-scholastics such as Francisco de Vitoria, who in 1532 insisted that war, though often righteous, is never "an argument for the truth of the Christian faith" and that it is "monstrous" to try to convert "barbarians" by it.[72] Rather, the missionaries stood in the tradition of sixteenth-century confreres involved in a humanistic reinvigoration of "holy war" doctrines amid the Wars of Religion and Iberian conquests across the globe.[73] Such positions were current enough among French Jesuits by the 1570s for the provincial at Paris, Oliver Manare, to refer to the infamous Bartholomew's Day massacre of Huguenots as "a catechism that had converted more heretics than all the other teachers of catechism . . . had converted during the previous twenty years."[74]

The missionaries stood in an older tradition, too—that of Crusade-era preachers who had redefined the Pauline ideal of the *miles Christi* as men who literally bore arms to advance Christ's reign on earth. They bore a family resemblance, as well, to the embattled clergymen of early medieval Europe who, in the face of Viking invasions and other existential threats to Christian kingdoms, abandoned an original monastic pacifism for a martial Christian ethos assimilated to Europe's indigenous warrior cultures and practices such as the blood feud.[75]

The mission sources evince a confident effort to acculturate French Catholicism to the warrior ethos of the Iroquois and other Eastern Woodlands nations. It was an important component of the Jesuits' larger project of adapting Christianity to indigenous ways and idioms.[76] An early example from the Huron mission is Paul Ragueneau's acceptance of the Huron term *Ondouate* as a name for the Christian God—a term the missionaries assumed meant "god of war," although the Hurons actually signified by it the leader of prewar rituals believed to spiritually empower warriors, or even the leader of attacks on Huron enemies.[77] Later, in his *Historiae Canadensis* (1664), François du Creux noted his missionary confreres' expectations that many young Native Americans who had lost kin in Iroquois raids would be affirmed in Christian conversions by the news that Louis XIV was planning a war against the Iroquois. They would have high "feelings," he wrote, when they learned that the French king had "reserved for himself the extermination of the Iroquois and the removal of that barrier to the Gospel erected by the arms and the cruelty of those barbarous tribes."[78]

A striking illustration of the Jesuit effort to acculturate Christianity to Native American outlooks on war and leadership comes from the western, not Iroquois, context. This is Allouez's address of June 4, 1671, to the chieftains and warriors gathered at Sault-Sainte-Marie, when Saint-Lusson claimed the Pays d'en Haut for Louis XIV. After the great cross with a French escutcheon was erected, Allouez spoke in an Algonquian tongue as follows, according to Dablon's account in 1672:

> Cast your eyes upon the cross raised so high above your heads: there it was that Jesus Christ . . . making himself man for the love of men, was pleased to be fastened and to die, in atonement . . . for our sins. . . . But look likewise at . . . the armorial bearings of the great captain of France whom we call King. . . . You [already] know about Onnontio [the governor at Quebec]. You know and feel that he is the terror of the Iroquois . . . now that he has laid waste their country and set fire to their villages. Beyond the sea there are ten thousand Onnontios like him, who are only the soldiers of that great captain, our great king. . . . When [Louis XIV] says "I am going to war," all obey him. . . . When he attacks, he is more terrible than the thunder: the earth trembles, the air and sea are set on fire by the discharge of his cannon; while he has been seen amid his squadrons, all covered with the blood of his foes, of whom he has slain so many with his sword that he does not count their scalps, but the rivers of blood he sets flowing. So many prisoners of war does he lead away that he makes no account of them.[79]

The subsequent history of western nations' dealings with the French suggests that such rhetoric was not ineffective, given the trading and military partnerships—and Christian conversions—cultivated in the period. War with the Iroquois was an intensifying reality for populations in the Pays d'en Haut.

With respect to the Iroquois themselves, the Jesuits regularly documented expectations that shows of deadly force by the French would inspire, not discourage, conversions, and not simply from fear but from newfound respect for French strength and battlefield prowess. And conversions, in turn, were only supposed to temper and reorient—not vitiate—the warrior ethos with which the Iroquois were typically raised from childhood. Indeed, the Iroquois converts most regularly lauded by the Jesuits were not suffering ascetics in the vein of the famous Saint Kateri Tekakwitha but, rather, courageous Christian warriors who, as often as not, survived to be honored for heroics favorable to the French and Catholic cause. Tekakwitha's early biographer, Claude Chauchetière, himself praised Christian Mohawk residents of Sault-Saint-Louis during the French-Iroquois conflicts of 1684 whose "faith . . . had united them with the French [and] cause[d] them to take arms against . . . their own nation." Other Jesuits later praised men and women of the mission who informed the French about "designs of the English and of [other] Iroquois" as they got wind of them.[80] Also, when requesting metropolitan aid for the same Iroquois mission, the Jesuits underscored military ventures in which resident warriors served loyally.[81] This seems to have been more than a prudential mode of communicating with civil authorities in France. The fathers at Sault-Saint-Louis documented that, during the Nine Years' War, they distributed supplies of clothing and other aid that they received from France especially to "valiant" mission residents who had "killed or captured" enemies of the French, and to warriors' widows and orphaned children.[82]

The Jesuits praised few converts so much as those who fought with spirit against the Iroquois and, later, the English. Illustrative are remarks of 1710 by Louis D'Avaugour, a Jesuit working at the Huron mission of Lorette. He was proud that the residents' "exact" and "abstemious" piety, while protecting them against temptations of the flesh, did not diminish their traditional "warlike spirit." Rather, their Christianity "merely impose[d] moderation . . . on their martial ardor." The Jesuit elaborated: "They never take up arms unless at the Governor's pleasure. . . . The French captains enlist no soldiers more willingly," knowing "that in the fray they will never desert the standard, or yield before the enemy's attack."[83]

D'Avaugour and his confreres were particularly impressed with a Huron chief named Thaovenhosen, who had taken part in the raid on Deerfield in 1704. He combined "skill in battle" and "Christian piety" to a degree the Jesuits regarded as excellent. After praising the Huron's intelligence and prayerfulness, D'Avaugour described Thaovenhosen as a model to the French and his own countrymen for how "to live well and to fight well." This was because he was "covered with honorable wounds received in battle." Had the French won more Indians like him to their side, "long ago no enemy of the French, no Iroquois would have been left." At the same time, this formidable warrior, always "the first to take up arms" when the call was sounded, displayed, too, "kindness and gentleness—with which the Christian law inspires him," but qualities that nevertheless "abated naught of the bravery of the warrior, or of the boldness of the Huron."[84]

Likewise a missionary named Sébastien Râle, himself famous for wartime activities in the early 1720s, lauded the martial exploits and "daring" of Christian Abenakis when fighting the English. In letters to his family members in France he described various exploits of Abenaki war parties—animated, in his words, by a strong "attachment to the Catholic faith"—as they faced down much larger groups of hostile English soldiers. One group of thirty Abenakis, for example, realizing they were surrounded by as many as six hundred enemy troops, "instantly formed six platoons of five men each; then, with a hatchet in one hand, and a knife in the other, they rushed upon the English with so much impetuosity and fury that, after having killed more than sixty men . . . they put the remainder to flight." Râle was impressed that "a handful of their warriors" could probably outmatch in fierceness "a body of . . . 3,000 European soldiers."[85]

The Jesuits not only held up male warriors for admiration but also honored, in print and in private communications, Native American women who either wielded weapons against enemies of the French—especially Iroquois—or who were killed during wartime. We see this in early mission sources such as Le Jeune's *Copie de Deux Lettres Envoiées de la Nouvelle France* (1656), wherein a story was told of the "courage of an Algonquin woman" who saved her husband from captivity by five Iroquois warriors. This woman, according to the Jesuits, "seized a hatchet and with two blows struck right and left, with astounding rapidity." Killing two of the "barbarians" right away after unbinding her husband, "she advanced to do the same to the three others, who, dismayed at the Amazon's furious onslaught, retained only sense enough to seek safety in flight."[86] Charlevoix heroized this same woman almost a century later. He explained that she was a resident of the Sillery mission and characterized her as an inspiration to other Indian Christians who were preparing themselves for war with the Mohawks. He dramatized the story more than the original report did. He called the woman a "courageous Christian" who saved her husband from bondage and returned to Sillery "in triumph" after she "seized a hatchet, drove it into the head of the chief of the party, and . . . tomahawked another," astounding other Iroquois with her "boldness."[87]

Charlevoix followed a pattern set earlier by Du Creux in the *Historia Canadensis* of praising Algonquin women already baptized, or desiring baptism, who had been taken captive during Iroquois raids but who had found ways to escape and return to their home villages and to the Jesuits—even in one instance at the cost of abandoning an infant child along the way. But Du Creux also singled out one story in which a woman had killed not in self-defense, long justified in Catholic moral theology by the seventeenth century (most famously by Aquinas in the *Summa Theologica*), but in an aggressive manner not necessitated by her circumstances:

> No more wonderful story . . . has ever been told than the . . . adventures of an Algonquin woman, who though not yet a Christian was afterwards, we may believe, baptized. This woman had been taken prisoner by the treacherous [Mohawks]. . . . For ten days she was in great distress, when one night while her enemies were sunk in sleep and she lay there bound by four cords . . . she found that one of the cords was a little loose and succeeded in freeing one of her arms. She had then no difficulty in freeing her other arm and presently her feet. . . . She was free and hurried past the prostrate bodies of her captors. *She might have made good her escape at once for the enemy were powerless, but she happened to find an axe . . . which she raised and brought down with all her might upon the head of one of the [Mohawks] who lay there.* The wretch . . . groaned heavily and waked the rest, who found him bathed in blood.[88]

Du Creux went on to spin a tale of the same woman's difficult days thereafter, running and hiding in the woods and even at one point in a swamp, holding her breath until a band of Iroquois men who were hunting her had passed by. She was eventually rescued by some Hurons allied with the French and, according to the story, this "brave and lucky woman" then searched for the French settlements, where she was met with kindness.[89]

Steadfast fidelity to the Gospel was, of course, also especially meritorious in the Jesuits' eyes, like that their heroic confreres such as Jogues and Brébeuf had exhibited in the late 1640s. In a letter penned to his brother in France in 1694, Chauchetière described the "martyrdom" of an old woman of Sault-Saint-Louis who was taken captive by some enemy Iroquois allied with the English during King William's War. Before being mutilated and lit on fire, "she knelt and exhorted all present to thank God for the favor that he conferred on her of suffering for him," urging one and all to accept Christianity "and to forsake their evil customs." Chauchetière likened the woman to the crucified Christ, attributing to her at the hour of her passion the words that Jesus had uttered from the cross: "My God, forgive them, for they know not what they do." Then, after describing what else the woman endured in gruesome detail, the Jesuit narrated that she "surrendered her blessed soul while praying, repenting of her sins, and sighing for the cross."[90]

But just like Jogues and Brébeuf, this unnamed woman—in the eyes of the Jesuit who memorialized her in print—was a martyr not only for Christ's heavenly kingdom, but also in a stymied holy war for the transatlantic expansion of "the most Christian kingdom" and an aspiring Bourbon imperial state.

CHAPTER 6

Cultivating an Indigenous
Colonial Aristocracy

Over time the Jesuits were aided in the work of Christianization by Native Americans who spoke about the French and their religion to neighbors. Sometimes these men and women urged friends and kin to relocate with them to mission villages. Mission superior Claude Dablon collected reports on such individuals while serving in Quebec from 1671 to 1693. In 1675 he recorded the story of an Oneida Iroquois captain who had led others of his nation toward Christianity and friendship with the French. The priest underscored that he was "one of the most notable men" among the Oneidas, an honored warrior who after public baptism with his wife became a catechist and lay preacher. The man made a virtual "chapel in the woods" out of his home, Dablon noted, and, given his position of influence, "he made even the infidels who hunted near him live like Christians." After the arrival of French brandy traders in his neighborhood, he moved his household about five miles away while making sure to travel back each Sunday to attend the Jesuits' Mass there.[1]

This man's influence enabled the missionaries to establish a chapter of a lay confraternity among the Oneidas. The Confraternity of the Holy Family, first established in Quebec, was akin to the Marian congregations for gentlemen at Jesuit churches in Europe but it was open to both men and women. It was promoted in France at the time as an American import.[2]

A shift had taken place in Jesuit engagements with Native Americans by the late seventeenth century. Earlier, in Paul Le Jeune's time, the missionaries had viewed most Natives as "poor" and in need of French benevolence. But in later years they came to regard some mission Indians as peers of the French lay elites who were so critical to the mission's development. They likened particular Native Americans to elevated European social types—gentlemen of talent and merit, charitable ladies, even royalty and members of the nobility. While still viewing many Natives as similar to France's rural and urban poor, they came to regard others as people of natural talent and virtue who had much to offer to France's young empire. The Jesuits thus increasingly trusted the collaborative initiative of individuals such as the Oneida captain, growing more comfortable, too, with the transmission of Catholicism through idioms and forms that were culturally familiar to mission residents.

This shift toward a more egalitarian, accommodating missionary approach accompanied increasing Jesuit dissatisfaction with particular French colonial influences, such as the expanding brandy trade. However, the Jesuits' evolving attitudes did not signify, as some have presumed, alienation from the French imperial cause or a conceptual severing in their minds of a spiritualized, transcultural Christianity from its European, Latinate historical trappings.[3] Their culturally adaptive approach was eminently French-imperial as well as evangelistic in purpose. We have seen hints of this already in how impressed the Jesuits were with converts such as Garakontié, a warrior who led a pro-French Onondaga faction and helped build New France's defenses. Likewise, they regarded as model converts residents of Sault-Saint-Louis and other missions who were willing to risk their lives as French allies in various conflicts, even when the enemy included members of their own kin groups.

The Jesuits de-emphasized paternalistic projects that aimed to render Native Americans more "civil" and externally "French," insofar as they came to see many indigenous leaders, women included, as more similar to meritorious French elites than they had first imagined. But, ironically, they did so at a time when colonial officials, especially Louis XIV's chief minister Jean-Baptiste Colbert, began pushing a new policy of faster assimilation of mission Indians into colonial settlements. The Jesuits resisted the effort as shortsighted, after they had come to identify indigenous examples of *civilité* and *police* that they believed enabled some populations, as they became Catholic, to serve as a pan-tribal, culturally mediating avant-garde of French empire.

Over time French-Indian intermarriages played an important part in the Jesuits' missionary and imperial strategy, as did marriages across tribal lines between Native men and women who were positively disposed toward the French—including marriages between baptized and unbaptized partners that differed from the prescribed, sacramental form of the Catholic Church. Partly to expand the population of individuals relatively friendly to Catholicism and the French presence, the Jesuits at times liberally encouraged marriages à la façon du pays, or according to local, indigenous customs, rather than indissoluble marriages in the ecclesiastically sanctioned form. This is surprising in light of another long-standing view of the missionaries: that the area in which they were *least* willing to accommodate indigenous ways was that of sexuality and marriage.[4]

The Jesuits' evolving, accommodating approach did not stem simply from increasing familiarity with diverse Native American societies. It arose from long experience of intertribal and colonial warfare and mounting frustration with some of their fellow Frenchmen, including colonial officials and investors who left New France relatively undefended and underdeveloped well into the eighteenth century. The missionaries also regarded the growing Franco-American population as insufficiently sharing in their political and social vision for New France. They became increasingly critical of French brandy traders and other groups whose influences upon mission communities differed from the courtly and urbane manners, aesthetics, consumption patterns, and identification with the French monarch that the Jesuits associated with true "Frenchness." Thus they sought in new ways to control which "French" manners, social groups, and political outlooks mission residents encountered.

In later years, the Jesuits along with many indigenous leaders also opposed what appeared to be French officials' high-handedness first in stationing garrisons near mission communities that had been loyal during wartime and, second, in restricting the latter's freedom to trade with groups unallied with the French. Risking accusations by colonial authorities that they opposed the assimilation of mission Indians into French colonial society, the Jesuits attempted to shield indigenous communities from certain French colonial influences, but they did this not from a desire to isolate them from a corrupt European civilization. Quite differently, their goals were to preserve trade and military alliances with New France, which sometimes had taken years to develop, and to safeguard a moral tone and social customs—organic intertwinings of indigenous and French forms of *civilité* and *police*—which the Jesuits believed were crucial for New France's cultural development in accord with the best of French civilization as they defined it.

To "Civilize" the Natives or "Play the Savage"?

In the *Relation* of 1661 Superior Jérôme Lalemant explained how his con-freres sometimes chose to live like the Native Americans among whom they preached, rather than to impose French ways on them. The missionaries ate the same food as the Natives, slept on the ground like them, learned indigenous languages and cultural symbols, and communicated Catholicism in terms that were comprehensible to the locals. Especially in mobile missions among the Montagnais and other hunter-gatherers, the Jesuits continuously battled the elements, including subarctic snows and chills. Difficult as all this was, the strategy seemed best for easing populations into lasting, faithful membership in the Church. "One must play the savage with them," Lalemant said, "and almost cease to live like a man, in order to make them live like Christians."[5]

"Play the savage" was a droll characterization for the metropolitan audience of a culturally accommodating approach to Christianization that the Jesuits had been developing for decades in the Eastern Woodlands. In private communications, missionaries were frank about the "long and slow martyrdom" the approach often represented for them. In a message of 1697 to his successors at the Saint-Xavier mission among the Montagnais, François de Crepeuil warned of unsanitary conditions, such as eating from dishes that had been "washed . . . with a greasy piece of skin, or . . . licked by the dogs." Children sometimes swarmed with "vermin" and were infected with scrofula, yet missionaries had little choice but to share common pots of food and drink with them. Crepeuil urged younger Jesuits to prepare themselves that life among the Montagnais would be "truly penitential and humiliating."[6]

Such language demonstrates continuity with encounter-era descriptions by Paul Le Jeune, who saw mission work as coming to the rescue of "poor" and "miserable" Natives. However, later mission sources often struck different notes, demonstrating respect for various people in the Eastern Woodlands. Still observing indigenous societies from a Francocentric perspective, the missionaries would liken some Native Americans to a wider range of social groups in France than the peasants and urban poor who featured in subtexts of the early *Relations*. For example, in the early eighteenth century, Gabriel Marest compared some tribes to borderland peoples in Europe conquered by the French. The Assiniboine Sioux, for example, were "serious and . . . phlegmatic," like peoples in the Low Countries dominated by the French since the 1660s. The Kriqs, differently, were "vivacious . . . always dancing or singing," like the people of Gascogne, a province incorporated into France at the end of the Hundred Years' War. The comparison held up, too, he noted, because "both tribes" were "brave" in wartime.[7] Marest insisted the comparison was valid despite the fact that neither indigenous nation had "villages or fixed dwellings," as the Flemish and Gascons had possessed for centuries. What mattered more to him were personal "dispositions," not environmental factors.

Other Jesuits likened Native American leaders to European royalty and aristocrats. In 1672 mission superior Dablon devoted ample space in a *Relation* to the Illinois nation's naturally good dispositions and their *civilité*, highlighting one chief who was both "gentle" in disposition and a "great warrior," and as much "respected in his cabin as a prince would be in his palace." He was, furthermore, surrounded by other "leading men . . . whom we might almost call courtiers, so becoming [*honneste*] and deferential was their demeanor."[8] A few years earlier Claude-Jean Allouez had described the Potawatomis on the western shore of Lake Michigan as both "warlike" and "docile," and as "disposed toward the French" and marked by "a certain sort of civility." One Potawatomi elder stood out because, after inviting Allouez to visit his cabin, "he arose from his seat to yield it," demonstrating in the Jesuit's view "the same formalities that politeness [*civilité*] demands of gentlefolk [*gens d'honneur*]" in France.[9] And in 1710 Louis D'Avaugour (himself descended from an old, Bretonnese noble family) described the Huron chief Thaovenhosen as an exceptional man who combined "the bravery of the warrior" with "remarkable kindness and gentleness," the latter partly inspired by "Christian law" and making him a moral exemplar to Frenchmen and Native Americans alike.[10]

Such missionary descriptions drew upon aristocratic ideals of masculinity current in France at the time, especially when linking some Native Americans' apparent gentleness and generosity with a formidable warrior ethos.[11] The Jesuits further compared indigenous warrior elites to those of the Old World. In the early 1660s Lalemant admitted that the fierce Iroquois impressed him in conflicts with the Hurons and the French because they distinguished themselves with "valiant deeds . . . as highly as could be expected [even] from the bravest warriors of Europe." The Mohawks, furthermore, were reminiscent of the ancient "Parthians, who gave the Romans of old so much trouble," so excellent was their tactical understanding and performance in war.[12]

Precisely because of the quality of Iroquois warrior elites who were so intractable in the face of European ambitions, the missionaries reacted with special enthusiasm whenever Iroquois leaders seemed open to friendship with the French. As the most formidable war-oriented society in the Eastern Woodlands, the Iroquois called to mind the warrior nobility from which many French aristocrats themselves claimed descent. The prospect of recruiting their best men as lay mission leaders and for military service to New France was extremely appealing. The Jesuits thus were eager to establish culturally adaptive missions in the heart of Iroquois Country and report not only on changes in religious belief and practice, but also on social attributes that they observed there. The fiercest warriors among the Onondagas, for example, struck the Jesuits with their "gentleness [*douceur*] in . . . conversation and a civility, which hardly savor[ed] in any wise of barbarism." Catholicism would progress especially well among them, it was hoped, and further strengthen such qualities.[13]

As the Jesuits assessed it, Christianity when introduced in a modest way in war-oriented societies invigorated and refined indigenous occurrences of gentleness and civility—gentlemanliness, we might say in English. Conversion gradually also conformed indigenous social virtues to French ones. Reporting to Quebec on the Onondaga mission in the wake of the Carignan-Salières campaigns, the missionary Jacques Frémin posited that the growing Christian community there was changing in this manner. "They speak to us with much more gentleness and are far more tractable than they formerly were," he wrote. One man in particular, the recently baptized Garakontié, whom he called a "prince and . . . orator," displayed "all the civility imaginable."[14]

The Catholic sacrament of Holy Eucharist was seen as a potent agent of indigenous civility's refinement. The Jesuits believed that Holy Communion had the special power to soften manners and effect social transformation. In an unpublished "Relation of 1679," Jacques Bigot observed that, in a Mohawk mission community, the "ceremony of the blessed bread" had replaced traditional practices of ritual cannibalism, and those who participated in Mass would also gather once a week for a meal at the home of a woman who prepared the hosts. "The civility that they show," he added, "has about it nothing of the savage, and these gatherings serve wonderfully in fostering fervor and charity."[15] Another report on the Mohawk mission boasted further that the reverence shown by Mass attendees suggested they would easily "before long . . . all become French." More than this, they would become like "the best-ordered families in France."[16] One Mohawk war widow, in particular, exhibited "all the good breeding of a French lady," tending to preparations before and during Mass with "modesty and self-possession."[17]

As the Jesuits more and more viewed particular Native Americans as part of an indigenous, natural aristocracy that could be cultivated for New France's benefit, Louis XIV's chief minister for colonial affairs, Colbert, attempted to impose a new Indian policy. In a communiqué to Intendant Talon of June 1666, Colbert demanded that the French in Canada do more to "civilize" the Natives. His use of the French infinitive *civiliser* appears, interestingly, to be the earliest such usage in extant sources pertaining to New France. What he signified by the term was Native Americans' adoption of several behaviors and social organizational forms he associated with being French. Baptized Natives were to live among the French in colonial villages and towns. They were to intermarry with the French wherever possible, to help populate settlements with Catholics of at least some French ancestry. Furthermore children were to be formally schooled and forced to speak French—something to which Colbert believed the Jesuits, specifically, should devote their resources. Beyond this the Natives were to dress in French styles and attend Mass in parishes, not mission chapels. Above all they were to serve the economic development of New France as farmers and lower-level laborers in fisheries, mines, the fur trade, and other colonial industries.[18]

Colbert's policy stemmed from a new vision of the French empire writ large, which was communicated from the royal court to various colonial officials, merchants, and missionaries. That empire was to be centered on lucrative trade and slavery-based cash-crop production in the Caribbean and Indian Ocean regions. Colbert imagined that New France, in service to the larger empire, should provide more agricultural produce, fish, furs, and other raw materials while serving, too, as a dependent consumer market for finished goods made in France. However, Colbert knew that the French population in Canada was smaller than it needed to be to achieve this. Even with increased emigration from France, newly encouraged by the Crown at the time, it would take generations to grow significantly. Native Americans could in the meantime make up the difference, he thought, by helping the French breed their way toward a more populous colony. But to be of value to the scheme, they needed to live among the French, as a subordinate class of laboring producers and consumers.

Colbert and eventually also Governor-General Frontenac identified the Jesuits' practice of ministering to Native Americans in mission reserves and Indian Country itself—and employing local languages and cultural forms while doing so—as a stumbling block to Canada's transformation along such lines. They urged the Jesuits to require baptized Natives to intermarry with the French and relocate to the Saint Lawrence settlements. They also urged the Jesuits to redirect energies to their young Collège de Québec and open new schools for Native and métis children in the same settlements.[19]

The Jesuits resisted this pressure. As a result they were accused by various critics, including Récollet missionaries favored by Frontenac, of opposing the spread of French ways and "civilization" in North America.[20] In reality the Jesuits believed their own approach was the more effective path to the same ultimate goal. At the same time, they insisted that promising and already collaborating Native American leaders, who were far from lacking in *civilité* of their own, be treated with diplomacy and deference. The Jesuits wished to incorporate these leaders and their kinship networks into New France as stakeholders in the French imperial enterprise, and therefore on terms that made sense to them. It would be counterproductive, indeed destructive of ties being cultivated patiently across different Native societies, if the French suddenly started treating baptized Natives as a subordinate population that existed to labor and breed at the pleasure of would-be French landlords, company officials, and government bureaucrats.

While wrapped up in some new, mercantilist ideas, Colbert's Indian policy was also in keeping with an older "civility before sanctity" approach to Christianization that had predominated in other areas of the Americas. The norm since the time of the conquistadors was to assimilate Natives quickly into colonial society, usually in the role of exploited laborers, before, or in conjunction with, baptizing them and teaching them rudimentary Christianity and European ways. Missionaries in Portuguese Brazil, including Jesuits Manuel da Nóbrega and José de Anchieta, came to favor the forced "reduction" of hunter-gatherer populations into European-style communities. John Eliot and other early English Puritan missionaries in North America, too, shared in the assumption that Christian conversions could unfold in lasting ways once Natives were assimilated to European town life, languages, and dress.[21]

Differently, the Jesuits of New France from an early period searched for indigenous forms of courteous manners and orderly political life—what they called *civilité* (or sometimes *honnesteté*) and *police*, respectively—in which Christianity could take root, and which conversion would in turn perfect.[22] As early as 1616 Pierre Biard had identified a "law of civility" among the Montagnais, but the missionaries referred to indigenous forms of *civilité* and *police* more regularly and optimistically in the latter half of the seventeenth century, especially as they became more familiar with settled and populous nations such as the Iroquois and Illinois.[23]

The Jesuits furthermore came to regard indigenous forms of civility and social order—especially once supernatural grace from the Church was at work in them—as a ground from which fraternal, effective collaboration with the French in trade and war would spring. They hoped Native American societies eventually would harmonize with the courtly and urbane French Catholic civilization the Jesuits were committed to spreading across the Atlantic. This is one reason the missionaries fixed so much hope, initially, on the Huron confederacy. The Hurons were seen as a people who, once Christian and cultivated as trade and military partners, had civilizational resources of their own to contribute to New France's maturation. Jean de Brébeuf early on had noted, for example, marks of Huron "political and civil life," such as "maintain[ing] peace and friendship with one another," "habit[s] of . . . conversing and reasoning very well," and regularly holding "councils . . . almost every day . . . on almost all matters" in which "everyone . . . has the right to express his opinion." He noted further that they even had their own word for what the French called *l'homme civil*—that is, *aiendewasti*.[24]

When contrasting the Jesuits' approach to Colbert's policy, it is useful to note that, at the time the latter was communicated to Intendant Talon, the Bourbon state was still itself in an early, experimental phase of assimilating culturally diverse populations in several borderland regions of France itself. These included Roussillon in the Pyrenees, Alsace near Germany, and other territories conquered and annexed by Louis XIV. Royal efforts toward linguistic, religious, and social assimilation in such places were slow-moving, with official policies only laxly enforced. Colbert's call to the Jesuits to focus on Indian schools in and around Quebec, for example, was made only a few years after the Crown sponsored a new Jesuit-run school for elite boys in Perpignan in Roussillon. Yet even there Jesuits were free to cater to local ways: they taught primarily in Catalan and Latin, not pushing French on students. Even later in the seventeenth century, French was far from universal in Roussillon even in the contexts of law and political administration, let alone in ordinary social and commercial interactions. Crown policy was lenient, too, in German-speaking Alsace and Flemish-speaking territories in the Low Countries. By the early eighteenth century—long after Colbert's policy for Native Americans was abandoned as impracticable—the Bourbon state had no standard language policy for annexed European regions but instead experimented with a range of practices, adapting to local circumstances.[25]

Jesuit resistance to Colbert's Indian policy hardly constituted, then, a radical, anti-imperial departure from an established mode of Frenchifying populations in culturally plural contexts. Furthermore, just because the Jesuits did not operate formal schools for Native American boys in the Saint Lawrence region, as Colbert and the Récollets urged, does not mean they were not engaged with informal education or the promotion of French cultural norms in mission settings. As with Christianity, however, the Jesuits instructed Natives about French ways in indigenous languages and in a peripatetic manner. In the early 1680s, for example, Jean de Lamberville employed a topographical print of Paris to lead Onondaga elders in a dialogue about French achievements and what a greater French presence among them might bring about. His goal, in which he reported succeeding, was to elicit wonder regarding the size of Paris, its commercial and infrastructural means of supporting a very large population, and its great buildings and artistic monuments. He pointed out, for example, "the Louvre; the bronze horse" (that is, the great equestrian statue of Henry IV, by Giambologna and Tacca, on the Pont Neuf); "the King's house, and those of the great [grands]; the general hospitals . . . the rare animals brought from various parts of the world . . . the superb churches, in which . . . 4,000 persons pray to God; the cemeteries; the colleges, where . . . 600 persons lodge in the same house." Lamberville also showed the men lifelike portraits of French personages, which he was pleased to see elicit admiration, among his interlocutors, for "the skill of . . . Europeans in representing persons to the life."[26] Some mission sources from the early 1700s suggest, too, that the missionaries regarded trade with the French, with the conversations and sharing of customs it involved, as a kind of schooling for Native Americans in French ways.

There were also practical or vocational lessons on offer: for example the Jesuits and voyageurs, or licensed fur traders, sometimes taught mission Indians in Illinois territory and elsewhere how to cultivate French wheat and grapes for wine-making.[27]

In addition to informal educational efforts in their missions, the Jesuits also believed they contributed invaluably to New France by forging ties with Native American leaders who in turn facilitated Christianization and French commerce in their communities. Some of these leaders were not even baptized or believing Christians. In 1680 Dablon recorded a story about two men of the Huron-Algonquin mission of Saint-Ignace de Michilimackinac in the Pays d'en Haut who deliberated in council over whether or not to plant a large cross in the midst of the village. One of them questioned the usefulness of such an object. The other was said to have responded, "One might as well ask . . . of what use are the [Jesuits]? . . . Of what use are the French, and all the comforts and advantages that we have received with prayer?" The latter's arguments prevailed, and the elders allowed the Jesuits to plant the cross in the center of Saint-Ignace. Afterward several village elders together with some Frenchmen in the vicinity "honored" the crucifix "by a volley from their guns."[28] The anecdote illustrates the confidence that the Jesuits in the Pays d'en Haut had that the leading men in their mission villages would, on their own accord and in their own time, reorient community life in favor of both Catholicism and the French. According to the missionary Vincent Bigot, it was the innate quality of such men that the missionaries could count on: the man who had successfully persuaded his peers in the council meeting was "possessed of an uprightness that seems natural to him, [who] lacks only Christianity to be a perfect man."[29] The Jesuits reserved such language for select individuals who appeared to have special charisma or influence in council settings, proven by the willingness of others to follow their lead in adopting new ideas and behaviors harmonious with Christianization and New France's development.

In view of the Jesuits' growing appreciation of the most "civil," "gentle," and socially prominent Native Americans they encountered, it becomes apparent that they resisted Colbert's push for more intermarriages, in particular, between natives and French persons out of concern that Indian Christians of naturally aristocratic qualities might indiscriminately mix with French persons of dubious social and moral caliber. In assessing the Jesuits' resistance to Colbert's assimilation program, we should keep in mind that, even by the late seventeenth century, French colonial society in the Saint Lawrence River Valley was still primitive compared to the socially elite quartiers of French cities the Jesuits identified positively with French ways. And at the time the Crown began to subsidize emigration to Canada in 1662, there were only about three thousand ethnically French individuals living in the Saint Lawrence settlements. More than half of these French persons lived in or near Quebec, the only settlement that was large enough to constitute a small provincial *ville* by French standards at that time. Furthermore, four out of five of these persons were male—a great many of them young and unmarried.[30]

While Colbert assumed this population problem and gender imbalance could be remedied by fecund marriages between colonists and baptized Native American women, the Jesuits were more discriminating than he was about which French colonials were fit to enter into marriage alliances with Indian women. Among the French inhabitants of Canada, only a handful of colonial officials, military officers, and estate owners were of aristocratic or urban-elite extraction. Many of the marriageable males were lower-ranking soldiers or engaged in construction, transport, maritime, or textile-related occupations.[31] Even the landed class of seigneurs in New France was generally not of exalted lineage by the standards of metropolitan notables. Furthermore—stemming from the seigneurs' lack of high status, disposable income, and connections in the transatlantic patronage system—less than 1 percent of their lands by the early 1660s had been parceled out for farming and infrastructural development. Integrating the daughters of leading Native American warriors and elders into *this* colonial society, and raising up a generation of métis children in it, would not have resulted in sufficient intermingling of "good" families of "merit," rank, dignity.[32] The Jesuits indeed, for decades, had approached the matter of marriages in the colonial setting in a different way.

Another of Dablon's reports on Native American collaborators with the mission included a lengthy death notice about a Huron convert named Jeanne Assenragenhaon. The Jesuits mourned her passing because she had been a great friend to them first in Huron territory and then in Quebec after time as a prisoner of war in Iroquois Country.

Jeanne's story as recorded is curious from the standpoint of the strict, post-Tridentine rigorism that Jesuits of the period are supposed by many to have been spreading through their missions. Jeanne, in fact, had married three different men, persuading two to embrace Christianity, but none of her marriages appear to have been solemnized in a Catholic ceremony. It is also unclear whether she remarried the first time before or after her original husband had died. Typically the Jesuits made it clear when Native American marriages were performed "before the Church" in a sacramentally valid way, and which therefore conformed to ecclesiastical prohibitions against divorce and remarriage without an annulment.[33]

The second marriage had occurred while Jeanne was among the Iroquois, but somehow Jeanne and her husband ended up back among the Hurons. When the Jesuits met the Iroquois spouse, he was submitting to Jeanne's instruction in Christian doctrines and practices. Shortly before his death the man was found by one Jesuit to be "thoroughly instructed" and ready for baptism. The third husband, Pierre Andaiakon, likewise was "pagan" at the time of the marriage. He, too, agreed not only to be taught Christianity by his wife but even to leave Huron territory to live among the French at Quebec, where Jeanne could more freely practice Catholicism. Once there, according to Dablon, Jeanne and Pierre "rendered most kindly services to the French" and other Native Americans. They took orphans into their home and hosted travelers stopping into Quebec "on Sundays and feast days" to attend Mass. And Jeanne in particular was a model of Christian social benevolence toward poorer Natives and French alike: "Not a week passed without her giving considerable alms—to such an extent that, after her death, it was found that she had given away . . . all that she had possessed."[34]

Jeanne had fulfilled social functions for an ethnically mixed colonial population that the Jesuits associated with elite, devout Catholic laywomen in France. She was a generous hostess to both clergymen and lay pilgrims, she was well instructed in Catholicism and passed on her knowledge to others in a domestic setting, and she practiced corporal works of mercy for the less fortunate. The Jesuits prioritized some of her behaviors and her influence over others above qualms they may have had about what appear to have been—from a strict Catholic viewpoint—irregularities in her marital history. Her first husband, if living at the time of her second marriage in Iroquois Country, would have been her true husband in the eyes of the Church. Regardless, Jeanne entered not once, but twice, into marriages with unbaptized partners despite having become Christian herself earlier in Huron territory. Such unions, in which there was a "disparity of cult" (*disparitas cultus*), had been discouraged by the Church since early medieval times. By the Jesuits' era they were prohibited barring a special dispensation by a bishop or ecclesiastical court.[35]

In France a woman with a questionable marital history would not have enjoyed status in devout circles. Yet in New France the Jesuits not only tolerated Jeanne but praised her "heroic" life. Her story hints at missionary accommodation where marriage was concerned when the advancement of Catholicism and the betterment of colonial society, especially by Natives perceived as elite and pro-French, were at stake. Indeed, to a surprising degree, the Jesuits actually encouraged marriages à la façon du pays among Catholic neophytes—often without priests present—to help increase the pro-French, "civil," and warrior-elite population of New France. And they practiced such accommodation not only deep within Indian Country but also in the vicinity of Quebec and Montreal.

Strict norms regarding marriage were promulgated by the Church especially from the time of the Council of Trent. The decree *Tametsi* (1563) forbade Christians to marry clandestinely without a clergyman present, without banns read prior to the marriage, and without a Trinitarian rite of blessing over the union. Except where rare dispensations were granted by a bishop, missionaries distant from metropolitan sees could not adjudicate marriage cases on their own, resulting sometimes in years of delay in obtaining permission to grant annulments or remarriages.

From an early period, the Jesuits determined that rigorous applications of ecclesiastical laws regarding marriage in New France would not only prevent the Christian population from growing at the rate it could, but also alienate prospective converts from Catholicism and the French. They preferred a flexible approach by which they could liberally bless marriages and dissolve some, too, without formal approval each time by ecclesiastical authorities in Europe. They sought approval for such flexibility from Rome, and to a limited degree they obtained it. Then, following the installation of a French bishop at Quebec in 1659, they enjoyed latitude in their mission stations when it came to pastoring men and women on conjugal matters.[36]

In the Eastern Woodlands societies that the Jesuits encountered, premarital sex, polygamy, and marital breakups followed by remarriages were common. The early *Relations* are therefore replete with commentary on difficulties the Jesuits had in drawing men and women, young and old, to Christian baptism once they understood that it would oblige them to reserve all future sexual activity for monogamous, indissoluble marriages. The missionaries frankly reported that many initially enthusiastic converts came later to find Catholic expectations for marriage burdensome, to the point that some abandoned their new religion and their spouses. Even where some Natives, especially widows and unmarried women, embraced celibacy with their new Christian identities, they not infrequently faced social rejection by neighbors and even violence from spurned suitors or parents trying to compel them into marriages. Furthermore, some indigenous leaders who approved of Christian instruction for women and children in their families cited Jesuit teachings about sex and marriage as primary reasons for rejecting baptism for themselves.[37]

From the beginning the missionaries did not simply condemn Native American customs and attitudes in this area of life. Rather, in 1636, they petitioned Pope Urban VIII for the "Privileges of the Indies" that had been granted almost a century before to Jesuits in Asia. In the apostolic constitution *Licet Debitum* (1549), Pope Paul III had permitted missionaries to act in lieu of a local bishop where matters required formal ecclesiastical adjudication. Given the absence of a local ordinary in New France in the early seventeenth century, the Jesuits hoped they, too, would be able to informally adjudicate marriage cases where they deemed it prudent to do so, without having to refer them each time to a bishop in France or the Roman Congregation de Propaganda Fide.[38]

A goal of the early petition to Rome was to be able to freely bless marriages between Catholic Frenchmen and unbaptized Native American women. The Jesuits had in mind, especially, marriages between the daughters of Native American chieftains and pious, well-mannered Frenchmen who had means of their own or material supports guaranteed by wealthy French patrons.[39] But unless the women were baptized right away—which the Jesuits opposed while prioritizing, first, catechesis and demonstrations of sincere, individuated faith—dispensations were required for such marriages to be solemnized in the Church. *Licet Debitum* had once allowed missionaries in Asia to dispense with this rule, especially to increase through childbirth populations favorably disposed to Christianity if not yet fully embracing of it. Requesting the same from Urban, mission leaders in Canada argued that the Natives, if permitted to intermarry with the French, would eventually desire Christian instruction and baptism of their own accord after coming to "love the French" as their kin. Practically, too, it would endear the French to some indigenous elders, who complained on occasion to the missionaries that due to local, intertribal conflicts there were shortages of eligible, fighting-age males in their communities. Intermarriage would thus offer expanded opportunities for Native women and, given the métis offspring that would result, help indigenous communities "create more warriors" and others who could "assist them . . . as their brothers and their kinsmen." At the same time, New France itself would be peopled with men and women loyal to France and the Church as well as to their maternal nations.[40]

Urban rejected the initial petition in 1638, which only emboldened the missionaries to press harder. They sent new requests to Rome and began justifying their case for the Privileges of the Indies in the *Relations*, which suddenly included ample material on the difficulties prospective Native

American converts had with Catholic teachings on marriage and sex. They presented a Huron "captain" named Aënons in a sympathetic light, citing his concern that marriages "binding for life" were a "stumbling-block" for Christianity among his people. Other leading Hurons were reported to have expressed interest in marriage alliances between their daughters and Frenchmen. The problem was, according to Le Mercier, "some obstacles were thrown in the way."[41] This was an oblique reference to Urban's opposition.

By the early 1640s, the Jesuits frankly reported that they were encouraging younger Native Americans who desired baptism to marry persons of their choice à la façon du pays, prior to sacramentally entering the Church. Attempting to elicit sympathy in Europe for young indigenous women who were drawn to the Jesuits' teachings, Barthèlemy Vimont explained that his confreres avoided baptizing even those especially desirous of the sacrament. He told the story of a teenager well instructed in the faith and desiring even to become godmother to her own mother. The Jesuits were pained to turn her away from baptism because they did not want to put her in the potentially hopeless situation, later, of being limited to a Catholic marriage when there were as yet scarcely any baptized men among her people upon whom she could rely for long-term fidelity.[42]

Beyond this the missionaries even encouraged some young people who *had* been baptized to marry outside the Church. "We deal leniently with them," Le Jeune declared in 1640, "allowing them to come to prayers," but not to receive Holy Communion. The Jesuits further hinted that it might be pastorally effective, if they had privileges granted by Rome, to *dissolve* marriages that had resulted in a believing Christian spouse's abandonment by another who had reverted to pre-Christian ways. Jérôme Lalemant in 1643 informed metropolitan readers that each Christian who married was "exposed, on the morrow of his nuptials, to the danger of being compelled to observe continence for the remainder of his life," because of the frequency with which marriages broke up in indigenous communities. The Jesuit asked rhetorically, "What therefore can a Christian young man do if . . . his wife should abandon the faith . . . ? Were he to burn with a passion a thousand times over, he must grow old in chastity without ever having made a vow to do so," because "the Church in this case has no sword."[43]

Lalemant left out of the *Relation* the fact that he and the Jesuit general in Rome were just at that time pressing for the mission's autonomy from Propaganda Fide and even from the bishop of Rouen who, at that time, was the French ordinary for New France. They were also requesting a privilege to freely dispense with ecclesiastical law regarding marriages they could solemnize sacramentally and others they could annul, especially where Christian spouses might quickly remarry partners more favorably disposed to Catholicism than their first.[44]

Eventually in 1648 a different pope granted the missionaries liberal dispensations for marriage cases. Innocent X allowed them to sacramentally bless marriages where there were canonical impediments, except in cases of bigamy or the murder of a prior spouse. The pope also lifted, for the mission context, the Church's prohibitions against marriages where there were impediments such as consanguinity in the third and fourth degrees, or where one or both persons seeking marriage were guilty of a serious crime—except rape or, again, the murder of a former spouse. Furthermore the missionaries could freely convalidate as sacramental, at a later date, marriages initially contracted à la façon du pays once it was clear both spouses had sincerely and lastingly converted from paganism. As for those already married outside the Church but who wished to marry another who was a good Catholic, the missionaries were granted the authority to dissolve prior marriages that previously required an annulment by ecclesiastical officials in Rouen or Rome, and only after a formal investigation in those cities.[45]

The Jesuits quickly took advantage of these new privileges. A report of 1650 from Jean De Quen at Tadoussac includes casual mention of marriages entered into in secret—contravening *Tametsi*—by baptized Christians in wintertime, when no Jesuit priest was present at the mission. Additionally the *Relation* of 1657 reveals that the Jesuits encouraged the first women in Iroquois Country who prepared for baptism to marry partners chosen from "the leading men of the country . . . brave warrior[s] and . . . good hunter[s]" who were relatively open to Christian instruction, so long as they were not seeking polygamous arrangements.[46]

Liberal as Innocent's dispensations were for the time, the missionaries did not obtain all they wanted. No explicit privilege was granted for the Jesuits to be able to freely dissolve sacramental marriages between baptized persons but in which one partner had renounced Christianity. In such cases the missionaries were still required to seek formal judgments from a bishop. But by 1659 such annulment cases could at least be adjudicated more locally rather than be referred to Rouen or Rome: New France was finally given its own episcopal see, and Bishop François-Xavier de Montmorency-Laval had arrived in Quebec to shepherd his new flock.

Although documentation is scarce on mission marriages during Laval's tenure, extant sources hint that the new colonial bishop permitted the Jesuits wide latitude. They employed it to encourage marital alliances—both sacramental and à la façon du pays—that contributed to their broader project of cultivating a population of "civil," "gentle" indigenous elites devoted to both Christianity and French law and order. Mission marriages thus were often formed across various lines: sometimes between Native Americans and French persons, more often between persons from different indigenous nations, and regularly between baptized and unbaptized partners.

Because of their resistance to Colbert's policy that, in this same period, favored more French-Indian marriages in the Saint Lawrence settlements, the Jesuits have been presumed by some to have opposed French-Indian couplings as a whole by the late seventeenth century.[47] There is evidence, in particular, that the missionaries opposed such marriages when the Frenchmen involved were *coureurs de bois* who flouted some colonial laws and whom the Jesuits deemed to be antisocial "solitaries," as Étienne de Carheil called them in a complaint to Quebec from Michilimackinac. By "solitaries" Carheil meant men who lived apart from other Frenchmen and were motivated more by self-interest than the collective interests of mission and colonial communities, and men whom the Jesuits (not entirely justly) believed drew women into sexual libertinage, disconnecting them from their kin groups as well as the Jesuits and settled French.[48] Otherwise missionaries approved French-Indian couplings and celebrated them at the altar when certain conditions were met. Both partners had to be deemed "capable" of long-term commitments; material support by the husband for the wife and future children had to assured in some way; the Frenchman in question had to be "associated together" with other French people, whether fellow traders or farmers; and the "consent" of both parties' parents, or instead the colonial bishop's, had to be given.[49] Sources from the early eighteenth century suggest further that the Jesuits strongly approved of marriages between French and Native American persons who demonstrated a similar degree of "gentle and polite manners," as well as "ardor in the practice of Christian virtues," as a missionary laboring among the Illinois put it. Such couples would then model such things to their children and neighbors.[50]

Otherwise marriages à la façon du pays between primarily Native American partners remained the norm even for many baptized and Communion-receiving mission residents. The Jesuits indeed encouraged such marriages between Native Americans when it helped increase the population of "notable" and warrior-elite families friendly to the French. Dablon for example referred in 1678 to "several captains and . . . elders" in the Onondagas' central village who had "embraced the faith" but were not "married before the church," as they were still being catechized by both the Jesuits and a "notable" layman among them who had led the way with such a marriage.[51] Claude Chauchetière, too, while working in the Iroquois mission reserves near Montreal noted that many of the warriors residing in them who had helped defend New France in wars against their own kin and the English "had been married in the savage fashion" *after* their baptisms. But some eventually, when "better instructed and better trained," remarried or had first marriages convalidated "according to the rites of the Church."[52] At least one of these men, a renowned Mohawk warrior attracted to La Prairie by the example of an Iroquois Christian couple, was explicitly encouraged by Jacques Frémin to leave the mission and find a woman of his own nation "who should please him most" and then bring her and other Mohawks back with him. The Jesuit urged this not only because there were few single Christian women at La Prairie at the time but also because this particular warrior was perceived to be a leader among his own people and able, by force of his "rank," "zeal," and "authority," to lead others to the mission. Reporting on this same man and others like him, Chauchetière noted with satisfaction, "The warriors [from Mohawk territory] have become more numerous at Montreal than . . . in their own country."[53]

The Jesuits most liberally accommodated indigenous marital situations that fell outside prescribed Catholic norms, when doing so increased the population of mission residents seen as socially and morally excellent. This applied to women as well as men. We have seen already the example of Jeanne Assenragenhaon. There was also a Mohawk woman named Marie Tsaouenté who was seen by Superior Dablon as "one of the most notable people" of her nation. She and her two sons were welcomed into the Huron mission at Lorette after she abandoned a husband. She remarried a Huron man while still technically married to someone else in the eyes of the Church. The two reared a daughter with the older boys. Dablon described Marie as "a very virtuous woman" whose qualities were passed on to her children, especially a son who displayed an "intelligence" and a "gentle" and "excellent" disposition that made him stand out "not only among the savages but also among the French."[54]

The Jesuits came to trust particular Native American women in irregular marriages who could lead others, including husbands and members of the wider community, not only toward Christianity but also toward a more settled, French-style existence. Exemplary in this regard was Jeanne Itaouinon, a resident of Sillery who ran an informal school for girls out of her home, which was admired by Bishop Laval and other colonial dignitaries. According to the missionary Jacques Bigot, Jeanne had to endure "a thousand slanders" from fellow *Christian* neighbors because she had married an unbaptized man named Paul, and not in a Catholic ceremony, after being abandoned by a previous husband. Bigot in 1682 noted that Paul was temperamentally difficult for Jeanne to live with, but she nevertheless patiently "taught him so well" that eventually he was docile to her wishes, enabling her to focus on her Christian educational labors. Bigot encouraged her, also, to ignore tongue-wagging neighbors who did not know what was truly in her "heart," as Jesus Christ did. God had visibly blessed her labors and "constancy," according to the Jesuit, because the girls in her school exhibited "greater modesty than the French girls" of New France. Even "gentlemen" who observed the school were utterly surprised by the quality of its graduates and their impact on the social tone of Sillery. Beyond this—illustrating Jeanne's value to the mission *because* of, not in spite of, her marital situation—Bigot recorded as a blessing the fact that her first husband eventually came to Sillery with his own second spouse and, impressed by Jeanne and other Christians there, amended his life and asked the Jesuits to allow him and his new wife a Catholic marriage.[55]

Stably married couples in the Jesuits' missions of course played a central role as exemplars to others, not only in their conjugal chastity and fidelity and in raising their children to be devout and well mannered, but also in giving alms to the poor. In the 1680s at the mission of Saint-François-Xavier near Montreal, a leading figure was a married woman who regularly met with other women of the village to organize charitable giving within the community. Likewise, their husbands who were "captains" in the village gathered others to help build homes and provide for widows and the sick.[56] In 1699 a missionary named Julien Binneteau reported on a number of households in the Illinois mission in which "husband and wife live in great fervor," setting moral examples for neighbors and advocating for the Jesuits against complaints by local shamans and "libertines." Some couples, too, regularly "assemble[d] in the cabin of one of the notable men of [their] village" to engage in extended "conversation" on spiritual matters. And some took needy children into their homes. Binneteau was sure to note that some couples who did this were mixed—the husbands French and the wives Illinois—and could readily serve as "a good example to the best regulated households in France."[57]

Important as marriages of different standing within the Church were to the missions, the Jesuits also encouraged some individuals to embrace strict Catholic standards of chastity outside the context of married life. A subtext regarding the socially elevated, even warrior-elite quality of such converts, especially women who fought off would-be seducers and rapists, is also present in missionary reports. A rhetoric of heroism, defense of personal honor, and warrior-like exertions of self-discipline and courage—indeed, classically aristocratic virtues—was central to Jesuit descriptions in this vein. For instance a woman of the Sillery mission was honored in the *Relation* of 1658 for the "courage of an Amazon" she exhibited while fending off a Frenchman who tried to rape her. The Jesuits attributed to her this narrative of the ordeal:

> Last night, this . . . crucifix [around my neck] saved my soul, which a French-man endeavored to ruin. . . . He took me by the hand, and . . . made me enter a house; then, suddenly and violently, threw me upon a bed. I at once began to cry out; repulsing him, I drew out my crucifix . . . and said to him in the heat of my anger: "Wretch! What do you seek to do? Do you wish to crucify again him who has given his blood and his life for you and me? If you do not fear to injure my honor, fear to offend him who may damn you. . . ." At these words, he loosened his hold, and, when I found myself delivered . . . I withdrew . . . into my cabin, and resolved to seek justice from the French captain.[58]

The anecdote underscores the woman's instinctive desire for "justice" from colonial authorities against her attacker. It is also reminiscent of a French Reform-era ideal of the chaste, devout gentlewoman who, while otherwise demure, was capable of almost manly self-assertion and defense of her own integrity when male protectors were nowhere to be found. Representative was Madame Miramion, later a foundress of religious organizations, who was imprisoned by the lustful comte de Bussy-Rabutin, Madame de Sévigné's cousin. A story went that when he was about to overcome her, she frightened him off with a bold profession of faith in divine retribution for sins such as rape. In the mission context we also find Chauchetière's later report that the "monster" of sexual "impurity," which began ravaging Iroquois society after the "introduction of liquor" by Europeans, "did not succeed" altogether because it was "vanquished" by many young women who "bravely" battled with it. Some women had even "been dragged into warehouses, where they were put to a choice," but they resisted sometimes by "striking blows upon the nose, and covering with shame and blood the faces" of men attacking them. Chauchetière likened such women to urban French *dévotes*: some of the women of "marriageable age" subjected to such experiences were, in the Sault-Saint-Louis reserve, otherwise "act[ing] like the Daughters of Mercy in France," busying themselves with "works of charity . . . for the poor and sick."[59]

Even very young Native American girls were capable of heroic behavior in the Jesuits' view. In 1671 Claude-Jean Allouez at the Mission de Saint-François-Xavier near Lake Michigan praised a teenager, Marie Movena, for the "courage" she demonstrated against her mother and stepbrother who sought to coerce her into a marriage with the latter. He did not appeal to Marie and he was not a Christian. Her will did not bend despite being subjected to beatings, denials of food, and even firebrand burns on her limbs by her own mother.[60] In an earlier *Relation,* a group of unmarried young women at Sillery were lauded for waving firebrands in the faces of several lusty young men who had asked them to spend the night with them in their cabins. "To be born into barbarism and act in this manner," a Jesuit author declared, "is to preach Jesus Christ boldly."[61]

The Jesuits, it should be noted, found such young men's modes of courtship to be rude, not just immoral because premarital sex was involved. The priests, familiar with European traditions of courtly love and ordinary French traditions such as organized *veillées* in which young men and women courted at dances, watched by family and friends, hoped Native American men would come to replace "rude way[s] of making love" with shows of gallantry, not just chastity.[62] Native American girls, then, who resisted—and *desired* to resist, whatever the consequences—certain kinds of advances, and encouraged others toward self-restraint and *sociabilité,* were assisting the Jesuits with a civilizing mission, not just the spread of Christian sexual ethics per se.

Frustrations with the Colonial French

As Dablon, Chauchetière, and other Jesuits rejoiced over diverse Native Americans who collaborated with the mission and the French imperial enterprise, they also penned sharply worded critiques of some Frenchmen. In 1694 Chauchetière stated to his brother in France that he and other missionaries desired to live "far away from the French with our beloved savages," who—"affable," "liberal," "moderate," and living "gently"— exhibited "fine remains of human nature which [was] entirely corrupt in civilized nations."[63] Likewise Jacques de Lamberville complained in a report of 1697 on the Mission de Saint-François Xavier near Montreal that local Frenchmen were causing "manifest injury to [a] nascent church, on account of the brandy" they sold to mission residents. French brandy traders were, in his view, motivated by "vile lucre" and unconcerned about destroying a "new vineyard of the Lord."[64]

Jesuit remarks in this vein have been viewed at times as evidence of deep ambivalence regarding an imperial project of North America's "Frenchification."[65] However, in their utopian overtones, they are out-lying remarks in the mission sources, uttered specifically in reference to the expanding brandy trade in New France and the attendant drunken-ness, brawling, and marital strife it generated in mission communities. Chauchetière otherwise supported the French colonial cause with some fervor.[66] Lamberville, too, was quite committed to the French imperial cause, especially the cultivation of community between mission Indians and the colony's morally and spiritually exemplary elites. In the same passage in which his condemnation of French love for "lucre" appears, the Jesuit also referred to the mission Iroquois' "happiness [in] becoming children of the Church and friends of the French," and he praised several French colonial elites as exemplary community leaders. These included a pious naval captain named Duluth; Marie-Madeleine de Chaspoux, wife of the colonial intendant; and Intendant Jean Bochart de Champigny himself, who was from a family devoted to royal service and who had recently installed an oversized bust of King Louis XIV, by Bernini, in the central market square of Quebec.[67]

The Jesuits opposed the brandy trade for two reasons that belie inter-pretations in an anti-imperial, civilization-escaping direction. First, the trade undermined their efforts to preach effectively even in their own mission stations, while at the same time eroding indigenous and acquired French forms of *civilité* in some Native American communities. Second, the brandy trade was like a cancerous growth in the heart of the French imperial enterprise they had long promoted, because it was spreading at the hands of Frenchmen that the Jesuits regarded as uncommitted to the political order and cultural values they identified with admired elites.

It was during Governor Frontenac's first term in office, beginning in 1672, that the brandy trade first became a plague to the missions. Frontenac adopted a liberal attitude toward it and to the opening of establishments offering liquor for sale. A Frenchman even opened a tavern at the La Prairie mission in 1673. The Jesuits could not stop him and felt betrayed by Frontenac. Chauchetière later noted that the French near La Prairie were specifically targeting mission Indians as customers, luring them toward a dependency on "drink" with Frontenac's full knowledge, despite the governor's earlier show of opposition to the trade.[68]

Brandy traders made inroads in Iroquois Country, too, during Frontenac's first term. Jesuits posted there wrote of the pernicious impact of alcohol, especially on young Iroquois men. They saw it as a threat both to Christianization and to indigenous *civilité* and social order as these had existed prior to contact with the French. Some Jesuits' lives were even endangered by young men who resented priestly moralizing against drunkenness and sexual sins (the latter of which the priests often blamed on the former). Carheil, for example, was at one point beaten and literally thrown out of the Cayuga village of Goiogouen by a group of hard-drinking residents. He later reported that village elders blamed the new disorders not simply on alcohol, but on the French generally.[69] This distressed Carheil, who at the time was concerned to cultivate effective military and trading partnerships for New France in Iroquois Country, as he would later do in the Pays d'en Haut.

By the early eighteenth century, the effects of the brandy trade on the missions were so extensive that the young priest Joseph-François Lafitau penned a memorial for the King's Council in 1718, detailing ways that the liquor trade was "entirely opposed to the well-being of the colony and of the state." He cited increases in fighting, domestic violence, and attendant marital breakups among mission Indians—some of them once great warriors and veteran allies of the French—who had succumbed to what later generations would identify as alcoholism. Significantly Lafitau informed the royal council that those who became addicted to alcohol would become so encumbered by financial debts to French creditors, who would "leave them not even their guns" when coming to collect, that they would sometimes flee to English territories—with their guns—to escape those pressing for repayment.[70]

For all their complaining about brandy and its effects on their missions, the Jesuits were not simply stern moralists—and certainly not teetotalers—where alcohol was concerned. In fact, in a letter of 1710, which included complaints to mission superior Joseph Germain about unscrupulous "tavern-keepers" who lured some Hurons into their establishments, the Jesuit D'Avaugour remarked on the excessive scrupulosity of some mission Indians who would not even accept "a goblet of wine offered to them" in friendship by the governor-general of New France. The missionaries even encouraged Native children to drink wine on festive occasions, a custom common in many elite French households. Furthermore the Jesuits supported plans for a central, government-controlled brewery in Quebec, which they believed would cause "a decrease in the use of intoxicating drinks" of high, unregulated alcohol content.[71]

We should keep in mind, too, that spirits such as brandy were almost as new to the French in the seventeenth century as they were to Native Americans. The Jesuits' reactions to them thus do not represent simply a form of clerical puritanism toward a phenomenon somehow typifying worldly civilization. Spirits were for the most part unknown in France before 1600, when the rise of the brandy trade began providing peasants and the urban poor with a cheaper alternative to wine and local beers and ciders than was traditionally available.[72] In short, the Jesuits' reaction to the trade in New France was part of a larger transatlantic story of French governmental, civic, and religious efforts to regulate a new trade and its impact on diverse communities.

Another problem the Jesuits had with the trade in New France was that brandy was peddled by a class of men the Jesuits generally disapproved—motivated more by profit than by a commitment to orderly community among French and Indians alike. Furthermore various Jesuit reports reveal frustration that, in some mission stations close to French settlements, military garrisons, and licensed trading posts, behaviors such as brawling, prostitution, and domestic violence—all of which the missionaries generally blamed on drunkenness—went unpoliced by the very authorities the missionaries had long identified with French *civilité* and service to the Bourbon state.

Effective policing of behaviors around missions by royally designated authorities was a primary goal of Jesuit complaints against brandy and some of the colonial French. This explains why the Jesuits wrote with special vehemence when agents of French power—for example, soldiers garrisoned near missions—appeared to disregard not only Christian morality, but also the values of French civilization. Carheil in 1702, for instance, demanded of Governor Callières that he intervene against French officers involved in the brandy trade and in the prostitution of Indian women for local Frenchmen near Michilimackinac. Carheil was disgusted that the French officers, of all people, sanctioned those "two infamous sorts of commerce" so much that "by their example . . . a general permission and assurance of impunity [were] assumed, [causing] them to become common to all the French who [came] to trade." The Native villages around Michilimackinac had become, in Carheil's words, "only taverns, as regards drunkenness; and sodoms, as regards immorality." But beyond this, the brandy trade and prostitution were also "injur[ing] . . . the ordinary trade of the voyageurs," or the licensed French fur traders who had to compete with others who skirted the law. Ironically, though, when the Jesuits dared to speak out against the vicious trades, *they* would be cast by leading officers as "opposing the King's service," insofar as they were "endeavoring to prevent a trade that he [had] permitted."[73] His exasperation over this quite evident, Carheil tried to convince the governor that the officers themselves were serving only their own interests, not the king's, and trying to deceive colonial authorities by framing the Jesuits with accusations of disloyalty to France, even to the point of demanding the missionaries be tried in court!

Carheil went on to complain to Callières that the king was being grossly misinformed about the state of New France and the missions. To punctuate his point he threatened to close down the mission at Michilimackinac and others and "abandon them to the brandy traders."[74] When no policing of the brandy traders and related disorders followed, the Jesuits made good on this threat. In 1705 they burned down their mission at Michilimackinac and departed for other areas with its Christian residents. This gained Louis XIV's attention: he ordered the reconstitution of the mission at the valuable location, under the leadership of Marest.[75]

In contrast with their portrayals of colonial leaders they regarded as renegades from the French imperial cause, the missionaries praised leading Native Americans—not always baptized Christians—who assisted in the moral and social policing of their villages. Frémin and Chauchetière noted the help of several Iroquois "captains" at La Prairie in "combating the vice of drunkenness." The Jesuits at Sillery, too, highlighted ways in which leading "captains" such as Étienne Neketucant proactively defended the village against imports of liquor by French traders. Neketucant, who was not yet baptized at the time, "displayed such fervor" in the year 1681, according to Jacques Bigot, when "repressing some disorders caused by drunkenness." He did this in one instance by taking an armed companion with him, another mission resident named François Xavier Haurawerunt, and warning at gunpoint a crew of French and Indian traders, who had arrived from Acadie, that they were not to set foot near Sillery if they had any plans to sell liquor.[76]

Jesuit reports of victories against the brandy trade were rare, however. Its destructive impact on indigenous communities was notorious by the time mission procureur Pierre-François-Xavier de Charlevoix produced his *Histoire et Description Générale de la Nouvelle-France* in the 1740s. He noted, for example, that a brief period of "seven or eight months" had been more than enough time to make a substantial number of Sault-Saint-Louis residents—who had taken refuge in Montreal during the Nine Years' War—"unrecognizable, both as regards morals and piety," due to the impact on their lives of heavy drinking and attendant sexual libertinage, as practiced by some of the colonists. Charlevoix went so far as to lament that the "fervor" those mission Indians had once displayed, to the "edification and admiration of New France," was virtually extinguished, because they had had "too much" social interaction with the French.[77]

Charlevoix, although he was writing decades after many of the events described in the *Histoire*, offered important perspective on the missionaries' purposes in trying to regulate contact between mission Indians and the French in general, not only brandy traders. He looked back on the earlier tensions between some colonial authorities and the Jesuits over the matter of "Frenchification," penning the following remarks on the missionaries' approach especially with regard to the Iroquois and Abenaki reserves near Montreal:

> His Majesty's Council . . . were convinced that [the Jesuits'] zeal was neither weak nor blind. The intercourse kept up by their neophytes with their relatives had no object but to people their [missions] with new proselytes, that is to say, diminish the number of [France's] enemies, and increase that of our allies, as daily happened. It was even admitted that the colony had no better soldiers than those who were in this way detached from the [Iroquois] cantons, and that the town at the Sault was one of its strongest bulwarks. . . .
>
> Experience, not of ten years but of more than a century, has taught us that the worst system of governing these people and maintaining them in our interest, is to bring them in contact with the French, whom they would have esteemed more, had they seen them less closely.
>
> In fine, there was no longer any doubt that the best mode of Christianizing them, was to avoid Frenchifying them. . . . The example of the Abénaqui nations, much further removed from the French settlements and whose attachment to our interest could go no further, alone sufficed to convince [Frontenac] of the fallacy of his principle. His complaints and his advice were little regarded at Court, where they were at last persuaded that his project [of Indian assimilation in the French settlements] was neither useful nor practicable.[78]

Far from trying to separate the Christianization of Native Americans from the French imperial project, the missionaries were on the contrary concerned that too much exposure to the French would adversely affect mission warriors and traders' opinions of the French, alienating them from earlier commitments to aid New France as allies. Moreover, in addition to monitoring the process of Frenchification in their mission stations, ensuring that only the right kinds of French influences were present, the Jesuits were concerned that the mission Indians not be Frenchified too much, so to speak, to the point that they would no longer be effective cross-cultural go-betweens upon whom the French could depend to expand their reach and eventual domination further out in Indian Country.

This calls to mind a colonial strategy of gradual, controlled assimilation seen closer to our own time in the modern French Third Republic's *mission civilisatrice*. Writing of colonial Algeria, for example, Fanny Colonna has described a practice whereby the best indigenous graduates of schools intended to "civilize" them were not to become *too* assimilated with the French, but rather to function in the colonial system as effective mediators between their home culture and the imperial French one.[79] In New France, centuries earlier, the missionaries did not want Christian conversion and assimilation to render mission Indians *too* gentle or docile—much as they valued such traits—to the point that they became ineffective warriors in a context of frequent conflicts that threatened New France and its allies. Rather, the Jesuits sought to preserve the warrior ethos and particular customs of indigenous peoples while reorienting them, as possible, away from the interests of the tribe per se and toward the defense and extension of a wider Indian-French and increasingly Catholic community.[80]

In the Jesuits' view, assimilation with the French was especially counterproductive to empire where it vitiated the spirit of self-discipline and controlled martial ardor characteristic of a strong warrior-elite class. Such a class was needed not only to effectively defend New France but also to help to lead the colony's social development along the lines of the aristocratic, urbane society the missionaries most valued in France itself. Furthermore, French authorities themselves thwarted the imperial project not only by a lack of commitment to effective policing but with heavy-handed, haphazard efforts to subdue mission Indians—by installing French garrisons among them, especially—when the latter sometimes pulled back from military and trading commitments out of justified dissatisfaction with the French. There is evidence, especially from the early eighteenth century, that the Jesuits found such moves by French authorities not only corrosive of empire-building efforts, but also grossly insulting given the rank, dignity, and history of loyal service to New France of the mission's warrior elites and their families.

Consider, for example, the terms in which Lafitau, on behalf of the

Jesuits and elders of Sault-Saint-Louis, protested to the King's Council in 1722 a plan to reinstall a French garrison in the mission's vicinity that had previously been posted there. He paraphrased the complaints of the Sault's chief men: "Our wives and our daughters are not safe with the French soldiers. Our young men . . . follow but too willingly the bad examples before their eyes; and a thousand vices that were formerly unknown among us have unfortunately been introduced in our midst. . . . In addition . . . the soldiers frequently seek by false reports to embroil us with the officer, and the officer with the governors, none of which things happened when we had no garrison."[81] Not only had the French soldiers disrupted the "tranquility and good order" of the Sault and caused a friction between the mission Indians and the colonial officials that had not been there before, but the very presence of a garrison was an affront to the honor of local Indian warriors who had fought so well for the French in past wars. "After so striking a proof of our attachment," the Jesuits wrote further, in the voice of the warriors, "it is desired, contrary to the well-being of our village, to show that we are distrusted, which is very insulting to us."[82]

Tellingly the Jesuits asserted that the warriors of Sault-Saint-Louis would be far less affronted if French garrisons were placed in the vicinity of all other Indian missions. They objected, then, to any group of mission Indians being singled out—treated not only as "slaves" of the French officers they had regarded as "brothers" during wartime but also as less than the peers of other missions' residents, especially after having shown grit and loyalty on the battlefield. This, the Jesuits said on their behalf, was "too shameful to endure"—language they hoped would resonate with honor-conscious nobles of the King's Council (see fig. 6).[83]

The terms in which the Jesuits defended the Iroquois of Sault-Saint-Louis and likewise mission communities in the Pays d'en Haut, against heavy-handed colonial policies (including in later years punishments for trading with the English) suggest that they sought to secure and protect *privileges* of mission communities that were not unlike those enjoyed by various titled elites, municipalities, and corporate institutions in France. For example the *princes étrangères*, whose once-independent domains had been incorporated into the French kingdom over time, and many lower-ranking nobles across France, enjoyed special hunting rights and exemptions from certain taxes as well as from having royal troops quartered without consent on their estates.[84] Nobles and urban magistrates in France typically could negotiate the terms by which the king's soldiers would interact with the local gentry, let alone their own family members. Some cities and communes also enjoyed special rights and privileges under the ancien régime. The Jesuits appear to have been concerned to secure similar treatment by the Crown for mission communities and their leaders, especially when indigenous elders explicitly requested fair and honorable treatment by French authorities in exchange for services rendered.

The missionaries, in short, regarded some French policies as affronts to the honor and rank of leading Native Americans, especially veteran Christian warriors they saw as *peers*, not subordinates, of the officials who mistreated them—subject to the same king, but with accumulating privileges and rights to be respected. In the same vein mission communities that had demonstrated loyalty to New France should have been permitted some self-governance within the French empire and freedom to accept or reject particular colonial policies that impinged upon them. Therefore it was *because* of a commitment to an expanding French empire dominated by the Bourbon state, and by a rising class of meritorious elites, that the Jesuits came to insist on a culturally accommodating approach that, on its surface, appeared to some observers over time to be anti-French.

CHAPTER 7

Losing Paris

By the early eighteenth century, Jesuit missionaries labored throughout the vast extent of eastern North America claimed by France. By 1710 there were nineteen permanent mission stations and several "flying missions," or mobile missions by which Jesuits followed along with hunter-gatherers' seasonal migrations.[1] Some missions were underdeveloped compared to Sault-Saint-Louis and the others close to Montreal and Quebec. And a handful of Jesuits, beginning with Paul du Ru in 1700, had traveled far afield of the Saint Lawrence and the Pays d'en Haut and were laboring in Lower Louisiana. They were based in New Orleans, which was incorporated in 1718. By 1724 this Louisiana mission was formally separated from its mother mission to New France. Jesuits based at New Orleans and at Kaskaskia in Illinois Country were thereafter answerable to their own major superior, not to Quebec.[2]

Despite its development since the founding era a century before, this network of missions was not the Christianizing success it had been intended to become. Nor was it the vanguard of the vigorously expanding French empire the missionaries had long envisioned. In the Saint Lawrence region, although the ethnically French population had increased considerably since the late seventeenth century, Quebec and Montreal remained modest by French standards. Settlers beyond them lived far from each other in isolated farmhouses or in small hamlets that dotted the landscape.[3] Colonial Louisiana was even less developed, despite momentary enthusiasm in Paris and at the courts of Louis XIV and the regent duc d'Orléans to build it up as a plantation colony after the fashion of Saint-Domingue and Martinique. Disappointed by this, Pierre-François-Xavier de Charlevoix, while serving as procureur for the Jesuits' American missions in both New France and Louisiana, lamented that the French had not forcibly taken more lands in the vicinity of the Lower Mississippi Valley, which had been neglected for decades by Spain. In his *Histoire et Description Générale de la Nouvelle France*, the Jesuit averred that France might have secured "all of the Gulf of Mexico" had there been the will, but that his countrymen, giving in to "lethargy," failed to consider "the fertility of the soil" there or the strategic benefits of "establishing a naval station in the Gulf."[4]

Several factors in the metropolitan, institutional development of the Jesuit enterprise in North America contributed to its declining fortunes in the late seventeenth and early eighteenth centuries. These included two events in the 1670s: the abrupt cessation of Chez Cramoisy's publication of the *Relations* and the relocation of the French royal court from Paris to Versailles. From the 1670s onward mission leaders had more difficulty reaching lay elites of Paris and officials at court with timely requests and news from New France. At the same time they had to compete for metropolitan attention more than in the past with, on the one hand, officials in the expanding colonial bureaucracy who did not always share the Jesuits' interests and, on the other, a corps of new writers on New France and other colonies and trading zones, including missionaries from rival orders.

Additionally the missionaries and their procureurs were plagued over time by a frosty relationship with the upper echelons of their own Jesuit bureaucracy headquartered in Paris. A contentious legal battle even played out over several decades involving funds originally set aside for the mission but diverted by leading Parisian Jesuits to projects within France. In fact, by the latter half of the seventeenth century, the mission to New France was a low priority among senior Jesuits of the French assistancy. This adversely affected the mission's staffing and financing. And it exacerbated the difficulty of securing steady support for projects in New France from lay officials and elites, who were increasingly presented with other investment and charitable opportunities in France's expanding overseas empire.

Finally, the cultural shifts of the early Enlightenment were transforming the priorities and social profile of the French officials and elites that the missionaries counted on for support. Crown officials and lay elites, especially in Paris, were becoming less preoccupied with religion and the afterlife than their parents and grandparents had been. They were no longer flocking to confraternities such as the Marian congregation at Église Saint-Louis, which had been critical to the mission's development in the era of Le Jeune and Cramoisy. Furthermore, elites who looked to profit from overseas ventures were less scrupulous than in the past about the profit motive itself. There was less pressure to invest only in colonial projects bound up with Christian proselytization efforts.

Resigned to these trends, some Jesuits attempted to spark new French interest in North America through publication efforts that, to a degree, shared in the zeitgeist of the literary clubs and salons. Joseph-François Lafitau's *Moeurs des Sauvages Amériquains* (1724) was among them. Charlevoix's *Histoire* also sought to renew elite interest in financial opportunities in North America. Some missionaries also tried to reach influential men of information and science through articles on discoveries in the natural world in North America, published for example in the *Mémoires de Trévoux*, an academic journal edited by Jesuits in Paris. Despite such efforts, well before the mid-century Seven Years' War and the shocking suppression of the Society of Jesus in France, most Jesuits of the mission understood that the heyday of intensive French interest in Catholic missions and colonial expansion in North America was long over.

The End of the Cramoisy Relations

During Louis XIV's long reign, from 1643 to 1715, French Catholicism became a truly worldwide presence. Among new missions launched at the time were the first French Dominican efforts in the Caribbean, those of Saint Vincent de Paul's Congrégation de la Mission in North Africa and Madagascar, and the early forays of the Société des Missions Étrangères de Paris (MEP) in East and Southeast Asia, Persia, and North America.

They were the fruit in part of new pressure put on Pope Alexander VII by the French Crown and elites such as the duchesse d'Aiguillon to begin breaking up the long-standing Iberian monopolies on mission fields around the world.

Even as he secured papal approval for French global expansion, a saber-rattling Louis affronted Alexander on another front. He seized the long-protected papal enclave of Avignon. He also attempted to install a magnificent equestrian statue of himself by Bernini between the Piazza di Spagna and Trinità dei Monti in Rome. Of course, Alexander opposed this and—with his Corsican guardsmen firing guns at Louis's ambassador and his men in 1662—rejected French assertions of diplomatic immunity for the vicinity of the French embassy at the Palazzo Farnese. Louis furthermore pushed for the nomination of more French cardinals at the Vatican. Alexander, and Clement IX and Clement X after him, retaliated by stalling French ecclesiastical appointments.[5]

The strain between Louis and the papacy put the Jesuits in both France and New France in an awkward position when in 1673 the Vatican newly required all prospective publications on Catholic missions to be approved by Propaganda Fide in Rome. The following year, mission procureur Paul Ragueneau and the printer Sébastien Mabre-Cramoisy—grandson and heir of the more famous Sébastien Cramoisy—had to choose between pleasing the king, by publishing that year's *Relation*, or displeasing him, either by submitting the planned book for Vatican review or not publishing it at all. They chose the last option as the only way to honor the king's opposition to Roman interference while also honoring Pope Clement X's new rule that was set forth in *Creditae Nobis Caelitus*.[6]

Although this papal brief mentioned the Jesuits by name, it was a general instruction for the Church, occasioned by squabbles between missionaries in East and South Asia. This was the era of the Chinese and Malabar rites controversies over the toleration of particular, indigenous rituals—such as the veneration of ancestors—by Jesuit missionaries in the tradition of Matteo Ricci and Roberto de Nobili. When issuing the brief, Clement had in mind a cessation of polemical volleys among Jesuits, Dominicans, Franciscans, and Augustinians regarding mission approaches in China and India. Unfortunately the Cramoisy *Relations* were caught in the crosshairs of the new requirement and royal displeasure with it.[7]

Published annually for more than four decades in Paris, the *Relations* by 1673 had survived their chief architects, Paul Le Jeune and the elder Cramoisy, by several years. Le Jeune had died in Paris on August 7, 1664. He was seventy-one and had spent his last years as a spiritual director primarily for women religious. Some of his spiritual advice to these women was published after his death.[8] Cramoisy, for his part, had handed over his publishing empire to his grandson in 1660.[9] Nevertheless he remained active in charitable endeavors, sitting on the board of the new Hôpital Général de Paris, serving as a liaison between French donors and the Hospitalières in Quebec, and taking up several new royal appointments. In 1656 he had been selected as director of the Dépôt des Publications at the Bibliothèque du Roy at the Louvre, the original incarnation of today's Bibliothèque Nationale de France. And in 1660 he was made Garde des Poinçons du Roy, or Keeper of the King's Stamps.[10] He filled these posts until his death on January 29, 1669, at the age of eighty-three.

In the meantime, young Mabre-Cramoisy had continued to publish the *Relations* in the same format as they had always appeared, ensuring what was for the era a striking consistency of form and quality for a book series of long standing.[11] The success of the series after four decades was undeniable. Their publisher and the Jesuits had every intention of carrying it forward at the time *Creditae Nobis Caelitus* was promulgated.

The *Relation* Mabre-Cramoisy published in 1673 bore no indication that it was the final installment of the series. It began with news about a new Huron mission, Notre-Dame de Foy, also known as Lorette and later the home of indigenous Christian warriors such as Thaovenhosen. It included reports of a journey to the Hudson Bay by a young colonial officer, Paul Denys de Saint-Simon, and the Jesuit Charles Albanel. The Jesuits indicated their hopes that the French would compete for furs in that region against the new Hudson's Bay Company, recently established by English traders in 1670.[12] Elsewhere in the *Relation*, Dablon wrote positively about Intendant Jean Talon's effort to discover overland routes to the Pacific, which would give the French in America access to China and

Japan. And the mission superior made it clear that he supported a policy of French naval expansion and further exploitation of North America's natural resources, such as copper in the vicinity of Lake Superior.[13]

Dablon planned to follow up on such matters with the French public in a *Relation* of 1674 as well as to detail the progress of the Jesuits' missions. But Ragueneau and Mabre-Cramoisy chose not to risk a breach with royal authority by submitting the text to the Vatican for approbation. This was logical, given how dependent the missionaries were on royal support.

By 1680 the mission fathers were in an awkward position as the king let it be known that he missed the Cramoisy *Relations* and wanted the series revived. While a drafted *Relation* was being prepared, General Oliva in Rome reiterated to Louis's confessor, the Jesuit François de La Chaise, that new *Relations* would be subject to prepublication Vatican authorization. La Chaise confirmed that this would be unacceptable to both the king and the Parlement de Paris.[14] So the series fully expired. That La Chaise himself was within a few years veritably at war with the general himself, regarding his loyalty to Louis XIV over the pope, only cemented the unlikelihood that the mission procureurs would ever be free to submit renewed installments of the *Relations* to authorities in Rome.[15]

The end of the *Relations* left the missionaries and Parisian procureurs in a position of having to address French officials and elites solely through private channels, one by one. Timely transatlantic communications had been challenging enough. The difficulty was further compounded by Louis's removal of the court to Versailles, some twelve miles from the Jesuits' headquarters in Paris. This transition unfolded over the years 1678–82, which were critical years for New France as the Iroquois Wars were renewed just as the French were opening new trade and missions in the Pays d'en Haut. Furthermore Louis's government consisted of an increasingly elaborate, layered bureaucracy, requiring missionaries and other colonial leaders to communicate needs through a chain of subordinates, clients, and, sometimes, relatives of France's secretaries of state.[16] By 1715 this bureaucracy included a new layer for colonial matters, the Conseil de la Marine, created by the younger Pontchartrain.

Thus when seeking royal support for particular projects, the Jesuits in

North America were more dependent than ever before on the amplification of their interests by colonial officials who were regularly in communication with secretaries of the Marine, who themselves had to compete for the king's ear at Versailles. But officials including Governor Frontenac and Secretary Colbert did not always share the missionaries' vision for New France. The Jesuits in the meantime were only sometimes successful in cultivating new ties with courtly elites. Several notables and royal councillors who did become friends of the mission in this era were Bernardin Gigault de Bellefonds, marshal of France, and Louis XIV's official court historian, Paul Pelisson, who was later abbot of Cluny. Both helped secure state funds for medical needs in the Jesuits' mission stations. Another supportive figure was Esprit Cabart de Villermont, who served for a time as a governor in colonial Cayenne and then on Louis's royal council. He maintained regular correspondence with several missionaries, including Jacques Gravier at Michilimackinac and Thierry Beschefer, mission superior from 1680 to 1704 and thereafter Parisian procureur. Villermont was also in touch with merchants and soldiers in New France. His correspondence with Beschefer devoted ample space to the colony's strategic position and military fortunes during the late seventeenth-century wars against the Iroquois and English.[17]

Even when the Jesuits secured royal funds or decrees in their favor, sources hint at a frustratingly slow, bureaucratized process. For example, in 1714 Pierre Cholenec requested funds from the colonial governor to relocate the Sault-Saint-Louis mission further up the Saint Lawrence and to fortify the new village. He had to follow up the next year with the colonial intendant to see whether the funds had formally been requested yet from the Crown. The intendant then communicated by letter in late 1715 with the new Conseil de la Marine, which finally approved in April 1716 an outlay of 2,000 francs for Sault-Saint-Louis. This amount, slow in reaching Cholenec, was much less than the Jesuit had asked for, even though the Conseil was aware that the fortress alone would cost 4,000 francs.[18]

Some of the mission's needs in this period were met by private outlays from French elites. The Jesuits maintained good relations with colonial officials' family members who resided in France, such as Marie Grisande de

Prouville, the daughter of Commander Prouville de Tracy. She made sure in 1672 that a major loan her father had intended for the Jesuits' Collège de Québec was transferred from Paris following his death.[19] Another patron of the mission was Marguerite d'Alégre, the marquise de Baugé, who was part of a noble family of Anjou and especially generous to the Abenaki mission. However, few names stand out from the records of the period as reliable donors on a par with the Ventadours, the Gamaches, Sillery, and others from the mission's founding era.

Adding to their communication difficulties, missionaries were unable without the *Relations* to quickly counter negative reports about their enterprise that began circulating in courtly circles toward the end of the seventeenth century. One critic was a clerk for the royal navy named Robert Challes, a Parisian better known for his travel writings on India, who had spent part of the 1680s engaged with the fur trade in Acadie. In Canada he formed a poor opinion of the Jesuits and later alleged to French political and mercantile elites that the Jesuits were to blame for New France's neglect. He charged them with having joined in with a group of deceitful "flatterers" earlier in the seventeenth century who had encouraged the Crown to invest more in Canada's fur trade than in agriculture and other sectors. He additionally accused the missionaries of caring more for profits than for Native American conversions.[20]

Negative reports were also disseminated by the Franciscan Récollets, the Jesuits' old missionary rivals for New France. At the request of Governor Frontenac, who was partial to them, the Récollets were able to return to North America in 1673 after a nearly fifty-year absence. They established a new mission at Port-Royal in Acadie and a friary in Montreal, and they relieved the Sulpicians of a stalling Iroquois mission at Kenté in southern Ontario.[21] In the early years of this revived mission, the Récollets, under the name of Friar Chrestien Le Clercq, produced a history of missionary activity in North America entitled *Le Premier Établissement de la Foi dans la Nouvelle-France*. Published in Paris in 1691, it deliberately defamed the Jesuits, claiming that, despite decades of Jesuit labor in New France, there was yet "scarcely any Christianity among the Indians, except some individuals . . . who would willingly abandon their religion for a mere nothing in the way of interest."[22] The book was immediately popular and was republished several times.

Because of the freeze on the *Relations*, the Jesuits were unable to respond quickly to such charges before a wide audience. The Récollets' book and other negative reports damaged the mission's reputation at a time when its staff and diversifying ministries were more dependent than ever on the goodwill of moneyed French elites and officials at Versailles.

By the early eighteenth century, with French officers returning from the North American theater of the War of the Spanish Succession and with the opening of the Lower Mississippi to French exploration and trade, more publications by lay authors began to appear on North American subjects. In addition, following the formal settlement of the Chinese Rites controversy in 1704, there was a renewal of French publication efforts by missionaries generally. Indeed, new reports by Jesuits posted around the world began appearing regularly from Parisian presses. But the mission to New France would not benefit significantly from this renaissance.

A House Divided

The mission's development over time was also influenced by an institutionalized bifurcation, within the Jesuit bureaucracy in France, between fundraising and staffing efforts for American ministries and those for increasingly voguish efforts in the Levant and East Asia. Relatedly, the mission's finances were at times limited more than they ought to have been by favoritism shown to other French Jesuit ministries by leading Jesuits of the Province of Paris.

Up to the 1650s the mission to New France enjoyed crown jewel status among the numerous ministries run by the Province of Paris. In 1653 a Jesuit advocating for a new French mission to Southeast Asia could justly complain—as Alexandre de Rhodes did from Avignon, earning only a rebuke from General Nickel in return—that the Society's leadership in Paris was reserving significant manpower for North America while giving little thought to other prospective mission fields.[23] However, by 1656 leading French Jesuits were seeking to downgrade the privileged status the Canadian mission had enjoyed since Richelieu's time. Parisian provincial Louis Cellot, for example, attempted to convince Nickel that his confreres in Canada were excessively caught up in trade and other worldly matters, even alleging that they were tolerating rampant prostitution in New France.[24]

Cellot planned by the summer of 1656 to reassign Le Jeune to an unglamorous post at the Rouen novitiate, terminating his development work for the Canadian enterprise. But Nickel intervened, reconfirming Le Jeune as mission procureur and, in a Christmas letter to mission superior Jean de Quen, expressing unwavering support for the Jesuits of New France. The following year Nickel also urged Cellot to press harder in Paris for the royal nomination of a bishop for New France, suggesting Cellot had been negligent in the matter.[25]

Cellot's successor as Parisian provincial, Jacques Renault, attempted to downgrade the Canadian mission a different way. He created a new office, *procureur général*, to supervise development for all French Jesuit missions abroad. The priest chosen for the post, Jean de Brisacier, would have authority over Le Jeune and funds raised for the American missions while prioritizing new French Jesuit efforts in Vietnam, the Ottoman Empire, and—it was hoped—China and India. Brisacier had useful connections with Jesuits of other nations laboring in Southeast Asia, as well as Portuguese diplomats and merchants, due to his time as the Society's visitor to the court of King João IV of Portugal.[26]

Renault favored Brisacier and new missions in Asia in part because young Jesuits by the 1650s were no longer requesting American postings with great enthusiasm. Instead the Levant and East Asia seemed more exotic and dangerous—and therefore attractive—to those with adventure in mind.[27] Renault thus wished to de-prioritize the comparatively well-staffed and well-funded mission to New France and focus new resources elsewhere. There was also hope that, as Le Jeune approached his last years, a procureur position devoted exclusively to American missions might be phased out.

Le Jeune objected to Renault's scheme and petitioned Nickel to preserve the independence of his office and of the North American mission. The scheme would be disastrous, he argued, because Brisacier had no experience with Canada and was unknown to important benefactors in France. In contrast, Le Jeune himself had spent years cultivating support at the French court, in Parisian society, and beyond the capital region.[28] Le Jeune further argued that Brisacier would alienate priests of the Société de Saint-Sulpice, who had just begun their own mission in New France in 1657 and with whom Jesuits in the colony and in Paris were building new relationships. Le Jeune's communications with Nickel were followed by others from François-Joseph Le Mercier and Paul Ragueneau in Quebec, who argued that Brisacier's imminent power over their enterprise would constitute a major setback for Christianization in North America.[29]

Nickel settled the matter by institutionalizing a division between development activities for the American missions and those for any Asian enterprises of the Province of Paris. In a letter of October 27, 1659, he insisted that Le Jeune retain his position as procureur in Paris—equal, not subordinate to, the new procureur for other French Jesuit missions—and that Brisacier take up the latter position and focus on existing and future French Jesuit ministries in Asia.[30]

This short-term victory for the mission to New France spawned a new rivalry between Jesuits seeking support for Asian versus American endeavors. It also occasioned new opportunities for favoritism toward the Asian missions by officials at the Maison Professe, especially when it came to financing projects and selecting candidates for mission posts. Some of the last *Relations* expressed grievances in this vein. At the beginning of the installment for 1669, for example, Le Mercier called upon Provincial Estienne Dechamps to send more missionaries to New France, implying there was a shortage of manpower that the Province of Paris could easily remedy.[31]

Factional divisions between Jesuits in Paris that had little to do with overseas missions per se may have factored into the tensions over the procureur positions. At a time when French Catholics were splitting into camps over Jansenism, Brisacier was a bold critic of the movement. In his book *Jansenisme Confondu* (1651), for instance, he attacked the nuns of Port-Royal as "mad virgins" who rejected the sacraments of the Church.[32] By the end of the decade he had authored several anti-Jansenist works, advancing the claim, among others, that the Jansenists were crypto-Calvinists. One of these books, published in 1657, was coauthored with François Annat, who was soon after chosen as Parisian provincial, and Claude de Lingendes, who had just served in the same office.[33]

Brisacier may have been favored by provincial leaders, then, as a new face for the Jesuit overseas missions in Paris while the latter were being defamed in the Jansenist press. Pascal, for one, in his *Lettres Provinciales,* accused Jesuit missionaries of a merely "human and political [*politique*]" attitude in their work, and of preaching "only a glorious . . . and not a suffering Jesus Christ." Pascal also charged Jesuits overseas with breaking from traditional points of Christian social teaching, such as the ancient condemnation of profiteering and the principle that the wealthy, when they had a "superfluity" of means, were duty bound to give significant alms to the poor.[34] Compared to Brisacier, Le Jeune and the Jesuits of New France had baggage in this area, given their longtime partnerships with colonial merchants, landholdings in Canada, and gentle coaxing of French elites to contribute some of their pocket change to the poor in North America.

Evidence of tension between provincial leaders and the Jesuits of New France is found in the paper trail of an ugly legal battle that took decades to resolve, transpiring over the years 1660–1720. At issue was a trust fund that had been set up for ministries in Quebec but that for many years was dipped into by the fathers at the Maison Professe for other projects of the Province of Paris.

Acting as a corporation, the Canadian mission in 1649 had purchased a small building that had belonged to the Maison Professe on the Rue Saint-Antoine in Paris. The missionaries originally hoped to use it to house a sister establishment of the Collège de Québec, to facilitate exchanges of students based in Paris and the colonial capital. Years earlier, the mission fathers had received a substantial gift from the Gamaches family, with the understanding that they would use it to develop the colonial college after the fashion of Jesuit schools in Europe. That college was to be used for educating young French colonials and, where practicable, Native American boys. It was also supposed to become a house of formation for young

Jesuits who would themselves teach at the college while completing higher studies there. But as late as 1660 the house on the Rue Saint-Antoine was run-down and not serving the colonial college as intended. Le Jeune informed the Jesuit general at the time that an anonymous layman was willing to renovate the building for the missionaries out of pocket, so long as his family might retain rights of use.[35]

Le Jeune required permission from General Nickel to go ahead with the plan, because he was running into opposition with his provincial and Brisacier at the Maison Professe. And sure enough, these Jesuits countered with a request that Nickel forbid Le Jeune from proceeding, on the grounds that the procureur for the American missions had no authority over the property. To Le Jeune's chagrin Brisacier obtained an order from Rome that Le Jeune hold off until the general further reviewed the matter.[36]

Tensions increased when, later that year, the fathers at the Maison Professe began charging mortgage payments on the property—to be paid with monies from the Gamaches trust earmarked for the Canadian mission. They claimed that the Maison Professe had never been paid for an original sale of the building. Additionally for years the Maison Professe was remiss in transferring to the mission fathers funds paid by the Gamaches since 1635.[37]

In 1666 Ragueneau, who had succeeded Le Jeune as procureur, attempted to persuade the Parisian provincial of the injustice of all this, but he was pressured into signing a contract by which the Maison Professe would retain ownership of the disputed property. The contract stipulated further that the Canadian mission was to pay 2,340 livres annually in rent payments—even as the mission fathers claimed the Maison Professe owed *them* annual payments of 2,787 livres from the Gamaches trust![38]

In short the mission fathers believed they were being robbed, by their own provincial leaders, of more than 5,100 livres annually. Ragueneau thus sought legal restitution. He showed the contract he had signed to members of the Parlement de Paris, who agreed that its terms, given the history the Jesuit told them, were unjust. But their opinion at that time did not nullify the contract.

Ragueneau complained that the funds owed to the mission were desperately needed in Quebec. According to one of his statements to the parlementaires, the fathers who resided at the Collège de Québec in the 1660s lived in a state of poverty "without equal" at any of the Jesuit colleges in France. They had no bedsheets and their meals consisted mostly of eels and occasionally mutton and even cowhide in place of beef. In Ragueneau's opinion the professed fathers in Paris, knowing the condition in which their colonial confreres were living, were acting without any "justice, charity, or prudence."[39]

Infighting between the mission procureurs and the Maison Professe over money and the building in the Marais continued for many decades. As late as 1720 mission fathers were still trying to access funds they were owed and to assert rights over the contested property. At this time Lafitau, who would serve as mission procureur himself a decade later, authored an account of the long-standing dispute after securing an order by the Jesuit general at the time, Michelangelo Tamburini, that the Maison Professe reimburse monies owed since the middle of seventeenth century.[40] In that order the general specified that the Maison Professe had to pay the missionaries 150,000 livres. This was much less than the mission fathers believed they were owed. By that time they calculated they were owed more than 600,000 livres, given all the improvements they had put into the Marais building, the losses owed in equity over many decades' worth of unjust embezzlement, and the inflation of French coinage since the mid-1600s.[41]

By the time Lafitau wrote his report, bad blood between factions of Jesuits within the Province of Paris was the last thing the mission needed. Unity was essential to adequately meet larger challenges mission developers faced in the metropole. First, the secularizing culture of elite, urban France was making support for overseas missions more of an afterthought than ever before, even among pious French Catholics with money and position. Second, there was growing indifference toward the value of colonies such as New France—let alone its indigenous inhabitants—to the expanding Bourbon state. Lafitau and other Jesuits of the mission attempted to navigate these difficulties in creative ways. But their efforts would be crippled by internecine Jesuit divisions that had hardened since the 1660s.

At the time the Jesuits in North America were preoccupied with the War of the Spanish Succession and its impact on their missions, they were attacked from an unexpected quarter in Europe. A layman who had served as a military officer in New France, Louis-Armand de Lahontan, targeted the missionaries in his book *Dialogues de M. le Baron de Lahontan et d'un Sauvage* (1703). Published in The Hague to skirt French Catholic censors, the book was widely circulated in France and favored in early Paris salons. In it Lahontan presented a rationalist critique of both Christianity and European cultural norms, including private property, through a fictional Huron mouthpiece named Adario.

Lahontan concentrated not on Jesuit dogmatism or fanaticism in preaching to Native Americans at the risk of their own lives, as we might expect from an Enlightenment-era critic. Rather, through Adario, Lahontan accused the missionaries of being as worldly-minded as French laymen involved in colonial development. Amplifying claims sounded by critics of the mission in the past, Lahontan suggested the Jesuits had pecuniary motives not only for propagating Christianity in America, but also for communicating it in ways adapted to indigenous cultures. As the fictional Huron sage Adario put it, "The Jesuits of Paris . . . have 'yours' and 'mine' . . . like the French; they are as acquainted with money as the French; and since they are more brutal and self-interested than the French it is not strange that they approve the manners of peoples who treat them with . . . friendship, and . . . give them presents."[42]

Unlike when the Récollets' damaging portrayal of the missionaries appeared in Paris, there was by this time a public forum at hand in which the Jesuits could counter Lahontan. Since 1701 a group of French Jesuits had been publishing a scholarly periodical, the *Mémoires de Trévoux*. An anonymous Jesuit thus took on Lahontan in its pages. However, as a sign of the times—if not an admission that there were grains of truth in Adario's words—the reviewer chose not to set the record straight about the missionaries per se. Rather, he attacked the messenger, alerting readers to Lahontan's skepticism regarding hallowed Christian doctrines and his ambivalence about French institutions: "Not only is it difficult to guess if [Lahontan] is Catholic or Protestant; one struggles to be persuaded that he is even a Christian. . . . He tears France apart, he rages against those powers most worthy of respect."[43]

Unfortunately for the Jesuits, the review in the *Mémoires de Trévoux* only brought more attention to Lahontan's writings, which already had the gleam of forbidden fruit. The growing popularity of the *Dialogues*, together with the defensive tone of the Jesuit reviewer, illustrates a new challenge mission developers faced by the early eighteenth century. French literate elites were growing more skeptical regarding the Catholic Church and its clergy. They were also growing more curious about the religious and philosophical traditions of parts of the world Christianity had not yet transformed. Even Christianity's old rival Islam suddenly seemed new and exciting, at least as it was inflected through orientalist literature such as Galland's French translation of *A Thousand and One Nights* (1704) and Montesquieu's *Lettres Persanes* (1721).[44] In aristocratic circles where Mass attendance perdured, some newly questioned the need to spread Christianity overseas. And in 1722 the duchesse d'Orléans memorably claimed that hardly a hundred people in Paris—priests included!—still believed in Christ's divinity.[45] She was greatly exaggerating, of course, but the fact that such a remark could circulate through high society as *un bon mot* illustrates the trending spread of blasé attitudes toward Catholicism and its universal mission.

Jesuit sources of the early eighteenth century evince concern that, even among French Catholics supportive in principle of overseas proselytization, pessimism had set in regarding the fruit a near-century-old mission could bear. Louis D'Avaugour, for example, acknowledged in 1710 to his superior Joseph Germain that there were many in France who believed "the soil of Canada [was] thoroughly sterile . . . that the heralds of the Gospel reap[ed] therefrom hardly any fruit in return for long and painful labor." But to disabuse others of that opinion, he highlighted conversions he had seen in his own mission of Lorette while counterproductively downplaying the success of other mission stations staffed by his confreres.[46]

Another challenging reality for early eighteenth-century mission procureurs was that, even in wealthy families in which Catholic piety was strong, less attention was being paid to otherworldly matters day to day. French Catholic elites in the period thought less often, and less anxiously, than their parents and grandparents had done about the destiny of their immortal souls. Symptomatic was a marked decline in end-of-life bequests to religious institutions. In this environment, foreign missions halfway across the globe could not compete well for donations alongside convents, charitable hospitals and schools, and other Catholic ministries more present to elites in their home environs.[47]

Relatedly, young men of talent, family, and ambition were not answering calls to the priesthood and religious life as often as their counterparts of previous generations had done. Although France's population grew from twenty-one million to twenty-five million between 1700 and 1770, the number of clergymen serving this population declined over the same period.[48] While young French and Francophone Belgian Jesuits were still being sent to North American posts with regularity up to the eve of the Seven Years' War, the mission was affected by the decline in vocations in Europe. Despite the presence of Lazarists, Oratorians, and numerous regular and secular clergymen throughout France, Jesuits were increasingly needed in parochial capacities, not only as confessors and educators, to meet the demand. Fewer members of the Society of Jesus, therefore, could be spared for permanent North American assignments, especially in an era of increasing competition for assignments in Asia.

The need for Jesuits to remain in France is apparent from the changing contours of missionaries' career trajectories in the early eighteenth century. Permanent American assignments, generally following candidates' ordinations to the priesthood, were common in the seventeenth century. This pattern continued into the eighteenth century, but over time there was also an increase in the percentage of Jesuits assigned to North America early on in their formation—sometimes before priestly ordinations, which would take place in Quebec—who then were called back to France to fill ordinary posts as teachers and ministers to French souls. Among the men sent to North America between 1715 and 1745, thirty out of eighty-three—more than a third—were recalled to France after a limited time overseas. And the average and median age of those men at the time of their return journeys was thirty-nine.[49]

One of these men, Pierre Nicolas Le Chéron d'Incarville, would, after sixteen years in Canada and a brief stint back home in France, go on to a missionary assignment and career in botany at the court of the Qianlong emperor in China. Several others would have illustrious careers in France. Lafitau was one of these: in his thirties the Bordeaux native spent six years among the Iroquois, primarily at Sault-Saint-Louis, before pursuing back home his famous work of analyzing, in proto-ethnographic terms, the North American societies he had encountered in Canada. Less well known was Jean Dumas, who spent fourteen years in Canada before returning to his native Lyons in his early forties to teach. Eventually he was appointed to the Société Royale de Lyons for his research in astronomy.[50] His work in geography and music also left an historical footprint.[51]

Beyond the impacts of broad cultural trends on the mission, the Society of Jesus itself experienced mounting opposition to its existence within France. On the one hand, there was a revival of Jansenism among French elites following the publication of both the final volumes of Antoine Arnauld's *Morale Pratique des Jésuites* (1692) and the papal condemnation of Pasquier Quesnel's teachings in the bull *Unigenitus* (1713). Not long after, in Montesquieu's *Lettres Persanes*, the Jesuits were lampooned for their didactic mode of combating Jansenist ideas and other positions they deemed heretical. On the other hand, the Jesuits' position within the French church—especially under Louis-Antoine de Noailles, the cardinal archbishop of Paris—was newly tenuous after 1700, when the Sorbonne condemned the Society for the Chinese Rites controversies while the Assemblée du Clergé, drawing upon Jansenist critiques, accused the Jesuits of promoting lax morality through their teaching.[52]

The Society was also falling out of favor with Louis XIV. As Catherine Northeast has explained in *The Parisian Jesuits and the Enlightenment* (1991), "The King's [increasing] desire to stifle religious dissent" in the wake of the Jansenist revival and his earlier revocation of the Edict of Nantes "meant that Jesuit controversialists became for the first time victims of royal displeasure."[53] This was despite the fact that Jesuits had been loyally serving the Crown as propagandists, as they had since Henry IV's time. Exemplary was Jean Étienne de Londel, whose dedication to Louis in *Les Fastes de Louis Le Grand* (1694) celebrated the king's military victories and compared his empire to ancient Rome's, claiming no other modern empire had approached its glory.[54] Unsurprisingly, waning royal favor led to decreased patronage for Jesuit publications, including on overseas missions.[55]

The declining prestige of the Jesuits in France, even in traditionally enthusiastic circles, is evidenced by a drop-off, by 1720, in aristocratic membership in the urban confraternities that had traditionally fertilized elite collaboration with the missionaries in North America. Louis Châtellier has documented the decline in the Congrégation des Messieurs de Paris, the confraternity in which Cramoisy, Sublet de Noyers, and others of the mission's founding era had been active. While the Messieurs de Paris who met regularly at Église Saint-Louis had been drawing about ten new upper bourgeois and noble members a year between 1670 and 1700, that average dropped to five per year in the ensuing decades. By the middle of the eighteenth century the Jesuits' confraternity for Parisian gentlemen welcomed one or two new members per year. A similar drop-off was seen in the Rouen congregation.[56]

Despite all this, the form of metropolitan indifference most noted by eighteenth-century Jesuits of the mission had little to do with religious and cultural trends. Rather, they tended to highlight French elites' tendency to underestimate New France's economic and strategic value to France itself. Charlevoix, for instance, noted that when the security of Acadie was in doubt during the War of the Spanish Succession, French officials were far less "attentive to the preservation of this province" than the British were to "taking steps to reduce it." Louis XIV's naval forces had arrived too late to save Acadie during the Siege of Port Royal in 1710. As a result, "a colony [that] might [have] in a short time become the source of the greatest trade" in the French empire was instead supplying the British with shiploads of codfish and other commodities. The Jesuit lamented that, even though the British had not succeeded in conquering the whole region, they nevertheless, through more enterprising behavior than his countrymen's, had "found means to enrich themselves by it, while we ourselves derived no advantage."[57] Likewise, after the French had reestablished trade in the Pays d'en Haut following a wartime hiatus, metropolitan officials failed to take the proactive step of exporting more manufactured goods to New France in order to lower prices for Native American traders in the region. Subsequently even residents of the Jesuits' missions who tended toward loyal trading partnerships with the French began taking their furs to Anglo-American markets, where they found better deals. Undervaluing the fur trade in North America, the French in Charlevoix's assessment had let it slip "almost exclusively in[to] the hands of the English," even as the French had developed trading relationships in places that would have allowed them to take greater advantage of it and simultaneously strengthen military and cultural ties with western Indian nations.[58]

Where new French interest in North America was piqued in the era, it was concentrated on Lower Louisiana, especially following the incorporation of New Orleans in 1718 and the reincarnation of an original merchant company for the region as the Compagnie des Indes. Notoriously, however, the Scotsman John Law, controller-general of finances during the regency of the duc d'Orléans, merged this company with several others involved in French overseas ventures *and* with a private bank he established that, remarkably, was guaranteed by the faith and credit of the Crown and christened La Banque Royale. The speculative frenzy that Law engendered in France promised returns as high as 200 percent annually on investments in prospective trading and mining ventures in the Mississippi Valley. But after the disastrous bursting of this "Mississippi Bubble" in 1720 and the French financial collapse that resulted, badly burned investors were naturally reluctant to get involved in North American enterprises. Safer bets for investors were to be found instead in the Caribbean, where after the War of the Spanish Succession the French had been able to corner the slave trade markets frequented by Spanish colonial purchasers. In addition, through the exploitation of their own slaves, French planters in Martinique and Saint-Domingue were seeing remarkable increases in sugar production and sales in Atlantic markets.[59]

Jesuits wishing to renew French metropolitan interest in North American development and missions were fully cognizant of these trends. Indeed some were close observers of the Caribbean: Charlevoix, notably, had spent time in Saint-Domingue following exploratory work he did for the Crown in North America in the 1710s. In his *Histoire de l'Isle Espagnole ou de S. Domingue* (1730), the future mission procureur and historian of New France studied economic and political factors in Saint-Domingue. Apparently untroubled by the slavery system there, Charlevoix praised the French naval secretary, Jean-Frédéric Phélypeaux de Maurepas, for overseeing the colony's emergence as "the richest and the most beautiful establishment that our [French] nation has in the New World."[60] As Jesuit publications on North America reappeared in the eighteenth century, writers including Charlevoix would attempt to attract French officials and investors to the missionary enterprise by appealing to economic opportunity and imperial state formation. Their success in this vein would prove to be quite limited, however.

Renewed Publishing Efforts for the Mission

It was amid the aftershocks of the Mississippi disaster that Lafitau's *Moeurs des Sauvages Amériquains* appeared from the Parisian presses of Saugrain the Elder, then best known as the publisher of a multivolume *Histoire Ecclésiastique* by the royal confessor Claude Fleury. *Moeurs* was an unusual book. In addition to being a seminal work of what would later be called modern ethnography, it was also the first new book in over fifty years to be authored by a Jesuit affiliated with the mission to New France.

In our own time, scholars have valued Lafitau's carefully wrought study of Native Americans' "virtues, talents," and broader cultural characteristics for the universalist anthropology and proto-ethnographic methodology it showcased and helped advance thereafter in academic discourses.[61] But *Moeurs* was not simply an intellectual exercise. With it Lafitau sought to revive French-elite interest in North America through creative comparisons of its indigenous societies with those of past centuries across the world, as the latter increasingly were coming to be known to Europeans through printed studies. In his preface, addressed to the regent of France, Lafitau proposed that the Natives of North America—including the Iroquois, whom he had gotten to know best during his time abroad and who had yet to submit to French rule—might still be of great "advantage" to the French "state" even after decades of lackluster French colonial efforts. However, the military, political, and economic service they might render would only be harnessed by those French elites willing to look beneath the Indians' "crude and uncultivated exterior" to see the inner, personal "resources" they possessed. These included "a love for their native land imprinted on their hearts, a natural passion for glory, a greatness of soul . . . at the test of peril," as well as an "impenetrable secrecy" when it came to sensitive political deliberations. The Natives of America also, in Lafitau's estimation, often demonstrated an "inborn scorn of death," something that was only "strengthened by training."[62]

Post-Enlightenment readers are disposed to interpret such language in light of discourses about the "noble savage." But what would have stood out more readily to the aristocratic readership that Lafitau addressed was a more concrete suggestion. That is, that there were many men and women across the Atlantic, who despite their "savage" language, dress, and customs were in their natural substances, so to speak, *like themselves*—like Europe's upper classes, traditional and newly rising, whether of noble ancestry or rewarded natural merit. Lafitau asked his readers to look beyond prejudices they may have harbored regarding surface-level qualities of indigenous American societies and to see that the people possessed, in abundance, personal qualities such as a "natural passion for glory" and a stoic attitude toward death—virtues that made them fit, for example, for military command and other forms of royal service. As Lafitau had gotten to know them, there were men and women in America's Eastern Woodlands who were capable of rare forms of courage, honorable and discreet service to rulers, patrons, or military commanders, beneficence toward their communities, and steadfast love of country. In elite Europeans' discourses about their own claims to govern others, such traits were the special marks of the *best* men, the first men of their nations—the men from among whom even kings chose their friends and confidants. Lafitau's purpose in elaborating on Native American cultural characteristics and "natural" qualities was not simply to encourage his contemporaries to respect the Natives of America as fellow human beings. He wished for public-spirited French elites to respect North America's Natives as potential fellow servants of the expanding Bourbon state, understood to be transatlantic in reach.

Lafitau's *Moeurs* was one of several items put forward in print by Jesuits affiliated with the mission in the early eighteenth century. But compared to the earlier Cramoisy *Relations* these publications appeared irregularly from various publishers. This may seem surprising in view of the efflorescence of French Jesuit journalism and printed missionary reportage in the Enlightenment era, as represented by two new series produced in France. These were the *Mémoires de Trévoux*, the monthly periodical launched in 1701, and the *Lettres Édifiantes et Curieuses*, a thirty-four-volume series launched in Paris in 1703 and featuring numerous missionary reports, mostly by French Jesuits, from all over the world.

The first of these, formally entitled *Mémoires pour l'Histoire des Sciences & des Beaux Arts*, was the brainchild of Jesuits Jacques-Philippe Lallemant—a formidable opponent of the Jansenists—and Michel Le Tellier. It was funded by the duc de Maine, one of Louis XIV's illegitimate sons.[63] First published in Trévoux near Lyons, it was from 1733 onward produced in Paris. Initially its aim was modest: to summarize new and notable books in a range of subject areas. However, the journal soon included broad-based evaluations of new works across the arts and sciences, often giving favorable if qualified reviews on the writings of *philosophes,* including eventually Diderot and D'Alembert.[64] Given the diversity of subjects treated in the *Mémoires*, the limited material in it concerning French North America tended to get lost in the shuffle. The editors furthermore were often preoccupied with Jansenism and therefore gave ample attention to relevant works on theological and philosophical controversy. The *Mémoires* as a result was not a go-to periodical for men of affairs at court or in mercantile and financial sectors interested in investment opportunities overseas.

At any rate, very little appeared in the *Mémoires de Trévoux* specifically related to New France and its missions. Among the few items that did was an article on astronomical observations by a Jesuit of the mission named Joseph-Pierre de Bonnécamps.[65] Not coincidentally this article appeared in the March 1747 issue of the journal during Charlevoix's tenure as mission procureur. Charlevoix had until recently been serving as the leading editor of that journal in Paris and therefore encouraged inclusion of Bonnécamps's findings.

By contrast, when the first volume of the *Lettres Édifiantes et Curieuses, Écrites des Missions Étrangères* first appeared in Paris, renewed potential for regularly reaching the French public about the mission was suddenly on the horizon. The series was conceived by a Jesuit named Charles Le Gobien and would see great success as a publishing venture through the eighteenth century. Not a veteran missionary himself, Le Gobien was a native of Saint-Malo who had taught philosophy at Alençon before being invited to Paris by the fathers at the Maison Professe to fill an administrative post that allowed him to pursue writing and editing projects. Chief among these was the *Lettres Édifiantes* series that continued to be published long after his death in 1708 under the direction of Jean-Baptiste du Halde, Louis Patouillet, and other Jesuits.[66]

But the launch of this new series was not a boon for the missionaries in North America. Their letters only occasionally made it into the volumes published almost annually by various printers, including P.G. Le Mercier and Nicolas Le Clerc, and not by a single house like Cramoisy's. But this lack of attention to North America by the editors was unsurprising, considering that the *Lettres Édifiantes* arose in the context of Le Gobien's administrative work, first as a secretary and then as procureur général, for the French Jesuits' Asian missions. In other words, Le Gobien was professionally the heir of Brisacier at the Maison Professe, not of Le Jeune and Ragueneau. The *Lettres* thus reflected the primarily Eastern preoccupations of its editors. Du Halde, for his part, while editing the series from 1709 to 1743, was much absorbed with the history and culture of China and thus with missionary correspondence from that part of the world. He is still today best known for his monumental work in this vein, the several-volume *Description Géographique, Historique, Chronologique, Politique et Physique de l'Empire de la Chine at de la Tartarie Chinoise* (1735)—a study admired by the philosophes Montesquieu and Voltaire.[67]

Over the many decades the series was published, only ten letters from New France and Louisiana were included in its volumes. Their inclusion stemmed from good relationships several procureurs for the American missions had with the fathers affiliated with the Eastern missions. The first two letters from North America to appear in the *Lettres Édifiantes* did so during Jean de Lamberville's tenure as procureur of the American missions, a post he held from 1692 until his death in 1714. Lamberville was close friends with a French Jesuit named Jean de Fontenay who was affiliated with the mission to China. Corresponding with him earlier in his career, Lamberville had expressed great hope that French Jesuits in China would pique interest in Christianity at the court of the Kangxi emperor "by means of the sciences," in the tradition of Matteo Ricci. He noted his sorrow, too, over the "persecution" suffered by the Jesuits in China at the hands of other European Catholics for their pioneering position in the Rites controversy.[68]

Several more reports, by the missionary Pierre Cholenec, appeared in the *Lettres* during the subsequent tenure of August Le Blanc as procureur. Le Blanc, too, was a mediating figure for the missionaries in New France and Parisian Jesuits preoccupied with Asia. In addition to serving briefly in Canada earlier in his career, he had also served in Istanbul, Armenia, and the Aegean Islands.[69] Six more letters then appeared during the tenure of Louis D'Avaugour in the same office, over the years 1720–32; another appeared later on during the Seven Years' War, when a veteran missionary and former professor of mathematics at the Collège de Québec, Charles Mesaiger, was metropolitan procureur.[70]

A key difference between these ten letters and the *Relations* of the previous century is that publication of the letters often occurred years after the events described in them had taken place. For example, the first letter from Canada to appear in the series, by the missionary Gabriel Marest and addressed to the procureur Lamberville, conveyed a full decade after they had been written the Jesuit's impressions during 1694 and 1695 of the region around Hudson Bay and the tensions there between the French and English over trade with local Natives. Marest had accompanied the French commander Pierre Le Moyne d'Iberville and his troops into the region, serving as a chaplain and interpreter during a mission to establish new trade and to capture York Factory, a strategically located English fur-trading post. This was in the midst of the Nine Years' War. Although the French public learned of Marest's still relevant impressions of the different Native American groups in the region, including his opinion that some were more amenable than others to Christian instruction, that public also received primarily a *relation* about the momentary success but ultimate failure of that French military and trading expedition, well after the Nine Years' War had given way to the War of the Spanish Succession.[71]

Another letter by Marest chosen for the collection, penned in Kaskaskia and dated November 9, 1712, sought to disabuse French readers of any impression that New France was full of towns and villages. It also painted a gloomy portrait of most of the Native American nations of the Illinois Country—except for the Illinois themselves, who were praised for their openness to the French—for example with the remark, "Reason must be greatly brutalized in these people." Furthermore it downplayed the appeal of the region, claiming it was far less "enchanting" than had recently been represented to the French in a published work by Henri de Tonti, a Sicilian explorer who had accompanied the Sieur de La Salle in some of his travels earlier in the previous century.[72]

Other letters from North America appearing in the *Lettres Édifiantes* were by or about Sébastien Râle, a missionary who worked primarily among the Abenakis and who is remembered for his role in the Fourth Anglo-Abenaki War—also known, indeed, as Râle's War—of 1722–25. The French public was treated to the sometimes remarkable events of French Jesuit and Christian Indian war-making against the Protestant New Englanders, many years after the fact. Although one of the letters by Râle himself appeared in relatively timely fashion in the volume for 1726 along with an account of his death in 1724, authored by a confrere, another of Râle's letters appeared in print in Paris years later in 1738.[73]

It was in the context of such haphazard, flagging attempts by mission procureurs to reach the French public that Charlevoix, following his own appointment to the position, produced his monumental *Histoire et Description Générale de la Nouvelle France*. It appeared from the presses of Rollin and the widow Ganeau two years into the Jesuit's seven-year tenure as procureur for the American missions. That he was able to complete such a monumental work while serving in the office of procureur, and while preoccupied with other publishing projects having nothing to do with North America, illustrates the degree to which the missions in Canada and the Great Lakes had become more of an academic concern than an active, administrative preoccupation, even to metropolitan Jesuits assigned to their upkeep. These other projects included another monumental work of history—a six-volume work on Paraguay—and ongoing service as a contributing editor to the *Mémoires de Trévoux*.[74]

Yet the *Histoire* was more than a narrative of North American events of the increasingly distant past. It was also, to a significant measure, Charlevoix's critique of French imperial policy and economic practice in North America in the early decades of the eighteenth century. Embedded in historical narratives and lengthy primary source excerpts from Jesuits and French officials were many practical suggestions for how the French might salvage what appeared to many to be a sinking colonial ship.

Charlevoix was critical of French officials and investors who had failed to take, by force, territories that had been neglected by Spain around the Gulf of Mexico. He argued further that the French had an opportunity to develop such spaces as productive farmlands and strategic sites for naval stations. In his critique the Jesuit blamed what he saw as a "get rich quick" mentality that led those who were disappointed by low initial returns to swing back into a general "lethargy" regarding the labor and patience needed for long-term development ventures. Some French interest, he noted, had been momentarily piqued by news of great "mines [in] New Mexico, and . . . in Lou[i]siana itself," but when it became evident after a few years "that this country produced neither gold nor silver, and that it was not easy to make the wealth, which New Spain possessed within it . . . the province fell under general censure." The Jesuit hoped his readers might, unlike other Frenchmen in the past, newly consider "the fertility of the soil" and the value to France's Atlantic empire of new naval bases in the region.[75]

Charlevoix was more than simply critical of his countrymen for what they had allowed to go to waste in North America. He offered what were for the time economically sophisticated explanations for some of the past financial losses the French had experienced in both New France and Louisiana. He also proposed ways the French could still correct structural problems and take new advantage of existing resources. He identified, for example, a trade imbalance that existed between France and New France, suggesting that the Crown had benefited more from the colony in the past when it was willing to invest more resources there:

> The King expends in that colony a hundred thousand crowns a year: the furs are worth about two hundred and eighty thousand livres; the oils and other minor products bring in twenty thousand livres; the pensions on the royal treasury paid by the King to individuals, and the revenues held by the bishop and seminaries in France, amount to fifty thousand francs. This makes six hundred and fifty thousand livres, on which all New France rolls. On this sum alone can it conduct its trade [with both Indian nations and the mother country]. . . . Its affairs were formerly on a better footing, the King spending a great deal more there; it shipped beaver to France to the amount of about a million, and was not so thickly settled; but it always drew more than it was able to pay, which ruined its credit with mercantile men, who are in our days not disposed to send goods to Canadian merchants without letters of exchange or a good security.[76]

The mission procureur's belief was that even though New France was seen as a dead weight on the French Atlantic economy, its now more sizable population, enlarged by both French settlement and expanded indigenous alliances through the Jesuits' missions, might begin to prove its long-term economic potential for the empire. However, Charlevoix insisted that, if New France was to become more productive for France, French creditors needed to act indulgently toward quarters of its population who were in debt to metropolitan firms or who were being drawn toward Anglo-American markets by lower prices. He recommended some forgiveness of debts by French creditors and more investment by French leaders in the form of royal funds for colonial ventures—including missions—and greater volumes of manufactured goods shipped from France, in order to present Native American and Franco-American traders alike with more competitive French prices.

Charlevoix offered other suggestions for New France's further development, hoping French officials and merchants might abandon what he saw as an old-fashioned mentality that colonies should not be permitted to develop manufacturing and export markets of their own. Cape Breton, for instance, had over the previous decades flagged in its potential as a highly productive, "natural entrepôt between Old and New France" because of a lack of sufficient investment capital to develop its fisheries and its "oil, coal, plaster, [and] timber" industries. Also problematic were restrictions—by overly "fearful" metropolitan authorities—on the liberty of Cape Breton and the Laurentian colony to conduct trade in finished, not just raw, commodities, semi-independently from the French Atlantic system. On this point the Jesuit sought to quiet the concerns of metropolitan elites that a liberalization of colonial economic activity would mean losses of wealth for France itself: "Profit made by Canada . . . will always return to the profit of the kingdom . . . New France cannot dispense with many articles from France. It will then draw a larger quantity and pay for them with the money which Cape Breton will give for its produce. . . . [And] it would be no great evil to France, if it did not export so much wheat or other things for maintaining life, for the cheaper provisions are, the more workmen it will have for its manufactures."[77]

Beyond this Charlevoix held out hope to metropolitan elites that, through more targeted investment and a looser regulatory hand, New France might come to assist France in penetrating Anglo-American colonial markets with its national specialty goods. He was confident especially that merchants in New England, Virginia, and elsewhere would be lured into regularly purchasing from Franco-American traders of French "wines, brandies, linens, ribbons, taffetas," and other goods that would be newly available from a richer, developed version of New France.[78]

But coming from a Jesuit in 1744 and buried in a dense history of New France and its missions, such ideas were not received with enthusiasm at the French court or in the Paris salons as they might have been in a different cultural moment. Charlevoix's era was one of intensifying anti-Jesuitism in France and across Europe. If the Jesuits of New France had ever had a chance to turn French leaders toward economically smarter and militarily more aggressive involvement in North America, as well as renewed commitment to the country's Christianization, the eve of the Seven Years' War and the suppression of the Jesuit order was not that juncture.

CHAPTER 8

A Mission with No Empire

By the middle of the eighteenth century, Jesuits affiliated with the mission to New France often served for only a limited time when young as part of their formation before receiving ordinary assignments back home. One such Jesuit was Julien-François Dervillé from the Loire Valley. He had entered the Society of Jesus at eighteen in September 1744. Six years later he was sent to Canada, well before his ordination to the priesthood. He completed some of his studies at the Collège de Québec and then served briefly in physically and spiritually demanding settings of the overseas mission. Within three years he was back in France, multitasking as a priest, confessor, teacher, and administrator for the Society of Jesus.

However, early in his priesthood, while not yet forty, Dervillé was commanded by the Crown of France to sever ties with the order. He and numerous Jesuits complied reluctantly with this painful outcome of the French political suppression of the Society over 1763–64. Dervillé subsequently reported to the bishop of Orléans to make himself useful in his home diocese. Over the next few decades he worked quietly as a parish priest. This was far from the adventurous, cosmopolitan career he had had in mind when joining the Jesuits in his youth.

Forty years after his time in New France, the now elderly Dervillé met with a martyr's death—in the heart of what had so recently been Europe's "most Christian kingdom." In 1791 he refused to swear the oath of loyalty to the new, revolutionary French regime that was suddenly required of clergymen throughout the country. He then went into hiding, in the home of a former nun, and ministered to souls in secret. Eventually, in the autumn of 1793 when Maximilien Robespierre's Reign of Terror was underway, Dervillé—disguised in women's clothing while out of the house—was identified by a zealous *citoyen* and hauled before the Committee on Public Safety in Paris. He was swiftly tried, sentenced, and guillotined on December 22, 1793.[1]

The year Dervillé was murdered, a few elderly ex-Jesuits were laboring in Canada, permitted to perform basic functions of their priesthood by a new, British colonial government there. Three decades earlier in 1763, the same year the Parlement de Paris pressured King Louis XV to suppress the Jesuit order in France, the French imperial map had been dramatically redrawn at the conclusion of the Seven Years' War. France had lost all of Canada to Britain, and the Louisiana territory to Spain.

The final years of the mission and the last men to serve it have generally been passed over in accounts of the Jesuits and New France as if they were a sorry footnote to an otherwise intriguing historical drama.[2] One scholar has even written that most Jesuits of the mission over the whole of the eighteenth century were "old, worn-out men who had long since abandoned dreams of turning Indians into Frenchmen."[3] But there is more to say than this, as Dervillé's story hints.

As a coda to the previous chapters of this book, several snapshots, so to speak, of the last Jesuits of French North America are offered here to illustrate ways in which the last men of the mission stood solidly in the tradition of their elder confreres where their commitment to French empire was concerned. Highlighted especially are the martial activities of some Jesuits who labored in borderland regions of New France and Louisiana on the eve of the Seven Years' War and during the war itself. Also examined are representative experiences of several Jesuits of the mission who either returned to France, as Dervillé did during the era of the Suppression, or witnessed unto the final hours of their lives the slow demise of the mission as no longer a French imperial enterprise or even, formally, a Jesuit one.

In the summer of 1720, ten years after Acadie had fallen to the British at the end of Queen Anne's War, the Province of Massachusetts Bay put a price of 100 pounds sterling on the head of the French Jesuit Sébastien Râle, whom we encountered in the previous chapter. A force of three hundred men was called up to find the priest, bring him back dead or alive, and collect scalps for ransom from the Abenakis among whom Râle was ministering. Râle escaped from the mission at Norridgewock early in 1722 when some of the English rangers were near to capturing him, but only after quickly consuming the Eucharistic hosts that were reserved in the mission chapel to protect them from desecration by Protestant attackers.[4]

Râle was detested in Massachusetts because he encouraged the Abenakis and other indigenous allies of New France to harass Anglo-American settlers in the borderlands of Maine and Nova Scotia. This territory traditionally belonged to the Eastern Abenakis, many of whom had embraced Catholicism and fought alongside the French in the recent war against the British and rival Native groups. The Abenakis also traded with the French, fully aware they were passing up advantages that trade with New England would have brought them, as Râle himself acknowledged in a letter to his nephew in France.[5] Furthermore the recent peace between Britain and France, signed across the Atlantic at Utrecht, had not been a boon for the Eastern Abenakis. The formal cessation of conflict had only emboldened Anglo-American settlers, who believed—as the Abenakis and the French did not—that the Treaty of Utrecht had actually subjected the Abenakis and their lands to the British Crown.[6] From the time of the treaty's signing in 1713 through the 1720s, the most anti-English Abenaki village was Norridgewock, known to the French as Kennebec. It was situated in the interior of the present-day U.S. state of Maine. Râle had been assigned there as a young priest in 1694 after some time in Illinois Country.

Râle hailed from France's Franche-Comté region, a war-torn borderland not so unlike Abenaki territory. As a teenager in Pontarlier, near the Swiss border, Râle saw his homeland taken twice by Louis XIV's armies, in 1668 and 1674. He spent formative years, then, in a setting marked by bloodshed over contested national boundaries and by shifting loyalties among Franche-Comté elites, some of whom antagonized family and friends when they committed themselves to the Bourbon state.

Following the failed attempt to capture Râle in 1722, upwards of forty Abenaki warriors attacked, with the Jesuit's blessing, the English settlement of Merrymeeting, sixty miles south of Norridgewock. Some homes and a mill were torched, but the inhabitants were spared except for five who were kidnapped in hopes of an exchange for Abenakis then imprisoned in Boston. This "moderation" of the Abenakis, as Râle called it, "did not have the effect that they hoped," as a retaliatory English party attacked sixteen unprepared Abenakis on a nearby island, killing five and wounding three.[7] Several days later, on July 25, the region's governor in Boston declared war on the Abenakis on the pretense that they were "rebels and traitors" to the British Crown.[8] War soon spread across Maine and into Nova Scotia. More Abenakis joined the effort against the English, as did many fighters residing in other Jesuit mission stations, including the Huron mission of Lorette.

The conflict climaxed at the Battle of Norridgewock on August 23, 1724. It was essentially a raid by New England militiamen and Mohawk allies. They were determined to kill Râle. They succeeded. The sixty-seven-year-old priest was captured and riddled by musket fire. A report penned several months later by Pierre La Chasse, the Jesuit superior at Quebec, claimed that Râle had in his last moments "fearlessly appeared before the enemy" in order to "procure the safety of his flock," but that as soon as the New Englanders saw him "a storm of musket-shots . . . was poured upon him" and he died "at the foot of a large cross that he had erected in the midst of the village." Seven Abenakis, reportedly trying to protect the priest, were killed with him.[9] The Jesuit's corpse was then mutilated and his scalp sent to Boston for ransom. In the meantime, about eighty more Abenaki men, women, and children were massacred.

La Chasse's report, later published in Paris in the *Lettres Édifiantes*, cast Râle and the Abenakis who died at Norridgewock as martyrs for a purely religious cause. The Abenakis, the story went, fought against the English due to "their attachment to their religion," while the English had fought to "extend their rule" and because of their "hatred" of Râle's "ministry and . . . zeal in establishing the true faith."[10] But Râle himself, in letters to his nephew and brother in France, indicated many times that he and the Abenakis of Norridgewock were animated, too, by fraternal feelings of loyalty to the French and diverse mission Indians in the Saint Lawrence region. They had fought and died due to bonds of alliance with those who shared both their Catholic faith and long experiences of conflict with "enemies" they saw as illegitimately occupying hunting zones, fisheries, and planting grounds they regarded as their own.

Because of the way he died, Râle is the Jesuit most associated with the Fourth Abenaki War, which ended badly for the Abenakis. Following a peace affirmed at Falmouth in 1727, Anglo-American settlers once again pushed into Abenaki lands, this time without serious resistance. But this was not from lack of effort by other Jesuits to confirm the Abenakis in armed opposition to New England. Two Paris-trained Jesuits, Étienne Lauverjat and Joseph Aubery, stand out in this respect.

Born in Bourges in 1679, Lauverjat by 1718 was stationed at the Abenaki village of Panouamské in Maine. There he counseled village elders against permitting English settlement in the vicinity. But the English came and the village suffered a major raid in March 1723. As Panouamské was drawn into the Fourth Abenaki War, Lauverjat supplied intelligence on Abenaki and English movements to the governor of New France, who secretly supplied money and arms to the Eastern Abenakis to aid their stand against New England. A price was set in Boston for Lauverjat's scalp, but the Jesuit survived the war and went on to serve at a new Abenaki mission in what became the U.S. state of Vermont. In the new location the Jesuit continued to inform officials in Quebec of Abenaki and Anglo-American relations while cultivating pro-French feeling through his mission. Eventually he was rewarded for his service to New France with a home near this Vermont mission and a French Canadian parish, Saint-Denis.[11]

Aubery was a native of Gisors, in Upper Normandy, who had entered the Society of Jesus at seventeen in 1690. He completed his Jesuit formation in North America at the Collège de Québec, where he also taught before being sent to Acadie in 1701, after learning the Abenaki language.

He founded a mission at Médoctec in Nova Scotia, where he cultivated pro-French feeling, not only interest in Catholicism, toward the end of the War of the Spanish Succession. From Médoctec he also attempted through communications with Versailles to assist French authorities in demarcating a clearer boundary between New France and New England. He failed to convince the French to boldly incorporate all territory traditionally inhabited by the Abenakis. Thereafter Aubery played a prominent role in the Anglo-Abenaki wars, urging hostilities, not conciliation, between the Abenakis and New England. Enthusiastic when the Abenakis declared war in 1718, the Jesuit attempted, again fruitlessly, to convince French authorities to send troops to secure Abenaki territory for New France. He also maintained communication with Governor Vaudreuil during Râle's War. Even as the Fourth Abenaki War quieted down, he continued pressing for more war after 1725, frustrated by what he regarded as a French lack of initiative regarding the ongoing borderland tensions.

During this era of Anglo-Abenaki conflict, Jesuits were also active more than 1,600 miles away in Lower Louisiana, assisting French efforts to secure indigenous alliances and define borders and spheres of influence vis-à-vis the English. The latter were increasingly present in the region of the present-day U.S. state of Mississippi. The French had been active in the region since 1699, when Pierre Le Moyne d'Iberville, the first governor of Louisiana, founded a settlement called Biloxi. A second settlement called Mobile, in what became the state of Alabama, was established three years later. The Natchez were the Native American group most dominant in the region at the time. The Jesuits as well as priests of the Société des Missions Étrangères de Paris established missions among them.

With missionary encouragement the Natchez traded peacefully for a time with the French while doing the same with the Chickasaws to the north and the English from the Carolinas to the east. However, conflict arose between the Natchez and the French in the 1710s and 1720s. The French then received assistance against the Natchez from the Choctaws, a Muskogean-speaking nation that proved welcoming to the Jesuits. Subsequently, new hostilities opened between the French and the Chickasaws, who had absorbed some of the defeated Natchez into their communities and were assisted by English officers with commercial stakes in the outcome.

During these Chickasaw Wars of 1721–52, the French in Louisiana and their Choctaw allies launched military campaigns under the command of Jean-Baptiste Le Moyne, sieur de Bienville, brother to the first governor of Louisiana and several times colonial governor himself. Several Jesuits took part in these campaigns as interpreters and military chaplains for the French. These were Antoine Sénat, Michel Baudouin, and Pierre de Vitry—men who were committed both to spreading Catholicism among the region's Natives and to expanding French trade in Mississippi, even where it required war with the English-allied Chickasaws.

In 1724 the Jesuits' Louisiana mission was formally separated from its mother mission to New France. Jesuits thereafter based at New Orleans and Kaskaskia in Illinois Country were answerable to a major superior in New Orleans itself. Only a handful of men served in this independent mission prior to the suppression of the Society of Jesus in France. Sénat was one of these. A native of Auch in southwestern France, he trained as a Jesuit in Toulouse and was sent directly to Louisiana in 1733. He then spent several years in Illinois Country, engaged in ordinary missionary labors. This was not the post he had requested: earlier he had asked to be sent to Madagascar, China, Indonesia, or, barring that, to remain in France to teach.[12]

On March 25, 1736—the feast of Palm Sunday that year—Sénat and several French officers were captured during a failed French and allied Indian assault on a Chickasaw village. Forced to retreat when the well-positioned Chickasaws were joined by some allies, the French could not rescue Sénat and the other captives. Although the story may be apocryphal, some Frenchmen who survived later reported that Sénat had had a chance to escape but remained with the other captives to provide spiritual succor to them in their dire circumstances. In any event, the Jesuit perished among the Chickasaws. The women of the fortified village set a ceremonial fire, into which Sénat and his compatriots were thrown after being beaten and tortured in a gauntlet. The young priest reportedly led the captured officers in a hymn as they died as prisoners of war.[13]

Baudouin and Vitry escaped the sort of sudden, violent end in Indian Country suffered by Sénat, whom the Jesuits quickly honored as a martyr. Baudouin, notably, was one of only several Jesuits of the pre-Suppression missions in North America to have been born in New France. His father and brother, both named Gervais, were employed as doctors in Quebec, and several of his sisters became nuns. When as a young man he decided to join the Jesuits, Baudouin crossed the Atlantic to enter a house of novitiate in his ancestral province of Bordeaux, receiving an Old World cultural education as well as an academic one, according to the Jesuits' *ratio studiorum*. Returning to Quebec for his last years of formation and his ordination to the priesthood, Baudouin was assigned to teach for several years at the colonial college. But he was reassigned in 1728 to the newly independent mission in Louisiana.

The Jesuits at that time were just beginning to preach among the Choctaws. Baudouin cut his teeth as a missionary among this people, whom he encouraged to enter into trading and military alliances with the French.[14] After his first ten years in this mission, he was recruited by Governor Bienville to serve as a chaplain in renewed war against the Chickasaws. The Jesuit readily accepted the assignment, up to the climactic moment of the campaign—a two-hour battle on May 26, 1738, which resulted in heavy losses for the French and their allies.

The role Baudouin played in that engagement is curiously contested. According to several reports, he was not present to tend to the wounded during and after the battle because he had taken ill and was almost captured as the fighting commenced. However, a French officer present, Jean-François-Benjamin Dumont de Montigny, composed a lengthy, three-part poem about the campaign. In it he blamed the French humiliation by the Chickasaws not on Bienville's strategic miscalculations but on Baudouin's excessive zeal for the French imperial cause. Two key verses from the second of the poem's three *chants* translate as follows:

> With us, we had Baudouin, a chaplain.
> He was a Jesuit with an excellent mind,
> Who, by this special talent, had the advantage

Of having won over our leader. And by his lovely words,
He gave orders more than the latter. When such pastors
Command in a clash, nothing but evil results.
He suddenly gave the order—knowing nothing
Of the precautions of war—to attack the enemy.
But we had, I confess, a very bad time . . .

The banners flying, we marched rank by rank,
Forming a single body, crying: *Vive la France!*
Baudouin, our chaplain, with good reason,
Should have given us his benediction.
"Let's go," he said, "claim the victory,
Which offers nothing to you but the sheer glory
Of defeating the enemy, who by your mere appearance,
Will quickly surrender weapons to you and respect you.
I can assure you of this, and my experience
Without a doubt, gives me assurance of such facts."[15]

Dumont attempted to publish his poetry in France on the eve of the
Seven Years' War. His verses were deemed mediocre by editors who did,
nevertheless, publish his prose memoirs. The poetic portrayal of Baudouin
is noteworthy all the same, for it suggests that Dumont's intended audience would have found it plausible enough to be amused by the notion
that a Jesuit in North America would have raced headlong into a battle,
leading an army of French and Indian fighters, shouting "Vive la France!"

Baudouin himself went on to recover from his difficult experiences in
1738 and labor many more years in the Choctaw mission. He then served
as superior of the Jesuits of Louisiana and Illinois Country from 1749 to
1763. At the end of his tenure, he witnessed the destruction of his order's
mission network in the region by colonial authorities who enforced there
the French royal suppression of the Society of Jesus.

Spared from the sorrows of the Suppression due to his earlier death was
Vitry, who also served as a chaplain in the Chickasaw Wars. Training as
a Jesuit in Nancy, Langres, and Paris before crossing the Atlantic in 1733,

Vitry spent early years of his priesthood with Baudouin in the Choctaw mission but was then recruited for chaplaincy work in a French expedition to build fortresses and warehouses at the junction of the Mississippi and Arkansas rivers. Setting out in late 1738 from New Orleans with French and allied Indian soldiers and traders, Vitry was present for the christening of a new military outpost, Fort de L'Assomption, upon its completion on August 16, 1739, the day after the Marian feast it honored. Put under the special protection of the Blessed Virgin, it was built some seventy miles north of an original planned site in order to facilitate French attacks on the Chickasaws.[16]

Vitry kept a journal during the expedition. Through it we encounter a Jesuit who supported the mission of the soldiers he served and was prone to emotional responses to patriotic pomp and circumstance. He was pleased with what he assessed to be firm loyalty to the French seen among mission Indians who arrived at Fort de L'Assomption in October 1739 with contingents of French Canadian troops. They had been mustered with Jesuit assistance to help secure trade and French expansion in Mississippi. Vitry rhapsodized over the "splendid army" he saw, whose men "were anxious to find an opportunity to prove their warlike spirit."[17] He went on in his journal, "The canoes of the French and . . . Indians are intermingled. . . . It is a beautiful sight. Now we can hear their drums; after firing three volleys, they shout three times 'Long live the King.'" Vitry also approved of an address to French officers at Assomption by a leading mission Indian from Canada, which included the lines, "We love the King of the French, he is our father. The great chief of Canada [i.e., the governor-general] told us that you wanted to eat your enemies who are also ours. We saw our brothers, the French, leave to wage a war against them, and we have followed."[18]

Vitry's French imperial fervor and even militancy, along with his confidence in mission Indians to serve the French cause, was consistent with the mentality of previous generations of Jesuits in North America. Recounting some of the fighting that took place during the expedition, he cited the discipline of the Christianized mission Indians on and off the battlefield and noted, also, the heroism of a Native American woman who had urged on French-allied fighters in the midst of a battle. Furthermore he actively participated in negotiations between, on one side, the French and their allies and, on the other, the Chickasaws and theirs. And he wrote uncritically, in the first-person plural, when recording the terms of a stern warning issued by the French to the Chickasaws: "'Your lives are in your hands,' *we* answered, 'you know the greatness of the Frenchman's power. We have armed all the tribes against you.'"[19]

Not long after he wrote this Vitry was made superior of the Louisiana Jesuits, preceding Baudouin in the post. He would serve in the office until his death, one month shy of his forty-ninth birthday, in April 1749.

The French and Indian War

The early years of Baudouin's tenure as mission superior in New Orleans and those of Superior Jean-Baptiste de Saint-Pé's second term in Quebec, starting in 1754, were a hopeful time for Jesuits in North America. In Louisiana they had been joined by a favorite sister order, the Ursulines, who assisted the local civilizing mission in crucial ways, running a hospital for the poor and sick in New Orleans and schooling the growing population of young French and creole women there.[20] In Quebec Saint-Pé and other senior missionaries were joined by many young recruits. The majority were from the Jesuits' Province of Paris. Eighteen young men, half of them in their twenties when they made the journey, arrived in New France between 1750 and 1755 alone.[21]

Among them was a new priest named Jean-Baptiste La Brosse. He was the son of elite landowners in Jauldes in southwestern France. After training with the Jesuits at Bordeaux, he was sent to Canada and worked initially among the Abenakis and a population of French Canadian and métis Acadian refugees who by the summer of 1755 were on the run from the British. La Brosse was almost captured at this time, but he escaped to serve as a hospital chaplain in Quebec and missionary at Odanak. There, in the tradition of Râle, he worked to maintain pro-French feeling among the Abenakis, who remained important allies to the French at a time of new tension with Britain. Eventually La Brosse accompanied the Abenakis into battle, when they aided the French during the fateful siege of Quebec in the summer of 1759. He was taken prisoner at that time but was quickly freed, due to his status as a military chaplain.[22]

Less fortunate than La Brosse was another young Jesuit, Claude-François-Louis Virot, who also served as an army chaplain during the war. Born in Besançon in 1721, Virot entered the Society at Toulouse while still a teenager.[23] Arriving in Canada in 1752, he was soon assigned to the Iroquois mission of Sault-Saint-Louis and then the Abenaki mission at Odanak. In the summer of 1757, after hostilities had formally opened between France and Great Britain, Saint-Pé allowed him and twenty Abenakis to travel into the Ohio Country to preach to the Delawares at Sawhunk, in western Pennsylvania.[24] Ohio Country was another contested borderland in which the French, British, and Iroquois vied for trade and military alliances. As war broke out there Virot and the Abenaki troops got caught up in the hostilities. The Jesuit was soon enlisted as a chaplain for Captain Charles-Philippe Aubry and a force of French regulars, militia, and mission Indians who were called to relieve besieged troops at Fort Niagara north of present-day Buffalo, New York. On July 24, the day they planned to attack, some of the French-allied Indians already there, who included Iroquois Christians from the reserves near Montreal, dissembled and hoped to parlay with the Iroquois who were allied with the British. The French went forward without them alongside Abenaki and western mission residents known to Virot. The Jesuit was himself killed by an Iroquois warrior during the battle while trying to minister to fallen comrades—possibly upwards of 350 men on the French and mission Indian side, versus twelve dead and forty wounded among the British and Iroquois.[25]

This battle was a turning point in the French and Indian War that had opened up more auspiciously for the French several years earlier. The hostilities in North America had commenced in the Ohio Country at Fort Necessity in July 1754, well prior to the formal declaration of war by Great Britain against France in the spring of 1756. Famously this was due to the role played by a young Anglo-American colonel, George Washington. A battle was fought between an army of just under four hundred British colonials and militiamen, under the command of the overeager

Washington, and a larger force of French regulars, militia, and allied Native Americans, including mission Indians mustered by the Jesuits. This battle precipitated a larger global conflict, the outbreak of which resulted in the largest influx of professional French soldiers in the history of New France.

The contingent of four thousand troops that arrived following the events at Fort Necessity was the kind of force the Jesuits had hoped for decades would be sent from France during other periods of conflict. But the British sent twice as many men across the Atlantic for the same fight. Although the early phase of the war held promise that the French and their indigenous allies might finally secure New France against British and Iroquois threats, French fortunes turned for the worse by the summer of 1759. Not only did the French lose Niagara, but a devastating British siege of Quebec commenced in late June, at the time of General James Wolfe's arrival at the Île d'Orléans. It concluded with the Battle of the Plains of Abraham outside the city walls on September 13.[26]

During this three-month siege, the leading Jesuit in Québec, Saint-Pé— now seventy-two years old—escaped to Montreal with other religious and churchmen, including Bishop Henri-Marie Dubreil de Pontbriand. Other Jesuits, however, did what they could to aid the French cause at close range. Eighty-year-old Lauverjat, for example, returned from Abenaki territory and while residing at the Collège de Québec was arrested for trying to convince British troops to defect to the French side.[27] Several Jesuit chaplains, including La Brosse and a Belgian-trained priest named Charles Germain, accompanied contingents of allied Native American warriors from their missions to the besieged capital, tending to them medically and spiritually when wounded or near death. Germain, who had been born in Luxembourg in 1707 and who had arrived in Canada in 1739 after years of study and teaching in France, was a veteran mission chaplain by this point. He had served French troops in Acadie at the time of a momentary British capture of Fort Louisbourg, during the War of the Austrian Succession. Following the fall of Quebec, he returned to Acadie, where he tried to convince the Abenakis that a French victory was still on the horizon. Even after capitulating to British authorities in Nova Scotia in 1761, in order to remain with his mission, he was suspected of fomenting Indian resistance against the British and even, years later, of facilitating anti-British espionage among Abenakis during the American Revolution.[28]

A handful of Jesuits proved less loyal to the French cause than these men, especially as hostilities dragged on past the fall of Quebec even while it was clear that the British would be the new rulers in Canada and the Pays d'en Haut. For example, Pierre-Luc du Jaunay, a Paris-trained Jesuit who had spent many years at Michilimackinac, was by 1760 concerned to prevent the French, the Ottawas, and the Ojibwas in the vicinity from violently resisting British forces, preaching acceptance of the new regime. The Ojibwas rejected the message, however, and in June 1763 some of their warriors massacred British troops garrisoned at Michilimackinac. Endangering his own life, Du Jaunay went out of his way to provide shelter to surviving British soldiers and to negotiate the release of other British soldiers held by the Ottawa chief Pontiac, three hundred miles southward near Fort Detroit. Eventually, when the French and Indians at Michilimackinac were pressed by the local commander to affirm loyalty to the British Crown, the Jesuit was the first in line. His concern was to ensure British protection of his mission, but his superiors soon ordered him to leave the post in 1765. He obeyed, but not before celebrating more Catholic baptisms in the region.[29]

Most remarkable, however, is the story of a Jesuit who defected from the French to devote years of his life to working for the British. This was Pierre-Joseph-Antoine de Roubaud, who turned spy for the British toward the end of the war. In the process he renounced his priestly vows, his membership in the Society of Jesus, and even his Catholic faith. He was motivated initially, it seems, by disillusionment over his country-men's manner of prosecuting the war—including a culture of disrespect among the French-born officer corps toward the allied Native American fighters whom the Jesuits had done so much to cultivate through their missions. Indeed, throughout the war, elite French officers were divided over whether or not Native American allies were even needed to save New France from the British. The marquis de Montcalm, commander of the French forces, was especially reluctant to employ any "sauvages" alongside his aristocratic, professional officers—the latter of whose honor was imperiled enough, in his view, by having to fight alongside uncouth Canadian militiamen to defend the colony.[30]

Roubaud observed firsthand many instances of French mistreatment of mission Indians, especially the Abenakis, whom he got to know during a brief period of years as a missionary. Born to a poor family in Avignon in 1723, he had attended the Jesuit college there and decided on a vocation with the Society. In the spring of 1756, just as the war was breaking out, he was sent to Canada to work at Odanak. This assignment brought him close to the war. He soon found himself traveling with armed Abenaki allies of the French in campaigns at Fort William Henry and Quebec.[31] In a report he penned during this period, after accompanying the Abenakis to Fort Vaudreuil in July 1757, the youthful Roubaud indicated how impressed he was by the spectacle of a general rendezvous of the French and allied Indian fighters. Each Indian nation gathered "under its own standard" as "two hundred canoes" approached nearby in "fine order." In a subtle swipe at the snobbery of the French officers, the Jesuit added of the Indians that they "formed a sight that Messieurs the French officers . . . did not deem unworthy of attention."[32]

But by September 1759 Roubaud's French and Indian American world—still new to him, as he had been in-country only three years—was crumbling to pieces, as Quebec fell to the British and, the following month, his own mission station of Odanak was destroyed. On October 3 the British ranger Robert Rogers and his men overran Odanak, taking as booty, among other things, a beautiful silver statue of the Virgin Mary that had been gifted to the Abenakis from the canons of Chartres Cathedral, long-standing patrons of the Jesuits in North America. Not long after this, while spending the winter in Montreal, Roubaud preached fiery homilies in which he blamed French professional soldiers for the loss of Quebec. In his view they were undisciplined both morally and militarily and had not put up a spirited defense of the colonial capital.

Roubaud was hardly the first Jesuit to blame the French for a slack defense of the colony. But Roubaud, in his mid-thirties and barely into his priesthood, appears to have sympathized keenly with the anger and betrayal the Abenakis themselves, now turning on the French, were feeling. By the winter of 1760–61, Roubaud had ingratiated himself with the new British governor in Quebec, James Murray—even staying at Murray's home, against the wishes of his superiors—and was secretly in communication with Sir William Johnson, the commanding officer for the Anglo-American militiamen and the Iroquois forces fighting on Great Britain's side. In a letter to Johnson from February 1761, the Jesuit described himself as French-born but not a "natural subject of the French king," declaring what an honor it was for him to become "acquainted with the English nation." He claimed further that the people of Canada were daily blessing their "destiny" of becoming British subjects.[33]

Soon after this, Roubaud renounced his Jesuit vows and his Catholic priesthood, moving to London to become an Anglican churchman. He took part as well in the international peace negotiations at The Hague, serving British delegates as a translator while peddling both French and British state secrets for money. Demonstrating how alienated he had become from the Society of Jesus, he also tried but failed to convince British officials to seize all Jesuit properties in Canada at the end of the war.[34] After all this, he settled down with an English bride and fathered several children. But the years thereafter were not kind to him. He made few friends in England and eventually returned to France, sick and destitute and without his family. He was taken in as a charity case by the Sulpician fathers of Paris on the eve of the French Revolution.[35]

The devastation at Odanak, the seizure of Jesuit properties in Quebec to serve as British barracks, and the battle deaths of Virot and many mission-based Native American Catholics were just some of the many losses suffered by the mission to New France during the war. Devastating, too, was a cutback in mission personnel at a time when some missionaries yet hoped to revitalize their enterprise under British toleration. Fourteen Jesuits, many under age thirty-five, were recalled from North America to France during the war, most after the fall of Quebec. Unfortunately for them, the "most Christian Kingdom" of France had become, by then, one of the least comfortable places in the world to be a Jesuit.[36]

Among the many men who spent only a few years with the mission to New France in later decades was Jean-François de La Marche from Quimper in Brittany. He arrived in Canada at twenty in 1720 to complete part of his Jesuit formation in a mission setting. He returned to France just three years later, and in his mature years he would go on to pen a philosophical defense of Christianity to counteract the rationalism and skepticism of the philosophes. The book was a kind of manual for French clerics and pious laypersons to reconvert their countrymen, especially urban elites who were embracing deism and naturalism. Employing a typical Jesuit tactic—used often in the North American missions—La Marche affirmed, rather than refuted outright, the core beliefs of his interlocutors. At the same time, he offered proofs that Christianity's tenets, including affirmations of divine revelation and the miraculous, did not contradict any conclusion of human reason so long as the latter was properly formed and applied. La Marche was convinced indeed that "faith and reason, far from being opposed, lend to each other . . . mutual aid to conduct men to the knowledge and love of virtue."[37]

La Marche's book was not published until 1762, and the Parisian firm that printed it, Brocas et Humblot, made a marketing decision to leave the Jesuit's name and affiliation off the cover page. By that point La Marche had crossed the Atlantic once again, after he was ordered in 1761 to assist with an investigation into the economic practices of his confreres in Martinique.[38] Falling ill and dying overseas, he would never see his book go to press or learn why the press had removed the byline to help sales: a major public scandal had broken out involving Antoine Lavalette, the superior of the Martinique mission, which quickly occasioned the suppression of the Society of Jesus by the Parlement de Paris and King Louis XV.[39]

Earlier, in 1756, the firm Lioncy Frères et Gouffre in Marseilles, a major creditor of Lavalette's wide-ranging real estate and commercial ventures in Martinique and Dominica, filed for bankruptcy when the Jesuit ignored its demands to begin repaying debts of over a million and a half livres owed to other creditors. Lavalette owed some four million beyond this to various firms. When it appeared he would default, the French creditors sought to prosecute him and seek repayment from the Jesuit order itself.[40] Juridically these moves were not so easily ventured, because the mission in Martinique was corporately part of the French assistancy of the Society of Jesus and, furthermore, under the executive authority of the Jesuit general in Rome. While trying to determine which person or administrative level of the Society to target as a defendant in a lawsuit, French magistrates passed the case from court to court and eventually to the Parlement de Paris. This spawned media attention and politicization, especially following a dramatic, unrelated event of January 5, 1757: an assassination attempt on the king by Robert-François Damiens, a man who had attended a Jesuit college in his youth. Although the perpetrator himself claimed he was influenced by rumors of royal corruption spread by Jansenist parlementaires, the Jesuits' enemies successfully employed a Jansenist periodical, the *Nouvelles Écclesiastiques*, to resurrect conspiracy theories about Jesuits from the era of Henry IV's assassination. Many in France soon were convinced that Damiens was a Jesuit stooge. The Society, seen as guilty by association, was newly demonized, bringing even more publicity to the Lavalette case.[41]

Taking advantage of growing public presumptions of Jesuit guilt, some parlementaires sensationalized the case and urged prosecution of the Society's entire French assistancy. They were emboldened after learning that the Portuguese had successfully suppressed the Society of Jesus within their kingdom and empire in 1759—news of which, when it reached Paris, led to celebratory bonfires and chants in the streets. By 1761 magistrates, including two Jansenists named Le Paige and Coudrette, launched a media campaign against the Society. The Jansenist press also disseminated satirical engravings that depicted Jesuits engaging in stereotypically worldly activities. In the spring, a parlementary arrêt demanded that the Jesuit order as a whole repay within twelve months all the money owed to Lioncy Frères et Gouffre, including interest and damages. The Society furthermore was deemed liable for numerous other debts suddenly being reported all over France, in a kingdom-wide frenzy, by creditors who had extended bills of exchange to the financial officers of various colleges and other Jesuit institutions.[42]

In the wake of this ruling a leading magistrate, the abbé de Chauvelin, issued a powerful indictment of the Society: "These men . . . by their state of life, by their vows, by the Constitutions cannot be . . . anything other than the blind and passive instrument of . . . a foreign general who must always reside in Rome." Such words echoed into the French provinces. Opposition to the Society intensified.

The French Suppression was accomplished through a series of arrêts issued by the Parlement de Paris between August 6, 1762 and April 1, 1763. These demanded of the king that the Society be banished from France, that each Jesuit individually break all ties with the order, and that any Jesuit in university studies or teaching posts renounce the Society's Constitutions, affirm the Gallican Articles of 1682, or lose their positions. Furthermore, the magistrates asserted power vis-à-vis the monarchy by claiming that the Jesuits had never obtained the Parlement's approval of their Constitutions, now deemed inconsistent with the laws of the Gallican Church, and that their original *lettres patentes* from past French kings were of doubtful validity. The Parlement raised, in short, a constitutional question: did not the Society of Jesus, with its vast network of schools, missions, and other ministries, depend solely on the will of kings for its existence in France? Was the Society not also a pawn of the papacy? How was this consistent with political order or Gallicanism?[43]

Reluctantly, after a long delay, Louis XV endorsed the arrêts and issued an edict in November 1764, abolishing the Society within his domains while asserting that the men of the order should not have to take any oaths as demanded by Parlement. He insisted, too, that former Jesuits be permitted to remain in French domains, quietly pursuing ministries under local bishops' purview and living as "good and faithful subjects" of the Crown. Older ex-Jesuits, additionally, would receive pensions from the state given all they had done for God and country.[44]

Thus the king effected a stunning reversal of what had been a fruitful, complex relationship between the Jesuits and the Crown since the time of Henry IV. Overseas that relationship had been in evidence right up to the eve of the Seven Years' War. In addition to the steady royal pensions that the missions and the Collège de Québec received, as well as the exemptions that the Jesuits enjoyed from transatlantic customs duties, some missionaries of New France's last days served the Crown in direct ways.[45] Exemplary was a Paris-trained Jesuit named Claude-Godefroy Coquart. Not long after his arrival in Quebec in 1739, Coquart as a young priest accompanied a military officer, Pierre Gaultier de La Vérendrye, on an exploratory mission as far west as Manitoba—one of several such ventures urged at the time by the French naval secretary, the comte de Maurepas. Later, in 1750, Coquart was commissioned by the royal intendant for New France, François Bigot, to visit French trading posts and report on their operations and output. Visiting Tadoussac, Le Sept Îles, La Malbaie, and many other posts, Coquart suggested improvements in his reports that might cost the Crown very little.[46] Echoing Charlevoix and other Jesuits' past critiques of the colonial French who staffed such posts, he argued that many royal trading posts were underperforming due to a lack of initiative at the leadership level and to indolence among many employees. At the same time, he praised La Malbaie as the best "tax farm" in New France, indicating a shared mentality with Absolutist-era officials who viewed centers of trade as sources of revenue for the centralizing monarchical state. It is not surprising, then, that Coquart was rewarded for his services to the Crown by successive colonial intendants.[47]

Shocking as the Suppression was, it was not immediately suffered in New France because the colony had fallen to the British during the war. Preoccupied with the British occupation in Quebec, the elderly Saint-Pé, still superior at the conclusion of the war, hoped to preserve what he could of the Jesuits' extensive properties and mission network. In an ironic historical twist, once he learned of the events in France, he and many local confreres were protected from having to renounce ties to the Society in Rome *because* of the new British, Protestant order being established in Canada. Indeed, prior to the final dissolution of the Society in France, Saint-Pé toward the close of 1763 oversaw the smooth transfer of control of the mission network to a younger, energetic superior who had arrived in Quebec from France in 1758. This was Augustin-Louis de Glapion, who was forty-three at the time. He would serve as superior until his death in 1790—well past the time of the suppression of the entire Jesuit order by Pope Clement XIV in 1773. Through deft negotiations with the new colonial authorities, Glapion even achieved British civil recognition of the Society of Jesus in Canada, even as the order lost its legal existence within the Catholic Church itself.

The tremors of the Suppression were felt more immediately in Lower Louisiana. At the end of the Seven Years' War, French colonial governance remained a daily reality for a short time despite a secret agreement of November 1762 that had transferred the territory to Spain. At that time there were thirteen Jesuits laboring in the Louisiana mission, nearly half of whom were posted in Illinois territory, and three of whom were working among the Alabamas and Choctaws. Others were based in New Orleans, where the Society owned a large plantation that was worked by thirty-six families of slaves. These men learned of their mission's fate in the summer of 1763.

Upon the arrival from France of a new attorney general for Louisiana, Nicolas Chauvin de La Frénière, the Council of New Orleans proceeded with its own investigation of the Constitutions of the Society of Jesus. It was understood from the beginning that the verdict would be damning, in accordance with the metropolitan precedent.[48] The council quickly found the Constitutions to be subversive of French royal authority, the rights of bishops, and public tranquility. A decree of July 9, 1764, ordered all priests and brothers of the Society in Louisiana to cease calling themselves "Jesuits." Furthermore the council required that all of the Jesuits' property—with the exception of personal items such as books and clothing—was to be confiscated by civil authorities. Artwork, Holy Communion chalices and patens, and other valuables from Jesuit churches and chapels were transferred to the Capuchins and, in the case of mission chapels in Illinois Country, to the royal procurator of the region.[49]

Over the next few days officials appraised the buildings, movable goods, livestock, and enslaved human beings owned by the Jesuits in New Orleans. Jesuits present for this activity were made to swear that they had not removed anything of value. Then a public sale was held, which netted for the colonial government nearly a million livres.[50] Following this the Jesuits were ordered to leave for France and present themselves to the secretary of the navy, the duc de Choiseul, who was supposed to distribute royal pensions to them. However, several of the missionaries took the opportunity to transfer to different Atlantic World locales. Louis-François Carette, who had been working among the Quapaws of the Arkansas River Valley, set off for Saint-Domingue, where the Jesuits had been operating a mission for slaves since 1704.[51] And Maximilien Le Roy departed first for Florida and then Vera Cruz in Mexico.[52]

In the Illinois territory, which had formally been ceded to Great Britain but was still de facto in French hands, Jesuits were rounded up as if they were common criminals. When brought to New Orleans, just before Christmas, they were shown mercy and provided with decent lodging before departing for France to claim what pensions might be available to them. Most crossed the Atlantic by the spring of 1764, not knowing the full extent of the Society's suppression in France until reaching their European port of arrival, the Basque city of San Sebastián (not far, as it happened, from Azpeitia, the birthplace of Saint Ignatius). But Sébastien-Louis Meurin, a fifty-six-year-old missionary originally from Champagne, returned to Illinois Country where, generally free from interference by British authorities, he continued to exercise the functions of his priesthood and instruct Native Americans until his death in 1777 at Prairie-du-Rocher, a few months shy of his seventieth birthday.[53]

Meurin's path illustrates the irony of the final years of the French Jesuits' enterprise in North America. On the one hand, the coincidence of the Society's suppression by France with the outcomes of the Seven Years' War enabled the mission to continue onward, albeit in a circumscribed way, in places where French rule had given way to British, Protestant domin-ion. On the other hand, Jesuits who returned to Catholic France had to navigate a political and cultural landscape that in some cases was more precarious than anything their confreres still in America faced toward the end of the eighteenth century.

Most missionaries who returned to France at the time of the Suppression settled into obscure, parochial assignments in their home dioceses. Many ministered for years and then passed away in peace in familiar French environs. Some, such as Joseph-Pierre de Bonnécamps, even fared quite well in worldly terms. He spent his final years at the lovely Château de

Tronjoly in Gourin, Brittany, not far from his hometown of Vannes, due to connections he had made with several French elites over the years.

Earlier in life Bonnécamps had trained as a Jesuit in Paris, La Flèche, Caen, and his hometown before he was sent to Quebec in 1744 to teach hydrography and mathematics at the colonial college. While there he secured financial assistance from the French naval secretary, Maurepas, to supply the college with a good telescope and even to build an observatory. Some of his astronomical observations were published in Paris.[54] Additionally, in 1749, he was able to join a French exploratory expedition in the Ohio Valley, chosen by Pierre-Joseph Céloron de Blainville for his reputed skills in surveying, cartography, and general observation of the natural world around him. The report he produced from that expedition gained him notice in France. He was befriended by Joseph-Nicolas Delisle, a naval officer caught up in the latest research in astronomy and geography, as well as by the French explorer—also a naval officer—Louis-Antoine, comte de Bougainville.[55] Eventually, after the fall of Quebec, Bonnécamps returned to France to teach at the Collège de Caen.

After the Suppression, Bonnécamps returned to North America. He was offered a chaplaincy in one of the few American territories that still remained in French hands after the war, the archipelago of Saint-Pierre and Miquelon off the coast of Newfoundland. There he befriended a young nobleman from his native French region of Brittany, François-Jean-Baptiste l'Ollivier de Tronjoly. Learning that his clerical friend from overseas was himself back in Brittany, laboring in a prison ministry at Brest, Tronjoly invited Bonnécamps to come live at the château in exchange for tutoring his children. The former missionary, professor, explorer, published scientist, and prison chaplain died in peace there at the age of eighty-two in May 1790, just after the new, revolutionary National Constituent Assembly had suppressed *all* Catholic religious orders in France.

Far less fortunate were two of Bonnécamps's brother veterans of the mission, Siméon Le Bansais and Julien-François Dervillé, who—like so many others at the time—fell victim to the French Revolution. Le Bansais had spent fifteen years in Canada before returning to France during the Seven Years' War. Born in 1719, he had been ordained to the secular priesthood in France before entering the Society of Jesus at Quebec in 1745, the same year he first crossed the Atlantic.[56] Of a scholarly bent, Le Bansais spent most of his time teaching at the Collège de Québec before the war disrupted his career. Once he was back in France he produced several devotional works, including a widely disseminated *Novena to the Holy Angels*. The edition of 1782, published in Avignon, where he was serving as a canon of Saint-Didier Cathedral, billed his theological and missionary credentials without referring to his former affiliation with the Jesuits.[57] He also published a lengthy reflection on the Lord's Prayer that included his thoughts on the "necessity of acts of contrition, faith, hope, and charity."[58]

Le Bansais's own faith would be tested in 1791 when, as a well-known clergyman based at the oldest city-center church in Avignon, he was pressured to swear his loyalty to the new revolutionary regime, as demanded by the National Constituent Assembly in Paris. While a handful of French bishops and about half of the French clergy swore the oath, numerous churchmen were unable in good conscience to swear to the principles that the Church was something lower than, or something that could be subordinated to, the French state, and that the pope in Rome only had authority over purely spiritual matters. Le Bansais himself, now in his seventies, refused to take the oath. He was imprisoned at Aigues-Morts, west of Marseilles, but was later found in a disheveled, sickly condition on a beach at Ville Franche, near Cannes. He died soon after in a charitable hospital for indigents and the infirm in Nice.[59]

Then there was Dervillé, with whom this chapter began. At the time of his arrest in late 1793 the elderly former missionary was residing on the Rue du Faubourg de Bourgogne in Orléans, in the home of a former nun named Marie-Anne Poullin, together with five other religious and a servant, all of them women. Apparently he was in fear for his life, as his arrest record indicates he was dressed as a woman to disguise himself while one day observing a ceremony around the city's liberty tree. After someone in the crowd tricked him into revealing his identity, Dervillé was precipitously manhandled and taken to his residence, where the building and his housemates were subjected to a search. He was taken prisoner when it was discovered that he possessed, as the revolutionaries called them, "all the resources of superstition and fanaticism: a rosary with medals, a round box full of 'enchanted bread' [Communion wafers], a large silver cross, a silver heart [probably the Sacred Heart], an encased relic, a ring with an image of the Virgin on the bezel . . . a Franciscan cord," and, tellingly, "a seal with *armes fleurdelisées*," that is, a signet with the heraldic symbols of the overthrown monarchy.[60] The women of the house were also taken prisoner and the group was hauled to Paris to face the dreaded Committee on Public Safety.

The five religious with whom Dervillé was arrested were all freed at the end of their quick trial, but Mademoiselle Poullin, her house servant, and Dervillé himself did not satisfy the Committee with their answers during the interrogation. Dervillé, in fact, admitted readily that he was a Catholic priest and a *Jesuit*—despite the order's suppression by Rome as well as France by that point—when faced with the certain prospect of martyrdom. He declared himself to be a servant of the "Apostolic and Roman Church," which, he also made clear, meant he could never swear to the oath required by the Civil Constitution of the Clergy. Reportedly he declared to his judges, "Laws must be subordinated to religion, and since the Catholic religion has God himself as her author, it is not for her to bend before laws, but rather for laws to bend before her."[61] Such convictions were sufficient in that revolutionary court of justice to constitute a crime against the French nation and, indeed, all of humanity. Dervillé—a short man in his late sixties, with white hair and gray eyes—was on December 21, 1793 fed to the guillotine, surrounded by a jeering mob at the Place de la Concorde in Paris.[62]

Quiet Death under British, Protestant Rule

Back across the Atlantic, the few French Jesuits remaining in North America spent their final years in relative peace. They tended to diverse ministries rooted in the French colonial past. At the same time, under Glapion's leadership, they managed the slow contraction and demise of a once vital, expansive missionary enterprise.

British rule in Canada brought with it a momentary hope that the

Jesuits might be permitted to recruit new men into their order, since the French royal suppression did not apply on British soil. In 1772 Bishop Joseph Briand of Quebec petitioned the British Crown to allow all religious orders present in his diocese to welcome novices.[63] But British toleration of Catholics extended only so far. It did not include a welcome mat for more Jesuits.

Then in 1773 the death knell tolled for the Society of Jesus as a whole, when Clement XIV issued *Dominus ac Redemptor*, dissolving the order worldwide. The Jesuits of what was once called New France faced the grim truth that, within a generation, their mission would literally die of old age. Indeed, with each priest and brother's death in the period, what remained of the French Jesuits' institutional presence in North America also dwindled. The secondary school at the Collège de Québec closed permanently in 1768 while the attached primary school remained open for eight more years. In 1777 and 1782, respectively, the Illinois mission and La Brosse's Tadoussac mission folded.

The last men of the ancien régime's mission to North America tried to make the best of their situation. For example, Germain, the veteran military chaplain from Luxembourg, convinced British authorities in Nova Scotia to permit him to stay in his mission at the end of the Seven Years' War. He even secured a pension from them. In exchange he promised to preach peace, not resistance, among the Natives of the region. Soon after, he relocated to Trois-Rivières, where he ministered to French Canadians and Indians for several years before he was granted a permanent appointment at Odanak—a revitalized mission renamed Saint-François-du-Lac. He served the predominantly Abenaki and French Canadian population there until his death in 1779 at age seventy-two.[64]

La Brosse, only in his thirties at the end of the war, tended to French and Native American Christians around Tadoussac until he died in 1782. His ministry centered on the cultivation of Catholic belief and worship among the Montagnais, whose language he studied closely while translating portions of the Bible into it. He also compiled a Montagnais dictionary. Although no longer a Jesuit in formal terms, he engaged in creative apostolic work among the Montagnais in ways that drew upon the long experience of the Society dating back to the time of Biard and Le Jeune. Working with a Scottish American printer named William Brown, La Brosse authored and saw the print production of thousands of copies of primers and devotional books in the Montagnais language. For decades he promoted literacy, instrumental and choral music, and Montagnais expressions of Catholic doctrine and liturgical practice, assisted in this work by lay Montagnais catechists whom he trained. He also engaged in medical work and developed a reputation as a skillful healer.[65]

Following a similar trajectory as La Brosse, but in a Huron context, was Pierre-Philippe Potier. A native of Hainaut in Wallonia, he entered the Society of Jesus at Douai in France at the age of twenty-one in 1729. Completing his formation in various French cities, Potier was sent to Quebec in 1743. He learned the Huron language at Lorette and relocated to the western Huron mission near Fort Pontchartrain du Détroit, which had been established in 1701. Mentored by an older Jesuit there, Armand de La Richardie, Potier took over the mission in 1746 only to witness its destruction by a war party from a rival Huron community. Over the next few years, with the help of a younger Jesuit recruit named Jean-Baptiste de Salleneuve, Potier and La Richardie reestablished the mission on the other side of the Detroit River, at the site of present-day Windsor, Ontario. This mission flourished even during the troubled years of the French and Indian War, after which in 1767 a new Catholic parish—Notre-Dame-de-l'Assomption—was approved for the site by the bishop of Quebec. Potier and his confreres were thus able to continue with their ministries under episcopal authority despite the royal suppression of their order in France. Potier engaged thereafter—until his last days in 1781—both in intensive study of the Huron language and culture and in the cultivation of Catholic piety in terms that made sense to the natives of the region. He, too, pursued in writing projects. His manuscripts, though not published in his lifetime, included a Huron grammar and many drafts of the sermons he preached in the Huron language.[66]

Several last Jesuits of the mission did not labor so quietly. Instead their stories reveal continuities with the mission's political past. Pierre-René Floquet and Joseph Huguet, in particular, caused trouble for the remaining Jesuits in Quebec and Montreal, who were trying to get along with British authorities. Affiliated with the Iroquois mission at Sault-Saint-Louis, they fell under suspicion for seditious sympathies with the American revolutionaries who had allied themselves with Louis XVI's France in their War of Independence.

Huguet, a Belgian-trained but French-born Jesuit, had been assigned to Sault-Saint-Louis in 1757 when he was thirty-two. The mission Indians there had kinship ties with British-allied Iroquois groups and they traded regularly with New York merchants. They were also bitter that the military services they had long rendered the French had, through many wars, resulted in heavy losses but only small rewards. Thus they were ambivalent in their commitment to a French victory during the French and Indian War and welcomed the British takeover of Canada with equanimity. Nevertheless, once the Thirteen Colonies declared independence from Britain, the residents of Sault-Saint-Louis proved friendlier to the revolutionaries than British authorities in Canada preferred. Huguet was suspected of encouraging this posture, especially after the Franco-American alliance was sealed in 1778. The Jesuit died under a cloud of suspicion at Sault-Saint-Louis in May 1783, a few months before Britain accepted the French and Americans' terms in the Treaty of Paris.[67]

Floquet for his part engaged in subversive communications with the revolutionaries. He had served briefly as a missionary at Sault-Saint-Louis in 1749 and 1750 but thereafter filled mostly administrative posts. Before the Seven Years' War he managed the finances of the Collège de Québec, but during the war he was appointed as superior of the Jesuits in Montreal. Still posted there once the American Revolution broke out, Floquet developed an attachment to the rebels' cause when contingents of the Continental Army temporarily occupied the city. Disobeying a directive of Bishop Briand in Quebec, Floquet in 1776 went out of his way to welcome an American delegation, led by Benjamin Franklin, which hoped to convince the Canadians to join the independence movement. The delegation included two Catholic revolutionaries from Maryland, Charles Carroll and his cousin John Carroll, the latter of whom was a Jesuit who would found Georgetown University in 1789 and serve as the first Catholic bishop appointed for the United States. Floquet defended his American sympathies to Bishop Briand. He freely owned not only to giving Holy Communion to French Canadian militiamen who joined the revolutionaries—something Briand had forbidden—but also to communicating with military men and clergymen in New York who had sided with the Patriots against the Loyalists. Briand put him under ecclesiastical interdict in 1777, forbidding him to exercise the functions of his priesthood. In the end the Jesuit submitted to the bishop's authority and was able to minister to souls again in Montreal, until his death in 1782.[68]

Partly due to suspicions surrounding the remaining Jesuits in Canada, the end of Glapion's tenure as superior in Quebec was plagued by aggressive claims on the priests' properties by British authorities. By the beginning of 1790, a few months shy of his death, the tired, seventy-one-year-old superior, representing himself and the three other living Jesuits of the mission—Bernard Well, Jean-Joseph Casot, and Étienne Thomas-de-Villeneuve Girault—handed over the properties "to the Canadian citizens," as he put it in a letter to the merchant Louis Germain Langlois. In that letter Glapion affirmed what he saw as rightful claims that the Jesuits had to lands and other possessions he was relinquishing, claims owed originally to the patronage and benefaction of the panoply of French officials and elites who had partnered with the missionaries in the early decades of the seventeenth century:

> The greater part of the property, estates, and possessions which have been, or still are, held by the Jesuits living in Canada . . . were given to them in full proprietorship by the King of France, the Duc de Ventadour, the trading company of Canada, and by generous individuals, for the maintenance of the said Jesuits, on the condition that they should be employed for the instruction of the savages and of the young Canadian French. The Jesuits so well acquitted themselves of both these obligations that, in acknowledgment of their merits, Louis XIV, of glorious memory, renewed and ratified in their favor, by his great charter . . . all those concessions and gifts which had been made to them. . . . But in October, 1789, the number of Jesuits living in Canada was reduced to four, all of them advanced in years. Consequently,

they were no longer able to fulfill the stipulated obligations. . . . For this reason, they renounce, unconditionally, voluntarily, and in good faith, all ownership and possession of the said gifts and concessions.[69]

The elderly Jesuits were permitted use of their chapel and residence hall in Quebec until the last of them died. The residence included a garden, a neighboring grove, and small utility buildings including a carriage house, stables, and a chicken coop. The priests were also permitted use of smaller properties at the Huron mission of Lorette and in Montreal. Additionally each man received a generous pension as a gift from the Canadian citizens, to provide for their needs and a genteel lifestyle in their last years. It was further agreed that the properties would be entrusted to the Catholic bishops of Quebec, so that they might be put to use again for their original purpose: "instruction of the savages and of the young Canadians."[70]

Well died in Montreal in 1791, and Girault in Quebec three years later. But it was not until after the turn of the next century, on March 16, 1800, that the last of the Jesuits of New France died in Quebec. This was Casot, who made it to the age of seventy-one. He was the son of French-speaking parents from a village called Peliseul in what was, at the time of his birth, the Habsburg duchy of Luxembourg. At twenty-five, late in 1753, he had joined the Jesuits, relocating to Paris to begin his novitiate. In 1757—just as the Seven Years' War was breaking out—he was sent to Quebec, where, through the duration of the hostilities, he toiled variously as a cook and as a director of the primary school of the Collège de Québec even while British soldiers were quartered on the college grounds. After the war he was appointed bursar of the college. Eventually, on December 20, 1766, at age thirty-eight, he was ordained a priest of the Society of Jesus by Bishop Briand, despite the order's suppression by several Catholic crowns in Europe by then.

During Casot's final days in Quebec, he probably wondered—perhaps while praying rosaries in the garden of the old Jesuit residence or sharing afternoon tea with polite British-colonial neighbors—how it was that a young man from the countryside in the Low Countries had come to be facing death in British Canada, without any Jesuit confreres beside him to offer words of consolation or to pray with him. He surely had knowledge, too, and questioned God's strange will in all of it, that revolutionary France had lately become a consulate after an ancient Roman fashion, under the sway of a dictatorial Corsican and probable atheist, and also that Catholics like himself were enjoying more religious freedom in British territories than they had been, of late, in the homeland of Saints Louis de France, Vincent de Paul, and Isaac Jogues. Furthermore, the great Society of Jesus that he had joined, probably with much hope and enthusiasm in the Paris of his youth, had become a scattered band of exiles and retirees like himself—biding their time in unlikely places such as Catherine the Great's Russia and the young United States and praying for the order's this-worldly resurrection.

That resurrection did come to pass, fourteen years after Casot's death. On August 7, 1814, a few months after Napoleon Bonaparte's abdication, Pope Pius VII restored the Society of Jesus to life around the world. Not long after, French-born, Francophone Belgian, French Canadian, and French American Jesuits would energetically reestablish ministries in and far beyond France. In North America, that process began in 1837 at Grand Coteau in Louisiana and in 1842 in Montreal.

This time, however, the only Europeans to whom the men of the Society laboring in North America formally answered were their Jesuit superiors and the pope. They had no avowed ties to any nation-state across the Atlantic, let alone to increasingly imperialistic France, whose partisans had begun proselytizing the world with a new trinitarian creed—*Liberté, Égalité, Fraternité*—and consecrating their own colonial ventures with blood.

CONCLUSION

In 1919, after Western powers had ravaged the world's peoples and landscapes with their Great War, Pope Benedict XV reprimanded Catholic missionaries who had helped fan the national-imperial zeitgeist. A genuinely Catholic missionary, he declared in *Maximum Illud*, "is always aware that he is not working as an agent of his country, but as an ambassador of Christ." The pontiff warned that an apostolic man should never "spend himself in attempts to increase and exalt the prestige of the native land he once left behind him," for this would "destroy his reputation with the populace. . . . If he has any object in view other than their spiritual good, they will find out about it."[1]

The following year, the same pope canonized the medieval girl-soldier Jeanne d'Arc—a saint exceedingly identified with French nationalism. During World War I, the archbishop of Paris had led French Catholics in public prayers to Jeanne, in hopes that from heaven she would help carry France to victory over the barbaric Germans. General Maxime Weygand and other Third Republic commanders also invoked her name before battles. The Maid of Orléans was recruited into imperial causes, too: Weygand later led an organization called the Alliance Jeanne d'Arc, which was devoted to maintaining French rule in Algeria.

Without more knowledge of modern history, our Jesuits of New France, if somehow presented with such facts, would have recognized themselves more in those invoking Saint Jeanne in battle and imperial contexts than in Pope Benedict's description of authentic Catholic missionaries. Sébastien Râle, for instance, might have puzzled over an assumption that his mission population—Abenakis who included veterans of New France's wars with New England—wanted only "spiritual" succor from priests. "It is not enough for me to perform the spiritual duties of my ministry," he had written in 1723, not long before perishing at Norridgewock from English and Mohawk gunfire; "I must also enter into their temporal affairs." He said this at a time when Jesuits were covertly helping to supply the Abenakis with French guns to fend off Anglo-Protestant settlers from their ancestral lands.[2] Even Saint Isaac Jogues, killed in Iroquois Country almost a century earlier, had without apparent scruple fulfilled simultaneously the functions of Catholic priest and intelligence-gathering agent for an aspiring colonial state. French ambitions, Jogues knew well, were exacerbating intertribal rivalries in the Eastern Woodlands and leading to the deaths of Indians and Europeans alike. Benedict's sharp distinction between serving Christ and exalting one's homeland would have been hard to grasp in the way most modern Christians now do, as if by second nature—whether from post-integralist, liberal embarrassment over the legacy of confessional politics or from repulsion by imperiously secularist states such as the *laïque* French Republic.

The Jesuits we have encountered in this book were apostles of French empire, not simply of the kingdom of Christ they strove to populate with Native American souls. Their story suggests that modern, post-revolutionary French imperialism, with its self-justificatory *mission civilisatrice*, has deep roots in post-Tridentine missionary Catholicism. These roots spanned continents; they may be discerned both in Jesuit practices in North America and in European print campaigns that were directed to a rising French national elite and reading public. The secular history of the mission indeed corrects a contemporary misperception that French missionaries only became swept up in a national-imperial *mission civilisatrice* after being pulled in that "modern" direction by nineteenth-century colonial experiences, away from a pre-Enlightenment fixation on religious conversion, moral purity, and otherworldly salvation.[3]

Shown in this book to have been some of the earliest, most enthusiastic

French imperialists, the Jesuits of New France now also contrast with many popular and academic images of them. When the legacy of their work in North America began to be defined in modern times—especially following the canonization of Jogues and other martyrs in 1930—their proactive commitment to empire was decorously downplayed. This has something to do with the emerging anti-nationalist, anti-imperial discourses of the time, represented for example by *Maximum Illud*. It also has to do with the exigencies of American Catholicism as it was maturing amid the liberal, Protestant culture of the world's rising superpower, the United States. English-language hagiographies, aimed at North American Catholics with no ties to a French empire, underscored heroic witness to the Gospel in wilderness settings wholly alien to European civilization.[4] The missionaries, committed to the Roman Church's otherworldly goals and the Christocentric spirituality of Saint Ignatius Loyola, were above all men willing to suffer—in Americanized recapitulations of the Paschal mystery—cold Canadian winters and lethal torture by belligerent Iroquois who detested the Gospel.

But even as academic authors later on offered disenchanted, historically more sensitive portraits of the American Natives together with the missionaries, the Jesuits' enterprising labors for French empire remained unaccounted for. On the one hand, studies that focused on the Jesuits themselves exaggerated mission elements that accorded with postcolonial and post-integralist missiological pieties: emergent preferences for dialogue over triumphalism; anticipations of the Second Vatican Council's view of mission as inculturation; emphases on penitential suffering in opposition to imperial conquest.[5] From this vantage point, the missionaries appeared supportive of colonization and trade in America, but in a spiritually detached, instrumentalizing way early in their enterprise. They also supposedly evolved toward a more progressive, less Eurocentric understanding of their mission while occasionally, reluctantly, getting drawn into colonial affairs. But the heart of their mission was the fulfillment of a "Jesuit ideal" of "helping indigenous people to adopt Christianity on their own terms," as Robert Michael Morrissey has put it.[6]

On the other hand, scholars in the vein of James Axtell and Bruce

Trigger, less hesitant to connect the Jesuits to French imperialism, nevertheless struggled to articulate some of the historical dynamics at play. They cast the relationship as a marriage of convenience between lay colonialists driven by motives of profit and political gain and clergymen indifferent to worldly affairs and operating with an allegedly medieval, stark *contemptus mundi* and apocalyptic zeal for saving souls. For such missionaries colonialism was just an expressway into heathen Indian Country. And Indian Country, once accessed, was virgin soil upon which the Gospel would be sown, epic battles between God and Satan would play out, and sincere—but probably deranged—Jesuits would win coveted crowns of martyrdom.

Such views of the missionaries now appear to reflect more than anything else an ingrained habit among post-Enlightenment Western intellectuals of drawing sharp distinctions—and presuming ruptures more than organic development—between the lay and "modern" on one side, and the clerical, "medieval," and militantly Christian on the other.[7] They stem, too, from a deep-seated tendency among contemporary Westerners to quarantine political and material considerations from theological and cosmological ones, even among those who take the latter seriously.[8]

Having studied the mission's secular edges across two centuries and a transatlantic horizon, we can see more clearly now what the Jesuits and their early modern Catholicism were about. These men were strangely medieval *and* modern, and quite intensely so in both regards. We hear their unnervingly literal calls for "holy war" in Iroquois Country while (perhaps discomfitingly) recognizing something of ourselves in their efforts to disenchant Native Americans regarding their "superstitions" and to begin evening out what they saw as transatlantic wealth disparities and inequities in terms of social and infrastructural development. The missionaries furthermore were making way not only for their "one, holy, catholic and apostolic Church," as they professed at Mass, but also for then-advanced medicines and hospital care, urban-elite standards of hygiene and decorum at table, and bourgeois understandings of thrift, property, and economy.

In short we see a militant, missionary Catholicism caught up in and engendering shifts we conventionally associate with the Enlightenment. The Jesuits of New France sought, over the long term, to spread European knowledge about the natural world, not only supernatural phenomena. They also worked to preoccupy French elites—and in time also Native American leaders—with the social transformation of North America, especially the alleviation of hunger and disease, by means of commerce and large-scale philanthropy. They framed social benevolence in terms of the divinely ordained destiny of the French to uplift the world's "poor" and unite them fraternally to a larger human family, living and dead. Significantly, that bonding of souls was not to be achieved solely through the sacraments and unity of belief of the universal Church. According to the missionaries, imperial France was God's chosen conduit for the Church at all levels of her mystical existence—*militans, dolens, triumphans*—as Native Americans' Christian communion was to be achieved through interleavings of grace and shared experiences with the French. The latter included fighting and suffering in wars against common enemies, sometimes marrying and raising families together, and jointly building an orderly society that benefited the many, not the few. Articulating this national-imperial project, the missionaries linked a Reform-era rhetoric of Christian charity with mercantile—and by Charlevoix's time, proto-liberal and capitalist—conceptions of the benefits of Atlantic commerce for both France and the colonized peoples it adopted.

The Jesuits of New France labored to form a transatlantic, French-American political community that was ecclesial and confessional in nature. In keeping with traditional conceptions of Christendom's expansion, spearheaded by baptized lords and their allies who swore fealty to Christ and his visible bride the Church, this community's elites were primarily baptized Catholics while including also meritorious, potential members of the Church. And like Christendom it was therefore more universal and inclusive than polities defined by ethnicity, tribe, or inherited feudal relationships. At the same time, the community was not simply another iteration of the medieval *Corpus christianum*. It was quite secularizing in character. It was defined at its limits less by persons' standing within the Church and more by their relationships to the French Bourbon state, authorized French traders and firms, and the values of *civilité* and *police* according to evolving courtly and Parisian norms.

This close but not one-to-one identification of the expanding Catholic spiritual community with an emerging French-American polity arose specifically out of the *Gallican* Catholic milieu of the mission's metropolitan germination. As Naomi Schor has observed, France from medieval times "drew from its privileged relationship to the Church [a] mission as a disseminator of a universalist creed," which itself was later transfigured in modern times as a "French universalism" oriented on a "civilizing mission" to the rest of the world. Schor has further suggested that it was the French Revolution, though it "did so much to destroy the power of the Gallican Church," that extracted the religious impetus of French universalism from the *nation*'s mission, enabling the latter "to perpetuate and propagate itself" with new vigor.[9] Yet, strikingly, we have seen in the Jesuit mission to New France that an expansionism no longer simply about the Church's universal mission, but also about France's unique civilizational mission to the world, was underway long before any such revolutionary rupture. It arose in a space of creative tension between the missionaries' ecclesial militancy and their vision of the absolutizing Bourbon state as the providential successor to Western imperial powers of the past. With political, mercantile, and religious interests coalescing in Paris during Richelieu and Louis XVI's eras, the Jesuits partnered enthusiastically with the elites of a Catholic nation-state that outstripped the Church and the Society of Jesus, on their own, with respect to the scale and scope of missionary endeavor it could attempt abroad. France, in short, was the vehicle in their midst that could advance simultaneously the Church's salvific mission to "all nations" and, on a secular plane, the *bonum commune* across broad oceanic and continental horizons. As the first Jesuit historian of Canada put it in 1664, "the light of the Gospel" and "the benefits of trade" had first begun, hand in hand, "to reach [the] miserable [American] peoples" in a previous era "through the instrumentality of the Spanish and the Portuguese," but in his own time, this sacred-and-secular mission would be achieved "especially through the French."[10] Paired with Paul Le Jeune's earlier, almost mystical meditation on the rising sun of French commerce over the Atlantic, such remarks bear an unmistakable family resemblance to the later utterances of the marquis de Condorcet and postrevolutionary champions of the "light" imperial France could exceptionally bestow on suffering, benighted peoples the world over.

The Jesuits' commitment to a simultaneously otherworldly and this-worldly mission in North America did not flag even as it became clear, by the eighteenth century, that French elites were not much interested in New France. The missionaries surely could have retreated to a more narrowly defined view of French empire after Jean-Baptiste Colbert tried to pressure them to focus on the integration of baptized Native Americans into a territorially, linguistically, and confessionally circumscribed colonial community in the Saint Lawrence River Valley. Instead, as time passed and French settlements and mission stations were left militarily vulnerable and underdeveloped by the French Crown, the missionaries looked to Native American leaders themselves—Christian and not yet Christian—to assist in the civilizational, not only ecclesial, expansion of New France. The Jesuits resolved to raise up a pan-tribal missionized population that would itself become an advance guard for French-American empire writ large—an empire that was ethnically and linguistically diverse yet drawn together by Catholic worship, trade, self-policing, French-cum-indigenous *civilité* and *sociabilité*, and military service to the state. There are family resemblances here, too, especially in the military service-and-reward system the Jesuits cultivated in mission "fortresses" such as Kahnawaké, to various mechanisms of the Third Republic's multi-phase integration of indigenous elites into the lower level of its military-bureaucratic colonial elite.[11]

To be sure, soul-saving Catholic worship of the Triune God, with the moral and spiritual fruits engendered by it, was the first and last goal of the Jesuits' mission. Yet it was also a well of resources—providing a social-spiritual glue, so to speak—for a new sort of transatlantic polity. Where the Jesuits labored in indubitably pioneering ways to communicate Catholicism in terms that made sense to local populations, rather than chauvinistically to impose French ways, it was *not* from growing dissatisfaction with European civilization. Nor did it stem from any discernible evolution toward the idea—favored by missiologists today—that their home civilization was dispensable, that its French cultural trappings, so to speak, could be dissociated from a disembodied, spiritual-ideational

Christian core or evangelical essence that would inspire a new, autochthonous Christian society. Rather, the missionaries were firmly confident not only in France's special calling to expand the Church into America, but also in its capacity, as a mature European power that could outdo ancient Rome's glories, to incorporate diverse populations and expressions of Christianity into a transatlantic community that was still eminently French and Catholic. Such confidence explains the almost shocking consistency we see, over time, among these Jesuits with respect to their willingness to sacrifice Native American and French lives, including their own, to New France's defense and expansion.

The earthly enterprise to which these early modern Jesuits were devoted was ultimately a failed trial run for imperial France. But there is no doubt that these men, their collaborators, and their missionary Catholicism bequeathed to modern French colonialism some of its structural and ideational furniture. Indeed, several of these men spent themselves in service to French national expansion to a degree that would not pass muster in the eyes of most of their latter-day coreligionists. Le Jeune, surely, would fall into this category, as would Râle, Antoine Sénat, and Claude Virot, who quite literally laid down their lives, in battle zones, on the altar of French empire. Those Jesuits were never, of course, raised to the honors of the Church's high altar as were Jogues and the other martyrs of the 1640s. But this perhaps has little to do with their relative personal worthiness alongside the mission's canonized saints, or with whatever closeness to God they may have known in moments of contemplative stillness. It has more to do with their laboring in the mission's mature phase, when the sheer politics of, and materialistic rationales for, national-imperial rivalries were vividly unfurled—in destructive ways increasingly difficult to identify with Christ Crucified, no matter how some apologists for empire, clerical and lay alike, still would try.

NOTES

ABBREVIATIONS

ARSI Archivum Romanum Societatis Iesu, Rome

DCB *Dictionary of Canadian Biography* edited by George W. Brown

JR *The Jesuit Relations and Allied Documents* by Reuben Gold Thwaites

LAC Library and Archives Canada, Ottawa

MNF *Monumenta Novae Franciae* by Lucien Campeau, SJ

OFM Order of Friars Minor

RAPQ *Rapport de l'Archiviste de la Province de Québec*

SJ Society of Jesus

INTRODUCTION

1. Anderson, *The Death and Afterlife of the North American Martyrs.*

2. Greer, *Mohawk Saint*; Deslandres, *Croire et Faire Croire*; Clair, "'Seeing These Good Souls Adore God"; Friant, "'Ils aiment bien leur chapelet'"; Morrissey, "Terms of Encounter"; Leavelle, *The Catholic Calumet*; Jetten, *Enclaves amérindiennes.*

3. E.g., Xavier and Županov, *Catholic Orientalism*; Gregerson and Juster, *Empires of God*; Stanwood, *The Empire Reformed*; Nexon, *The Struggle for Power in Early Modern Europe*; Pestana, *Protestant Empire.*

4. See especially Vidal, *Français?*; Røge, "A Natural Order of Empire"; Rushforth, *Bonds of Alliance*; Lavoie, *Le Domaine du Roi, 1652–1859*; Banks, *Chasing Empire across the Sea*; Chapman, *Private Ambition and Political Alliances*; Pritchard, *In Search of Empire*; Frêlon, *Les Pouvoirs du Conseil souverain*; Quinn, *The French Overseas Empire.*

5. White and Daughton, *In God's Empire*; Curtis, *Civilizing Habits*; Daughton, *An Empire Divided.*

6. Robert, *Christian Mission*, 45–47; Walls, "The Eighteenth-Century Protestant Missionary Awakening," 29; Bosch, *Transforming Mission*, 254–55.

7. Châtellier, *The Europe of the Devout*.

8. Forrestal, *Vincent de Paul*; Schen, *Charity and Lay Piety in Reformation London*; McHugh, *Hospital Politics in Seventeenth-Century France*; Dinan, *Women and Poor Relief*; Diefendorf, *From Penitence to Charity*.

9. Greer, *Mohawk Saint*; Leavelle, *The Catholic Calumet*; Clair, "'Seeing These Good Souls Adore God'"; Vélez, "'A Sign that We Are Related to You'"; Bilodeau, "'They Honor Our Lord'"; Sleeper-Smith, *Indian Women and French Men*.

10. Beresford, *Black Robe*; Deslandres, "French Catholicism in the Era of Exploration and Early Colonization," 213; Melzer, *Colonizer or Colonized*, 105–6; Randall, *Black Robes and Buckskin*, 5; Havard and Vidal, *Histoire de l'Amérique française*, 337–38; Anderson, *Betrayal of Faith*, 8; Greer, *Mohawk Saint*, 7–9, 82–83; Blackburn, *Harvest of Souls*, 15–17; Dorsey, "Going to School with Savages."

11. Deslandres, *Croire et Faire Croire*, 23; Tuttle, *Conceiving the Old Regime*, 81–83; Pilleul, "Le discours sur la Nouvelle-France et son évolution"; Simard, *La Réduction*, 26; Goddard, "Canada in Seventeenth-Century Jesuit Thought," 191; Goddard, "Converting the 'Sauvage,'" 221; Blackburn, *Harvest of Souls*, 17; Axtell, *The Invasion Within*, 39, 60–62.

12. Abé, *The Jesuit Mission to New France*, 114, 149–50; Boucher, *France and the American Tropics to 1700*, 56; Randall, *Black Robes and Buckskin*, 11; Greer, *The People of New France*, 82–84; Trigger, *The Children of Aataentsic*, 1:468; Axtell, *The Invasion Within*, 39, 60–62; Jaenen, "The Frenchification and Evangelization of the Amerindians"; Eccles, *Canada under Louis XIV, 1663–1701*, 87; Healy, "The French Jesuits and the Idea of the Noble Savage," 152–53.

13. Robert, *Converting Colonialism*, 2.

14. The classic nineteenth-century accounts are Parkman, *The Jesuits in North America*; Rochemonteix, *Les Jésuites et la Nouvelle-France au XVIIe siècle*; and Rochemonteix, *Les Jésuites et la Nouvelle-France au XVIIIe siècle*. Brief acknowledgments of Jesuit collaboration with French empire builders include Monet, "The Jesuits in New France"; Cushner, *Why Have You Come Here?*, 153–54; Richter, *Facing East from Indian Country*, 88; Blackburn, *Harvest of Souls*, 11, 129; Eccles, *The French in North America, 1500–1783*; Greer, *The People of New France*, 84; O'Neill, *Church and State in Colonial Louisiana*, 108–9; Kennedy, *Jesuit and Savage in New France*, 81, 129.

15. Clossey, *Salvation and Globalization in the Early Jesuit Missions*; Abé, *The Jesuit Mission to New France*, 201.

16. Martin, *The Jesuit Mind*, 187–98.

17. Compare to Friedrich, *Der lange Arm Roms?*, 433–35.

18. Leavelle, *The Catholic Calumet*; Anderson, *The Betrayal of Faith*; Vincent, "L'Iroquois est un loup pour l'homme"; Greer, "Conversion and Identity"; Devens, *Countering Colonization*; Richter, "Iroquois versus Iroquois"; Harrod, "Missionary Life World and Native Response"; Ronda, "'We Are Well as We Are.'"

19. Gitlin, *The Bourgeois Frontier*, 2–4.

20. Randall, *Black Robes and Buckskin*; Leavelle, *The Catholic Calumet*.

21. True, *Masters and Students*.

22. Le Bras, *L'Amérindien dans les Relations du père Paul Lejeune*, 17. The major nineteenth-century scholars who worked with the *Relations* are Laval University's Abbé Charles-Honoré Laverdière (1826–1873), the New York based Catholic historian and journalist John Gilmary Shea (1824–1892), the French Jesuit Camille de Rochemonteix (1834–1923), Harvard University's Francis Parkman (1823–1893), and the American Library Association's Reuben Gold Thwaites (1853–1913), who spearheaded the *Relations'* and numerous other mission documents' translation into English. In recent decades, the *Relations* and other missionary writings from New France have occasioned fruitful work by literature scholars. See especially Brazeau, *Writing a New France*; Le Bras, *L'Amérindien dans les Relations du père Lejeune*; Melzer, *Colonizer or Colonized*; Pioffet, *La tentation de l'épopée dans les Relations des jésuites*; Ouellet et al., *Rhetorique et conquête missionnaire*.

23. In addition to the *Relations'* availability online in English translation through Creighton University, and in both the original French and in English via Alexander Street Press, Thwaites's volumes are also available on Google Books and the original Cramoisy imprints are also digitally available through Early Canadiana Online (ECO). Collections of selected texts from the *Relations* are available as classroom-worthy textbooks: e.g., Greer, *The Jesuit Relations*; Randall, *Black Robes and Buckskin*.

24. Du Creux, *Historiae canadensis seu Novae Franciae libri decem*; Hamel, "Les *Historiae Canadensis* (1664) du père François Du Creux."

25. Charlevoix, *Histoire et description générale de la Nouvelle France*; Charlevoix, *History and General Description of New France*.

26. Lafitau, *Moeurs des sauvages amériquains*; Lafitau, *Customs of the American Indians*.

27. Starkloff, *Common Testimony*; Motsch, *Lafitau et l'émergence du discours ethnographique*; Pagden, *The Fall of Natural Man*, 198–209.

28. Blackburn, *Harvest of Souls*, 12; Dostie, *Le Lecteur suborné dans cinq textes missionnaires de la Nouvelle-France*.

29. Anderson, *Chain Her by One Foot*; Jennings, *The Invasion of America*, 57.

30. JR 51:67.

31. Newman, *An Essay on the Development of Christian Doctrine*, 1–2.

1. A MISSION FOR FRANCE

1. Matt. 28:19–20 (Douay-Rheims version).

2. JR 5:21.

3. JR 46:197–99, 291.

4. Pioffet, "L'arc et l'épée," 41–52; Axtell, *The Invasion Within*, 91.

5. JR 5:9. Compare to MNF 2:298.

6. Beik, *Urban Protest in Seventeenth-Century France*, 96.

7. Registries of novices at the Paris novitiate, 1615, ARSI, *Franc. 11*, 40v; *Franc. 22*, 115.

8. Brémond, *Histoire littéraire du sentiment religieux en France*, vol. 2, 450.

9. Benedict, *Cities and Social Change in Early Modern France*, 132; Mousnier, *Paris capitale au temps de Richelieu et de Mazarin*, 159–64; Jacquart, "Paris: First Metropolis in the Early Modern Period," 105.

10. These were Paschase Bröet, Jean Codure, Claude Le Jay, and Pierre Favre.

11. Martin, *The Jesuit Mind*, 18.

12. Martin, *The Jesuit Mind*, 1–2; Bergin, *Church, Society, and Religious Change in France, 1580–1730*, 112–13; Martin, *Henry III and the Jesuit Politicians*, 137–44.

13. Nelson, *The Jesuits and the Monarchy*, 57–69, 78.

14. Bangert, *A History of the Society of Jesus*, 256.

15. Haudrère, "Collège royal de La Flèche, l'esprit missionnaire et le Canada."

16. Bangert, *A History of the Society of Jesus*, 123; Guillermou, *Les Jésuites*, 39; Haudrère, "Collège royal de La Flèche."

17. Declaration of the Parisian Jesuits, January 31, 1612, ARSI, *Gal. 62*, 90.

18. Bangert, *A History of the Society of Jesus*, 128. See also Blet, "Jésuites et libertés gallicanes en 1611," 168–70; Blet, "Jésuites gallicans au XVIIe siècle?," 55–84.

19. Nelson, *The Jesuits and the Monarchy*, 228.

20. Delattre, *Les Établissements des jésuites en France depuis quatre siècles*, 3:1307–8.

21. McGregor, *Paris from the Ground Up*, 155–67.

22. Delattre, *Les Établissements des jésuites en France*, 3:1140.

23. Shea, *History of the Catholic Missions Among the Indian Tribes of the United States*, 191; Campeau, *Biographical Dictionary*, 177.

24. Campeau, *Biographical Dictionary*, 179.

25. Campeau, *Biographical Dictionary*, 218; Rochemonteix, *Les Jésuites et la Nouvelle-France au XVIIe siècle*, 1:139.

26. MNF 2:278.

27. Trigault, *Relation des cruels Martyres que 118 Chrestiens*.

28. Trigault, *Histoire des martyrs du Japon*; Trigault, *Histoire de ce qui s'est passé à la Chine*.

29. JR 5:105, 6:23, 8:271. Compare to Abé, *The Jesuit Mission to New France*.

30. Jesuits of Paris, *Solennité de la canonization de saint Ignace et de S. François Xavier, Apostre des Indes*; Morin, *La vie du glorieux S. Ignace de Loyola*.

31. MNF 2:59–75.

32. MNF 2:63; Fischer, *Champlain's Dream*, 394.

33. Deffain, *Un voyageur français en Nouvelle-France au XVIIe siècle*, 4–5.

34. Thierry, *La France de Henri IV en Amérique du Nord*, 7.

35. Pagden, *Lords of All the World*, 32–33; Thierry, *La France de Henri IV*, 31–32.

36. Kennedy, *Jesuit and Savage*, 15.

37. Boucher, *Les Nouvelles Frances*, 5; Frazee, *Catholics and Sultans*, 82; Ruiu, "Conflicting Visions of the Jesuit Missions to the Ottoman Empire, 1609–1628."

38. Rodríguez, *Monumenta Mexicana*, vol. 8, 3, 14.

39. Brasseaux, *The Founding of New Acadia*, 151–52; Thierry, *La France de Henri IV*, 369–77.

40. Faragher, *A Great and Noble Scheme*, 2, 23.

41. JR 3:141–55.

42. JR 3:25, 141–55.

43. MNF 1:509; my translation.

44. JR 3:137–39; Faragher, *A Great and Noble Scheme*, 24.

45. Fischer, *Champlain's Dream*, 313; Habig and Bacon, "L'ouvre des Récollets missionnaires en Nouvelle-France," xxxvi.

46. Habig and Bacon, "L'ouvre des Récollets missionnaires en Nouvelle-France," xxxvii; Carroll, *Noble Power during the French Wars of Religion*, 24.

47. MNF 2:99, 136; Trudel, *The Beginnings of New France: 1524–1663*, 136–37.

48. JR 4:403–5.

49. Fischer, *Champlain's Dream*, 397; Banks, *Chasing Empire across the Sea*, 16.

50. MNF 2:273–79; Campeau, *Biographical Dictionary*, 70, 238.

51. Sagard, *The Long Journey to the Country of the Hurons*, 171, 185.

52. Compare to True, *Masters and Students*, 31; Galland, *Pour la Gloire de Dieu et du Roi*, 139–75.

53. JR 3:33–39; MNF 1:462.

54. Fischer, *Champlain's Dream*, 404–5.

55. Trudel, *La seigneurie des Cent-Associés*, 419–20.

56. Châtellier, *The Europe of the Devout*, 108.

57. Châtellier, *The Europe of the Devout*, 100; Fouqueray, *Histoire de la Compagnie de Jésus en France des origines à la suppression*, 3:252.

58. JR 9:105.

59. Compare to Ranum, *Richelieu and the Councillors of Louis XIII*, 100–119; Lefauconnier, "François Sublet de Noyers (1589–1645)."

60. Martin, *Print, Power, and People*, 223.

61. Febvre and Martin, *The Coming of the Book*, 127; Martin, *The French Book*, 7, 196.

62. Martin, "Un grand éditeur parisien," 179, 188.

63. Jacquet, "Cramoisy," 1161.

64. Martin, *Print, Power, and People*, 223.

65. Martin, *Print, Power, and People*, 224. Compare to Rochemonteix, *Les Jésuites et la Nouvelle-France au XVIIe siècle*, 3:412–13; Neveu, *Érudition et religion aux XVIIe et XVIIIe siècles*.

66. Febvre and Martin, *The Coming of the Book*, 223–24.

67. MNF 2:78.

68. Martin, *Print, Power, and People*, 224.

69. Superior General to Sébastien Cramoisy (various letters), 1622–1666, ARSI, *Gal. 46 I*, 116v, 118v, 119v, 120v, 127, 134v, 135v, 136, 140, 144, 146, 147, 149v, 164v–165, 167v, 171v–172, 176, 190v, 202v, 206, 233v, 238–38v, 242v, 251v, 273v–74, 276, 282; *Gal. 46 II*, 293, 295v, 298, 324, 330, 334v, 337–37v, 339v, 342, 344, 348, 349v, 371v, 377v, 383, 386, 402–3v, 424v, 513v.

70. Richelieu, *Harangue prononcée en la sale du petit Bourbon le XXIII Fevrier 1615*.

71. Jacquet, "Cramoisy," 1162; Martin, *Print, Power, and People*, 225; Martin, "Un grand éditeur parisien," 180. Compare to Bibliothèque nationale de France, *L'Art du livre à l'Imprimerie nationale des origines à nos jours*.

72. Trudel, *La seigneurie des Cent-Associés*, 419–20.

73. Pouliot, *Étude sur les Relations des Jésuites de la Nouvelle-France*; Correia-Afonso, *Jesuit Letters and Indian History*. Compare to Friedrich, "Circulating and Compiling the *Litterae Annuae*," 3–39.

74. MNF 2:280–95.

75. JR 5:11.

76. True, *Masters and Students*, 10.

77. Masse, "Nouveaux Mondes (Mexique, Inde)," 229–49.

78. Vaulx, *Histoire des Missions Catholiques Françaises*, 65.

79. Hsia, *Sojourners in a Strange Land*, 19.

80. Rochemonteix, *Les Jésuites et la Nouvelle-France au XVIIe siècle*, 1:180–85.

81. JR 5:9, 15–21.

82. JR 15:219–21.

83. JR 15:235–37.

84. Solomon, *Public Welfare, Science and Propaganda*, 105–8.

85. Renaudot, *Nouvelles ordinaires*, 23 July 1632, reprinted in *Recueil des Gazettes nouvelles*, 282–83; my translation.

86. Church, *Richelieu and Reason of State*, 113, 124; Klaits, *Printed Propaganda under Louis XIV*, 7.

87. Nelson, *The Jesuits and the Monarchy*; Pelletier, *Apologie ou Défense pour les pères Jésuites*; Petiot, *Panegyricus Ludovico XIII*. Compare to Church, *Richelieu and Reason of State*, 142.

88. [Le Moyne], *Le Portrait du Roy*, 35–36.

89. Boisrobert, *Le sacrifice des Muses au grand cardinal de Richelieu*, n.p.; my translation; Boisrobert, *Palmae Regiae invictissimo Ludovico XIII*; Boisrobert, *Epicinia musarum, eminentissimo cardinali duci de Richelieu*; Boisrobert, *Le Parnasse Royal*.

90. JR 8:217; 15:217.

91. JR 11:47.

92. JR 47:113; 53:271; 58:240.

93. Ott, "Pope Urban VIII."

94. Duffy, *Saints and Sinners*, 234; Bireley, *The Jesuits and the Thirty Years' War*, 168.

95. JR 7:241–43.

96. MNF 2:184, 212–13. Compare to Boucher, *The Shaping of the French Colonial Empire*, 7.

97. JR 7:241–43.

98. JR 7:311–13.

99. Collins, *The State in Early Modern France*, 57.

100. Elliott, *Richelieu and Olivares*, 116–17.

101. Collins, *The State in Early Modern France*, 55, 58–59.

102. *Mercure françois* 19:223, 258–59, 671–681.

103. JR 7:243; 8:45.

104. JR 8:9–13.

105. Bireley, *The Jesuits and the Thirty Years' War*, 170.

106. JR 8:13–15.

107. Boucher, *The Shaping of the French Colonial Empire*, 4.

108. JR 8:217.

109. JR 9:151–53.

110. JR 9:153, 167–69.

2. THE "POOR MISERABLE SAVAGE"

1. JR 7:7–9. This chapter revises a previously published article. See McShea, "Presenting the 'Poor Miserable Savage' to French Urban Elites."

2. JR 7:7–9.

3. Beik, *A Social and Cultural History of Early Modern France*, 8–25; Farr, *The Work of France*, 78–110; Vardi, *The Land and the Loom*, 110–21; Briggs, *Early Modern France*, 36; Daniel Roche, *Histoire des choses banales*, 239; Hoffman, *Growth in a Traditional Society*, 81–142; Appleby, "Grain Prices and Subsistence Crises in England and France."

4. Farr, *The Work of France*, 63, 69; Vardi, *The Land and the Loom*, 20, 26–27; Beam, *Laughing Matters*, 210–20; Dewald, *The European Nobility*, 47–49; Courcelles, *Histoire généalogique et héraldique des Pairs de France*, vol. 16, s.v. "De Loynes."

5. Dewald, *The European Nobility*, 98–105.

6. Compare to Brazeau, *Writing a New France*.

7. Forrestal, *Vincent de Paul*; Diefendorf, *From Penitence to Charity*; McHugh, *Hospital Politics in Seventeenth-Century France*; Dinan, *Women and Poor Relief in Seventeenth-Century France*; Châtellier, *The Religion of the Poor*.

8. JR 5:21, 57–59; 7:187; Chill, "Religion and Mendicity in Seventeenth-Century France," 402; Jütte, *Poverty and Deviance*, 12.

9. Dickason, *The Myth of the Savage*, 64.

10. Champlain, *Premiers récits de voyages en Nouvelle-France, 1603–1619*; Champlain, *Derniers récits de voyages en Nouvelle-France et autres écrits, 1620–1632*.

11. Sagard, *Histoire du Canada et Voyages que les freres Mineurs Recollects*.

12. Diefendorf, *From Penitence to Charity*, 8.

13. John 12:8.

14. Davis, *Society and Culture in Early Modern France*, 17–64; Solomon, *Public Welfare, Science, and Propaganda*, 29–59; Yves de Paris, OFMCap, quoted in Christophe, *Les pauvres et la pauvreté*, 63.

15. JR 3:31–33.

16. JR 3:113.

17. JR 9:185, 189.

18. JR 9:191.

19. JR 8:9–11.

20. Axtell, *The Invasion Within*, 39, 60–62; Greer, *The Jesuit Relations*, 6, 13; Ronda, "The European Indian," 385; Goddard, "Canada in Seventeenth-Century Jesuit Thought," 191–93; Vecsey, *The Paths of Kateri's Kin*, 25, 51–53. The Jesuits themselves employed the verb "Frenchify" (*franciser*) in writing by the 1660s. JR 41:27, 29; 55:187.

21. JR 268–71.

22. JR 9:133–35.

23. JR 11:43–45.

24. Axtell, *The Invasion Within*, 131–78; Stevens, *The Poor Indians*, 6–17, 34–61.

25. DePauw, *Spiritualité et Pauvreté à Paris au XVIIe siècle*, 133.

26. MNF 3:267. Compare to JR 9:187.

27. MNF 2:307; 3:269. Compare to JR 5:83; 9:189.

28. JR 9:189; 8:9–11.

29. Pinkard, *A Revolution in Taste*, 57–58; MNF 4:272–73. Compare to JR 15:225.

30. MNF 3:88; JR 6:249; 7:219–21.

31. MNF 2:412; my translation. Compare to JR 5:95.

32. Rey, *Dictionnaire Historique de la Langue Française*, 1:406; Dauzet, *Nouveau Dictionnaire Étymologique et Historique*, 160.

33. JR 6:273.

34. Pinkard, *A Revolution in Taste*, 73; Goubert, *The French Peasantry*, 87, 91; Jütte, *Poverty and Deviance*, 73–75; Roche, *Histoire des choses banales*, 87, 241, 247.

35. JR 5:101, 263; 7:43; Braudel, *The Structures of Everyday Life*, 190.

36. Pinkard, *A Revolution in Taste*, 3, 111.

37. JR 5:101; 6:223; 7:53; Vardi, *The Land and the Loom*, 20; Goubert, *The French Peasantry*, 91, 258.

38. JR 7:81; Soyer, *Pantropheon*, 337; Toussaint-Samat, *A History of Food*, 255–56.

39. Dickason, *The Myth of the Savage*, 12.

40. MNF 2:413–14; my translation. Compare to JR 5:99–101.

41. Knox, "Gesture and Comportment," 303.

42. Elias, *The Civilizing Process*, 61, 87; Chartier, *The Cultural Uses of Print*, 71–109.

43. Braudel, *The Structures of Everyday Life*, 284; Roche, *Histoire des choses banales*, 258.

44. JR 5:87–89.

45. JR 6:267.

46. Braudel, *The Structures of Everyday Life*, 206.

47. Roche, *Histoire des choses banales*, 259.

48. MNF 2:609; my translation. Compare to JR 6:261–69.

49. JR 7:43; 6:259–63.

50. JR 7:43; 5:167.

51. Braudel, *The Structures of Everyday Life*, 275–76, 278, 283; Farr, *The Work of France*, 63, 69; Vardi, *The Land and the Loom*, 20, 26–27; Jütte, *Poverty and Deviance*, 62–63, 70; Hufton, *Bayeux in the Late Eighteenth Century*, 84. Compare to Chill, "Religion and Mendicity in Seventeenth Century France," 402.

52. JR 5:121; 8:103.

53. MNF 2:652; my translation. Compare to JR 7:35.

54. MNF 3:97; my translation. Compare to JR 8:103.

55. Hussey, *Paris*, 146–47; Jones, *Paris*, 142; Ranum, *Paris in the Age of Absolutism*, 87–88, 114–15.

56. Ranum, *Paris in the Age of Absolutism*, 90; Hussey, *Paris*, 166; Newman, *Cultural Capitals*, 77–78; Beik, *A Social and Cultural History of Early Modern France*, 102–4.

57. JR 5:85–87, 161–63; 7:111.

58. Jütte, *Poverty and Deviance*, 65. Compare to Darnton, *The Great Cat Massacre*, 37.

59. Braudel, *The Structures of Everyday Life*, 203.

60. MNF 3:552; my translation. Compare to JR 11:121.

61. JR 11:119–21.

62. JR 13:149–51; MNF 3:730–731.

63. Compare to Goddard, "Converting the 'Sauvage,'" 219–39.

64. JR 6:203–5; MNF 2:585; Groethuysen, *The Bourgeois*, 19.

65. Sagard, *The Long Journey to the Country of the Hurons*, 78, 171, 185.

66. JR 6:181, 211–15; 9:123.

67. JR 6:177–81.

68. JR 6:203; Anderson, *The Betrayal of Faith*, 24, 29; Speck, *Naskapi*, 5, 20.

69. JR 6:175–77.

70. Anderson, *The Betrayal of Faith*, 23–24.

71. See for example Question 75, Article 3 in the First Part of the *Summa Theologica*.

72. Denzinger, *The Sources of Catholic Dogma*, 169.

73. JR 5:165–67.

74. JR 5:165–67; 6:177–79.

75. JR 8:121; 10:157–61.

76. JR 10:147, 159.

77. JR 5:99; 10:157, 177.

78. Virgil, *The Aeneid*, 53–54.

79. JR 6:251; 7:9.

80. JR 7:53–57.

81. MNF 3:612; my translation. Compare to JR 12:45.

82. JR 12:63–65.

83. JR 12:45.

84. JR 5:21; Burke, *Popular Culture in Early Modern Europe*, 207.

85. JR 6:101–3.

86. JR 6:161–63; Beam, *Laughing Matters*, 210–18.

87. JR 10:199–201.

88. Deslandres, "Indes intérieures et Indes lointaines," 369–77; Deslandres, *Croire et faire croire*; Martin, *The Jesuit Mind*, 212–13; Châtellier, *The Religion of the Poor*, 35–36. Compare to Croix and Roudaut, *Les Bretons, la mort et Dieu*, 227–28.

89. JR 13:77–79.

90. Davis, *Society and Culture in Early Modern France*, 97–123.

91. JR 12:179.

92. JR 12:5–7.

93. Burke, *Popular Culture in Early Modern Europe*, 273–74. Compare to Muchembled, *La sorcière au village (Xve– XVIIe siècle)*.

94. Brockliss and Jones, *The Medical World of Early Modern France*, 230–37. Compare to Solomon, *Public Welfare, Science, and Propaganda in Seventeenth Century France*, 21–59.

95. Jacquet, "Cramoisy," 1162; Châtellier, *The Europe of the Devout*, 130, 135; Chaussé, "Le Pere Paul Le Jeune," 221; Jamet, *Les Annales de l'Hôtel-Dieu de Québec*, xvii, 9.

96. JR 3:115; Burke, *Popular Culture in Early Modern Europe*, 273. Compare to Sonnet de Courval, *Satyre contre les charlatans*.

97. JR 7:255, 8:215, 11:45.

98. Grafton, *New Worlds, Ancient Texts*; Elliott, *The Old World and the New*; Kupperman, *America in European Consciousness*, 2–5. Compare to Brazeau, *Writing a New France*; Greenblatt, *Marvelous Possessions*.

3. THE BEAVER WARS AND THE FRONDE

1. Wilkinson, *Louis XIV*, 25.
2. JR 41:213.
3. Anderson, *The Death and Afterlife of the North American Martyrs*; Boss, "Writing a Relic," 211–34.
4. Trudel, *The Beginnings of New France*, 187; Campeau, *Les Finances publiques de la Nouvelle-France sous les Cent-Associés*, 7–9; Blackburn, *Harvest of Souls*, 14.
5. Briggs, *Early Modern France*, 104; Du Creux, *The History of Canada or New France*, 1:207.
6. Trudel, *The Beginnings of New France*, 180, 187.
7. Hunt, *The Wars of the Iroquois*, 71–74. Compare to JR 5:207, 213; 6:59; 8:61–63.
8. Dubé, *The Chevalier de Montmagny*, 164–66; Hunt, *The Wars of the Iroquois*, 74–75.
9. JR 17:219–25.
10. Châtellier, *The Europe of the Devout*, 93; Nelson, *The Jesuits and the Monarchy*, 1–2.
11. MNF 5:238.
12. JR 21:269–73; 22:31–33; MNF 5:45, 226–27.
13. MNF 5:226–27.
14. MNF 5:230–31.
15. JR 21:61–79.
16. MNF 5:162–63 (emphasis added); JR 21:117–19.
17. JR 22:31–33; MNF 5:42; Dubé, *The Chevalier de Montmagny*, 166.
18. JR 21:269–73; MNF 5:226–27.
19. Fouqueray, *Histoire de la Compagnie de Jésus en France des origines à la suppression*, 5:414; MNF 5:232–35.
20. MNF 5:369–70.
21. JR 23:281–85; MNF 5:649–650.
22. JR 25:75–77.
23. JR 24:301–3.
24. Campeau, *Biographical Dictionary*, 163.
25. Trigger, *The Children of Aataentsic*, 2:638; Richter, *The Ordeal of the Longhouse*, 61.
26. Brandão, *Your Fyre Shall Burn No More*, 55–56.
27. JR 24:295–97.
28. JR 24:271–73, 289–91.
29. MNF 5:637; 6:8.
30. MNF 5:789.
31. JR 25:45.
32. MNF 5:782. Compare to JR 25:47.
33. JR 25:47.
34. JR 25:47.

35. JR 25:65; MNF 6:489.

36. MNF 6:490–92.

37. MNF 6:491–93.

38. MNF 6:494.

39. Parkman, *The Jesuits in North America*, 193.

40. MNF 7:126.

41. JR 31:105–7.

42. JR 29:49, 57–61. Compare to Trigger, *The Children of Aataentsic*, 2:654–655; Brandão, *Your Fyre Shall Burn No More*, 102–7.

43. JR 29:61.

44. JR 30:219–21, 227; 31:107; Anderson, *The Death and Afterlife of the North American Martyrs*, 25.

45. MNF 6:514; my translation. Compare to JR 28:139–41.

46. Trigger, *The Children of Aataentsic*, 2:762–770.

47. JR 34:55.

48. Martin, "Un grand éditeur parisien," 186; Jacquet, "Cramoisy," 1162.

49. Collins, *The State in Early Modern France*, 70.

50. Ranum, *The Fronde*, 182; Jacquet, "Cramoisy," 1162; Parlement de Paris, *Arrest de la Cour de Parlement donné toutes les Chambres assemblées, le 6 jour de Janvier 1649*; Parlement de Paris, *Arrest de le Cour de Parlement, pour la diminution des loyers des maisons dans la ville & fauxbourgs de Paris, du 10 avril 1649*; Parlement de Paris, *Arrest de le Cour de Parlement, portant injonction à tous les subjets du Roy d'obéir à la déclaration de mars dernier*; Parlement de Paris, *Arrest de la Cour de Parlement toutes les chambres assemblées contre le Cardinal Mazarin, du samedy 11 mars 1651*. Cramoisy helped distribute a number of other mazarinades in the period.

51. Banks, *Chasing Empire across the Sea*, 20.

52. MNF 8:15. Compare to JR 36:73.

53. JR 36:75–81, 105; MNF 8:2–4.

54. MNF 8:6.

55. Trudel, *The Beginnings of New France*, 222,

56. McCoy, *Jesuit Relations of Canada*, 139.

57. JR 34:79–81.

58. JR 34:147.

59. JR 35:89.

60. JR 34:215, 225.

61. Campeau, MNF 7:570–571; Ragueneau, *Relation de ce qui s'est passé en la mission des Pères de la Compagnie de Jésus aux Hurons*; Ragueneau, *Narratio historica eorum quae Societatis Iesu in Nova Francia*; Ragueneau, *Verhael Van t'gheen gheschiet is in de Missie van de PP. der Societeyt Iesu*. Compare to McCoy, *Jesuit Relations of Canada*, 152–73.

62. Ranum, *The Fronde*, 199; Parlement de Paris, *Arrest de la Cour de Parlement, portant injonction à tous marchands & artisans de cette ville & fauxbourgs de Paris*; Parlement de Paris, *Arrest de Parlement en faveur de toutes les revenderesses de poisson et autres denrées dans les Marché-Neuf*.

63. Collins, *The State in Early Modern France*, 75; Briggs, *Early Modern France*, 36; Jones, *Paris*, 155–56.

64. JR 38:45, 49.

65. JR 38:45–47.

66. JR 27:139.

67. JR 26:201; 27:65–67, 89–91.

68. MNF 8:262–65, 270, 426; 9:43, 188.

69. Charlevoix, *History and General Description of New France*, 2:245.

70. MNF 8:539.

71. Dennis, *Cultivating a Landscape of Peace*, 180; Anderson, *The Death and Afterlife of the North American Martyrs*, 72–76; Chartrand, *The Forts of New France*, 13.

72. MNF 8:665–666.

73. JR 43:161.

74. JR 36:149, 37:94; 43:251–53.

75. MNF 7:625–626; my translation.

76. Eccles, *Canada under Louis XIV*, 1–2.

77. Boucher, *France and the American Tropics to 1700*, 142, 158; Singer and Langdon, *Cultured Force*, 40.

78. Bouton, *Relation de l'Establissement des François depuis l'an 1635 en l'isle de la Martinique*, 33, 83, 93–104.

79. Singer and Langdon, *Cultured Force*, 25.

80. JR 45:259.

81. JR 46:291.

82. JR 45:187–91.

83. JR 45:201.

84. JR 45:197.

85. JR 45:201.

86. JR 46:196–98; my translation.

87. Richter, *Before the Revolution*, 219; Delâge, *Bitter Feast*, 237; Anderson, *Chain Her by One Foot*, 53–54.

88. Lynn, *Giant of the Grand Siècle*, 104; Collins, *The State in Early Modern France*, 94.

89. McCluskey, "'Les Ennemis du Nom Chrestien.'"

90. JR 46:147–49.

91. JR 46:149, 153.

92. Compare to Dennis, *Cultivating a Landscape of Peace*, 214–15.

93. MNF 8:411–12, 425.

94. Robinson, Introduction to Du Creux, *History of Canada*, xii.

95. Du Creux, *History of Canada*, 1:5.

96. Du Creux, *History of Canada*, 1:6–8.

97. Du Creux, *History of Canada*, 2:486, 491.

98. Du Creux, *History of Canada*, 2:754.

99. Robinson, Introduction to Du Creux, *History of Canada*, 1:xiv–xv. Compare to Hamel, "François Du Creux"; Hamel, "Translating as a Way of Writing History."

100. Du Creux, *History of Canada*, 2:439, 442.

101. Du Creux, *History of Canada*, 2:440. Compare to Du Creux, *Historiae Canadensis*, 453–54.

102. Du Creux, *History of Canada*, 2:442.

103. Du Creux, *History of Canada*, 2:483.

104. JR 45:191–95.

105. JR 49:212–14; my translation.

4. EXPORTING AND IMPORTING CHARITY

1. JR 53:59–61.

2. Charas, *Histoire naturelle des animaux, des plantes & des minéraux*.

3. JR 49:59; 50:271; 53:69–75; 59:37; 66:129; 68:67.

4. Alchon, *A Pest in the Land*, 99; Watts, *Epidemics and History*, 92.

5. Abé, *The Jesuit Mission to New France*, 159–60; Anderson, *The Death and Afterlife of the North American Martyrs*, 32–33; Beaulieu, *Convertir les fils de Caïn*, 98–101; Trigger, *Natives and Newcomers*, 249–50.

6. E.g., Théry, "Femmes missionnaires en Nouvelle-France," 89–99.

7. Bosch, *Transforming Mission*, 255; Robert, *Christian Mission*, 45–47; Walls, "The Eighteenth-Century Protestant Missionary Awakening in Its European Context," 29. Compare to Clair, "'Seeing These Good Souls Adore God'"; Brockey, *Journey to the East*, 350–64; Higashibaba, *Christianity in Early Modern Japan*, 22–27.

8. Châtellier, *The Europe of the Devout*; Lazar, *Working in the Vineyard of the Lord*; Bowers, *Plague and Public Health in Early Modern Seville*; Terpstra, *Cultures of Charity*; Gavitt, *Gender, Honor, and Charity in Late Renaissance Florence*.

9. E.g., JR 11:49; 12:23; 18:241.

10. JR 9:105; 65:85.

11. Châtellier, *The Europe of the Devout*, 130; Dinan, "Motivations for Charity in Early Modern France," 187; Dinan, *Women and Poor Relief in Seventeenth-Century France*, 68, 74, 97; McHugh, "The Hôpital Général," 235–36.

12. JR 18:137.

13. JR 6:143.

14. Deffain, *Un voyageur français en Nouvelle-France au XVIIe siècle*, 4–5; Jacquet, "Cramoisy," 1162; Châtellier, *The Europe of the Devout*, 130, 135; Jamet, *Les Annales de l'Hôtel-Dieu de Québec*, xvii, 9.

15. JR 16:25–29; 20:241; Procuration of Marie de Vignerot [duchesse d'Aiguillon] for taking possession of lands ceded by the Compagnie de la Nouvelle France, March 29, 1637, LAC, MG3-III; Taking of possession by the Hospitalières of lands accorded to the duchesse d'Aiguillon, January 26, 1640, LAC, MG8-A23; Donation by the duchesse d'Aiguillon to the Réligieuses Hospitalières of the Hôtel-Dieu de Québec, January 31, 1640, LAC, MG17-A10, 228–36; Dinan, "Motivations for Charity in Early Modern France," 187n.

16. Hughes, *History of the Society of Jesus in North America*, vol. 2, 243.

17. JR 18:96–97. Compare to JR 20:233.

18. JR 16:101–9; 19:9–11; 20:241.

19. JR 22:155–57; Lynch, *Individuals, Families, and Communities in Europe*, 156.

20. JR 24:159.

21. JR 24:185.

22. JR 23:313.

23. JR 23:305–7.

24. JR 20:237.

25. JR 18:65–75.

26. JR 23:307.

27. JR 16:135; 20:237–39; 23:305–7; Diefendorf, *From Penitence to Charity*, 221, 234; Forrestal, *Vincent de Paul*.

28. Procuration by the Hôpital de la Miséricorde de Québec to Sébastien Cramoisy, October 1, 1658, and October 6, 1666, LAC, MG8-A23.

29. Compare to Châtellier, *The Europe of the Devout*, 103.

30. JR 36:61; 51:107; 52:103–7.

31. Sébastien Cramoisy to Mother Marie de St-Bonnaventure, April 18, 1654, LAC, MG17-A10, 5–10.

32. JR 11:49–51.

33. JR 18:243–45; 43:221–23; 53:59–61.

34. JR 13:113–15.

35. JR 34:51; 35:33–39. On the Jesuits' landholdings in New France, see Coates, *The Metamorphoses of Land*, 15–17.

36. JR 34:99, 199.

37. JR 34:51, 99, 199, 215; 35:39, 53, 89, 211.

38. JR 34:215.

39. JR 35:89.

40. JR 35:207–11; 36:55.

41. JR 35:19; 36:193.

42. Elmore, "The Origins of the Paris Hôpital Général," 74.

43. JR 36:61.

44. JR 36:55.

45. JR 37:181; Labelle, *Dispersed but Not Destroyed*, 161–62.

46. JR 44:47–49.

47. JR 11:53–5; 16:33–35; 21:111, 137–39.

48. JR 22:173; 37:153; 57:47–49; 62:179–81, 247.

49. JR 52:125.

50. JR 62:95–97.

51. JR 63:73, 85.

52. JR 65:91.

53. JR 66:213.

54. JR 20:257; 22:173.

55. JR 24:189; emphasis added.

56. MNF 8:786–787; 9:7–8; JR 43:23.

57. Pouliot, "Les procureurs parisiens de la Mission de la Nouvelle-France," 42–43. Compare to Jamet, *Les Annales de l'Hôtel-Dieu de Québec*, 226n.

58. JR 20:249–51; 37:147–49.

59. JR 37:151.

60. JR 64:109–13.

61. MNF 8:792–793.

62. Stevens, *The Poor Indians*, 7.

63. Dinan, "Motivations for Charity in Early Modern France," 181–82; Hickey, *Local Hospitals in Ancien Régime France*, 17–44.

64. Binet, *Le Riche sauvé par la porte dorée du Ciel*, 569–570.

65. Binet, *Le Riche sauvé par la porte dorée du Ciel*, n.p., 131, 471–86.

66. JR 9:107; emphasis added. Compare to MNF 3:243.

67. Luke 6:20–21.

68. Boulle, "French Mercantilism, Commercial Companies, and Colonial Profitability," 239–41.

69. Conklin, *A Mission to Civilize*, 61–64, 76–80; Daughton, *An Empire Divided*, 14, 37.

70. JR 54:239–41.

71. Lafitau, *Customs of the American Indians*, 2:17.

5. CRUSADING FOR IROQUOIS COUNTRY

1. JR 51:67.

2. JR 55:111–13.

3. JR 53:27.

4. Banks, *Chasing Empire across the Sea*, 24–25.

5. JR 45:201.

6. JR 49:189–91; 50:159.

7. Richaudeau, *Lettres de la Révérende Mère Marie de l'Incarnation (née Marie Guyard)*, 2:309.

8. JR 49:253–55.

9. JR 49:179; 50:127–49, 181–87; Verney, *The Good Regiment*, 37–53, 90–91.

10. JR 50:141; Richter, *Before the Revolution*, 260.

11. JR 50:239.

12. JR 51:121.

13. JR 51:169–71.

14. JR 51:205–9.

15. JR 51:235.

16. JR 51:241–43.

17. Richter, *Trade, Land, Power*, 106; St-Arnaud, *Pierre Miller en Iroquoisie au XVIIe siècle*, 82–86.

18. JR 62:99; Richter, *The Ordeal of the Longhouse*, 142–44.

19. White, *The Middle Ground*, 1.

20. White, *The Middle Ground*, 28–29, 35; Skinner, *The Upper Country*, ix–x.

21. White, *The Middle Ground*, 29; Skinner, *The Upper Country*, 40.

22. Margry, *Découvertes et Établissements des Français dans l'oeust et dans le sud de l'Amérique septentrionalle*, vol. 2, 215–20.

23. JR 62:151–55. Compare to White, *The Middle Ground*, 30.

24. Richter, *The Ordeal of the Longhouse*, 144.

25. JR 62:107, 153.

26. JR 62:157, 161.

27. JR 62:157–63.

28. JR 62:163.

29. Desbarats, "The Cost of Early Canada's Native Alliances," 610–12.

30. Dubé, *La Nouvelle-France sous Joseph-Antoine le Febvre de la Barre*, 92, 101. Compare to AC, C11A, vol. 6, 134–35, 143–44.

31. Calloway, *The World Turned Upside Down*, 118–19.

32. Richter, *The Ordeal of the Longhouse*, 144.

33. JR 64:255–57.

34. JR 64:249–53.

35. JR 64:259.

36. JR 63:269–79.

37. Charlevoix, *History and General Description*, 4:19–36.

38. Pritchard, *In Search of Empire*, 335; Banks, *Chasing Empire across the Sea*, 29.

39. JR 64:33–35.

40. JR 64:35.

41. Charlevoix, *History and General Description*, 4:57–58.

42. Charlevoix, *History and General Description*, 4:19–20.

43. Charlevoix, *History and General Description,* 4:46–47; emphasis added.

44. Charlevoix, *History and General Description,* 4:245–47, 276–77.

45. Richter, *Before the Revolution*, 317.

46. JR 64:109–13.

47. Richter, *Facing East from Indian Country*, 159.

48. Bruyas, *Radical Words of the Iroquois Language.*

49. Charlevoix, *History and General Description*, 5:104.

50. Havard, *The Great Peace of Montreal of 1701*, 74.

51. Havard, *The Great Peace of Montreal of 1701*, 68.

52. Pritchard, *In Search of Empire*, 27.

53. JR 65:223–25; emphasis added.

54. Dandelet, *The Renaissance of Empire in Early Modern Europe*, 246–47; Miquelon, "Envisioning the French Empire," 653.

55. Pritchard, *In Search of Empire*, 394.

56. Quoted in Haefeli and Sweeney, *Captors and Captives*, 75.

57. Haefeli and Sweeney, *Captors and Captives*, 77.

58. Pritchard, *In Search of Empire*, 394.

59. Demos, *The Unredeemed Captive*, 34–39, 151–52.

60. Charlevoix, *History and General Description*, 5:253.

61. JR 66:195.

62. JR 66:193–95.

63. JR 66:199–203.

64. Charlevoix, *History and General Description*, 5:253.

65. Charlevoix, *History and General Description*, 5:252–53.

66. JR 46:65.

67. JR 45:209.

68. JR 51:123.

69. JR 57:127.

70. Pascal, *Pensées*, 218.

71. Quoted in Bell, *The First Total War*, 59.

72. Pagden and Lawrence, *Vitoria*, 272.

73. Reinhardt, "Introduction: War, Conscience, and Counsel in Early Modern Catholic Europe," 443–44.

74. Quoted in Martin, *The Jesuit Mind*, 102.

75. Smith, *War and the Making of Medieval Monastic Culture*, 96–110; Dawson, *Religion and the Rise of Western Culture*, 102.

76. Compare to True, *Masters and Students*, xv.

77. Steckley, *Words of the Huron*, 196–98, 210. Compare to JR 10:183; 23:153.

78. Du Creux, *History of Canada*, 1:10.

79. JR 55:111–13.

80. JR 63:241–43; 64:111.

81. Desbarats, "The Cost of Early Canada's Native Alliances," 620.

82. JR 64:111–13.

83. JR 66:159–61.

84. JR 66:167–69.

85. JR 67:105, 203–5.

86. JR 41:215.

87. Charlevoix, *History and General Description*, 2:261.

88. Du Creux, *History of Canada*, 2:460–46; emphasis added. For Thomas's discussion, see Article 7 of Question 64 in the *Summa*'s "Secunda Secundae Partis."

89. Du Creux, *History of Canada*, 2:462.

90. JR 64:127–29.

6. AN INDIGENOUS ARISTOCRACY

1. JR 59:241–43.

2. Confraternité de la Sainte-Famille, *La solide dévotion à la très Sainte-famille de Jésus, Marie et Joseph*.

3. Havard, "'Les forcer à devenir Cytoyens'"; Morrissey, "The Terms of Encounter"; Jaenen, "The Frenchification of the Amerindians"; Jetten, *Enclaves amérindiennes*; Axtell, *The Invasion Within*, 39, 60–62.

4. Blackburn, *Harvest of Souls*, 15; Anderson, *Chain Her by One Foot*, 9; Delâge, *Bitter Feast*, 201–3; Deslandres, *Croire et Faire Croire*, 319; Pesantubbee, *Choctaw Women in a Chaotic World*, 75; Tuttle, *Conceiving the Old Regime*, 81–83.

5. JR 46:78–80; my translation.

6. JR 65:43–47.

7. JR 66:109.

8. JR 55:209–11.

9. JR 51:27–29.

10. JR 66:167–69; Pouliot, "Les procureurs parisiens," 45.

11. Crouch, *Nobility Lost*, 21.

12. JR 45:209.

13. JR 43:285.

14. JR 54:111–13.

15. JR 61:213.

16. JR 57:89–91.

17. JR 59:282–85.

18. Jean-Baptiste Colbert to Jean Talon, January 5, 1666 and February 20, 1668, RAPQ (1930–1931), 45, 94–95.

19. Colbert to Talon, February 20, 1668, RAPQ (1930–1931), 94–95; Delanglez, *Frontenac and the Jesuits*, 42.

20. Leclercq, *Premier établissement de la foy dans la Nouvelle-France*, 224.

21. Hosne, *The Jesuit Missions to China and Peru*, 75–76; Metcalf, *Go-Betweens and the Colonization of Brazil*, 111–12; Prien, *Christianity in Latin America*, 156–57; Cogley, *John Eliot's Mission to the Indians before King Philip's War*, 7.

22. Compare to Elias, *The Civilizing Process*, 61, 87; Chartier, *The Cultural Uses of Print in Early Modern France*, 71–109; Febvre, "*Civilisation*," 224–26.

23. JR 3:87, 97, 276–77.

24. JR 10:210–13.

25. Sahlins, *Boundaries*, 116–18; Cohen, "Linguistic Politics on the Periphery," 167, 180.

26. JR 62:57–59.

27. JR 66:219–21; my revision of Thwaites's translation; Bernard, *Relations de la Louisiane et du fleuve Mississippi*, 25–26.

28. JR 61:133–35.

29. JR 61:15.

30. Dennis, *Cultivating a Landscape of Peace*, 202–5; Trudel, *Beginnings of New France*, 251–52.

31. Choquette, *Frenchmen into Peasants*, 107–13.

32. Trudel, *Beginnings of New France*, 202; Allain, "Colbert and the Colonies," 16.

33. JR 59:241.

34. JR 60:297–301.

35. Saad, *Les Mariages Islamo-Chrétiens*, 112, 132–33.

36. JR 59:279.

37. MNF 9:39; JR 22:229; 24:47; 43:227–29; 65:67; 67:175.

38. MNF 3:35; Codignola, "The Holy See and the Conversion of the Indians in French and British North America, 1486–1760," 200–201; Županov, *Missionary Tropics*, 174, 184, 189; Ward, *Women Religious Leaders in Japan's Christian Century*, 133, 140.

39. JR 14:63; Melzer, *Colonizer or Colonized*, 106.

40. MNF 3:35, 37–38.

41. JR 13:169–75, 187; 14:15–21.

42. JR 15:125; 16:59, 89, 229.

43. JR 23:187.

44. MNF 6:16.

45. MNF 6:517; 7:234–36.

46. JR 42:139.

47. Tuttle, *Conceiving the Old Regime*, 91; White, *The Middle Ground*, 69–70.

48. JR 65:239.

49. JR 60:255; 65:237–47.

50. JR 66:219–21.

51. JR 61:219.

52. JR 63:185–87.

53. JR 63:175–79.

54. JR 61:39

55. JR 62:115, 141.

56. JR 62:179–81.

57. JR 65:67–69.

58. JR 43:2276–29; my revised translation of Thwaites's.

59. JR 63:201–5.

60. JR 54:239.

61. JR 18:132.

62. JR 3:99–101; Desan, "Making and Breaking Marriage," 8–9.

63. JR 64:131.

64. JR 65:29–31.

65. E.g. Axtell, *The Invasion Within*, 65; Moore, *Indian and Jesuit*, 194.

66. JR 62:168; 63:241–43.

67. JR 65:29–33.

68. JR 63:181.

69. JR 62:101.

70. JR 67:39–45.

71. JR 47:293; 51:173–75; 66:159.

72. Cullen, *The Brandy Trade under the Ancien Régime*, 1–9.

73. JR 65:193–95.

74. JR 65:191.

75. Peyser and Brandão, *Edge of Empire*, xxxii.

76. JR 62:111; 63:181.

77. Charlevoix, *History and General Description*, 4:198.

78. Charlevoix, *History and General Description*, 4:197–98.

79. Colonna, "Educating Conformity in French Colonial Algeria," 346–70.

80. JR 66:159–61.

81. JR 67:73–75.

82. JR 67:75.

83. JR 67:75.

84. Liebersohn, *Aristocratic Encounters*, 17.

1. Kennedy, *Jesuit and Savage in New France*, 50–51. Compare to JR 63:71.

2. Delanglez, *The French Jesuits in Lower Louisiana*, and O'Neill, *Church and State in French Colonial Louisiana,* remain the most comprehensive accounts of pre-suppression Jesuit activity in the Lower Mississippi region.

3. Dennis, *Cultivating a Landscape of Peace*, 202.

4. Charlevoix, *History and General Description*, 6:11–12.

5. Dandelet, *The Renaissance of Empire*, 233; Duffy, *Saints and Sinners*, 236; Bergin, *Crown, Church and Episcopate Under Louis XIV*, 228.

6. Bilio, *Bullarum diplomatum et privilegio sanctorum romanum pontificum*, vol. 18, 393.

7. Pouliot, *Étude sur les Relations des Jésuites de la Nouvelle-France*, 12–15.

8. Le Jeune, *Épistres spirituelles, escrites à plusieurs personnes de piété*; Le Jeune, *Solitude de dix jours*.

9. Martin, *Print, Power, and People*, 282.

10. Jacquet, "Cramoisy," 1162; Burke, *The Fabrication of Louis XIV*, 49–59.

11. Martin, "Un grand éditeur parisien," 185.

12. JR 55:249; 56:149.

13. JR 55:237.

14. Brucker, Reviews, *Études religieuses, historiques et littéraires*; Pouliot, *Étude sur les Relations des Jésuites de la Nouvelle-France*, 14; Rochemonteix, *Les Jésuites et la Nouvelle-France au XVIIe siècle*, 1:lii–liv.

15. Gay, *"Voués à quel royaume?"*

16. Banks, *Chasing Empire across the Sea*, 22–23.

17. JR 63:269–79, 283.

18. JR 67:25–27.

19. Loan and repayment schedule for the Collège de Québec by Marie de Grisande de Prouville October 19, 1672, LAC, MG3-III.

20. Challes, *Mémoires de Robert Challes, écrivain du Roi*, 79, 88.

21. Kennedy, *Jesuit and Savage*, 46.

22. Le Clercq, *First Establishment of the Faith in New France*, vol. 1, 255.

23. MNF 8:541–542.

24. MNF 8:626.

25. MNF 8:799, 826; 9:51.

26. MNF 9:339, 404; Alden, *The Making of an Enterprise*, 249.

27. ARSI, *Fondo Gesuitico Indepetae 26*.

28. MNF 9:340.

29. MNF 9:352, 405.

30. MNF 9:362.

31. JR 51:159. Compare to JR 49:189–91.

32. Brisacier, *Le Jansénisme confondu dans l'advocat du Sr Callaghan*; Brodrick, *The Economic Morals of the Jesuits*, 55; Strayer, *Suffering Saints*, 95.

33. Brisacier, *Les Jansénistes reconnus Calvinistes par Samuel Desmares*; Annat et al., *Responses aux Lettres provinciales publiées*.

34. Pascal, *Les Provinciales*, 75–76, 88, 120–21.

35. MNF 9:428–429.

36. MNF 9:530–531.

37. Report by Paul Ragueneau, ca. 1663, ARSI, *Gal. 109 I*, 24–25; Lafitau to Tamburini, 1720, ARSI, *Gal. 110 I*, 117–21v; Anonymous report, ca. 1720, ARSI, *Gal. 110 III*, 382–83.

38. Anonymous report, ca. 1720, ARSI, *Gal. 110 III*, 382–83.

39. Report by Paul Ragueneau, ca. 1663, ARSI, *Gal. 109 I*, 24–24v.

40. Lafitau to Tamburini, 1720, ARSI, *Gal. 110 I*, 117–21v.

41. Anonymous report, ca. 1720, ARSI, *Gal. 110 III*, 383.

42. Lahontan, *Dialogues de M. le baron de Lahontan et d'un Sauvage*, 71; my translation.

43. Review, *Mémoires pour l'histoire des Sciences et des beaux Arts . . . Juillet 1703*, 1110.

44. McCabe, *Orientalism in Early Modern France*, 277.

45. Bangert, *A History of the Society of Jesus*, 298.

46. JR 66:147–49.

47. Garrioch, *The Making of Revolutionary Paris*, 186–87.

48. Garrioch, *The Making of Revolutionary Paris*, 198.

49. JR 70:164–75.

50. Formey, *La France Littéraire, ou Dictionnaire des auteurs François vivans*, 43.

51. Guillot, *Les Jésuites et la musique*, 171–72.

52. Northeast, *The Parisian Jesuits and the Enlightenment*, 5.

53. Northeast, *The Parisian Jesuits and the Enlightenment*, 7.

54. Quoted in Dandelet, *The Renaissance of Empire*, 224.

55. Northeast, *The Parisian Jesuits and the Enlightenment*, 13.

56. Châtellier, *The Europe of the Devout*, 177.

57. Charlevoix, *History and General Description*, 5:201.

58. Charlevoix, *History and General Description*, 5:265.

59. Banks, *Chasing Empire across the Sea*, 32.

60. Charlevoix, *Histoire de l'Isle Espagnole ou de S. Domingue*, 1:iv.

61. Certeau, "Writing vs. Time"; Motsch, *Lafitau et l'émergence du discours ethnographique*; Pagden, *The Fall of Natural Man*, 198–209; Sayre, *Les Sauvages Américains*.

62. Lafitau, *Customs of the American Indians*, 2–3.

63. Backer and Backer, *Bibliothèque des écrivains de la Compagnie de Jésus*, 3:428.

64. Van Kley, *The Jansenists and the Expulsion of the Jesuits from France*, 148; Bangert, *A History of the Society of Jesus*, 303–4.

65. Bonnécamps, "Observation météorologique faite à Québec en Canada," 572–74.

66. Rétif, "Brève histoire des Lettres edifiantes et curieuses."

67. McCabe, *Orientalism in Early Modern France*, 125.

68. JR 64:239–59.

69. Pouliot, "Les procureurs parisiens," 44.

70. Pouliot, "Les procureurs parisiens," 45, 47.

71. JR 66:67–119.

72. JR 66:223; Tonti, *Dernières découvertes dans l'Amérique septentrionale de M. de la Salle*.

73. Le Long et al., *Bibliothèque historique de la France*, vol. 3, 661–62.

74. Charlevoix, *Histoire du Paraguay*; Bangert, *A History of the Society of Jesus*, 303–4.

75. Charlevoix, *History and General Description*, 6:11–12.

76. Charlevoix, *History and General Description*, 5:287.

77. Charlevoix, *History and General Description*, 5:289.

78. Charlevoix, *History and General Description*, 5:290–91.

8. A MISSION WITH NO EMPIRE

1. Sabatié, *Le Tribunal révolutionnaire de Paris*, 269–70.

2. E.g., Monet, "The Jesuits in New France," 196.

3. Richter, *Trade, Land, Power*, 94.

4. Grenier, *The First Way of War*, 47–48. Compare to JR 67:113–15.

5. JR 67:95.

6. Haefeli and Sweeney, *Captors and Captives*, 227.

7. JR 67:117.

8. Haefeli and Sweeney, *Captors and Captives*, 229.

9. JR 67:233–235.

10. JR 67:231, 247.

11. Beauharnois and D'Aigremont to Ministre, October 1, 1728 and October 1, 1733, Vaudreuil to Conseil de Marine, October 31, 1718, La Jonquière to Ministre, October 9, 1749, and Deliberation of the Conseil de Marine, April 1722, LAC, CIIA, 17–22v, 57–64v, 157–62v, 181–82, 509–511v; JR 66:345; DCB 3.

12. Delanglez, *The French Jesuits in Lower Louisiana*, 309–10.

13. JR 68:309–11; Rochemonteix, *Les Jésuites et la Nouvelle-France au XVIIIe siècle*, 1:367–88; Delanglez, *The French Jesuits in Lower Louisiana*, 303–7.

14. JR 70:14, 241.

15. Villiers, "L'établissement de la province de la Louisiane," 344, 347; my translation.

16. Delanglez, *The French Jesuits in Lower Louisiana*, 316–17.

17. Quoted in Delanglez, *The French Jesuits in Lower Louisiana*, 319.

18. Wedel, *A Jean Delanglez, S.J., Anthology*, 41–45.

19. Wedel, *A Jean Delanglez, S.J., Anthology*, 50–51, 52–59; my emphasis.

20. Clark, *Masterless Mistresses*, 41–122.

21. JR 71:178–80.

22. DCB 4.

23. United States Catholic Historical Society, *Historical Records and Studies*, vol. 1, 40.

24. JR 70:91; Rochemonteix, *Les Jésuites et la Nouvelle-France au XVIIIe siècle*, 2:185.

25. Rochemonteix, *Les Jésuites et la Nouvelle-France au XVIIIe siècle, 2:144*; Bausman, *History of Beaver County, Pennsylvania*, vol. 2, 1135; Banks, *Chasing Empire across the Sea*, 41.

26. Banks, *Chasing Empire across the Sea*, 40.

27. Trudel, *L'Église canadienne sous le Régime militaire*, vol. 1, 31.

28. DCB 4.

29. DCB 4.

30. Osman, "Pride, Prejudice, and Prestige," 196. Compare to Crouch, *Nobility Lost*, 102–6.

31. Masse, "Pierre Roubaud," 316; Calloway, *The Western Abenakis of Vermont*, 192.

32. JR 70:103–5.

33. O'Callaghan, *The Documentary History of the State of New York*, vol. 4, 337.

34. Meehan and Monet, "The Restoration in Canada," 393.

35. Masse, "Pierre Roubaud," 317; Sullivan, *The Papers of William Johnson*, vol. 3, 279.

36. JR 71:171–81.

37. [La Marche], *La Foi justifiée de tout reproche de contradiction avec la Raison*, xxiv.

38. Rochemonteix, *Le père Antoine Lavalette à Martinique*, 247–48.

39. Van Kley, *The Jansenists and the Expulsion of the Jesuits from France*.

40. Thompson, "The Lavalette Affair," 206–39; Thompson, "French Jesuits, 1756–1814," 183.

41. Fumaroli, "Between the Rigorist Hammer and the Deist Anvil, 682–685.

42. Thompson, "The Lavalette Affair," 216.

43. Fumaroli, "Between the Rigorist Hammer and the Deist Anvil," 686.

44. Bangert, *A History of the Society of Jesus*, 377–79.

45. JR 65:181–83.

46. JR 69:81–27.

47. DCB 3.

48. Delanglez, *The Jesuits in Lower Louisiana*, 501–3.

49. JR 70:218–21.

50. Delanglez, *The Jesuits in Lower Louisiana*, 515.

51. Duval, *The Native Ground*, 87; Alvord, *Collections of the Illinois State Historical Library*, 100.

52. JR 71:178.

53. JR 71:174.

54. Bonnécamps, "Observation météorologique faite à Québec en Canada."

55. DCB 4.

56. JR 71:175.

57. Le Bansais, *Neuvaine à l'honneur des Sts Anges*.

58. Le Bansais, *Paraphrase du Pater*.

59. JR 71:175; Backer and Backer, *Bibliothèque des écrivains de la Compagnie de Jésus*, 4:38.

60. Quoted in Sabatié, *Le Tribunal révolutionnaire de Paris*, 269; my translation.

61. Sabatié, *Le Tribunal révolutionnaire de Paris*, 269–70; my translation.

62. Duchateau, *Histoire du Diocèse d'Orléans*, 378.

63. Bangert, *A History of the Society of Jesus*, 408.

64. DCB 4.

65. [La Brosse], *Nehiro-iriniui aiamihe massinahigan*; [La Brosse], *Akitami kakikemesudi-arenarag' auikhigan, Messiui Arenâbak Uäbanakéuiak uitsi Pépâmkamigék éitsik*; DCB 4; Hébert, *Histoire ou légende?*.

66. DCB 4; Toupin, *Les écrits de Pierre Potier*.

67. Rochemonteix, *Les Jésuites et la Nouvelle-France au XVIIIe siècle*, 2:218; DCB 4.

68. Rochemonteix, *Les Jésuites et la Nouvelle-France au XVIIIe siècle*, 2:217–18; DCB 4; Charland, "La mission de John Carroll au Canada."

69. JR 71:101–3. The letter was signed on December 31, 1789.

70. JR 71:103–5.

CONCLUSION

1. Benedict XV, *Maximum Illud*.

2. JR 67:181.

3. Daughton, *An Empire Divided*, 18.

4. Compare to Habermas, "Mission im 19. Jahrhundert," 632–33.

5. Second Vatican Council, *Ad Gentes*, 6.

6. Morrissey, "The Terms of Encounter," 44.

7. Siedentop, *Inventing the Individual*, 350.

8. Lilla, *The Stillborn God*, 7–8.

9. Schor, "The Crisis of French Universalism," 44. Compare to Pitts, *A Turn to Empire*, 166.

10. Du Creux, *History of Canada*, 1:24.

11. Conklin, *A Mission to Civilize*, 246–49; Colonna, "Educating Conformity in French Colonial Algeria."

BIBLIOGRAPHY

The author has divided the bibliography into four sections: Archives, Early Print Sources, Additional Primary Sources, and Secondary Sources. She wishes by this means to draw extra attention to the central role dictinctive genres of primary sources play in the analysis, especially early print sources not traditionally linked to the history of Jesuits in North America and critical editions of primary texts that gave shape to the modern historiography critiqued in this book.

ARCHIVES AND EARLY PRINT SOURCES

ARSI. Archivum Romanum Societatis Iesu, Rome, Italy
    Fondo Gesuitico, *Indipetae 26, Gallia 1633–1761*
    Franc. 11
    Franc. 22, *Catalogi Breves 1558–1639*
    Gal. 46 1–2, *Epist. Generalium ad Externos 1613–1672*
    Gal. 62, *Oeuvres et épreuves de la Compagnie de Jésus en France depuis son origin jusqu'à nos jours; Documents généraux et particuliers*
    Gal. 109 1–4, *Historia Missionis Canadensis 1611–1659*
    Gal. 110 1–2, *Historia Missionis Canadensis 1660–1769*
LAC. Library and Archives Canada, Ottawa, Ontario, Canada
    C11A, *Fonds des colonies*
    MG3-3, *Étude XLIII*
    MG8-A23, *Fonds de greffes de notaires du Québec*
    MG17-A10, *Correspondance*

Annat, François, SJ, Jean de Brisacier, SJ, Claude de Lingendes, SJ, and Jacques Nouet, SJ. *Responses aux* Lettres provinciales *publiées par le secrétaire de Port-Royal contre les PP. de la Compagnie de Jésus*. Liège: J. M. Hovius, 1657.

Bernard, Jean-Frederic, ed. *Relations de la Louisiane et du fleuve Mississippi*. Amsterdam: Jean-Frederic Bernard, 1720.

Biard, Pierre, SJ. *Relation de la Nouvelle France, de ses terres, natural du Païs, & de ses Habitans, item, du voyage des Pères Jesuites ausdictes contrées, & de ce qu'ils y ont faict jusques à leur prinse par les Anglois*. Lyon: Louys Muguet, 1616.

Binet, Étienne, SJ. *Le Riche sauvé par la porte du Ciel, et les Motifs sacrez, & grande puissance de l'Aumosne*. Paris: Sébastien Cramoisy, 1627.

Boisrobert, François Le Métel de, ed. *Epinicia musarum, eminentissimo cardinali duci de Richelieu*. Paris: Sébastien Cramoisy, 1634.

——. *Palmae Regiae invictissimo Ludovico XIII, Regis christianissimo a praecipius nostri aevi poetis in trophaeum erectae*. Paris: Sébastien Cramoisy, 1634.

——. *Le Parnasse Royal, où les immortelles actions du tres-chrestien et tres-victorieux monarque Louis XIII*. Paris: Sébastien Cramoisy, 1635.

——. *Le sacrifice des Muses au grand cardinal de Richelieu*. Paris: Sébastien Cramoisy, 1635.

Bonnécamps, Joseph-Pierre de, SJ. "Observation météorologique faite à Québec en Canada, le 12 de Juin 1746." In *Mémoires pour l'histoire des Sciences et des beaux Arts . . . Mars 1747*, 572–74. Paris: Chaubert, 1747.

Bouton, Jacques, SJ. *Relation de l'establissement des François depuis l'an 1635: En l'isle de la Martinique*. Paris: Sébastien Cramoisy, 1640.

Brisacier, Jean de, SJ. *Le Jansénisme confondu dans l'advocat du Sr Callaghan*. Paris: F. Lambert, 1651.

——. *Les Jansénistes reconnus Calvinistes par Samuel Desmares*. Paris: Sébastien Cramoisy et Gabriel Cramoisy, 1652.

——. *L'Innocence et la vérité reconnues dans les preuves invincibles de la mauvaise foy du Sr. Jean Callaghan, Ibernois, pour servir de responce au livre intitulé* L'Innocence et la vérité deffenduës *et à tous les autres mensonges du Port Royal*. Paris: Society of Jesus, 1653.

Charas, Moyse. *Histoire naturelle des animaux, des plantes & des minéraux qui entrent dans la composition de la thériaque d'Andromachus*. Paris: Olivier de Varennes, 1668.

Charlevoix, Pierre-François-Xavier de, SJ. *Histoire et description générale de la Nouvelle France*, 3 vols. Paris: Rolin Fils, 1744.

——. *Histoire du Paraguay*. 6 vols. Paris: Desaint, 1757.

——. *Histoire de l'Isle Espagnole ou de S. Domingue*. 2 vols. Paris: F. Didot, 1730–1731.

Confraternité de la Sainte-Famille. *La solide dévotion à la très Sainte-famille de Jésus, Marie et Joseph*. Paris: Florentin Lambert, 1675.

Du Creux, François, SJ. *Historiae Canadensis, seu Novae-Franciae libri decem*. Paris: Sebastien Cramoisy, 1664.

Formey, M. *La France Littéraire, ou Dictionnaire des auteurs François vivans*. Berlin: Haude et Spener, 1757.

Jesuits of Paris. *Solennité de la canonization de saint Ignace et de S. François Xavier, Apostre des Indes: Faicté à Paris au Collège de Clermont . . . le 28 juin de juillet*. Paris: Sébastien Cramoisy, 1622.

Kirwitzer, Venceslaus Pantaleon, SJ. *Histoire de ce qui s'est passé au royaume de la Chine en l'année 1624*. Paris: Sébastien Cramoisy, 1629.

[La Brosse, Jean-Baptiste de, SJ.] *Akitami kakikemesudi-arenarag' auikhigan, Messiui Arenâbak Uâbanakéuiak uitsi Pépâmkamigék éitsik*. Quebec: Brown and Gilmore, 1770.

———. *Nehiro-iriniui aiamihe massinahigan*. Quebec: Brown and Gilmore, 1767.

Lafitau, Joseph-François, SJ. *Moeurs des sauvages amériquains, comparées aux moeurs des premiers temps*. Paris: Saugrain l'aîné & Charles Estienne Hochereau, 1724.

Lahontan, Louis-Armand de Lon d'Arce de. *Dialogues de M. le baron de Lahontan et d'un sauvage*. The Hague: Frères L'Honoré, 1703.

Le Bansais, Siméon, SJ. *Neuvaine à l'honneur des Sts Anges*. Avignon: Antoine Offray, 1782.

———. *Paraphrase du Pater, en forme de sentimens et affections, avec des réflexions sur la nécessité des actes de contrition, de foi, d'espérance et de charité*. Paris: Lesclapart Fils, 1779.

Leclercq, Chrestien, OFM. *Premier établissement de la foy dans la Nouvelle-France*. Paris: Amable Auroy, 1691.

Le Jeune, Paul, SJ. *Épistres spirituelles, escrites à plusieurs personnes de piété, touchant la direction de leur intérieur*. Paris: Florentin Lambert, 1665.

———. *Solitude de dix jours, sur les plus solides véritez et sur les plus saintes maximes de l'Évangile*. Paris: Florentin Lambert, 1665.

Le Long, Jacques, et al., eds. *Bibliothèque historique de la France: contenant le catalogue des ouvrages, imprimés & manuscrits, qui traitent de l'histoire de ce royaume*. Vol. 3. Paris: Jean-Thomas Herissant, 1771.

[Le Moyne, Pierre, SJ.] *Le Portrait du Roy passant les Alpes, dedie aux Reynes, par un religieux de la Compagnie de Jesus*. Paris: Sébastien Cramoisy, 1629.

Mémoires pour l'histoire des Sciences et des beaux Arts . . . Juillet 1703. Trévoux: Étienne Ganeau, 1703.

Mercure François: ou Suitte de l'Histoire de nostre temps. 24 vols. Paris: Estienne Richer, 1605–43.

Morin, Pierre, SJ. *La Vie du glorieux S. Ignace de Loyola, fondateur de l'ordre de la Compagnie de Jesus*. Paris: Sébastien Cramoisy, 1622.

Parlement de Paris. *Arrest de la Cour de Parlement donné toutes les Chambres assemblées, le 6 jour de Janvier 1649*. Paris: Les Imprimeurs et Libraires ordinaires du Roy, 1649.

———. *Arrest de Parlement en faveur de toutes les revenderesses de poisson et autres denrées dans les Marché-Neuf*. Paris: Sébastien Cramoisy, 1649.

———. *Arrest de la Cour de Parlement, portant injonction à tous marchands & artisans de cette ville & fauxbourgs de Paris, de tenir leurs boutiques ouvertes*. Paris: Les Imprimeurs et Libraires ordinaires du Roy, 1649.

———. *Arrest de la Cour de Parlement, portant injonction à tous les subjets du Roy d'obéir à la déclaration de mars dernier*. Paris: Les Imprimeurs & Libraires ordinaires du Roy, 1649.

———. *Arrest de la Cour de Parlement, pour la diminution des loyers des maisons dans la ville & fauxbourgs de Paris, du 10 avril 1649*. Paris: Les Imprimeurs et Libraires ordinaires du Roy, 1649.

———. *Arrest de la Cour de Parlement toutes les chambres assemblées, contre le Cardinal Mazarin, du samedy 11 mars 1651*. Paris: Les Imprimeurs et Libraires ordinaires du Roy, 1651.

Pelletier, Le Sieur. *Apologie ou Défence pour les Pères Jésuites, Contre les calomnies de leurs ennemis*. Paris: Sébastien Cramoisy, 1626.

Petiot, Étienne, SJ. *Panegyricus Ludovico XIII, vindici rebellionis, domitori Elementorum, aeterno Triumphatori: Pro Fracta Britannica, pro subjugato Oceano, pro triumphata Rupello*. Paris: P. de la Court, 1629.

Ragueneau, Paul, SJ. *Narratio historica eorum quae Societatis Iesu in Nova Francia fortiter egit et passa est annis M.DC.XLIIX et XLIX*. Translated by Georgio Gobat, SJ. Innsbruck: Hieronymus Agricola, 1650.

———. *Relation de ce qui s'est passé en la mission des Pères de la Compagnie de Jésus aux Hurons, pays de la Nouvelle-France ès années 1648 et 1649*. Lille: La veuve de Pierre de Rache, 1650.

———. *Verhael Van t'gheen gheschiet is in de Missie van de PP. der Societeyt Iesu een landt van Niew Vrancriick of de jaeren 1648 ende 1649*. Translated by Franciscus de Smidt, SJ. Antwerp: Cornelis Woons, 1651.

Recueil des Gazettes nouvelles, Relations & autres choses Memorables de toute l'Année 1632. Paris: Bureau d'Adresse, 1633.

Richelieu, Armand Jean du Plessis, cardinal duc de. *Harangue prononcée en la salle du petite Bourbon le XXIII Fevrier 1615, à la cloture des Estats tenus à Paris*. Paris: Sébastien Cramoisy, 1615.

Sagard, Gabriel, OFM. *Histoire du Canada et Voyages que les freres Mineurs Recollects y ont faicts pour la conversion des Infidelles*. Paris: Claude Sonnius, 1636.

Sonnet de Courval, Thomas. *Satyre contre les charlatans, et pseudomedecins empyriques*. Paris: Jean Millot, 1610.

Tonti, Henri de. *Dernières découvertes dans l'Amérique septentrionale de M. de la Salle.* Paris: J. Guignard, 1697.

Trigault, Nicolas, SJ. *Histoire de ce qui s'est passé à la Chine, tirée des lettres escrites ès années 1619, 1620, & 1621, adressées au R.P. Mutio Vitelleschi.* Translated by Pierre Morin, SJ. Paris: Sébastien Cramoisy, 1625.

——. *Histoire des martyrs du Japon depuis l'an 1612 jusques à 1620.* Translated by Pierre Morin, SJ. Paris: Sébastien Cramoisy, 1624.

——. *Relation des cruels Martyres que 118 Chrestiens ou environ, endurèrent au Japon, l'an 1622.* Translated by [unidentified]. Paris: Sébastien Cramoisy, 1924.

ADDITIONAL PRIMARY SOURCES

Alvord, Clarence Walworth, ed. *Collections of the Illinois State Historical Library.* Vol. 10. Springfield: Illinois State Historical Library, 1915.

Archives de la Province de Québec. *Rapport de l'Archiviste de la Province de Québec pour 1930–1931* (RAPQ). Quebec: Rédempti Paradis, 1931.

Benedict XV, Pope. *Maximum Illud.* Apostolic Letter. Rome, November 30, 1919.

Bilio, Cardinal Aloysius, ed. *Bullarum diplomatum et privilegio sanctorum romanum pontificum.* Vol. 18. Turin: A. Veccio et al., 1869.

Bruyas, Jacques, SJ. *Radical Words of the Iroquois Language, With Their Derivatives.* New York: Cramoisy Press, 1862.

Calloway, Colin G., ed. *The World Turned Upside Down: Indian Voices from Early America.* Boston: Bedford/St. Martin's, 1994.

Campeau, Lucien, SJ. *Monumenta Novae Franciae.* 9 vols. Rome: Monumenta Historica Societatis Iesu, 1967–2003.

Challes, Robert. *Mémoires de Robert Challes, écrivain du Roi: Un colonial au temps de Colbert.* Paris: Plon, 1931.

Champlain, Samuel de. *Derniers récits de voyages en Nouvelle-France et autres écrits, 1620–1632.* Edited by Mathieu d'Avignon. Quebec: Presses de l'Université de Laval, 2010.

——. *Premiers récits de voyages en Nouvelle-France, 1603–1619.* Edited by Mathieu d'Avignon. Quebec: Presses de l'Université de Laval, 2009.

Charlevoix, Pierre-François-Joseph de, SJ. *History and General Description of New France,* 6 vols. [1866–1872]. Translated by John Gilmary Shea. Chicago: Loyola University Press, 1962.

Denzinger, Henry. *The Sources of Catholic Dogma.* Translated by Roy J. Deferrari. Fitzwilliam NH: Loreto Publications, 2004.

Du Creux, François, SJ. *The History of Canada or New France.* Edited by James B. Conacher. Translated by Percy J. Robinson. 2 vols. Toronto: Champlain Society, 1951–52.

Lafitau, Joseph-François SJ. *Customs of the American Indians Compared with the Customs of Primitive Times.* 2 vols. Edited and translated by William N. Fenton and Elizabeth L. Moore. Toronto: Champlain Society, 1974 and 1977.

[La Marche, Jean-François, de SJ.] *La Foi justifiée de tout reproche de contradiction avec la Raison, et l'incrédulité convaincue d'être en contradiction avec la Raison dans ses raisonnemens contre la Révélation.* Paris: Brocas et Humblot, 1762.

Le Clercq, Chrestien, OFM. *First Establishment of the Faith in New France.* Vol. 1. Translated by John Gilmary Shea. New York: John G. Shea, 1881.

Le Jeune, Paul. *Lettres spirituelles écrites à plusieurs Personnes de Piété vivant en religion et dans le Monde, touchant la Direction de leur Intérieur.* Edited by R. P. Fressencourt, SJ. Paris: Victor Palmé, 1875.

Margry, Pierre, ed. *Découvertes et Établissements des Français dans l'ouest et dans le sud de l'Amérique septentrionale (1614–1754): Mémoires et documents originaux.* Vol. 2. Paris: D. Jouast, 1877.

O'Callaghan, E. B., ed. *The Documentary History of the State of New York.* Vol. 4. Albany: Charles van Benthuysen, 1851.

Pascal, Blaise. *Les Provinciales.* La Flèche: Brodard & Taupin, 2005.

———. *Pensées.* Edited by Dominique Descotes. Paris: Garnier-Flammarion, 1976.

Peyser, Joseph L., and José António Brandão, eds. *Edge of Empire: Documents of Michilmackinac (1671–1716).* East Lansing: Michigan State University Press, 2008.

Richaudeau, L'Abbé, ed. *Lettres de la Révérende Mère Marie de l'Incarnation (née Marie Guyard).* 2 vols. Paris: Librairie Internationale Catholique, 1876.

Rodríguez, Miguel Angel, SJ. *Monumenta Mexicana, Volume 8 (1603–1605).* Rome: Institutum Historicum Societatis Iesu, 1991.

Sagard, Gabriel, OFM. *The Long Journey to the Country of the Hurons.* Translated by H. H. Langton. Toronto: Champlain Society, 1939.

Second Vatican Council. *Ad Gentes.* Decree. Rome, 1965.

Sullivan, James, ed. *The Papers of William Johnson.* Vol. 3. Albany: University of the State of New York, 1921.

Thwaites, Reuben Gold, ed. *The Jesuit Relations and Allied Documents: Travels and Explorations of the Jesuit Missionaries in New France, 1610–1791.* 73 vols. Cleveland: Burrows Brothers, 1896–1901.

Toupin, Robert, SJ, ed. *Les écrits de Pierre Potier.* Ottawa: University of Ottawa Press, 1996.

United States Catholic Historical Society. *Historical Records and Studies.* Vol. 1. New York: United States Catholic Historical Society, 1900.

Villiers, Marc de. "L'établissement de la province de la Louisiane avec les moeurs des sauvages, leurs danses, leurs religions, etc.: Poème composé de 1728 à 1742 par Dumont de Montigny." *Journal de la Société des Américanistes* 23, no. 2 (1931): 273–440.

Virgil. *The Aeneid.* Translated by Robert Fagles. New York: Penguin Books, 2006.

SECONDARY SOURCES

Abé, Takao. *The Jesuit Mission to New France: A New Interpretation in the Light of the Earlier Jesuit Experience in Japan*. Leiden: Brill, 2011.

Alchon, Suzanne Austin. *A Pest in the Land: New World Epidemics in Global Perspective*. Albuquerque: University of New Mexico Press, 2003.

Alden, Dauril. *The Making of an Enterprise: The Society of Jesus in Portugal, Its Empire, and Beyond, 1540–1750*. Stanford: Stanford University Press, 1996.

Allain, Mathé. "Colbert and the Colonies." *The French Experience in Louisiana*. Edited by Glenn R. Conrad. Lafayette: Center for Louisiana Studies, 1995.

Anderson, Emma. *The Death and Afterlife of the North American Martyrs*. Cambridge: Cambridge University Press, 2013.

———. *The Betrayal of Faith: The Tragic Journey of a Colonial Native Convert*. Cambridge MA: Harvard University Press, 2007.

Anderson, Karen L. *Chain Her by One Foot: The Subjugation of Women in Seventeenth-Century New France*. London: Routledge, 1991.

Appleby, Andrew B. "Grain Prices and Subsistence Crises in England and France, 1590–1740." *The Journal of Economic History* 39, no. 4 (December 1979): 865–87.

Axtell, James. *The Invasion Within: The Contest of Cultures in Colonial North America*. Oxford: Oxford University Press, 1985.

Backer, Augustin de, SJ, and Alois de Backer, SJ. *Bibliothèque des écrivains de la Compagnie de Jésus*. 7 vols. Liège: L. Grandmont-Donders, 1853–61.

Balteau, J., M. Barroux, M. Prévost, et al., eds. *Dictionnaire de Biographie Française*. Paris: Letouzey et Ané, 1932–2001.

Bangert, William V., SJ. *A History of the Society of Jesus*. St. Louis: The Institute of Jesuit Sources, 1972.

Banks, Kenneth J. *Chasing Empire across the Sea: Communications and the State in the French Atlantic, 1713–1763*. Montreal: McGill-Queen's University Press, 2006.

Bauer, Arnold J. *Goods, Power, History: Latin America's Material Culture*. Cambridge: Cambridge University Press, 2001.

Bauer, Ralph. *The Cultural Geography of Colonial American Literatures: Empire, Travel, Modernity*. Cambridge: Cambridge University Press, 2003.

Beam, Sara. *Laughing Matters: Farce and the Making of Absolutism in France*. Ithaca NY: Cornell University Press, 2007.

Beaulieu, Alain. *Convertir les fils de Caïn: Jésuites et amérindiens nomades en Nouvelle-France, 1632–1642*. Montreal: Nuit Blanche Editeur, 1990.

Beik, William. *A Social and Cultural History of Early Modern France*. Cambridge: Cambridge University Press, 2009.

———. *Urban Protest in Seventeenth-Century France: The Culture of Retribution*. Cambridge: Cambridge University Press, 1997.

Bell, David A. *The First Total War: Napoleon's Europe and the Birth of Warfare as We Know It*. Boston: Houghton Mifflin, 2007.

Belmessous, Saliha. *Assimilation and Empire: Uniformity in French and British Colonies, 1541–1954*. Oxford: Oxford University Press, 2013.

Benedict, Philip. *Cities and Social Change in Early Modern France*. London: Unwin Hyman, 1989.

Beresford, Bruce, dir. *Black Robe*. Santa Monica CA: Metro Goldwyn Mayer, 1991.

Bergin, Joseph. *Church, Society, and Religious Change in France, 1580–1730*. New Haven: Yale University Press, 2009.

———. *Crown, Church and Episcopate Under Louis XIV*. New Haven: Yale University Press, 2004.

Bibliothèque Nationale de France. *L'Art du livre à l'Imprimerie nationale des origines à nos jours*. Paris: Imprimerie nationale, 1951.

Bilodeau, Christopher. "'They Honor Our Lord among Themselves in Their Own Way': Colonial Christianity and the Illinois Indians." *American Indian Quarterly* 25, no. 3 (Summer 2001): 352–77.

Bireley, Robert. *The Jesuits and the Thirty Years' War: Kings, Courts, and Confessors*. Cambridge: Cambridge University Press, 2003.

Blackburn, Carole. *Harvest of Souls: The Jesuit Missions and Colonialism in North America, 1632–1650*. Montreal: McGill-Queen's University Press, 2000.

Blet, Pierre, SJ. "Jésuites gallicans au XVIIe siècle?" *Archivum Historicum Societatis Iesu* 29 (1960): 55–84.

———. "Jésuites et Libertés Gallicanes en 1611." *Archivum Historicum Societatis Iesu* 24 (1955): 165–88.

Bosch, David J. *Transforming Mission: Paradigm Shifts in Theology of Mission*. Maryknoll NY: Orbis Books, 1991.

Boss, Julia. "Writing a Relic: The Uses of Hagiography in New France." In *Colonial Saints: Discovering the Holy in the Americas, 1500–1800*, edited by Allan Greer and Jodi Bilinkoff, 211–34. London: Routledge, 2003.

Boucher, Philip P. *France and the American Tropics to 1700: Tropics of Discontent?* Baltimore: Johns Hopkins University Press, 2007.

———. *Les Nouvelles Frances: France in America, 1500-1815*. Providence: John Carter Brown Library, 1989.

———. *The Shaping of the French Colonial Empire: A Bio-Bibliography of the Careers of Richelieu, Fouquet, and Colbert*. New York: Garland Publishing, 1985.

Boulle, Pierre H. "French Mercantilism, Commercial Companies, and Colonial Profitability." In *The Organization of Interoceanic Trade in European Expansion, 1450–1800*, edited by Pieter Emmer and Femme Gaastra, 233–54. Aldershot UK: Ashgate, 1996.

Bowers, Kristy Wilson. *Plague and Public Health in Early Modern Seville*. Rochester NY: University of Rochester Press, 2013.

Brandão, José António. *Your Fyre Shall Burn No More: Iroquois Policy toward New France and Its Allies to 1701*. Lincoln: University of Nebraska Press, 2000.

Brasseaux, Carl A. *The Founding of New Acadia: The Beginnings of Acadian Life in Louisiana, 1765–1805*. Baton Rouge: Louisiana State University Press, 1987.

Brazeau, Brian. *Writing a New France, 1604–1632*. Farnham UK: Ashgate, 2009.

Braudel, Fernand. *The Structures of Everyday Life: Civilization & Capitalism, 15th-18th Century*. Vol. 1. Translated by Siân Reynolds. New York: Harper & Row, 1981.

Brémond, Henri. *Histoire littéraire du Sentiment Religieux en France depuis la fin des guerres de religion jusqu'à nos jours*. Vol. 2. Grenoble: Éditions Jérôme Millon, 2006.

Briggs, Robin. *Early Modern France: 1560–1715*. Oxford: Oxford University Press, 1998.

Brockey, Liam Matthew. *Journey to the East: The Jesuit Mission to China, 1579–1724*. Cambridge MA: Belknap Press, 2007.

Brockliss, Laurence, and Colin Jones. *The Medical World of Early Modern France*. Oxford: Clarendon Press, 1997.

Brodrick, J., SJ. *The Economic Morals of the Jesuits: An Answer to Dr. H.M. Robertson*. London: Oxford University Press, 1934.

Brown, George W., et al., eds. *Dictionary of Canadian Biography*. 12 vols. Toronto: University of Toronto Press, 1966–90. http://www.biographi.ca/index-e.html.

Brucker, Joseph, SJ. Reviews. *Études religieuses, historiques et littéraires* 52 (1891): 513–14.

Burke, Peter. *The Fabrication of Louis XIV*. New Haven: Yale University Press, 1992.

———. *Popular Culture in Early Modern Europe*. New York: New York University Press, 1978.

Calloway, Colin G. *The Western Abenakis of Vermont, 1600–1800: War, Migration, and the Survival of an Indian People*. Norman: University of Oklahoma Press, 1994.

Campeau, Lucien, SJ. *Biographical Dictionary for the Canadian Missions in Acadia and New France: 1602–1654*. Translated by William Lonc, SJ. Midland on: Steve Catlin, 2004.

———. *Les Finances publiques de la Nouvelle-France sous les Cent-Associés, 1632–1665*. Montreal: Éditions Bellarmin, 1975.

Carroll, Stuart. *Noble Power during the French Wars of Religion: Guise Power and the Catholic Cause in Normandy*. New York: Cambridge University Press, 1998.

Certeau, Michel de. "Writing vs. Time: History and Anthropology in the Works of Lafitau." Translated by J. Hovde. *Yale French Studies* 59 (1980): 37–64.

Chapman, Sarah E. *Private Ambition and Political Alliances: The Phélypeaux de Pontchartrain Family and Louis XIV's Government, 1650–1715*. Rochester NY: University of Rochester Press, 2004.

Charland, T.-M. "Las mission de John Carroll au Canada en 1776 et l'interdict du P. Floquet." SCHÉC *Rapport* 1 (1933–34): 45–56.

Chartier, Roger. *The Cultural Uses of Print in Early Modern France*. Translated by Lydia G. Cochrane. Princeton: Princeton University Press, 1987.

Chartrand, René. *The Forts of New France: The Great Lakes, the Plains and the Gulf Coast, 1600–1763*. Oxford: Osprey Publishing, 2010.

Châtellier, Louis. *The Religion of the Poor: Rural Missions in Europe and the Formation of Modern Catholicism, c. 1500–c. 1800*. Translated by Brian Pearce. Cambridge: Cambridge University Press, 1997.

——. *The Europe of the Devout: The Catholic Reformation and the Formation of a New Society*. Translated by Jean Birrell. Cambridge: Cambridge University Press, 1989.

Chaussé, Gilles. "Le Père Paul Le Jeune, SJ, missionnaire-colonisateur." *Revue d'histoire de l'Amérique française* 12, no. 2 (1958): 56–79, 217–46.

Chill, Emanuel. "Religion and Mendicity in Seventeenth-Century France." *International Review of Social History* 7, no. 3 (1962): 400–425.

Choquette, Leslie. *Frenchmen into Peasants: Modernity and Tradition in the Peopling of French Canada*. Cambridge MA: Harvard University Press, 1997.

Christophe, Paul. *Les pauvres et la pauvreté, IIe partie: Du XVIe siècle à nos jours*. Paris: Desclée, 1987.

Church, William F. *Richelieu and Reason of State*. Princeton: Princeton University Press, 1972.

Clair, Muriel. "'Seeing These Good Souls Adore God in the Midst of the Woods': The Christianization of Algonquian Nomads in the *Jesuit Relations* of the 1640s." *Journal of Jesuit Studies* 1, no. 2 (2014): 283–301.

Clark, Emily. *Masterless Mistresses: The New Orleans Ursulines and the Development of a New World Society, 1727–1834*. Chapel Hill: University of North Carolina Press, 2007.

Clendinnen, Inga. *Ambivalent Conquests: Maya and Spaniard in the Yucatan, 1517–1570*. Cambridge: Cambridge University Press, 1987.

Clossey, Luke. *Salvation and Globalization in the Early Jesuit Missions*. Cambridge: Cambridge University Press, 2008.

Coates, Colin M. *The Metamorphoses of Land: Community in Early Québec*. Montreal: McGill-Queen's University Press, 2000.

Codignola, Luca. "Jesuit Writings according to R. G. Thwaites and Lucien Campeau, SJ: How Do They Differ?" In *Little Do We Know: History and Historians of the North Atlantic, 1492–2010*, edited by Matteo Binasco, 219–40. Cagliari: Instituto di Storia dell'Europa Mediterranea del Consiglio Nazionale delle Ricerche, 2011.

Cogley, Richard W. *John Eliot's Mission to the Indians before King Philip's War*. Cambridge MA: Harvard University Press, 1999.

Cohen, Paul. "Linguistic Politics on the Periphery: Louis XIII, Béarn, and the Making of French as an Official Language in Early Modern France." In *When Languages Collide: Perspectives on Language Conflict, Language Competition, and Language*

Coexistence, edited by Brian D. Joseph et al., 165–200. Columbus: Ohio State University Press, 2003.

Collins, James B. *The State in Early Modern France*. Cambridge: Cambridge University Press, 1995.

Colonna, Fanny. "Educating Conformity in French Colonial Algeria" [1975]. Translated by Barbara Henshaw. In *Tensions of Empire: Colonial Cultures in a Bourgeois World*, edited by Frederick Cooper and Ann Laura Stoler, 346–70. Berkeley: University of California Press, 1997.

Conklin, Alice L. *A Mission to Civilize: The Republican Idea of Empire in France and West Africa, 1895–1930*. Stanford: Stanford University Press, 1997.

Conrad, Glenn R., ed. *The French Experience in Louisiana*. Lafayette: Center for Louisiana Studies, 1995.

Correia-Afonso, John, SJ. *Jesuit Letters and Indian History, 1542–1773*. London: Oxford University Press, 1969.

Courcelles, Le Chevalier de. *Histoire généalogique et héraldique des Pairs de France des grands Dignitaires de la Couronne, des principales familles nobles du Royaume, et des Maisons princières de l'Europe*. Vol. 16. Paris: l'Autour et Arthus Bertrand, 1826.

Croix, Alain, and Fanch Roudaut. *Les Bretons, la mort et Dieu: de 1600 à nos jours*. Paris: Messidor/Temps actuels, 1984.

Crouch, Christian Ayne. *Nobility Lost: French and Canadian Martial Cultures, Indians, and the End of New France*. Ithaca NY: Cornell University Press, 2014.

Cullen, L. M. *The Brandy Trade under the Ancien Régime: Regional Specialisation in the Charente*. Cambridge: Cambridge University Press, 2002.

Curtis, Sara A. *Civilizing Habits: Women Missionaries and the Revival of French Empire*. Oxford: Oxford University Press, 2010.

Cushner, Nicholas P. *Why Have You Come Here?: The Jesuits and the First Evangelization of Native America*. Oxford: Oxford University Press, 2006.

Dandelet, Thomas James. *The Renaissance of Empire in Early Modern Europe*. Cambridge: Cambridge University Press, 2014.

Darnton, Robert. *The Great Cat Massacre and Other Episodes in French Cultural History*. New York: Basic Books, 1999.

Daughton, J. P. *An Empire Divided: Religion, Republicanism, and the Making of French Colonialism*. Oxford: Oxford University Press, 2006.

Dauzet, Albert. *Nouveau Dictionnaire Étymologique et Historique*. Paris: Librairie Larousse, 1964.

Davis, Natalie Zemon. *Society and Culture in Early Modern France*. Stanford: Stanford University Press, 1975.

Dawson, Christopher. *Religion and the Rise of Western Culture: Gifford Lectures Delivered in the University of Edinburgh, 1948–1949*. London: Sheed & Ward, 1950.

Deffain, Dominique. *Un Voyageur français en Nouvelle-France au XVIIe siècle: étude lit-téraire des relations du père Paul Le Jeune, 1632–1641.* Tübingen: M. Niemeyer, 1995.

Délâge, Denys. *Bitter Feast: Amerindians and Europeans in Northeastern North America, 1600–1664.* Translated by Jane Brierly. Vancouver: University of British Columbia Press, 1993.

Delanglez, Jean, SJ. *Frontenac and the Jesuits.* Chicago: Institute of Jesuit History, 1939.

———. *The French Jesuits in Lower Louisiana (1700–1763).* Washington DC: The Catholic University of America, 1935.

Deslandres, Dominique. "French Catholicism in the Era of Exploration and Early Colo-nization." In *The Cambridge History of Religions in America,* vol. 1, edited by Stephen J. Stein, 200–218. Cambridge: Cambridge University Press, 2012.

Delattre, Pierre, SJ. *Les Établissements des jésuites en France depuis quatre siècles.* 6 vols. Enghien, Belgium: Institut supérieur de Théologie, 1949–1957.

Demos, John. *The Unredeemed Captive: A Family Story from Early America.* New York: Vintage Books, 1995.

Dennis, Matthew. *Cultivating a Landscape of Peace: Iroquois-European Encounters in Seventeenth-Century America.* Ithaca NY: Cornell University Press, 1993.

DePauw, Jacques. *Spiritualité et Pauvreté à Paris au XVIIe siècle.* Paris: La Boutique de l'Histoire, 1999.

Desan, Suzanne. "Making and Breaking Marriage: An Overview of Old Regime Mar-riage as a Social Practice." In *Family, Gender, and Law in Early Modern France,* edited by Suzanne Desan and Jeffrey Merrick, 1–25. University Park: Penn State University Press, 2009.

Desbarats, Catherine. "The Cost of Early Canada's Native Alliances: Reality and Scarcity's Rhetoric." *The William and Mary Quarterly* 52, no. 4 (October 1995): 609–30.

Deslandres, Dominique. *Croire et Faire Croire: Les missions françaises au XVIIe siècle (1600–1650).* Paris: Fayard, 2003.

———. "Indes intérieures et Indes lontaines: Le modèle français d'intégration socio-religieuse au XVIIe siècle." In *La France-Amérique (XVIe–XVIIIe siècles): Actes du XXXVe colloque international d'études humanistes,* edited by Frank Lestringant, 369–77. Paris: Honoré Champion Éditeur, 1998.

Devens, Carol. *Countering Colonization: Native American Women and Great Lakes Missions, 1630–1900.* Berkeley: University of California Press, 1992.

Dewald, Jonathan. *The European Nobility, 1400–1800.* Cambridge: Cambridge Uni-versity Press, 1996.

Dickason, Olive Patricia. *The Myth of the Savage and the Beginnings of French Colonization in the Americas.* Edmonton: University of Alberta Press, 1984.

Diefendorf, Barbara. *From Penitence to Charity: Pious Women and the Catholic Refor-mation in Paris.* Oxford: Oxford University Press, 2004.

Dinan, Susan E. *Women and Poor Relief in Seventeenth-Century France: The Early History of the Daughters of Charity*. Aldershot UK: Ashgate, 2006.

———. "Motivations for Charity in Early Modern France." In *Reformation of Charity: The Secular and the Religious in Early Modern Poor Relief*, edited by Thomas Safley, 176–92. Leiden: Brill, 2004.

Dorsey, Peter A. "Going to School with Savages: Authorship and Authority among the Jesuits of New France." *The William and Mary Quarterly* 55, no. 3 (July 1998): 399–420.

Dostie, Pierre. *Le Lecteur suborné dans cinq texts missionnaires de la Nouvelle-France*. Sainte-Foy QC: Les Éditions de la Huit, 1994.

Dubé, Jean-Claude. *The Chevalier de Montmagny (1601–1657): First Governor of New France*. Translated by Elizabeth Rapley. Ottawa: University of Ottawa Press, 2005.

Dubé, Pauline, ed. *La Nouvelle-France sous Joseph-Antoine le Febvre de la Barre, 1682–1685: Lettres, mémoires, instructions et ordonnances*. Sillery QC: Septentrion. 1993.

Duchateau, L'Abbé. *Histoire du Diocèse d'Orléans depuis son origine jusqu'à nos jours*. Orléans: H. Herluison, 1888.

Duffy, Eamon. *Saints and Sinners: A History of the Popes*. New Haven: Yale University Press, 2006.

Duprat, F. A. *Histoire de l'Imprimerie Impériale de France*. Paris: Imprimérie Impériale, 1861.

Duval, Kathleen. *The Native Ground: Indians and Colonists in the Heart of the Continent*. Philadelphia: University of Pennsylvania Press, 2011.

Eccles, W. J. *Canada under Louis XIV, 1663–1701*. Toronto: McClelland and Stewart, 1964.

———. *The French in North America: 1500–1783*. East Lansing: Michigan State University Press, 1998.

Elias, Norbert. *The Civilizing Process: Sociogenetic and Psychogenetic Investigations* [1939]. Translated by Edmund Jephcott. Malden MA: Blackwell Publishing, 2000.

Elliott, J. H. *Richelieu and Olivares*. Cambridge: Cambridge University Press, 1989.

———. *The Old World and the New, 1492–1650*. Cambridge: Cambridge University Press, 1970.

Elmore, Richard F. "The Origins of the Paris Hôpital Général." PhD dissertation, University of Michigan, 1975.

Evennett, H. Outram. *The Spirit of the Counter-Reformation*. Cambridge: Cambridge University Press, 1968.

Faragher, John Mack. *A Great and Noble Scheme: The Tragic Story of the Expulsion of the French Acadians from their American Homeland*. New York: W. W. Norton, 2005.

Farr, James R. *The Work of France: Labor and Culture in Early Modern Times, 1350–1800*. London: Rowman & Littlefield, 2008.

Febvre, Lucien. "*Civilisation*: Evolution of a Word and Group of Ideas" [1930]. In *A New Kind of History: From the Writings of Lucien Febvre*, edited by Peter Burke, 219–57. London: Routledge & Kegan Paul, 1973.

Febvre, Lucien, and Henri-Jean Martin. *The Coming of the Book*. Translated by David Gerard. London: Verso, 1976.

Fischer, David Hackett. *Champlain's Dream: The European Founding of North America*. New York: Simon & Schuster, 2008.

Forrestal, Alison. *Vincent de Paul, the Lazarist Mission, and French Catholic Reform*. Oxford: Oxford University Press, 2017.

Fouqueray, Henri, SJ. *Histoire de la Compagnie de Jésus en France des origins a la suppression*. 5 vols. Paris: Bureaux des Études, 1910–25.

Frazee, Charles A. *Catholics and Sultans: The Church and the Ottoman Empire, 1453–1923*. Cambridge: Cambridge University Press, 1983.

Frêlon, Elise. *Les Pouvoirs du Conseil souverain de la Nouvelle France dans l'édiction de la norme (1663–1760)*. Paris: L'Harmattan, 2002.

Friant, Emmanuelle. "'Ils aiment bien leur chapelet': Le discours jésuite sur la transmission du religieux aux Hurons par l'objet de pieté (1634–1649)." *Études d'histoire religieuse* 77 (2010): 7–20.

Friedrich, Markus. *Der lange Arm Roms? Globale Verwaltung und Kommunikation im Jesuitenorden 1540–1773*. Frankfurt: Campus Verlag, 2011.

———. "Circulating and Compiling the Litterae Annuae: Towards a History of the Jesuit System of Communication." *Archivum Historicum Societatis Iesu* 77, no. 154 (July–December 2008): 3–40.

Fumaroli, Marc. "Between the Rigorist Hammer and the Deist Anvil: The Fate of the Jesuits in Eighteenth-Century France." In *The Jesuits II: Cultures, Sciences, and the Arts, 1540–1773*, edited by John W. O'Malley, SJ, et al., 682–90. Toronto: University of Toronto Press, 2006.

Galland, Caroline. *Pour la gloire de Dieu et du Roi: Les Récollets en Nouvelle-France au XVIIe et XVIIIe Siècles*. Paris: Cerf, 2012.

Garrioch, David. *The Making of Revolutionary Paris*. Berkeley: University of California Press, 2004.

Gavitt, Philip. *Gender, Honor, and Charity in Late Renaissance Florence*. Cambridge: Cambridge University Press, 2013.

Gay, Jean-Pascal. "Voués à quel royaume? Les Jésuites entre voeux de religion et fidelité monarchique. À propos d'un memoire inédit du P. de La Chaize." *XVIIe siècle* 2, no. 227 (2005): 285–314.

Gitlin, Jay. *The Bourgeois Frontier: French Towns, French Traders, and American Expansion*. New Haven: Yale University Press, 2009.

Goddard, Peter A. "Canada in Seventeenth-Century Jesuit Thought: Backwater or Opportunity?" In *Decentering the Renaissance: New Essays on Canada, 1500–1700*, edited by Germaine Warkentin and Carolyn Podruchny, 186–99. Toronto: University of Toronto Press, 2002.

———. "Converting the 'Sauvage': Jesuit and Montagnais in Seventeenth-Century New France." *The Catholic Historical Review* 84, no.2 (April 1998): 219–39.

Goubert, Pierre. *The French Peasantry in the Seventeenth Century*. Translated by Ian Patterson. Cambridge: Cambridge University Press, 1986.

Grafton, Anthony. *New Worlds, Ancient Texts: The Power of Tradition and the Shock of Discovery*. Cambridge MA: Belknap Press, 1992.

Greenblatt, Stephen. *Marvelous Possessions: The Wonder of the New World*. Chicago: University of Chicago Press, 1991.

Greer, Allan. *Mohawk Saint: Catherine Tekakwitha and the Jesuits*. Oxford: Oxford University Press, 2005.

———. "Conversion and Identity: Iroquois Christianity in Seventeenth-Century New France." *Conversion: Old Worlds and New*, edited by Kenneth Mills and Anthony Grafton, 175–98. Rochester NY: University of Rochester Press, 2003.

———. *The Jesuit Relations: Natives and Missionaries in Seventeenth-Century North America*. Boston: Bedford/St. Martin's, 2000.

———. *The People of New France*. Toronto: University of Toronto Press, 1997.

Gregerson, Linda, and Susan Juster, eds. *Empires of God: Religious Encounters in the Early Modern Atlantic*. Philadelphia: University of Pennsylvania Press, 2011.

Grenier, John. *The First Way of War: American War Making on the Frontier, 1607–1814*. Cambridge: Cambridge University Press, 2008.

Groethuysen, Bernard. *The Bourgeois: Catholicism vs. Capitalism in Eighteenth-Century France*. Translated by Mary Ilford. New York: Holt, Rinehart, and Winston, 1968.

Guillermou, Alain. *Les Jésuites*. Paris: Presses Universitaires de France, 1961.

Guillot, Pierre. *Les Jésuites et la musique: La Collège de la Trinité à Lyon, 1565–1762*. Liège: Pierre Mardaga, 1991.

Habermas, Rebekka. "Mission im 19. Jahrhundert—Globale Netze des Religiösen." *Historische Zeitschrift* 287 (2008): 629–79.

Habig, Marion A., OFM, and René Bacon, OFM. "L'ouvre des Récollets missionnaires en Nouvelle-France." *Dictionnaire biographique des Récollets missionnaires en Nouvelle-France: 1615–1645—1670–1849*. Edited by Odoric Jouve. Montreal: Éditions Bellarmin, 1996.

Haefeli, Evan, and Kevin Sweeney. *Captors and Captives: The 1704 French and Indian Raid on Deerfield*. Amherst: University of Massachusetts Press, 2005.

Hamel, Amélie. "Translating as a Way of Writing History: Father du Creux's *Historiae Canadensis* and the *Relations jésuites* of New France." *Renaissance Studies* 29, no. 1 (February 2015): 143–61.

———. "François Du Creux, historien et apologiste." *Revue de Bibliothèque et Archives nationales du Québec* 3 (2013). http://id.erudit.org/iderudit/1017687ar.

———. "Les *Historiae Canadensis* (1664) du père François Du Creux: enjeux et problèmes littéraires." *Tangence* 92 (Winter 2010): 67–82.

Harrod, Howard L. "Missionary Life World and Native Response: Jesuits in New France." *Studies in Religion* 13, no. 2 (1984): 170–92.

Haudrère, Philippe. "Collège royal de La Flèche, l'esprit missionnaire et le Canada." *Encyclopédie du patrimonie culturel de l'Amérique française.* Edited by Martin Fournier. 2007. http://www.ameriquefrancaise.org/fr/article-95/Collège_royal_de_La_Flèche,_l'esprit_missionnaire_et_le_Canada.html.

Havard, Gilles. "'Les forcer à devenir Cytoyens': État, Sauvages et citoyenneté en Nouvelle-France (XVIIe–XVIIIe siècle)." *Annales* 64, no. 5 (2009): 985–1018.

———. *The Great Peace of Montreal of 1701: French-Native Diplomacy in the Seventeenth Century.* Translated by Phyllis Aronoff and Howard Scott. Montreal: McGill-Queens's University Press, 2001.

Havard, Gilles, and Cécile Vidal. *Histoire de l'Amérique française.* Paris: Champs Flammarion, 2003.

Healy, George R. "The French Jesuits and the Idea of the Noble Savage." *The William and Mary Quarterly* 15, no. 2 (April 1958): 143–67.

Hébert, Léo-Hébert. *Histoire ou légende? Jean-Baptiste de La Brosse.* Montreal: Éditions Bellarmin, 1984.

Hickey, Daniel. *Local Hospitals in Ancien Régime France: Rationalization, Resistance, Renewal, 1530–1789.* Montreal: McGill-Queen's University Press, 1997.

Higashibaba, Ikuo. *Christianity in Early Modern Japan: Kirishitan Belief and Practice.* Leiden: Brill, 2001.

Hoffman, Philip T. *Growth in a Traditional Society.* Princeton: Princeton University Press, 1996.

Hosne, Ana Carolina. *The Jesuit Missions to China and Peru, 1570–1610: Expectations and Appraisals of Expansionism.* New York: Routledge, 2013.

Hsia, Florence C. *Sojourners in a Strange Land: Jesuits and Their Scientific Missions in Late Imperial China.* Chicago: University of Chicago Press, 2009.

Hufton, Olwen. *Bayeux in the Late Eighteenth Century: A Social Study.* Oxford: Clarendon Press, 1967.

Hughes, Thomas, SJ. *History of the Society of Jesus in North America: Colonial and Federal.* 4 vols. London: Longmans, Green, and Co., 1908.

Hunt, George T. *The Wars of the Iroquois: A Study in Intertribal Trade Relations.* Madison: University of Wisconsin Press, 1940.

Hussey, Andrew. *Paris: The Secret History.* New York: Bloomsbury, 2006.

Jacquart, Jean. "Paris: First Metropolis of the Early Modern Period." In *Capital Cities and their Hinterlands in Early Modern Europe,* edited by Peter Clark, 105–18. Aldershot UK: Scolar Press, 1996.

Jacquet, M. "Cramoisy (Famille)." *Dictionnaire de biographie française.* Vol. 9. Paris: Letouzey et Ané, 1961.

Jaenen, Cornelius J. "The Frenchification and Evangelization of the Amerindians in the Seventeenth Century New France." *CCHA Study Sessions* 35 (1968): 57–71.

Jamet, Albert. *Les Annales de l'Hôtel-Dieu de Québec, 1636–1716.* Quebec: Hôtel-Dieu de Québec, 1984.

Jennings, Francis. *The Invasion of America: Indians, Colonialism, and the Cant of Conquest.* New York: W. W. Norton, 1976.

Jetten, Marc. *Enclaves amérindiennes: Les 'réductions' du Canada, 1637–1701.* Sillery QC: Septentrion, 1994.

Jones, Colin. *Paris: The Biography of a City.* New York: Penguin Books, 2004.

Jütte, Robert. *Poverty and Deviance in Early Modern Europe.* Cambridge: Cambridge University Press, 1994.

Kennedy, J. H. *Jesuit and Savage in New France.* New Haven: Yale University Press, 1950.

Klaits, Joseph. *Printed Propaganda under Louis XIV: Absolute Monarchy and Public Opinion.* Princeton: Princeton University Press, 1976.

Knox, Dilwyn. "Gesture and Comportment: Diversity and Uniformity." In *Cultural Exchange in Early Modern Europe,* edited by Robert Muchembled and William Monter, 289–307. Cambridge: Cambridge University Press, 2007.

Kupperman, Karen Ordahl, ed. *America in European Consciousness, 1493–1750.* Chapel Hill: University of North Carolina Press, 1995.

Labelle, Kathryn Magee. *Dispersed but Not Destroyed: A History of the Seventeenth-Century Wendat People.* Vancouver: University of British Columbia Press, 2013.

Lavoie, Michel. *Le Domaine du roi: 1652–1859: souveraineté, contrôle, mainmise, propriété, possession, exploitation.* Quebec: Septentrion, 2010.

Lazar, Lance Gabriel. *Working in the Vineyard of the Lord: Jesuit Confraternities in Early Modern Italy.* Toronto: University of Toronto Press, 2005.

Leavelle, Tracy Neal. *The Catholic Calumet: Colonial Conversions in French and Indian North America.* Philadelphia: University of Pennsylvania Press, 2012.

Le Bras, Yvon. *L'Amérindien dans les Relations du père Paul Lejeune (1632–1641).* Sainte-Foy QC: Les Éditions de la Huit, 1994.

Lefauconnier, Camille. "François Sublet de Noyers (1589–1645): Ad majorem regis et Dei gloriam." PhD dissertation, École nationale de chartes, 2009.

Liebersohn, Harry. *Aristocratic Encounters: European Travelers and North American Indians.* Cambridge: Cambridge University Press, 2001.

Lilla, Mark. *The Stillborn God: Religion, Politics, and the Modern West.* New York: Knopf, 2007.

Lynch, Katherine A. *Individuals, Families, and Communities in Europe, 1200–1800: The Urban Foundations of Western Society.* Cambridge: Cambridge University Press, 2003.

Lynn, John A. *Giant of the Grand Siècle: The French Army, 1610–1715*. Cambridge: Cambridge University Press, 1997.

Martin, A. Lynn. *The Jesuit Mind: The Mentality of an Elite in Early Modern France*. Ithaca NY: Cornell University Press, 1988.

———. *Henry III and the Jesuit Politicians*. Geneva: Droz, 1973.

Martin, Henri-Jean. *The French Book: Religion, Absolutism, and Readership, 1585–1715*. Translated by Paul Saenger and Nadine Saenger. Baltimore: Johns Hopkins University Press, 1996.

———. *Print, Power, and People in 17th-Century France*. Translated by David Gerard. Metuchen NJ: Scarecrow Press, 1993.

———. "Un grand éditeur parisien au XVIIe siècle: Sébastien Cramoisy." *Gutenberg-Jahrbuch* (1957): 179–88.

Masse, Caroline. "Pierre Roubaud, polygraphe et faussaire au Siècle des lumières." *Voix et Images* 20, no. 2 (1995): 314–21.

Masse, Vincent. "Nouveaux Mondes (Mexique, Inde) et premières lettres missionnaires imprimées en langue française, 1532–1545." In *De l'Orient à la Huronie—Écritures missionnaires et littérature d'édification auX XVIe et XVIIe siècles*, edited by Guy Poirier, Marie-Christine Gomez-Géraud, and François Paré, 229–49. Quebec: Presses de l'Université Laval, 2011.

McCabe, Ina Baghdiantz. *Orientalism in Early Modern France: Eurasian Trade, Exoticism, and the Ancien Régime*. Oxford: Berg, 2008.

McCluskey, Phil. "'Les Ennemis du Nom Chrestien': Echoes of the Crusade in Louis XIV's France." *French History* 29, no. 1 (2015): 46–61.

McCoy, James C. *Jesuit Relations of Canada, 1632–1673: A Bibliography*. Paris: A. Rau, 1937.

McGregor, James H. S. *Paris from the Ground Up*. Cambridge MA: Belknap Press, 2009.

McHugh, Tim. *Hospital Politics in Seventeenth-Century France: The Crown, Urban Elites and the Poor*. Aldershot UK: Ashgate, 2013.

———. "The Hôpital Général, the Parisian Elites and Crown Social Policy during the Reign of Louis XIV." *French History* 15, no. 3 (2001): 235–53.

McShea, Bronwen Catherine. "Presenting the 'Poor Miserable Savage' to French Urban Elites: Commentary on North American Living Conditions in Early Jesuit Relations." *The Sixteenth Century Journal* 44, no. 3 (Fall 2013): 683–711.

Meehan, John, SJ, and Jacques Monet, SJ. "The Restoration in Canada: An Enduring Patrimony." In *Jesuit Survival and Patrimony: A Global History, 1773–1900*, edited by Robert A. Maryks and Jonathan Wright, 386–98. Leiden: Brill, 2014.

Melzer, Sara E. *Colonizer or Colonized: The Hidden Stories of Early Modern French Culture*. Philadelphia: University of Pennsylvania Press, 2011.

Metcalf, Alida C. *Go-Betweens and the Colonization of Brazil, 1500–1600*. Austin: University of Texas Press, 2006.

Miquelon, Dale. "Envisioning the French Empire: Utrecht, 1711–1713." *French Historical Studies* 24, no. 4 (Fall 2001): 653–77.

Monet, Jacques, SJ. "The Jesuits in New France." In *The Cambridge Companion to the Jesuits*, edited by Thomas Worcester, 186–98. Cambridge: Cambridge University Press, 2008.

Moore, James T. *Indian and Jesuit: A Seventeenth-Century Encounter*. Chicago: Loyola University Press, 1982.

Morrissey, Robert Michael. "The Terms of Encounter: Language and Contested Visions of French Colonization in the Illinois Country, 1673–1702." In *French and Indians in the Heart of North America, 1630–1815*, edited by Guillaume Teasdale and Robert Englebert, 43–75. East Lansing: Michigan State University Press, 2013.

Motsch, Andreas. *Lafitau et l'émergence du discours ethnographique*. Paris: Presses de l'Université de Paris-Sorbonne, 2001.

Mousnier, Roland. *Paris capitale au temps de Richelieu et de Mazarin*. Paris: Pedone, 1978.

Muchembled, Robert. *La sorcière au village (Xve–XVIIIe siècle)*. Paris: Gallimard-Folio, 1991.

Nelson, Eric. *The Jesuits and the Monarchy: Catholic Reform and Political Authority in France (1590–1615)*. Aldershot UK: Ashgate, 2005.

Neveu, Bruno. *Érudition et religion aux XVIIe et XVIIIe siècles*. Paris: Bibliothèque Albin Michel, 1994.

Newman, John Henry. *An Essay on the Development of Christian Doctrine* [1845]. Edited by Stanley L. Jaki. Pinckney MI: Real View Books, 2003.

Newman, Karen. *Cultural Capitals: Early Modern London and Paris*. Princeton: Princeton University Press, 2007.

Nexon, Daniel H. *The Struggle for Power in Early Modern Europe: Religious Conflict, Dynastic Empires, and International Change*. Princeton: Princeton University Press, 2009.

Northeast, Catherine M. *The Parisian Jesuits and the Enlightenment, 1700–1762*. Oxford: Voltaire Foundation, 1991.

O'Malley, John W., SJ. *The First Jesuits*. Cambridge: Harvard University Press, 1995.

O'Malley, John W., SJ, Gauvin Alexander Bailey, Steven J. Harris, SJ, and T. Frank Kennedy, SJ. *The Jesuits II: Cultures, Sciences, and the Arts, 1540–1773*. Toronto: University of Toronto Press, 2006.

O'Neill, Charles Edwards. *Church and State in Colonial Louisiana: Policy and Politics to 1732*. New Haven: Yale University Press, 1950.

Osman, Julia. "Pride, Prejudice, and Prestige: French Officers in North America during the Seven Years' War." In *The Seven Years' War: Global Views*, edited by Mark H. Danley and Patrick J. Speelman, 191–211. Leiden: Brill, 2012.

Ott, Michael. "Pope Urban VIII." In *The Catholic Encyclopedia*, vol. 15. Edited by Charles G. Herbermann. New York: Robert Appleton Company, 1912. http://www.newadvent.org/cathen/15218b.htm.

Ouellet, Réal, et al. *Rhétorique et conquête missionnaire: Le Jésuite Paul Lejeune*. Sillery QC: Septentrion, 1993.

Pagden, Anthony. *Lords of All the World: Ideologies of Empire in Spain, Britain and France, c. 1500-c. 1800*. New Haven: Yale University Press, 1995.

———. *The Fall of Natural Man: The American Indian and the Origins of Comparative Ethnology*. Cambridge: Cambridge University Press, 1982.

Pagden, Anthony, and Jeremy Lawrence. *Vitoria: Political Writings*. Cambridge: Cambridge University Press, 1991.

Parkman, Francis. *The Jesuits in North America in the Seventeenth Century*. Boston: Little, Brown, and Company, 1867.

Pesantubbee, Michelene E. *Choctaw Women in a Chaotic World*. Albuquerque: University of New Mexico Press, 2005.

Pestana, Carla Gardina. *Protestant Empire: Religion and the Making of the British Atlantic World*. Philadelphia: University of Pennsylvania Press, 2009.

Pilleul, Gilbert. "Le discours sur la Nouvelle-France et son évolution." *Mémoires de Nouvelle-France: De France en Nouvelle-France*, edited by Philippe Joutard and Thomas Wien, 133–53. Rennes, France: Presses Universitaires de Rennes, 2005.

Pinkard, Susan. *A Revolution in Taste: The Rise of French Cuisine, 1650–1800*. Cambridge: Cambridge University Press, 2009.

Pioffet, Marie-Christine. *La tentation de l'épopée dans les* Relations *des jésuites*. Sillery QC: Septentrion, 1997.

———. "L'arc et l'épée: les images de la guerre chez le jésuite Paul Lejeune." In *Rhétorique et conquête missionnaire: Le jésuite Paul Lejeune*, edited by Réal Ouellet, 41–52. Sillery QC: Septentrion, 1993.

Pitts, Jennifer. *A Turn to Empire: The Rise of Imperial Liberalism in Britain and France*. Princeton: Princeton University Press, 2005.

Pouliot, Léon, SJ. "Les procureurs parisiens de la Mission de la Nouvelle-France." *Lettres du Bas-Canada* 22 (1968): 38–52.

———. *Étude sur les Relations des Jésuites de la Nouvelle-France (1632–1672)*. Paris: Desclée de Brouwer & Cie, 1940.

Prien, Hans-Jürgen. *Christianity in Latin America*. Translated by Stephen Buckwalter. Leiden: Brill, 2012.

Pritchard, James S. *In Search of Empire: The French in the Americas, 1670–1730*. Cambridge: Cambridge University Press, 2004.

Quinn, Frederick. *The French Overseas Empire*. Westport CT: Praeger, 2000.

Randall, Catharine. *Black Robes and Buckskin: A Selection from the Jesuit Relations*. New York: Fordham University Press, 2011.

Ranum, Orest A. *The Fronde: A French Revolution, 1648–1652*. New York: W. W. Norton & Company, 1993.

———. *Paris in the Age of Absolutism: An Essay.* University Park: Pennsylvania State University Press, 2002.

———. *Richelieu and the Councillors of Louis XIII: A Study of the Secretaries of State and Superintendants of Finance in the Ministry of Richelieu.* Oxford: Clarendon Press, 1963.

Reinhardt, Nicole. "Introduction: War, Conscience, and Counsel in Early Modern Catholic Europe." *Journal of Early Modern History* 18 (2014): 435–46.

Rétif, André. "Brève histoire des Lettres edifiantes et curieuses." *Neue Zeitschrift für Missionswissenschaft* 7 (1951): 31–50.

Rey, Alain, ed. *Dictionnaire Historique de la Langue Française.* Paris: Dictionnaires le Robert, 1993.

Richter, Daniel K. *Trade, Land, Power: The Struggle for Eastern North America.* Philadelphia: University of Pennsylvania Press, 2013.

———. *Before the Revolution: America's Ancient Pasts.* Cambridge MA: Belknap Press, 2011.

———. *Facing East from Indian Country: A Native History of Early America.* Cambridge MA: Harvard University Press, 2001.

———. *The Ordeal of the Longhouse: The Peoples of the Iroquois League in the Era of European Colonization.* Chapel Hill: University of North Carolina Press, 1992.

———. "Iroquois versus Iroquois: Jesuit Missionaries and Christianity in Village Politics, 1642–1686." *Ethnohistory* 32, no. 1 (Winter 1985): 1–16.

Robert, Dana L. *Christian Mission: How Christianity Became a World Religion.* Oxford: Wiley-Blackwell, 2009.

———, ed. *Converting Colonialism: Visions and Realities in Mission History, 1706–1914.* Grand Rapids MI: Eerdmans, 2008.

Roche, Daniel. *Histoire des choses banales: Naissance de la consommation dans les sociétés traditionnelles (XVIIe–XIXe siècle).* Paris: Fayard, 1997.

Rochemonteix, Camille de, SJ. *Le père Antoine Lavalette à Martinique, d'après beaucoup de documents inédits.* Paris: Picard et Fils, 1907.

———. *Les Jésuites et la Nouvelle-France au XVIIe siècle.* 3 vols. Paris: Letouzey et Ané, 1895–96.

———. *Les Jésuites et la Nouvelle-France au XVIIIe siècle.* 2 vols. Paris: Alphonse Picard et Fils, 1906.

Røge, Pernille. "A Natural Order of Empire: The Physiocratic Vision of Colonial France after the Seven Years' War." In *The Political Economy of Empire in the Early Modern World*, edited by Sophus Reinert and Pernille Røge, 32–52. London: Palgrave Macmillan, 2013.

Ronda, James P. "'We Are Well As We Are': An Indian Critique of Seventeenth-Century Christian Missions." *The William and Mary Quarterly* 24 (1977): 66–82.

———. "The European Indian: Jesuit Civilization Planning in New France." *Church History* 41, no. 3 (September 1972): 385–95.

Ruiu, Adina. "Conflicting Visions of the Jesuit Missions to the Ottoman Empire, 1609–1628." *Journal of Jesuit Studies* 1, no. 2 (2014): 260–80.

Rushforth, Brett. *Bonds of Alliance: Indigenous and Atlantic Slaveries in New France.* Chapel Hill: University of North Carolina Press, 2012.

Saad, Charles. *Les Mariages Islamo-Chrétiens.* Paris: L'Harmattan, 2005.

Sabatié, A.-C. *Le Tribunal révolutionnaire de Paris: Origine, évolution, principaux procès et ses victimes dans le clergé.* Paris: P. Lethielleux, 1912.

Sahlins, Peter. *Boundaries: The Making of France and Spain in the Pyrenees.* Berkeley: University of California Press, 1989.

Sayre, Gordon M. *Les Sauvages Américains: Representations of Native Americans in French and English Colonial Literature.* Chapel Hill: University of North Carolina Press, 1997.

Schen, Claire S. *Charity and Lay Piety in Reformation London, 1500–1620.* London: Routledge, 2017.

Schor, Naomi. "The Crisis of French Universalism." *Yale French Studies* 100 (2001): 43–64.

Shea, John Gilmary. *History of the Catholic Missionaries among the Indian Tribes of the United States.* New York: E. Dunigan and Brother, 1855.

Siedentop, Larry. *Inventing the Individual: The Origins of Western Liberalism.* Cambridge MA: Belknap Press, 2014.

Simard, Jean-Jacques. *La Réduction: L'Autochtone inventé et les Amérindiens d'aujourd'hui.* Sillery QC: Septentrion, 2003.

Singer, Barnett, and John Langdon. *Cultured Force: Makers and Defenders of the French Colonial Empire.* Madison: University of Wisconsin Press, 2004.

Skinner, Claiborne A. *The Upper Country: French Enterprise in the Colonial Great Lakes.* Baltimore: Johns Hopkins University Press, 2008.

Sleeper-Smith, Susan. *Indian Women and French Men: Rethinking Cultural Encounter in the Western Great Lakes.* Amherst: University of Massachusetts Press, 2001.

Smith, Katherine Allen. *War and the Making of Medieval Monastic Culture.* Woodbridge UK: Boydell Press, 2011.

Solomon, Howard M. *Public Welfare, Science, and Propaganda in Seventeenth Century France: The Innovations of Théophraste Renaudot.* Princeton: Princeton University Press, 1972.

Soyer, Alexis. *Pantropheon; or, History of Food, and Its Preparation, from the Earliest Ages of the World.* London: Simpkin, Marshall, & Co., 1853.

Speck, Frank G. *Naskapi: The Savage Hunters of the Labrador Peninsula.* Norman: University of Oklahoma Press, 1935.

Stanwood, Owen. *The Empire Reformed: English America in the Age of the Glorious Revolution*. Philadelphia: University of Pennsylvania Press, 2011.

Starkloff, Carl F., SJ. *Common Testimony: Ethnology and Theology in the Customs of Joseph Lafitau*. St. Louis: Institute of Jesuit Sources, 2002.

St-Arnaud, Daniel. *Pierre Miller en Iroquoisie au XVIIe siècle: Le sachem portrait la soutane*. Sillery QC: Septentrion, 1998.

Steckley, John. *Words of the Huron*. Waterloo ON: Wilfrid Laurier University Press, 2007.

Stevens, Laura M. *The Poor Indians: British Missionaries, Native Americans, and Colonial Sensibility*. Philadelphia: University of Pennsylvania Press, 2004.

Strayer, Brian E. *Suffering Saints: Jansenists and Convulsionnaires in France, 1640–1799*. Brighton: Sussex Academic Press, 2008.

Terpstra, Nicholas. *Cultures of Charity: Women, Politics, and the Reform of Poor Relief in Renaissance Italy*. Cambridge MA: Harvard University Press, 2013.

Théry, Chantal. "Femmes missionnaires en Nouvelle-France: dans la balançoire de la rhétorique jésuite." In *Rhétorique et conquête missionnaire: Le Jésuite Paul Lejeune*, edited by Réal Ouellet, 89–99. Sillery QC: Septentrion, 1993.

Thierry, Éric. *La France de Henri IV en Amérique du Nord: De la création de l'Acadie à la fondation de Québec*. Paris: Honoré Champion Éditeur, 2008.

Thompson, D. Gillian. "French Jesuits, 1756–1814." In *The Jesuit Suppression in Global Context: Causes, Events, and Consequences*, edited by Jeffrey D. Burson and Jonathan Wright, 181–98. Cambridge: Cambridge University Press, 2015.

———. "The Lavalette Affair and the Jesuit Superiors." *French History* 10, no. 2 (1996): 206–39.

Toussaint-Samat, Maguelonne. *A History of Food*. Translated by Anthea Bell. Chichester UK: Wiley-Blackwell, 2009.

Trigger, Bruce G. *The Children of Aataentsic: A History of the Huron People to 1660*. 2 vols. Montreal: McGill-Queen's University Press, 1987.

———. *Natives and Newcomers: Canada's "Heroic Age" Reconsidered*. Montreal: McGill-Queen's University Press, 1985.

Trudel, Marcel. *La seigneurie des Cent-Associés, 1627–1663*. Vol. 1. Montreal: Fides, 1979.

———. *The Beginnings of New France: 1524–1663*. Translated by Patricia Claxton. Toronto: McClelland and Stewart Ltd., 1973.

———. *L'Église canadienne sous le Régime militaire, 1759–1764*. Vol. 1. Montreal: Institut d'Histoire de l'Amérique Française, 1956.

True, Micah. *Masters and Students: Jesuit Mission Ethnography in Seventeenth-Century New France*. Montreal: McGill-Queen's University Press, 2015.

Tuttle, Leslie. *Conceiving the Old Regime: Pronatalism and the Politics of Reproduction in Early Modern France*. Oxford: Oxford University Press, 2010.

Van Kley, Dale K. *The Jansenists and the Expulsion of the Jesuits from France*. New Haven: Yale University Press, 1975.

Vardi, Liana. *The Land and the Loom: Peasant and Profit in Northern France, 1680–1800*. Durham NC: Duke University Press, 1993.

Vaulx, Bernard de. *Histoire des Missions Catholiques Françaises*. Paris: Librairie Arthème Fayard, 1951.

Vecsey, Christopher. *The Paths of Kateri's Kin*. Notre Dame IN: University of Notre Dame Press, 1997.

Vélez, Karin. "'A Sign that We Are Related to You': The Transatlantic Gifts of the Jesuit Mission of Lorette, 1650–1750." *French Colonial History* 12 (2011): 31–44;

Verney, Jack. *The Good Regiment: The Carignan-Salières Regiment in Canada, 1665–1668*. Montreal: McGill-Queen's University Press, 1992.

Vidal, Cécile, ed. *Français? La nation en débat entre colonies et métropole, XVIe–XIXe siècle*. Paris: Éditions EHESS, 2014.

Vincent, Grégoire. "'L'Iroquois est un loup pour l'homme, ou la difficulté de 'convertir les Loups et Agneaux' dans les écrits des missionnaires de Nouvelle-France au dix-septième siècle." *Québec Studies* 54 (2012/2013): 17–30.

Walls, Andrew F. "The Eighteenth-Century Protestant Missionary Awakening in Its European Context." In *Christian Missions and the Enlightenment*, edited by Brian Stanley, 22–44. Grand Rapids MI: Eerdmans, 2001.

Ward, Haruko Nawata. *Women Religious Leaders in Japan's Christian Century, 1549–1650*. Aldershot UK: Ashgate, 2009.

Warkentin, Germaine, and Carolyn Podruchny. *Decentering the Renaissance: New Essays on Canada 1500–1700*. Toronto: University of Toronto Press, 2002.

Watts, Sheldon J. *Epidemics and History: Disease, Power, and Imperialism*. New Haven: Yale University Press, 1997.

Wedel, Mildred Mott, ed. *A Jean Delanglez, S.J., Anthology: Selections Useful for Mississippi Valley and Trans-Mississippi American Indian Studies*. New York: Garland Publishing, 1985.

White, Owen, and J. P. Daughton, eds. *In God's Empire: French Missionaries and the Modern World*. Oxford: Oxford University Press, 2012.

White, Richard. *The Middle Ground: Indians, Empires, and Republics in the Great Lakes Region, 1650–1815*. Cambridge: Cambridge University Press, 1991.

Wilkinson, Richard. *Louis XIV*. London: Routledge, 2007.

Witek, John W., SJ. *Controversial Ideas in China and in Europe: A Biography of Jean-François Foucquet, SJ. (1665–1741)*. Rome: Institutum Historicum Societatis Iesu, 1982.

Xavier, Ângela Barreto and Ines G. Županov. *Catholic Orientalism: Portuguese Empire, Indian Knowledge*. Oxford: Oxford University Press, 2015.

Županov, Ines G. *Missionary Tropics: The Catholic Frontier in India (16th–17th Centuries)*. Ann Arbor: University of Michigan Press, 2005.

INDEX

Figures are indicated by F with a number

Capuchins, 17, 38, 243
Carette, Louis-François, 244
Carheil, Étienne de, 135, 142–43, 145–46, 178, 185, 187–88
Caribbean area, 11, 80, 88, 166, 195, 212–13
Carignan-Salières Regiment/campaigns, 3, 129, 131–32, 135
Carnival, 59–60
Carolinas, 147, 228
Carroll, Charles, 250
Carroll, John, 250–51
Cartier, Jacques, 12, 38
Casot, Jean-Joseph, 251, 252–53
catechesis, xvi, 53, 59, 104, 145, 148, 153, 159, 175, 179, 249
Catholic Church, xv, xviii, xxiii, xxviii; affecting Native Americans, 168; France and, 246, 262; Jesuit missionaries and, 51, 133, 162, 257, 258–60; Jesuits suppressed by, 243; laypersons and, 98; Native American marriages in, 161, 172–73, 175–77, 179–81; papal instructions for, 196; Reformation affecting, 5; skepticism toward, 208
Catholicism, xv–xvi, xix, xx, xxvi–xxviii; alliances and, 31; ceremonies of, 73, 165; commerce and, 16, 43, 229; elites and, 18–19, 37, 60, 64, 102, 206; French divisions and, 27–28, 203, 217; French ties of, 3–4, 11–12, 13–18, 29, 67, 75, 98, 130, 134, 151–52, 166, 170, 195–96, 228, 255–56; Great Britain and, 248, 253; marriage and, 161, 166, 173–77, 180–81; Native Americans and, 52–53, 54, 56, 153, 160, 162, 168, 248–49; political community and, xxi, 259-262; Protestantism and, 257; Rome and, 93; skepticism toward, 208–9, 236, 238; social charity and,

258; warrior ethos and, 154–55, 156, 164–65, 190. *See also* Christianity
Catholic Reformation, xx, xxi, xxvii, 120. *See also* Council of Trent; Tridentine reforms
Cayugas, 134–35, 142, 145, 185
celibates and celibacy, xvi, 49, 174. *See also* virginity
Cellot, Louis, 201–2
Cent-Associés. *See* Compagnie de la Nouvelle France
Chabanel, Noël (saint), 66
Challes, Robert, 200
Châlons-sur-Marne, 5
Champagne region, 4–5, 19, 47
Champigny, Jean Bochart de, 184
Champlain, Samuel de, 4, 11, 15, 16, 33, 46
chaplains, military, xviii, 130, 131–32, 218, 229, 230–32, 233–34, 235, 245, 248
charity, 116–19; challenges in providing, 97–98, 105, 109–11, 115–16, 119–20, 123–24; conversions encouraged by, 102, 108; housing as, 104–5; in Huron refugee crisis, 108–12; as Jesuit concern, 96–97, 122–23; laypersons involved in, 97–99, 105–6, 109; medical care as, 100–104; metropolitan elites involved in, 114–15, 120–22; Native Americans involved in, 112–14; Paul Le Jeune encouraging, 99–100
Charles Emmanuel I, duc de Savoy, 29
Charles Garnier (saint), 66
Charlet, Étienne, 70
Charlevoix, Pierre-François-Xavier de, 141, 143, 150, 156–57, 211, 213, 219–21; *Histoire et Description Générale de la Nouvelle-France*, 188–89, 194, 195, 218–19
Chaspoux, Marie-Madeleine de, 184
chastity, 6, 176–77, 181

India, missions in, 196–97, 202

Indian Country, xxiii, xxvi, 166, 173, 190, 230, 258

Indians. *See* Native Americans

Innocent X (pope), 177–78

Iroquois (Five Nations), xv, xxvii; alcohol and, 182, 185, 188, 189; captives of, 127, 148; Christian, 113, 119, 134–35, 154–55, 172; compared to French, 84; as expansionists, 135–36, 137–39; Jesuit beliefs about, 150–52; Jesuit economic plans for, 133; Jesuit policy toward, 80–81; Jesuits as missionaries among, 77–78, 86, 119, 129, 164; Jesuits defending, 191; Jesuits fortifying against, 86; Jesuits negotiating peace with, 132; Jesuits threatening, 133–35; Jesuits urging war against, 66–67, 69–70, 73–74, 81, 85, 88–90, 91–92, 129–31, 137–38, 152–53; killings by, 234; as "little Turk of New France," 3, 89; marriage among, 179; as mission population, 184; negotiating peace, 144; relations of, with Algonquins, 127, 132, 156–57; relations of, with Dutch, 67; relations of, with English, 129, 136, 143, 148–49, 250; relations of, with French, 66, 68, 82, 106, 129, 131–34, 139, 141–46, 148–49; relations of, with Hurons, 66, 68, 73, 79, 83–84, 97, 108, 109, 132; relations of, with Miamis, 136–37; relations of, with the Illinois, 136–37; as threat to Christianization, 70; as traders, 76; warrior ethos of, 153, 164. *See also* Cayugas; Mohawks; Oneidas; Onondagas; Senecas

Iroquois Country, xvii, 72, 111–12, 140, 177, 258. *See also* Iroquois (Five Nations)

Iroquois Wars, 66–67, 79, 82, 89, 107, 136, 151, 198

Isaac Jogues (saint), F 4, *xv*; background and character of, 72–73; death of, 78, 92; information gathering by, 74–76, 256; as martyr, 66, 67; Mohawks and, 73–74, 77–78; *Novum Belgium*, 75–77; rescue of, 74, 75; speech attributed to, 93

Islam, 12, 91, 208

Istanbul, 217

Itaouinon, Jeanne, 180–81

Jacquinot, Barthèlemy, 11, 22

Jansenisme Confondu (Brisacier), 203

Jansenists, 203–4, 210, 240

Japan, missions in, 9–10

Jean de Brébeuf (saint): on Carnival, 60; Crown and, 70–71; on Hurons, 50, 56–57, 60; as martyr, 10, 66, 83–84; as missionary, 10, 15, 107–8

Jeanne d'Arc (saint), 255

Jean de Lalande (saint), 66

Jesuits, xv–xvi, xvii–xxiii, xxvi–xxvii, xxviii; alcohol, attitude toward, 184–88; alliances of, 129–30; British and, 236–38, 247–53, 251–52, 288n69; business interests of, 71, 204; in conflict with French policy, 165–69, 190–92; contemporary views on, 257–58; on conversion, 151; cultivating patron-client relationships, 118; cultural adaptation by, 153–54, 160, 162–64; cultural life of, 87; difficulties facing, 97–98, 119–20, 123, 199–201, 240–41; dispersal of, 243–44; donors to, 111, 114, 118–19; early days in Canada, 15–16; economics and, 42–43, 63, 195; as expansionists,

Villermont, Esprit Cabart de, 141, 198

Vimont, Barthèlemy, 8, 9, 70, 71, 73–74, 103–4, 176

Vincent de Paul (saint), 106, 120, 195, 252

Virginia, 13, 14, 33, 221

virginity, xvi, 203. *See also* celibates and celibacy

Virot, Claude-François-Louis, 234, 262

Vitelleschi, Mutius, 9, 10, 21, 69, 70–71

Vitoria, Francisco de, 152

Vitry, Pierre de, 229, 230, 231–33

Walker, Hovenden, 148–50

war as language, 152

warfare, xvii, 123, 130, 151–58, 161

War of the Spanish Succession, 130, 146–50, 207, 211

warrior ethos, xviii, 130, 151–56, 179–80, 181, 190, 214

warrior nobility. *See* warrior ethos

Wars of Religion, 5, 6, 153

Washington, George, 234–35

Well, Bernard, 251, 252

West India Company (Dutch), 69, 76. *See also* New Netherland

Weygand, Maxime, 255

wine, 46–47, 133, 186

Winthrop, John, the Younger, 81

women, Native American: bravery of, 127, 156–57, 181–83; charitable activities of, 113, 181; marriage and, 112, 121, 171, 175–76, 180–81

women religious, 96, 98, 197. *See also* Hospitalières (Augustinian Canonesses); Ursulines

World War I, 255

Xavier, Francis (saint). *See* Francis Xavier (saint)

To order or obtain more information on these or other University of Nebraska Press titles, visit nebraskapress.unl.edu.

To order or obtain more information on these or other University of Nebraska Press titles, visit nebraskapress.unl.edu.

CPSIA information can be obtained
at www.ICGtesting.com
Printed in the USA
LVHW021449241121
704328LV00004B/491